"Humberto Casanova has walked boldly into the thick complexity of biblical language. He is deeply informed by the claim and function of metaphor and invites his readers to a quite fresh discernment of their potential. He deals with the trickiness of catching the inscrutable holy God in human articulation and does so with an alert critical edge. This book will be of immense value for those who work at the communication of serious faith in an increasingly skeptical culture. Casanova's careful scholarship is a great service to our common work of interpretation."

—**Walter Brueggemann**
 Columbia Theological Seminary, author of *The Prophetic Imagination*

"Accessible and profoundly complex, Humberto Casanova's new study explores myth and meaning in the literatures of the Ancient Near East and Mediterranean world, relating recurring patterns of content and thought to contemporary media and messaging. With clarity, the work introduces and applies a wide range of theoretical approaches employed in studies of comparative religion and mythography. An important thread in this thought-provoking book deals with reception history and the ways in which people read and purposely misread biblical myth thereby shaping and reinforcing particular worldviews."

—**Susan Niditch**
 Amherst College, author of *Ancient Israelite Religion*

"In his book Humberto Casanova makes use of the conceptual metaphor theory, as first introduced by Lakoff and Johnson. His analysis offers two strong claims about fundamentalism in religion, especially in Christianity. First, the church presents the idea of God through anthropomorphization. Second, the worldview of the church cannot be reconciled with that found in today's democratic societies. The basic problem with these conceptual metaphors, Casanova contends, is that they cannot be taken literally because they are incongruous with what people know about the world today."

—**Zoltán Kövecses**
 Eötvös University, Hungary, author of *Where Metaphors Come From*

"Humberto Casanova reflects wide learning in ancient, medieval, and modern sources on religion and argues compellingly that the concepts of 'myth' and 'metaphor' are essential for the study of religion."

—Marc Zvi Brettler
> Duke Trinity College, author of *The Bible and the Believer: How to Read the Bible Critically and Religiously*

"Humberto Casanova joins the increasing number of scholars who affirm that the Bible has not just been influenced by myth, *it is myth*. Where Casanova moves the conversation forward is in his argument that this categorical misinterpretation of the Bible is at the root of the current state of religious affairs—more and more people are finding religion irrelevant to the modern world and are therefore leaving religious organizations altogether. . . . In *Imagining God*, Casanova makes the compelling argument that the ancients constructed their ideas of God using metaphors drawn from their own cultural surroundings, and so should we, thus calling for a new theology that embraces the Bible's mythical nature, is in dialogue with the natural sciences, and that takes seriously the criticisms of today's youth."

—Amy L. Balogh
> Regis University, author of *Moses Among the Idols*

"Humberto Casanova offers a cogent assessment of the reception and use of biblical imagery in the Western theological imagination through a lucid and in-depth examination of the categories of myth and metaphor. . . . His diagnosis of the current crisis of Christian theology traces the problem to a reliance upon metaphors that are disconnected from contemporary life. The remedy calls for no less than a 'radical new vision of God,' one that replaces outdated source domain images with fresh metaphors generated by the institutions and values of today."

—Dexter E. Callender Jr.
> Miami University, author of *Adam in Myth and History*

Imagining God

IMAGINING GOD

Myth and Metaphor

Humberto Casanova

foreword by Barry L. Bandstra

WIPF & STOCK · Eugene, Oregon

IMAGINING GOD
Myth and Metaphor

Copyright © 2020 Humberto Casanova. All rights reserved. Except for brief quotations in critical publications or reviews, no part of this book may be reproduced in any manner without prior written permission from the publisher. Write: Permissions, Wipf and Stock Publishers, 199 W. 8th Ave., Suite 3, Eugene, OR 97401.

Wipf & Stock
An Imprint of Wipf and Stock Publishers
199 W. 8th Ave., Suite 3
Eugene, OR 97401

www.wipfandstock.com

PAPERBACK ISBN: 978-1-5326-8818-8
HARDCOVER ISBN: 978-1-5326-8819-5
EBOOK ISBN: 978-1-5326-8820-1

Manufactured in the U.S.A.   FEBRUARY 3, 2020

The front cover shows a picture of a bas-relief from the palace of Ashurnasirpal II (883–859 BCE). See page 184 for an explanation of the relief.

To Deanne Busker Casanova

CONTENTS

List of Illustrations and Tables | viii
Permissions | ix
Foreword by Barry L. Bandstra | xi
Abbreviations | xiii
Introduction | xvii

Chapter 1   Myth and Metaphor | 1
Chapter 2   Anthropomorphism | 52
Chapter 3   Divine World | 125
Chapter 4   Case Study: Monarchy | 162
Chapter 5   Critical Assessment of the King Metaphor | 193

Glossary | 237
Bibliography | 241
Index of Ancient Sources | 277
Index of Bible Citations | 289
Index of Authors | 301
Index of Subjects | 307

LIST OF ILLUSTRATIONS AND TABLES

Journey as source domain | 5

Our bodily experience as main source for metaphors | 56

The expression *sons of* as a common idiom | 66

The majority of platonic attributes for god do not come from the Bible | 99

The gods get married and have children | 113

Hebrew Bible terms used to refer to the gods | 142

Two different renditions of Psalm 82 | 158

Metaphorical basis of myth | 162

Main empires in the Ancient Near East and the Mediterranean | 173

The healing of a possessed/lunatic boy | 222

Description of the disease | 223

PERMISSIONS

We express our gratitude for having been granted permission to use material taken from:

Cavanaugh, William T., and James K. A Smith, eds. *Evolution and the Fall*. Grand Rapids: Eerdmans, 2017.

Foster, Benjamin R. *Before the Muses: An Anthology of Akkadian Literature*. Bethesda, MD: CDL, 2005.

Jacobsen, Thorkild. *The Harps that Once . . . : Sumerian Poetry in Translation*. New Haven, CT: Yale University Press, 1987.

Jenkins, Jack. "'Nones' Now as Big as Evangelicals, Catholics in the US." *Religion News Service*, March 23, 2019.

Martin, Michel. "The Moral Question of Trump's Border Wall." NPR, *All Things Considered*, January 27, 2019.

Parker, Simon B., ed. *Ugaritic Narrative Poetry*. Chico, CA: SBL Scholars, 1997.

Peacocke, Arthur. *Theology for a Scientific Age*. Minneapolis: Fortress, 1993.

Rahlfs, Alfred. *Septuaginta*. Stuttgart: Deutsche Bibelgesellschaft, 1935.

Smith, Nelle. "When You Argue with a Fundamentalist, You Don't Know What You're Asking For." *Religious Dispatches*, March 27, 2018.

"Ultimate Mars Challenge." *NOVA*, November 14, 2012. WGBH Media Library and Archives.

Wansbrough, Henry, ed. *The New Jerusalem Bible*. London: Darton, Longman & Todd, 1985.

FOREWORD

Sometimes I ask students in my introductory Hebrew Bible course whether they feel they have to believe in the cosmology and metaphysical world of the Bible (after we've unpacked those terms, of course) in order to uphold belief in the truth of the Bible. We pursue the question by wondering: Should we believe there are invisible but real angels attending us right now? Does the deity of the Bible reside in a space up there beyond the stratosphere in a place called heaven, though space explorers have never found evidence of it? Must one believe in all of the different manifestations of deity in the Bible, including Yahve, the warrior-god of the Hebrews in the book of Exodus? Or a hell-dwelling devil who actively promotes social havoc and personal felony as the promoter of evil in our world? And what about notions of immortality and life after death? Must we believe in the actuality of all these things, or, if not, why not?

These are probably challenging questions for Bible-believing Christians, and they may have serious implications. If such matters are not real in a matter-of-fact sense, then what does that do to the truth value of the biblical text? At the very least it prompts discussion of what is truth as it applies to the two-thousand-year-old book called the Holy Scriptures. How does one decide what of the Bible is literally real and what is not? Is it up to us to decide, and how do we go about doing so? Does the very asking of these questions undermine the veracity of Scripture or indicate a lack of true faith on the part of the asker?

Humberto Casanova, in this scholarly tour de force, does not give us the option of brushing aside such questions. Instead, he applies the latest findings of scholarship on the ancient literature and history of the biblical world by situating the Bible in its authentic context. The evidence he gathers is massive, as he ranges over the textual corpuses of the biblical period, including Mesopotamian, Egyptian, Canaanite, Greek, Roman, and of course Israelite cultures. He relentlessly gathers the relevant texts and synthesizes the literary and textual data to own the problem and ask the question: Should we accept the Bible's worldview at face value?

His conceptual toolkit consists of three well-defined tools: anthropomorphism, metaphor, and myth. He explains and unpacks them in rich and interesting chapters, and then goes on to illustrate them with case studies demonstrating their implications. His conclusions are based soundly on the evidence of the texts themselves. And while some readers might find the conclusions unsettling because their inherited assumptions of a biblically based metaphysical world end up getting shaken, others might find in this study a grand liberation from the mythological inheritance of the ages.

If you want to ask serious questions about the world of the Bible, or have yourself had serious questions but have not had an authoritative resource to help you identify and articulate your uneasiness, this study is a must-read. As for me in my teaching, I now have a scholar's resource to put in the hands of my students who ask the existential question of the Bible: What then is really real and how do I know so?

Barry L. Bandstra, PhD (Yale University, Department of Near Eastern Languages and Civilizations) is professor of religion at Hope College, Holland, Michigan

ABBREVIATIONS

General

Akk.	Akkadian language
adj.	adjective
adv.	adverb
Atra.	*Atraḫasīs*
BCE	Before the Common Era
BDAG	*Greek-English Lexicon of the New Testament* (see Bauer in the bibliography)
BDB	*Hebrew and English Lexicon of the Old Testament* (see Brown in the bibliography)
CAT	*The Cuneiform Alphabetic Texts from Ugarit, Ras Ibn Hani and Other Places* (see Dietrich 1995 in the bibliography)
CE	Common Era
conj.	conjunction
CTA	*Corpus des tablettes en cunéiformes alphabétiques: Découvertes à Ras Shamra-Ugarit de 1929 à 1939* (see Herdner in the bibliography)
En. el.	*Enūma Eliš*
En. Nin.	*Enki and Ninmaḫ*
ETCSL	Electronic Text Corpus of Sumerian Literature (website)
Ges.	*Gesenius' Hebrew Grammar* (see Kautzsch in the bibliography)
Gilg.	*Gilgameš*
Gk.	Greek language

Heb.	Hebrew language
impf.	imperfect
impv.	imperative
inf.	infinitive
IDB	*The Interpreter's Dictionary of the Bible* (see Buttrick in the bibliography)
KTU	*Die Keilalphabetischen Texte aus Ugarit* (see Dietrich 1976 in the bibliography)
lit.	literally
Ludlul	*Ludlul bēl nēmeqi* (see Annus in the bibliography)
mss.	manuscripts
MT	Masoretic Text
paral.	parallel text(s)
pers.	person
pl.	plural
pres.	present
ptc.	participle
sing.	singular
Sum.	Sumerian language
Theo.	*Theogony* (see Most in the bibliography)
Ugar.	Ugaritic language
v.	verse
vv.	verses

Journals

AA	*American Anthropologist*
AJA	*American Journal of Archaeology*
AJT	*Asia Journal of Theology*
AS	*Anatolian Studies*
AOAT	*Alter Orient und Altes Testament*

ABBREVIATIONS

BA	Biblical Archaeologist
BASOR	Bulletin of the American Schools of Oriental Research
BJRL	Bulletin of the John Rylands Library
BO	Bibliotheca Orientalis
BSOAS	Bulletin of the School of Oriental and African Studies
CBQ	Catholic Biblical Quarterly
DSD	Dead Sea Discoveries
ExpT	Expository Times
FI	Free Inquiry
HTR	Harvard Theological Review
JANER	Journal of Ancient Near East Religions
JAOS	Journal of the American Oriental Society
JBL	Journal of Biblical Literature
JCS	Journal of Cuneiform Studies
JNES	Journal of Near Eastern Studies
JSHJ	Journal for the Study of the Historical Jesus
JSS	Journal of Semitic Studies
JTS	Journal of Theological Studies
NABU	Nouvelles Assyriologiques Brèves et Utilitaires
NTS	New Testament Studies
PEQ	Palestine Exploration Quarterly
UF	Ugarit-Forschungen
VT	Vetus Testamentum
WTJ	Westminster Theological Journal
ZDPV	Zeitschrift des deutschen Palästina-Vereins
ZAW	Zeitschrift für die Alttestamentliche Wissenschaft
ZRG	Zeitschrift für Religions- und Geistesgeschite

Bible Versions

Aquila	Greek version of the Hebrew Bible by Aquila Sinope (*ca.* 130 BCE)
ASV	American Standard Version (1901)
NJB	New Jerusalem Bible (1985)
JPS	Holy Scriptures, Jewish Publication Society (1917)
KJV	King James Version (1769)
LXX	Greek version of the Hebrew Bible (see Rahlfs in the bibliography)
NASB	New American Standard Bible (1977)
NIV	New International Version (2011)
NLT	New Living Translation (2007)
NRSV	New Revised Standard Version (1989)
PER	La Biblia del Peregrino (2006)
Simaco	Greek version of the Hebrew Bible (*ca.* second century CE)
TJPS	*Tanakh: A New Translation of The Holy Scriptures According to the Traditional Hebrew Text.* Philadelphia: Jewish Publication Society of America, 1985.
Vg.	*Vulgata latina* (R. Weber et al. *Biblia Sacra Iuxta Vulgatam Versionem.* Stuttgart: Deutsche Bibelgesellschaft, 2013)

INTRODUCTION

IN FINAL ANALYSIS, THIS book deals with a pastoral problem. An ever growing number of Christians are becoming increasingly uncomfortable with the language of faith. They are uneasy with the stories of the Bible and the tenets of the church. People are having a hard time believing in the worldview of the Bible. Statistics show that these feelings easily escalate into a crisis of faith, and for now the predicament is being resolved by leaving the church. Therefore, we urgently need to clarify what we mean when we talk about the gods of theism. Unraveling the puzzle of *the language of faith* may help solve what has become an unbearable situation regarding faith. In doing so, we need to approach the stories of the Bible and its language from within the larger context of the Ancient Near East and the Mediterranean, because the Bible was not produced in a vacuum. By providing context, this approach proves to be tremendously helpful in trying to understand the language used to talk about the gods. In chapter 5, we'll see that this is not just an academic affair; it is a profoundly pastoral problem. We encourage the leaders and ministers of the church to read this book and to confront the current crisis, and we specially urge them to listen to the youth's agony and to our dying world.

Chapter 1

Metaphor is the main concept leading to an understanding of the language of faith. In this chapter we develop several anchoring topics. We begin with a minimal definition of myth as *stories about the gods* made possible by the use of metaphors. Then we explain metaphor as a cognitive mechanism by which we seek to understand one area of experience in terms of another, and we give some examples of how metaphor operates in our daily life and cognitive routines. These ideas enable us to expand on the *narrative nature* of myth as an extended metaphor that borrows images and expressions from our human world in order to construct a divine universe. In fact, theism can be defined as the envisioning of a divine world by means of metaphors, particularly anthropomorphism. We give some examples of how myth was used in the ancient world. In this way we further illuminate the nature and function of myth. In order to set an additional foundation, we pause to warn the reader about the mind-controlling nature of metaphor.

However, it is not enough to only define myth. We also thought it necessary to present some rival definitions, so that the reader may assess them in the light of the evidence we provide in the rest of the book. One theory argues that myth never refers to only one god whose actions occur on earth. Instead, myth always presents stories about the gods (polytheism) whose actions take place in a heavenly world. Another definition claims that myth portrays the gods in charge of only the cyclical operations of nature, but not in control of the linear functioning of history. These definitions claim that while biblical narratives transmit "historical events," pagan myths are fictional stories that occur in heaven or in connection with nature. We refute these claims, presenting preliminary evidence that will be further substantiated in the course of our study. The truth is that Israel's neighbors believed in gods who were in control not only of nature but also of the social, political and military affairs of humanity, for no part of human life was outside the control of the gods.

Additionally, it is essential to show that myth and legend are not completely separate genres. There are many gray areas between them, and we even find the intrusion of myth within historical narratives. The rest of the book will expand on the subject by means of numerous examples, but it was necessary to show at the very beginning the consensus among scholars regarding these gray areas. Finally, an excursus at the end of the chapter substantiates that even if we hold a very narrow definition of myth, in the Scriptures we find beautiful mythical stories which inherit numerous traits from the myths of other religions.

Chapter 2

The only way to talk about the gods of theism is via metaphorical language, and its central metaphor has always been *anthropomorphism*. Therefore, in chapter 2 we first discuss anthropomorphism as a universal cognitive mechanism that helps us function in the world. People ascribe human qualities and behavior to everything around them. Next we highlight the physical and human characteristics ascribed to the gods. This humanizing of the gods envisions them as having human bodies. The gods have eyes, ears, arms, hands, emotions, intentions, hunger, thirst, etc. So we peruse several stories that depict the gods as actually having physical bodies and acting in this world.

Then we describe how philosophy started rejecting any narrative that would describe the gods as bodily creatures, and this trend propelled a new way of interpreting Bible narratives. However, the hostility against anthropomorphism was mostly directed against any portrayal of the gods which would ascribe them both immoral behavior and human-physical bodies. For even Plato conceived the gods as idealized human beings. He only shifted the emphasis away from the physical to focus on human moral qualities. The truth is that without anthropomorphism there is no god. However, the more interpreters and theologians withdrew from a humanized god, the more their god became unknown and distant. God became incomprehensible, immutable, essentially distinct from the world, etc. At the end of the chapter, a case study illustrates the crisis in biblical interpretation.

Chapter 3

This chapter provides additional background in order to build a better framework for understanding the world of the Bible. The humanizing of the universe creates meaning by ascribing human qualities and intentions to the impersonal world around us. In other words, the natural and historical forces steering human life are presented as personal agents working behind the scenes. The result is meaning: "things happen for a reason." This creates a polarity that describes the gods both as impersonal forces and as humanized-personal beings. In addition, the world of the gods was structured by mimicking the earthly system of government. The divine realm became a monarchy with a god-king at the top of a hierarchy. This senior god was the leader of a divine assembly. We also refer to the important figure of the hero who stands out as a human being who attains divine nature and prestige due to his birth, deeds or divine purpose. We then discuss the concepts of heaven and the underworld. And finally we examine Psalm 82 as an additional case study regarding biblical interpretation.

Chapter 4

Up to this point, we have argued that theism uses *metaphorical language* to tell stories about the gods. Then we established *anthropomorphism* as the central metaphor of theism. In this chapter we prove that *monarchy* was the most important anthropomorphism used by all the religions of the Ancient Near East and the Mediterranean.

In this chapter we concentrate particularly on the conceptual metaphor GOD IS KING, which was the primary concept used to understand the world of the gods. Conditioned by its time and culture, myth perceived the universe as a cosmic kingdom imitating the earthly monarchies of the time. This metaphor was the foundation of imperialism. The gods were warrior-kings and the earthly kings were gods. Religion was at the service of the power of the state.

Chapter 5

Our modern democratic ideals require us to assess whether there is any value in monarchy as a theological construct, and we ask ourselves what kind of god we want to imagine today. We also spell out the inescapable collision between ancient and modern worldviews, and wonder how we would construct a new theology for this day and age. We conclude that a better understanding of the nature of the language that the Bible uses to refer to the gods should enable us to move beyond the *literal* interpretation of Scripture. In closing, we invite Christians to recreate their myths by using our current cultural context as *source domain* and to consider building a worldview which obliterates imperialistic-monarchical understandings of reality, and instead focuses on egalitarian-humanistic values.

I would like to thank my dear wife, Deanne, for all her valuable help reading and editing these pages, and always asking the magic question, "What do you want to convey in this sentence?"

—**Humberto Casanova,** Grand Rapids, Michigan, 2020

Ring the bells that still can ring.
Forget your perfect offering.
There is a crack in everything,
that's how the light gets in.

—LEONARD COHEN[1]

Chapter 1

MYTH AND METAPHOR

1.1 Myth: Definition

1.1.1 Narrative, Gods, Metaphor and Community

GEOFFREY KIRK DOUBTS WHETHER it is possible to construct a universal definition of myth capable of embracing all the myths we know in one single designation.[2] This is particularly impossible when trying to formulate a general definition of its *social function*. However, a quick review of the scholarly research will highlight some key elements that frequently surface in the description of myth: First, myth entails a *narrative* and, in fact, that's the meaning of the Greek word *muthos* (= narrative, story, tale). Second, scholars agree that myth is distinctively a *story about the gods* or a story in which *the gods are key participants*[3] and, therefore, it is a unique kind of narrative. If we combine these two components, we could say that myth is a "theological narrative." Myth portrays the gods acting both in a divine world and in the history of humankind. Third, myth is an *extended meta-*

---

1. Cohen, "Anthem."
2. Kirk, "On Defining Myth," 54–55. Kirk is content with a very general definition: myth is "traditional oral tale" (57). Cf. "It would be hard to find a definition of myth that would be acceptable to all scholars and at the same time intelligible to no specialists. Then, too, is it even possible to find *one* definition that will cover all the types and functions of myths in all traditional and archaic societies?" (Eliade, *Myth and Reality*, 5).
3. Cf. "By myth we refer to the many stories about the gods" (Lambert, "Mythos," 3).

phor, that is, myth is a metaphor that has been expanded into a narrative (§1.1.3). Fourth, myth often has the following functional component: it is "a narrative about the deeds of gods and heroes . . . of collective significance to a particular social group or groups."[4] Myth is not the possession of the individual but it belongs to the collective consciousness.[5] To summarize: *myth is composed by a set of metaphors and symbols elaborated in the form of a narrative. The cumulus of these narratives and expressions serve the purpose of forming a conceptual metaphor. In other words, the sum of all these stories forms a concept of the divine.*

The above definition refers to a *literary genre*, and it is not to be confused with the popular use of the term *myth* by which we indicate a false belief or statement. A person may say: "the idea that antibiotics kill viruses is nothing but a myth," that is, this belief is false and has no basis in reality. Note that in this case there is no mention of a narrative about the gods or a story supporting social values. In contrast, the literary genre known as myth (and legend) has been employed as the certified vehicle for transmitting aspirations, values and customs belonging to a community. These values shape, unify and protect a social system by way of stories carved into the collective consciousness. A myth or legend may retain a factual or historical element, but that is not where its importance resides. A myth is "true" not because of its historical accuracy but because it conveys values that are considered essential to the life of the community. When those values change or are abandoned, the myth dies (§5.2).

1.1.2 Metaphor[6]

Metaphor is the lifeblood of mythical thinking and, therefore, we need to describe how it functions. First, George Lakoff and Mark Johnson explain that "the essence of metaphor is understanding and experiencing one kind of thing in terms of another."[7] Like in the following example:

> If Mr. Conwell wants his business proposal to be approved by the board, he needs to *build* a stronger argument.

---

4. Buxton, *Imaginary Greece*, 14.

5. See Jung, *Archetypes*; Robertson, *Jungian Archetypes*.

6. See Black, *Models and Metaphors*; Davidson, "What Metaphors Mean"; Frye, *Myth and Metaphor*; Gibbs, *Cambridge Handbook of Metaphor*; Kittay, *Metaphor*; Kövecses, *Where Metaphors Come From*; Kövecses, *Metaphor*; Lakoff and Johnson, *Metaphors We Live By*; Ortony, *Metaphor and Thought*; Richards, *Philosophy of Rhetoric*; Ricoeur, *Rule of Metaphor*; Winter, *Clearing*.

7. Lakoff and Johnson, *Metaphors We Live By*, 5.

This statement understands the field of *business* in terms of what happens in the realm of *construction*. Similarly, Zoltán Kövecses explains that a metaphor is a way of "conceptualizing one domain of experience [*business*] in terms of another [*building*]. The domain of experience that is used to comprehend another domain is typically more physical, more directly experienced, and better known than the domain we wish to comprehend, which is typically more abstract, less directly experienced, and less known."[8] This happens because the foundation of our knowledge is corporeal: "our experiences with the physical world [that is, movement, space, vision, smell, temperature, etc.] serve as a natural and logical foundation for the comprehension of more abstract domains."[9] Through their bodily experience, humans first acquire the physical meaning of a word, and then use that word metaphorically. For example, we first experience the cozy feeling of warmth, and then we say: "They gave her a warm welcome" (= they welcome her with love and hospitality). Other examples: "He's a *bitter* guy"; "they *inflamed* what was already a troublesome situation." The physical experience of the predominance of the right hand has created an almost universal metaphor: "I have always said that Mario is my right hand" (= he is my most useful worker). The Scriptures use the same human experience to talk about its god: "The right hand of Yahve does mighty things" (Ps 118:15). The physical fact that containers are filled "up" allows us to create metaphors like: "I'm up to my eyeballs with him" (= I'm really tired of this person); or: "I'm fed up with the situation." In all these examples, concrete experiences with the physical world serve to explain what is more abstract.

Second, by means of metaphors we build *concepts* that help us understand reality. This means that metaphor is more than just a *figure of speech*. Popular understanding degrades it to a mere occasional rhetorical ornamentation, to a comparison between two expressions. For example, if we read the inaugural address of President Reagan (1985), we may think that the expression "mountains yet to climb" is nothing more than oratory décor:

> We are creating a nation once again vibrant, robust, and alive.
> But there are many mountains yet to climb.

The truth is, however, that this isolated instance is part of the conceptual metaphor LIFE IS CLIMBING A MOUNTAIN, by which we understand one domain (*life*) in terms of another (*climbing, alpinism*). And when we talk

---

8. Kövecses, *Where Metaphors Come From*, 2. See Kövecses, *Metaphor*, 4; Lakoff and Johnson, *Metaphors We Live By*, 5.

9. Kövecses, *Metaphor*, 7. For a good exposition regarding the fact that human experience and knowledge rests in an embodied foundation, see Lakoff and Johnson, *Philosophy in the Flesh*.

about a *conceptual metaphor* we refer to a host of individual metaphors that together *form a concept*; a way of interpreting a segment of our experience. Let's see other examples:

- We are almost at the peak; let's keep moving up until we finish this project.
- I admit this business venture has its cliffs, but the rewards at the summit make it worth the risk.
- She kept climbing all the way up to the championship.
- I've been lucky to have an experienced scout who taught me how to climb the mountains of life.

These instances show that the comparison President Reagan made between hill-walking and the challenges of government was not an isolated statement but an individual manifestation of how life is understood in terms of mountain climbing. Metaphor is not just a lexical phenomenon. It is rather a way of conceptualizing, a way of shaping our *understanding and experience* of the world. A conceptual domain shapes the way we interpret another: "In short," says Lakoff, "the locus of metaphor is not in language at all, but in the way we conceptualize one mental domain in terms of another."[10]

Third, we are capable of interpreting one realm of life in terms of another because we establish a set of *correspondences* or similarities between two domains. For example, we can compare the concept of *love* to a *journey*, and say: "our relationship has entered a bumpy road." In this sentence, a love-relationship is understood in terms of a difficult journey via comparison.

Fourth, metaphor allows a segment of reality to act as a storehouse from which we borrow expressions that help us understand another segment of life. The point of supply is called *source domain*. And the area in need of explanation is called *target domain*.[11] For example: The conceptual domain *journey* is a very common *source* supplying a multitude of expressions which are employed to talk about other areas of life, things like love, arguments, etc.[12] This is possible because our physical movement from one place to another is a well understood universal experience. Steve Winter quotes a famous psalm, and correctly explains that its images fall under the conceptual metaphor LIFE IS A JOURNEY:[13]

10. Lakoff, "Contemporary Theory of Metaphor," 203.
11. Kövecses, *Metaphor*, 4.
12. See Kövecses, *Metaphor*, 3–4. Lakoff, "Contemporary Theory of Metaphor," 206–8; Lakoff, "What Is a Conceptual System," 41–43; Lakoff and Johnson, *Metaphors We Live By*, 44, 85, 89–91; Winter, *Clearing*, 16, 20, 60.
13. Winter, *Clearing*, 20. Cf. "In the middle of life's road, I found myself in a dark

> Even if I should walk through a dark valley,
>> I fear no harm.
> For you are with me;
>> your rod and your staff,
> they reassure me (Ps 23:4).[14]

Again, the source domain known as *journey* provides many expressions that are used to understand the target domain *life*:[15]

Journey as source domain

Metaphor	Meaning
In life, I take the road less traveled.	= I do not conform to the way in which other people behave.
Stop the world, I want to get off.	= I don't want to live in a world like this.
She doesn't let anyone get in her way.	= She won't let people prevent her from getting what she wants.
Light is at the end of the tunnel.	= Success comes after a period of adversity.
In our lives we'll find bumps in the road.	= We always experience problems in life.
He had a head start in life.	= He began his life benefiting from many family advantages.
He's without direction in his life.	= His life has no purpose.

In all these examples, the source domain *journey* acts like a stockroom providing linguistic expressions that help explain the target domain *life*. The sum of all these expressions creates the conceptual metaphor LIFE IS A JOURNEY, that is, we are able to form a concept of *life* via metaphors.

1.1.3 Narrative Nature of Myth

How are we going to write a *narrative* about the gods when the only thing we know is this world? The only way to talk about the gods would be by using our human experience to understand the divine world in terms of

---

wood" (Dante's *Divine Comedy*, quoted in Kövecses, *Metaphor*, 53).

14. The author of this book often uses his own translation of the Bible and other literature. When this is not the case we specify the source.

15. For the life is a journey metaphor, see Kövecses, *Metaphor*, 11, 34, 50, 53–55, 80; Kövecses, *Where Metaphors Come From*, 9; Lakoff, "What Is a Conceptual Metaphor"; 63–65. Winter, *Clearing*, 16, 108.

this world. Antiquity provided a host of expressions taken from this world to help build a concept of god. As we shall see, it is crucial to underline here that the areas of human life that the Bible uses to describe the divine stemmed from the Ancient Near East[16] and were conditioned by the time and culture in which they originated.

As we shall see in more detail (§4), *monarchy* produced a multitude of terms and images associated with its organization. And monarchy was used as a storehouse providing an abundance of linguistic expressions (*source domain*) used to explain the more elusive concept of god (*target domain*). The sum of all these expressions produced the conceptual metaphor GOD IS KING, which the Hebrew Bible articulates by saying: "Elohim is king" (Ps 47:8), or "Yahve is king" (Ps 10:16). Again, by *conceptual metaphor* we do not refer to an isolated metaphorical expression, like "I saw Adonay sitting on a throne" (Isa 6:1). The conceptual metaphor GOD IS KING is rather built by the sum of all such expressions. A host of images and expressions associated with the *monarchy* were knitted together to produce many mythological narratives and, in this way, an imaginary divine world, that is, a concept of god.

Let's give an example of a *story* based on the king metaphor. In 1 Kings 22, Ahab and Jehoshaphat asked the prophets for a word from Yahve. They wanted to know whether they would succeed in their plans of waging war against Syria. The prophets delivered a promissory oracle (vv. 5–6). Then they consulted the prophet Micaiah, who warned Ahab that Yahve had already set a trap to kill him in battle. If we ask: how did Micaiah know about the coming threat? The answer is that the prophet was granted a vision into the council of the gods in which they discussed how to eliminate Ahab (cf. Jer 23:18, 22).[17] First Kings 22:19–22 illustrates the conceptual metaphor YAHVE IS KING by means of an individual story describing the divine-royal assembly gathered in a council meeting:

> [19] Then [Micaiah] said: Therefore, hear the word of Yahve: I saw Yahve sitting on his throne, and all the host of heaven[18] standing by him, on his right and on his left.

---

16. The label "Near East" is a Eurocentric expression on which there is no agreement regarding its meaning (see Fisher, *Middle East*; Held, *Middle East*). We use it here to refer to the territory covering from Anatolia (now part of Turkey) to the Levant (Palestine, Syria, etc.), Egypt, the Arabic Peninsula (today Saudi Arabia, Yemen, etc.), Mesopotamia (Iraq) and Iran.

17. This scene is part of a prophetic narrative that reports how Elijah's prophesy against Ahab was fulfilled (see 1 Kgs 21:18–24). Its fulfillment is clear in 22:38, when the dogs lick the king's blood, just as the prophet foretold.

18. The expression "host of heaven" points to the stars of the sky. These heavenly

²⁰ And Yahve asked: Who will deceive¹⁹ Ahab into marching to his death at Ramoth-Gilead? Some proposed one thing, and some another, ²¹ until a spirit came forward and stood before Yahve, saying: I will deceive him.

²² And Yahve asked him: How?

[The spirit] replied: I will go out as a deceptive spirit in the mouth of all his prophets.

Then [Yahve] responded: You will prevail in deceiving [him]; go forth and do so.²⁰

By imitating the earthly monarchy, the mythographer is able to create a narrative that talks about a meeting of the heavenly council under the leadership of king Yahve—just like in the previous narrative, where Jehoshaphat consulted with his prophets. The topic under discussion is how to kill Ahab. A spirit suggests a *modus operandi*, and the god approves. The narrative transfers (*metaferō*) the semantic content of one realm (monarchy) into another (divine world). In other words, the divine domain is understood in terms of a worldly monarchy. The passage has extended the metaphor into a story that imitates an aspect of the monarchic system.²¹ The scene transpires in Heaven and only the gods participate in it. But note that the divine court is discussing how to intervene in the human world. Myth is not limited to the activities of the gods within the divine realm, but oftentimes it has to do with the plans and actions of the gods within the political and military affairs of humanity.

Of course, the story does not belong to the empirical world it imitates. Although the prophet says "I saw Yahve" (v. 19), his vision is not bodily sensorial, but it's only the mental representation of an imaginary world that is known only in terms of its metaphorical language. Yahve is not *literally* a king that deliberates with his council. We only imagine him *as if* he were a king. This metaphorical description is not different from "Yahve is my fortress" (Ps 18:2). We understand that the god is obviously not a fortified compound with defense works to resist a military attack.²²

---

bodies are at the same time gods who serve Yahve (Ps 103:21). See §3.1.

19. In Jer 20:7 and Ezek 14:9, Yahve is the subject of the same verb $pātā^h$ (= to deceive).

20. In Job 1:6–12; 2:1–6, we find a similar situation in which the prosecutor proposes a plan, and Yahve approves it.

21. In §4 we'll talk in some detail about the conceptual metaphor god is king.

22. When we talk of any god as our Father, we are not saying that he is *literally* our father. Unless the god had intercourse with our mother, and we are the product of that relationship, the god is not "Our Father." Likewise, Jesus is not *literally* Good Shepherd,

1.1.4 Some Uses of Myth

It is impossible to produce a universal definition of myth in terms of its social function because the stories about the gods were used in so many different ways. Among its many uses, sheer *entertainment* was one of them. For example, an old Sumerian genre was the *debate* or *disputation* (a-da-min),[23] whose *Sitz im Leben* was the school for scribes. The scribes invented this literary genre "for royal entertainment or religious festivals. These [stories] pitted imaginary antagonists against each other—shepherd and farmer, summer and winter, cattle and grain, pickaxe and plow, silver and copper."[24] At the end of each debate, the gods decided who the winner was in the competition.

Another use of myth was to *explain the most profound experiences of our existence*. Life and death form a binary concept in need of explanation. *Life* is nature's capacity to reproduce, breed and spawn all types of biological life. In ancient times, this mind-blowing experience was explained by calling on the gods. This is why the most important gods of the Ancient Near East were fertility and weather-gods (Enlil, Baal, Yahve, etc.). They were thought to be the force behind the production of all weather-phenomena which foster life (§1.2.3; §1.3.3). Another all-embracing and overpowering experience is *death*. As the opposite of life and fertility, death was also explained by a plethora of anthropomorphisms: "Cruel Death cuts off mankind";[25] "Death holds me fast"; "Death, the ruler of men"; "He snatched me from the mouth of death."[26] The furious fight between Baal and Yamm (§1.3.3) or between Baal and Mot (§1.3.4) is nothing more than the battle between life and chaos, between life and death. And these two realities of life and death, says *Gilgameš*, are under the control of the gods:

> The Anunnaki, the great gods, held an assembly,
> Mammitum, maker of destiny, fixed fates with them:
> both Death and Life they have established,

Lamb of God, Vine, Husband, etc.

23. The term a-da-min is comprised by *ada* = "strife, debate, dispute" + *min* = "two," that is, a dispute between two individuals. On the subject of Sumerian debates, see Alster, "Sumerian Literary Dialogues," 2; Vanstiphout, "Mesopotamian Debate Poems, Part I," 271–318; Vanstiphout, "Mesoptamian Debate Poems, Part II," 339–67; Vanstiphout, "Lore, Learning and Levity," 23–46. For debates and fables in Akkadian (*teṣētu*), see Lambert, *Babylonian Wisdom*, 150–212.

24. Hallo, *Oldest Literature*, 722. See Vanstiphout, "Lore, Learning and Levity," 31–2. Cf. Judg 9:8–15; 2 Kgs 14:9.

25. *Gilg.* x.305, in Foster, *Gilgamesh*, 82.

26. Cf. "Mutu," 317.

but the day of Death they do not disclose.[27]

More particularly, myth was used to *explain the perplexing course of nature.* Things like infertility, the high index of stillborn babies, and the death of so many women during parturition were tragedies in need of explanation. Why and how had it all started? *Atra-ḫasīs* (*ca.* 1700–1600 BCE) claims that all these tragedies occur because at the beginning of the world the gods decided to inflict these calamities on humankind in order to prevent overpopulation, and for this same purpose, a caste of priestess was created to remain celibate. *Atra-ḫasīs* explains it this way:

> In addition, let there be a third [category][28] among the peoples,
> (Let there be) among the peoples women who bear
> > and women who do not bear.
> Let there be among the peoples the *Pāšittu*-demon,[29]
> > to snatch the baby from the lap of her who bore it . . .
> Let's establish (priestess) *Ugbabtu*-women,
> > *Entu*-women, and *Igiṣītu*-women . . .
> And let them be taboo,
> > and so stop childbirth.[30]

Today we know that infertility is not the result of a decision made by the gods in primeval times. The death of babies and mothers was not the product of demons and gods. The truth is that "birth in Mesopotamia was a very precarious affair," says Erle Lichty. "Due to the lack of proper medicine and medical knowledge, the lack of proper diet, and the lack of sanitation, miscarriages, still-births, and infant mortality ran at a very high rate. For the same reasons, death in childbirth was also frequent."[31] For lack of a better explanation, ancient people humanized the forces of nature into personal gods that had a "reason" for sending death or demons to kill mothers and/or their babies. Consequently, people resorted to incantations, charms, amulets and potions to protect themselves from gods and demons. This tradition

---

27. *Gilg.* x.319–22, in George, *Epic of Gilgamesh*, 87.

28. The text does not clarify what is this "third" thing. Lambert and Millard, conjecture a "third category" (*Atra-ḫasīs*, 103); while Foster thinks it may refer to a: "third woman" (*Before the Muses*, 253); and Bottéro and Kramer propose a "third law" (*Cuando los Dioses*, 567).

29. *Pāšittu* = annihilator, exterminator.

30. *Atra.* III.vii.1–8 (cf. Lambert and Millard, *Atra-ḫasīs*, 103). For celibate priestess who lived in a cloister and were part of the upper class, see Tetlow, *Women*, 88; Marsman, *Women in Ugarit*, 490–2.

31. Lichty, "Demons and Population Control," 23.

passed to Judaism, Islam and Christianity. Lichty refers to an old Christian conjuration designed to scare the witch who snatches babies. We quote the text more extensively:

> O, Evil Spirit! mayest thou be killed and cursed by the terrible and glorious name of the Trinity, and by the 360 holy fathers of the Council of Nicaea. May X remain clear and shining through the dew of the Holy Spirit as on the day in which his mother bore him; for ever and ever, Amen.[32]

People explained diseases as misfortunes sent by planets and stars. The Gospel of Matthew maintains that the moon assailed a young man with epilepsy: "Lord, have mercy on my son, for he's been stricken by the moon" (Matt 17:15).[33] Today the modern world has no use for this function of myth, even when many religious people still explain earthquakes, hurricanes and other disasters as punishments from god.

Myth tries to make sense of deeply disturbing experiences like guilt, suffering and evil. Paul Ricoeur maintains that "if there is one human experience ruled by myth, it is certainly that of evil."[34] Humans cannot avoid using metaphors to express experiences like guilt, death and suffering. When people lament, says Ricoeur, the experience of evil becomes the voice (wailing, sobbing) of meaningless evil. And this lamenting "connects suffering to language only by joining a question to its moaning. 'Why evil?' 'Why children die?' 'Why me?' In turning itself into a question, lamentation itself appeals to myth,"[35] for it demands an explanation which can only be constructed anthropomorphically in order to sound somewhat rational. Suffering is the breeding ground for stories like the myth of *cosmos versus chaos*, a topic developed in Psalm 74 (§1.3.6). In the presence of meaningless pain and misery, myth provides meaning by creating stories depicting *personal* gods who intervene in human life. Many stories insist that people suffer because the gods are punishing them for their sins. Ernst Cassirer labels this dogma as the doctrine of "mythical causality,"[36] and explains that while empirical thought would talk about, let's say, a disease in terms of a particular case of an *impersonal* natural law, mythic thinking would take

---

32. Gaster, "Two Thousand Years," 142.

33. The Greek text does not say "he is an epileptic" (NRSV), nor "he is demented" (NJB) or "he has seizures" (NIV). See §5.2 for a full explanation of this text.

34. Ricoeur, "Evil," 2897. Evil could be physical: sickness, earthquakes, droughts, floods, hurricanes, etc. Or it could be moral evil: war, murder, unfaithfulness, lies, social injustice, etc.

35. Ricoeur, "Evil," 2898. See also Ricoeur, *Symbolism of Evil*.

36. Cassirer, *Mythical Thinking*, 43.

the same disease as the expression of a *personal* will, whether of a god or a demon. For example, in February of 2010, an earthquake devastated Haiti killing more than 200,000 people. The empirical perspective explained the event as a particular case of tectonic-plate layering at the point of crust-plate boundaries. But the Reverend Pat Robertson expressed the mythic perspective by saying that the earthquake was god's punishment over Haiti for having made a covenant with the devil.[37] However, if we live in a universe ruled by *impersonal* laws and chance, then we have to admit that these impersonal forces know nothing about punishment, justice or compassion. A person may deeply grieve the loss of a loved one in the earthquake but she cannot ask whether that death was just or unjust. As pain longs for a framework of meaning, people can't avoid the temptation of *ascribing personal* attributes to the forces that assault and diminish human life.

Myth was used to explain political and military events. In §1.2.3, we'll mention the fall of the Agade Empire (*ca.* 2159 BCE) in terms of Enlil's revenge. We'll also credit the gods for the fall of Croesus' empire (*ca.* 546 BCE). The biblical tradition explains the fall of Jerusalem (587 BCE) as Yahve's retribution for Judah's apostasy (§5.1). Psalm 82 tries to explain social injustice in general by blaming the gods (§3.3.4.e). After the terrorist attack of 9/11, Pat Robertson and Jerry Falwell said that the fall of the Twin Towers was god's punishment on America for having driven god out of the public square and schools, and also because of pagans, abortionists, feminists, gays, lesbians, and the American Civil Liberties Union (*700 Club*, September 13, 2001). Today this "providential" use of myth is obsolete.

Myth was used to explain or support cultural norms. Within Israel's patriarchal society, the subordination of women was thought to be a "value," that is, something to be protected as part of the structure of society. Women's subordination was reinforced by inventing a story in which the rationale for creating Eve was to be a "helper adequate for him" (Gen 2:18, 20), or it was explained as a punishment for Eve's sin (Gen 3:16). We do not believe these stories to be true anymore, not because they are fictional but because today we see them as endorsing oppression. Our current values of equality and democracy have made the stories obsolete. Nonetheless, this function of myth may be the most fruitful use of myth today for it helps to communicate values that support our communities.

---

37. In Job 36:15, Elihu resorts to the didactic use of myth to explain evil: "By means of afflictions, [god] delivers the afflicted, and gets their attention by means of suffering" (cf. Ps 119:67, 71).

1.1.5 A Word of Caution: The Power of Metaphor

We already mentioned that popular culture misunderstands metaphor as a casual ornamentation. The truth is that metaphors have the power to bewitch us in such a way that we believe the metaphor to be true in a literal way. Metaphorical images have the power to carry us into an imaginary world capable of controlling mind and behavior, because metaphor is a way of *knowing and understanding* and, therefore, it can easily be turned into a tool for disfiguring reality.

Another way of demeaning metaphor occurred during the Enlightenment, when figurative language got a bad reputation. John Locke called it "the art of fallacy," and wrote a whole paragraph against it:

> Since wit and fancy finds easier entertainment in the world, than dry truth and real knowledge, figurative speeches . . . will hardly be admitted as an imperfection or abuse of it. I confess, in discourses, where we seek rather pleasure and delight, than information and improvement, such ornaments as are borrowed from them, can scarce pass for faults. But yet if we would speak of things as they are we must allow that . . . all the artificial and figurative application of words eloquence hath invented, are for nothing else but to insinuate wrong ideas, move the passions, and thereby mislead the judgment, and so, indeed, are perfect cheats . . . It is evident how much men love to deceive, and be deceived, since rhetoric, that powerful instrument of error and deceit, has its established professors . . .[38]

Subsequent studies of metaphor have both corrected the narrow understanding of metaphor as sheer rhetorical ornamentation and have vindicated its good reputation against the accusation that it only serves as an "instrument of error and deceit." Metaphor is not just a *figure of speech*; it is part of the way we *think*. It is not merely that we use metaphors, but that our thinking is to a large extent metaphorical. Metaphor is *a way of knowing and understanding*. Modern studies have established that metaphor is a powerful cognitive tool essential to reasoning and perception.[39] Metaphor is a universal and inevitable aspect of our daily thinking process, and it is a pivotal vehicle for explaining complex and unclear concepts.

But having sung the praises of metaphor, we should also add a word of caution regarding the use of metaphorical expressions and narratives.

---

38. Locke, *Essay Concerning Human Understanding*, 372–73.

39. See Lakoff and Johnson, *Metaphors We Live By*; Lakoff, "Contemporary Theory of Metaphor."

Sometimes metaphorical language is flatly inappropriate. Suppose that a heart attack ends sending a person to the emergency room. After some exams, the doctor says to the patient: "Your ticker is acting a bit antisocial but some tough love from your butcher will force him to be nice." It is obvious that in this case the language does not help to understand what the actual problem is or how it can be solved.

In other cases, metaphorical language can only be accepted as a provisional explanation waiting to be confirmed in some other way, if possible. For example, trying to prove that war drones are safe for civilians caught in combat zones, John Brennan used a metaphor comparing this weapon to a surgical procedure:

> In addition, compared against other options, a pilot operating the aircraft remotely, with the benefit of technology and with the safety of distance, might actually have a clearer picture of the target and its surroundings, including the presence of innocent civilians. It's this surgical precision—the ability with laser-like focus to eliminate the cancerous tumor called an al-Qaida terrorist, while limiting damage to the tissue around it—that makes this counterterrorism tool so essential.[40]

Brennan created a metaphorical narrative that helped him explain the use of a combat weapon (*target domain:* war) in terms of a surgical procedure that removes a tumor with the precision of a laser scalpel (*source domain:* medicine). In his narrative, the terrorist appears *as if* he were a tumor; the drone *as if* it were a scalpel; and civilians *as if* they were surrounding tissue. The story instills a sense of safety as our imagination flees to the operating room. But don't be fooled, in real life the terrorist is not a tumor, the drone is not a scalpel, and civilians are not surrounding tissue. Brennan has not yet proven the safety and precision of the weapon. This is a matter which needs to be established by scientific means and not by metaphorical narratives. And yet there's nothing wrong with this story. It can be understood as a pedagogical resource, as a way of explaining a complex issue. However, as Brennan never added any technical data substantiating what he said metaphorically, his narrative sounds more like demagoguery.

Politicians are experts in using metaphors to avoid responding to difficult questions. In December of 2016, the British public opinion blasted Prime Minister Theresa May for not being able to give any specifics on how her government was planning to withdraw Great Britain from the European Union. When a journalist asked her about it, May responded saying: "Actually we want a red, white and blue Brexit: that is the right Brexit for the UK,

---

40. Brennan, "Ethics and Efficacy."

the right deal for the UK."[41] Instead of providing concrete operational details, May alluded to the colors of the British flag. Did she mean a patriotic transition!? The metaphor doesn't make any sense and it was obviously a way of evading the question.

Religious language easily lends itself to deception. C. S. Lewis was notorious for his abuse of metaphor which he employed often to "validate" a point without really proving anything. For example, in his book *Mere Christianity* Lewis argues that Christians receive new life through baptism, faith and the Lord's Supper. He explains that he believes this on Jesus' authority. And immediately adds:

> Do not be scared by the word authority. Believing things on authority only means believing them because you have been told them by someone you think trustworthy . . . I believe there is such a place as New York. I have not seen it myself. I could not prove by abstract reasoning that there must be such a place. I believe it because reliable people have told me so.[42]

We can't blame Mark Rubinstein for scolding him: "In examples such as the existence of a place called New York, all authorities agree, and their conclusions follow from observation and reason. But religious beliefs are qualitatively different. Religion is inherently controversial since it speculates about the unseen or uninferred. Authorities do not agree. As a result, there may be no authority you can reliably depend on."[43] The key point here is "religious beliefs are qualitatively different." Lewis is comparing apples to oranges. The confidence we have on the guaranteed knowledge regarding New York is illegitimately transferred to the religious arena.

And now let's illustrate the hellish use of metaphor with an example borrowed from the Second World War. Hans M. Frank (1900–1946 CE) declared that Poland was filled with "Jews and lice." Once the metaphor was established, Germany created a narrative arguing that the elimination of Jewish people was a matter of national health. Paul-Otto Schmidt, German Foreign Minister, declared: "The Jewish question is not a question of humanity, and it is not a question of religion; it is solely a question of political hygiene" [*eine Frage der politischen Hygiene*].[44]

---

41. O'Donnell, "May Says She'll Seek."

42. Lewis, *Mere Christianity*, 62.

43. Rubinstein, "C. S. Lewis and Proof by Metaphor," 14.

44. Hilberg, *Destruction of the European Jews*, 1097. Even a metaphorical action could give the impression of producing a real effect: "Pilate . . . took some water and washed his hands before the crowd" (Matt 27:24). We wash our hands to eliminate dirt and impurity, but Pilate's literal washing seems to extend its efficacy to the realm

As hatred is irrational, it is unable to find expression in language other than figuratively. When hate brings down language, it takes refuge in metaphor in order to express the unspeakable. Dehumanization can only be achieved by the power of metaphor, for metaphor has the capacity to *control how we perceive the world*.[45] The Nazis created a narrative that equated Jewish people with lice. In this way they were able *to see* them and treat them likewise. In a similar fashion, Augustin Bizimungy, Rwanda's army general, called the Tutsi population "cockroaches" and then started the genocidal killing of 800,000 people in 1994. The church fathers Gregory of Nazianzus and Isidore of Seville "compare monkeys to pagans and deny both the faculty of reason."[46] In 1854, Samuel G. Morton, Josiah C. Nott and George R. Gliddon published *Types of Mankind: Ethnological Researches*, in which they materialized the monkey metaphor by genetically linking the African population to chimpanzees, gorillas and orangutans. This pseudoscience was only a tool for materializing the metaphor of the animal. The animalization of people from other countries or ethnic groups has been the favorite metaphor to dehumanize and exterminate them. To think of people as animals is to treat them as such:

> African slaves were shackled and muzzled like animals, beaten like animals, branded like animals, bought and sold like animals, had their children taken from them like animals, and had their humanity and individuality ignored, just as humans do with animals. They were property just as animals were, and could be legally killed by their property owner, just as animals could.[47]

President Trump has described immigrants as animals: "You wouldn't believe how bad these people are. These aren't people. These are animals."[48] And he tweeted complaining that illegal immigrants "infest our country."[49] Consequently, his administration treated immigrants as animals.

Finally, the Rev. O'Neal Dozier declared (2003) that homosexuality was "something so nasty and disgusting that it makes God want to vomit."[50]

---

of morality and justice, something completely disconnected with the washing of the hands. Nonetheless, Pilate feels authorized to conclude that he's "innocent" regarding Jesus' fate, when Jesus' execution could not have happened without his approval.

45. See Smith, *Less Than Human*, where he deals with the relation between metaphor, slavery and genocide.
46. Hund, *Semianization*, 44.
47. DeMello, *Animals and Society*, 265.
48. Trump, "Remarks by President Trump."
49. @realDonaldTrump 9:52 AM, June 19, 2018.
50. Quoted in Weinstein, "Gays 'Make God Want to Vomit.'"

This powerful metaphor does not prove anything but the feelings of the speaker. Traditional theology teaches that the Christian god is spiritual. God does not have a physical body able to feel the involuntary need to regurgitate. However, the metaphor is an incredibly effective tool to "move the passions, and thereby mislead the judgment" (Locke) without proving how god really "feels." The metaphor evades our analytic capacities and hits our emotions directly.

1.2 Myth: Faulty Definitions

1.2.1 Stories about the Origins of the World

Some scholars would define myth as a story about the origins of the world. Aland Dundes explains it this way: "A myth may be defined as a sacred narrative explaining how the world or how humans came to be in their present form."[51] This definition is incorrect. It is true that there are many myths dealing with the creation of the world,[52] but we also have myths about life, death, love, war, etc.[53] For example, the Sumerian myth *The Bridal Sheets* tells the story of how Utu (the Sun god) made arrangements for the wedding of his sister Inana (Venus). In the story, he insinuates that a wedding is on the horizon by telling her that she needs new sheets for her bed. Inana gets the message and starts fretting about the whole deal, but then she's filled with joy when she finds out that the chosen groom is the god she loves.[54] Further, the well-known myth of the battle between Baal and Yamm makes no reference to creation motifs.[55] Job 1:1—2:10 portrays a mythical scene that has no connection to the beginning of the world. Therefore, it

---

51. Dundes, *Flood Myth*, 1. Similarly Childs, *Myth and Reality*, 17–19; Eliade, *Myth and Reality*, 5.

52. There is plenty. See Genesis 1–3; Atra-ḫasīs: The Babylonian version of creation and the flood (*ca.* 1646 BCE); Ziudsura: The Sumerian version of creation and the flood (*ca.* 1600 BCE); Enki (Namma) and Ninmah: The creation of humanity (*ca.* 2000 BCE); A bilingual story of the creation of humanity: KAR 4 (*ca.* 1000 BCE); Inana, Gilgameš and the Huluppu tree (*ca.* 2000 BCE); Before Creation (*ca.* 2112-2004 BCE); *Enūma Eliš*: The exaltation of Marduk (*ca.* 1126–1105 BCE); Marduk: The creator of the world (*ca.*1200–1000 BCE); Creation according to the Barton cylinder (*ca.* 2300 BCE); Hesiod, *Theogony*, etc.

53. Heimpel, "Mythologie," 546–48, provides a complete list of myths with no connection to the origins of the world. The themes are birth, love, marriage, death, war, rank, fame.

54. *Bridal Sheets*, in Jacobsen, *Harps that Once*, 13–15.

55. See Smith, "Baal Cycle."

is important to reject any definition that limits myth to stories about the origins of the world.

1.2.2 Tendentious Definition

Until the middle of the twentieth century, a large segment of Christian scholarship denied that the Bible contains myths; or it was argued that the few myths that do show up were taken from the surrounding cultures and neutralized into poetic rhetoric. These conclusions were reached by claiming that "the presuppositions for forming myths are lacking in the soil of the OT religion. Its monotheistic tendency and its organic connection with history... prevent Israel from creating myths of its own."[56] Two concepts stand out here: monotheism and the "organic connection to history," which are supposed to be the scriptural antidotes against myth. Roderick MacKenzie's definition elaborates on these two ideas:

> The simplest definition of myth is "a story about gods." Essentially, mythology is polytheist; two gods are the very minimum *dramatis personae* that will suffice for it. But in the Israelite narratives there is only the one God, Who therefore cannot be acted upon by any other. On the supernatural level, there can be no conflict. Once Yahve intervenes, the question is settled; what He does is final, irresistible, definitive. Further, there is here [in the Bible] no possibility of a story on the divine level only. There are myths from Ras Shamra and Babylon, in which the whole action is performed in the divine world, with gods and goddesses as the actors; such a *genus* is simply impossible in Israel. All this prehistory deals with human actors, whose proceedings are judged and settled by unconditioned divine action.[57]

Note carefully that for a story to be considered myth, it has to fulfill two requisites: First, *myth is polytheistic*. To qualify as a myth, a narrative must contain a minimum of two gods. Otto Eissfeldt echoed the same old song: "A real myth presupposes at least two gods, the one contesting with the other."[58] This definition is completely arbitrary, for what makes a narrative a myth is not the number of gods present in a story, but the fact that the story uses anthropomorphic language.[59] As we shall see, the fundamental metaphor of

---

56. Weiser, *Old Testament*, 58.
57. MacKenzie, "Before Abraham Was," 136.
58. Eissfeldt, *Old Testament*, 35.
59. See §1.1.3; §2.4.6–7.

theism happens to be anthropomorphism (§2.1.3), and its central anthropomorphism is the king-metaphor (§4). First Kings 22:19–22 (§1.1.3) is a mythical narrative, not because it contains "gods" in plural, but because it replicates metaphorically what happens in the court of an earthly king. In this case the chief god (henotheism) is portrayed as being surrounded by the gods of his own council.[60] Our study will establish that to define a myth on the basis of how many gods appear in a narrative is incorrect. It is a clear maneuver to exempt Yahve from the definition.

Second, MacKenzie insists that *myth describes events that happen only in the divine world*. Again, this definition does not emerge from an impartial analysis of the evidence but from the need to protect the "historicity" of the biblical stories and the uniqueness of Yahve. But even assuming the accuracy of this definition, we still find passages in the Scriptures that meet these conditions. We already showed that 1 Kings 22:19–22 presents an event that transpires only in the divine realm, but Yahve is not alone in the story. He's accompanied by the "host of Heaven" (= gods). He interacts with them and with a spirit (§1.1.3). In chapter three, we'll see that Psalm 89:5–8[6–9] portrays a scene that takes place only in the divine world with the participation of Yahve and other gods (§3.3.4.d). Psalm 82 is an exquisite mythical narrative in which only Yahve and the gods play a part (§3.3.4.e). What befalls in Job 1:6–12 happens in Heaven with the participation of "the sons of elohim" and a divine prosecutor (§3.3.4.c). All these passages meet the conditions postulated by MacKenzie. The events happen only in the divine world and with the participation of more than one god. In §1.3, we'll also examine other biblical narratives that involve more than one god and which occur in the divine world.

1.2.3 Bogus Argument: The Gods Are Limited to the Realm of Nature

Some scholars have argued that Israel's interest was centered in historical events. This prevented her from embracing mythical narratives. In contrast, we are told that pagans were obsessed with the cyclical character of nature, and this led them to the invention of myths. Yahve was supposed to be the god of history while the pagan gods belonged to the sphere of nature.[61]

60. If people complain that these are angels, not gods, we should remind them that the members of Yahve's pantheon (or assembly) were in fact gods. Daniel refers to them as "holy gods" (*'ĕlāhîn qaddîšîn*, Dan 4:8, 9, 18[5, 6, 15]; 5:11; and see §3.3.4b). As we shall demonstrate later, the angels are the gods of Yahve's council: "Elohim stands up in the assembly of El, in the midst of the gods he pronounces judgment" (Ps 82:1; and see §3.3.4.e).

61. George E. Wright was the poster child for the argument that Yahve acts in

Bertil Albrektson produced a seminal study (1967) that established that the cultures surrounding Israel clearly believed that their gods were in control of history. He pointed out that instead of providing evidence, theologians only created a slogan which is taken as "almost self-evident which is not in need of further demonstration or proof."[62] But if we dare read Ancient Near East and Mediterranean literature honestly, we'll learn that the argument about the "gods of nature" has been fabricated by a sector who doesn't want to see what is in plain sight.[63] Long before Israel appeared in history, the Ancient Near East had already produced a theology that portrayed the gods as rulers of the universe and the destiny of the human race.[64]

Let's look at some of the evidence. Until the appearance of Marduk, Enlil was the unquestionable king of the gods (§4.2.1).[65] As a weather-god, En-lil was the Lord (*en*) of the wind (*lil²*). He was also the inventor of the pick-axe used for working the soil and building cities.[66] He was the god of farmers and herdsmen.[67] His wife was the grain goddess Ninlil, and his son was Ninĝirsu (or Ninurta, §4.2.1), the god of the plough and spring rains.[68] As such, Enlil was the supreme god of nature's abundance:

---

history, while the gods do so only in nature. He makes his case in a chapter about "Dios y los Dioses" (Wright, *Arqueología*, 145–48). See also the arguments of Barr, "Meaning of Mythology," 8; Eissfeldt, *Old Testament*, 35; Von Rad, *Teología*, 53, 185, 190, 214; Weiser, *Old Testament*, 57–58.

62. Albrektson, *History and the Gods*, 14. See also the excellent criticism of the old view by Davies, "Approach to the Problem"; McKenzie, "Myth and the Old Testament"; Oden, *Bible Without Theology*; Smith, "Mythology and Myth-Making"; Thompson, *Mythic Past*; Wyatt, *Mythic Mind*.

63. In the context of social justice, Dr. William Baxter has said something applicable to the discipline of Bible studies: "those in power will ignore what they do not want to see as long as we let them," in Barber, *Third Reconstruction*, 55. The denial of the fact that the Bible is a mythological book has a clear political purpose, the supremacy of Christianity in the world. See §4.3.4-6.

64. Later on (§4.3.4) we'll examine how the gods directed history and won victories for their kings.

65. Kramer, *Sumerians*, 119.

66. In *Song of the Hoe* (ca. 1900–1600 BCE), we are told that Enlil created the world and made humans grow like plants. He also created the pickax (ETCSL t.5.5.4), which he praised by saying: "The hoe makes everything prosper, the hoe makes everything flourish. The hoe is good barley . . . it cultivates the right kind of fields. It is you, hoe, that extends the good agricultural land!" (*Song of the Hoe* i.94–106; see Black, *Literature of Ancient Sumer*, 314).

67. He is himself: "Enlil, the good shepherd of (herds) multiplying one like the other, the herdsman and leader of all in which is breath of life, exercises his great princely office awe-inspiringly, has the holy verdant crest-crown green" (*Hymn to Enlil* 92–94, in Jacobsen, *Harps that Once*, 107).

68. Jacobsen, *Treasures*, 99.

> Thou art Lord! Thou art master!
>> Enlil, thou are lord! Thou art master!
>> Nunamnir,[69] thou art lord! Thou art master!
> A lord carrying great weight,
>> lord of the storehouse,
>> art thou!
> The lord making the barley sprout forth,
>> the lord making the vines sprout forth,
>> art thou!
> Lord of heaven, lord making yields be,
>> and lord of the earth
>> art thou!
> Lord of heaven, lord making yields be,
>> and lord of the earth
>> art thou!
> Enlil being lord, Enlil being master,
>> and inasmuch as a lord's word
>> is a thing unalterable,
> his sagacious word
>> cannot be changed![70]

But Enlil was also the warrior-god of *history, politics and military might* (§4.3.4.a). Enlil "assumed the form of a human executive gathering all the threads of complex management, and making all major decisions."[71] A hymn conveys clearly this idea, by saying:

> He is the one prince of heaven,
>> the monarch of earth,
> august, tutelary god
>> of the gods of high descent.
> Accordingly he makes decisions by himself
>> –no god looks on.[72]

---

69. According to Edzard, the word "Nunamnir" (^{d}nu-nam-nir) means "he who is respected" ("Die Mythologie," 60).

70. *Enlil and Ninlil* i.142–53, in Jacobsen, *Harps that Once*, 179.

71. Jacobsen, *Treasures*, 99–100.

72. *Hymn to Enlil* i.100–103, in Jacobsen, *Harps that Once*, 107.

As the highest executive god, nothing happened without his approval, not only in nature but *in human affairs*. The following hymn clearly states that without him:

> no city could be built,
> > no population settled therein,
> no byre built,
> > its sheepfold not set up.
> No king could be raised to office,
> > no lord installed,
> no high priest or high priestess
> > designated by the (omen-)kid,
> no general or lieutenant
> > could be had by the army.[73]

Moving from human society back to nature, the same hymn adds that without Enlil:

> The waters of the carp-flood at its height
> > could not dredge the canals . . .
> The sea could not give birth
> > to the heavy souther with its rain,
> the freshwater fish could not spawn
> > in the canebrake,
> the birds of heaven not base their nests
> > on the broad earth.
> In the sky the rain-laden clouds
> > could not open their mouths,
> in the fields the tilth could not sprout
> > the mottle barley . . . [74]

Enlil was not confined to the realm of nature but was involved in military affairs. Samuel Kramer explained that *The Cursing of Agade* is a story that revealed why the Empire of Agade (*ca.* 2340–2159 BCE) came to an end.[75] This *historical* event was explained in terms of the intervention of a powerful god.

73. *Hymn to Enlil* i.110–13, in Jacobsen, *Harps that Once*, 108.

74. *Hymn to Enlil* i.114–21, in Jacobsen, *Harps that Once*,108. See Kramer, *Sumerians*, 120–21.

75. The story was written *ex eventu*, "reflecting the ideological interests of the kings of the Ur III dynasty (2112–2004) . . . In their explanation of the fall of the Agade empire, they cast themselves in the role of its heirs" (Kuhrt, *Ancient Near East*, 58).

The story is "one of the earliest recorded attempts to interpret a historical event in the framework of a currently held world view. In searching for the causes behind the humiliating and disastrous Gutian invasion, the author comes upon what he thinks is undoubtedly the true answer ... According to the author, [king] Naram-Sin had sacked [the city of] Nippur and committed all sorts of desecrating and defiling acts against Enlil's sanctuary [of E-kur], and Enlil had therefore turned to the Gutians ... to destroy Agade and avenge his beloved temple."[76] Naram-Sin (*ca.* 2213–2176) triggered the fall of his empire when he destroyed Enlil's city and sanctuary,[77] for in revenge the warrior-god caused the fall of the greatest empire of that era:

> Enlil, the roaring storm that subjugates the entire land,
> the rising deluge that cannot be confronted,
> was considering what would be destroyed in return for the wrecking of his beloved E-kur.
> He lifted his gaze towards the Gubin mountains, and made all the inhabitants of the broad mountain ranges descent.
> Enlil brought out of the mountains those who do not resemble other people,
> who are not reckoned as part of the Land ...
> Because of Enlil, they stretched their arms out across the plain like a net for animals.
> Nothing escaped their clutches,
> no one left their grasp.[78]

Trying to calm Enlil, the gods turned to curse Agade:

> Enlil, may the city that destroyed your city
> be treated as your city has been treated!

Now we turn to Utu (or Šamaš). The meaning of his name is "sun," but this doesn't mean that his only function in the world is to regulate the days and seasons of the solar system. It would be totally false to claim that Utu's actions and influence were limited to nature while Yahve's primary concern was with "history" (§3.1). Contrary to this idea is the fact that Utu was an omniscient god (= light) and, therefore, his main duty was to act as the

---

76. Kramer, *Sumerians*, 62.
77. *Cursing of Agade* i.100–148, in Black, *Literature of Ancient Sumer*, 120.
78. *Cursing of Agade* i.149–175, in Black, *Literature of Ancient Sumer*, 120–21.

universal "incorruptible judge";[79] as the "Lord of truth and justice";[80] as the one who judges "the case of the oppressed man and woman."[81] A legend presents him helping king Lugalbanda when he laid wounded in a cave.[82] Šamaš also helped Gilgameš and Enkidu to kill Humbaba, the guardian of the forest.[83] In all these cases, Utu is involved in human affairs. The prayers to Šamaš clearly portray him as a god of history:

> O Shamash, King of heaven and earth,
>> judge above and be[low,
>> lord of the dead, gui]de of the living,
> You are preserver of life, the great leader of humankind . . . [84]
>> Oh Shamash, judge of heaven and earth,
>> judge of upper and lower regions,
> Who administers the people of this land,
>> who releases the prisoner,
>> who revives the moribund . . . [85]

Finally, glyptic art represents Šamaš not as an impersonal force of nature but as a humanized god. For example, the famous *Stele of Hammurabi* portrays Šamaš as a bearded man seated on his throne wearing a crown with horns, while King Hammurabi is standing in front of him receiving the laws that made him famous.[86] William Ward also discusses images of Šamaš carved in several cylinder seals in which the god is represented as a man with his foot set on a mountain and wearing a tiara and a long garment open in front.

---

79. *Against a Curse* i.3, in Foster, *Before the Muses*, 732. Cf. Ps 9:8; 58:11[12].

80. *Against a Snake* i.2, in Foster, *Before the Muses*, 729. Cf. Ps 33:5

81. *Against Ghosts* i.10, in Foster, *Before the Muses*, 731 (cf. Ps 103:6; 146:7). In the epilogue of Lipit-Ishtar's (1870–1860 BCE) legislation, the king makes clear the involvement of the gods in the legislative affairs of the nation: "In accordance with the true Word of the god Utu, I made the lands of Sumer and Akkad hold fair judicial procedure. In accordance with the utterance of the god Enlil, I, Lipit-Ishtar, son of Enlil, eradicated enmity and violence" (*Laws of Lipit-Ishtar* xxi.5–17, in Roth, *Law Collections*, 33).

82. *Lugalbanda in the Mountain Cave*, in Black, *Literature of Ancient Sumer*, 11–22.

83. *Gilg.* v.135–79. See George, *Epic of Gilgamesh*, 42.

84. *Against Impending Evil* i.1–2, in Foster, *Before the Muses*, 728.

85. *Against a Known Sorcerer* i.1–2, in Foster, *Before the Muses*, 729. See Starr, *Queries to the Sungod*, where he elaborates on the political influence of Šamaš in the kingdoms of Esarhaddon and Assurbanipal.

86. For the stela, see https://www.louvre.fr/en/oeuvre-notices/law-code-hammurabi-king-babylon. For other human representations of the sun god, see Frankfort, *Cylinder Seals*, 68, 95–7, 130, 137, 160–64.

Another seal shows rays coming from his shoulders, his foot again upon a mountain and with his notched sword in his hand.[87]

The gods were in charge of the universe. *Atraḫasīs* (ca. 1700–1600 BCE) explains that the gods "determined the destinies" (*šimati*) of humankind,[88] and *Gilgameš* adds that the gods established death as their fate:

> The tavern keeper said to him, to Gilgamesh:
> Gilgamesh, wherefore do you wander?
> The eternal life you are seeking you shall not find.
> When the gods created humankind,
> They established death for mankind,
> And withheld eternal life for themselves.[89]

King Assurbanipal (669–627 BCE) believed that he was "king of the universe . . . , king of the four world-regions." And he built this expansionist ideology on the will of the gods who control history:

> The great gods in their council decreed a favorable destiny (*šimat*) . . . the lands of my enemies they counted into my hands.[90]

The gods not only ruled history in general but their control was also displayed at a very personal level. Long before the book of Job, the Babylonians produced a poem about the suffering of the righteous. The work was known as *Ludlul bēl nēmeqi* (= "I will praise the Lord of Wisdom"), and was written sometime during the Kassite period (1300–1155 BCE).[91] This lament talks about a man who lost everything in life: his social status as governor, his wealth, his family and health, until Marduk had mercy on him and restored his life. The poem operates under the assumption that Marduk is the cosmic ruler who has the power to destroy or to give life. While there were many

---

87. Ward, *Cylinders*, 87–9.

88. *Atra.* i.219.

89. *Gilg.* x.77–81, in Foster, *Gilgamesh*, 75.

90. *Inscription of Ashurbanipal* edition B column i, in Piepkorn, *Historical Prism*, 29.

91. The translations by Pfeiffer, "I Will Praise the Lord of Wisdom," 434–37; Biggs, "I Will Praise the Lord of Wisdom," 596–600; and Lambert, *Babylonian Wisdom*, 21–62, all contain several gaps in the text. A notable gap is the omission of almost all of the first part of the first tablet. Using a Tablet discovered at Nimrud, Wiseman, "New Text," 101–7, was able to provide the translation for the sections i.13–46 and ii.111–20. Another tablet allowed George and Al-Rawi, "Tablets from the Sippar Library," 187–206, to provide a wonderful edition of the whole first tablet. At the moment, the edition by Annus and Lenzi, *Ludlul bēl nēmeqi*, has no competition. See also Foster, "Self-Reference of an Akkadian Poet," 123–30; Foster, *Before the Muses*, 392–409; Horowitz and Lambert, "New Exemplar," 237–45; and Moran, "Notes on the Hymn," 255–60.

gods in Babylon, the only true and sovereign god was Marduk. The belief in a personal almighty god unleashes a tremendous crisis in the presence of wanton evil:

> The Lord, he sees [eve]rything in the heart of the gods,
> > but no on[e among the god]s knows his way.
>
> Marduk, he sees [eve]rything in the heart of the gods,
> > but no god can learn his counsel ...
>
> Without his consent, who could assuage his striking?
> > Apart from his intention, who could stay his hand?[92]

The sufferer of the story complains that Marduk can do anything he wants, even assigning guilt without warning: "He speaks and imputes guilt."[93] When life takes a random turn it is only because Marduk controls human destiny and he is able to play with people like the cat plays with a mouse:

> In one moment a person is worried,
> > then suddenly becomes exuberant.
>
> In one instant he sings with jubilation,
> > the next he groans like a mourner.
>
> Their destiny changes in a blink of the eye.[94]

Only when Marduk's anger subsides does the suffering end and the chains are broken:

> After the heart of the Lord was sti[ll],
> > The min[d] of the merciful Marduk was app[eased].
>
> After [he accept]ed my prayer ...
>
> His [bene]volent attention was sweet ... [95]

Moving to the Mediterranean, we find Homer partaking in the doctrine of Providence, that is, the belief that the gods control human life. At the very beginning of the *Odyssey*, it is made clear that it was the gods who decided to bring Odysseus back home to his sweet Penelope:

> ... the gods had ordained that he should return home to Ithaca ...
> all the gods pitied him ... [96]

---

92. *Ludlul* i.29–33. Cf. Ps 76:8[7]; Job 11:10.
93. *Ludlul* i.23.
94. *Ludlul* ii.40–43, 48. Cf. Amos 3:5, 6; Isa 45:7; 54:15; Lam 3:37–39; Eccl 7:14.
95. *Ludlul* iii.51–4.
96. Homer, *Odyssey* i.17–8, in Murray, *Odyssey 1–12*, 13. In *Odyssey* iii.208–10,

Then the goddess Athena volunteers to go to Ithaca to incite (*epotrunō*) Odysseus' son to sail on an expedition to look for his father.[97] So Athena visits Telemachus,[98] and she recruits a group of men to form a crew for the ship. She also visits king Nestor. In all these visits, Athena appears in the form of a human being who persuades, interacts, dines and talks with people in order to carry out the divine plan of bringing Odysseus back home.

In the first part of his *Histories*, Herodotus narrates the time when king Croesus (595–547 BCE) asked Solon to disclose who was the most fortunate man he's ever met. The sage responded that this type of questions can only be answered once the person has died, because:

> He who has constantly enjoyed most of these [advantages], and then ends his life in tranquility, this man, in my judgment, O king, deserves the name 'happy.' Therefore, we ought to consider the end of everything, in what way it will terminate; for the Deity having shown a glimpse of happiness to many, has afterward utterly overthrown them.[99]

History showed that Croesus became one of those who was successful at the beginning but ended in ruin. Herodotus recounts the death of his son and how Cyrus conquered his empire. According to Herodotus, these tragic events were sent by the gods as punishment for his arrogance:

> After the departure of Solon, the indignation of the gods fell heavily upon Croesus because he thought of himself the most happy of all men.[100]

We should point out that the downfall of Croesus entailed a significant divine intervention in the political and military aspects of human life. The gods had triggered the fall of a powerful king who had managed to conquer almost all Asia Minor.

Xenophon (431–354 BCE) also touches on the role of the gods in terms of rewards or punishments over human behavior. Regarding the fall of Sparta (371 BCE), he says:

> Now one could mention many other incidents, both among Greeks and barbarians, to prove that the gods do not fail to take heed of the wicked or of those who do unrighteous things; but

---

Telemachus complains that the gods have not decreed for him the joy of avenging his father.

97. *Odyssey* i.16–17, 88–89.
98. See §2.2.4.a.3.
99. Herodotus, *Histories* i.32.9, in Cary, *Herodotus*, 14.
100. Herodotus, *Histories* i.34.1, in Cary, *Herodotus*, 15.

at present I will speak of the case which is before me [which is Sparta].[101]

Conclusion

These few examples show that the gods were not just in control of the cycles of nature but that they were also in charge of ruling history. Both Yahve and the gods claimed they were in control of history. It is ridiculous to claim that Israel had the monopoly of historical consciousness for all human beings are aware of both historical and cyclical time.

1.2.4 Myths and Legends: Gray Areas

A quick review of the academic literature shows that scholars agree that there are no strict boundaries between myth and legend. Kirk starts by setting a useful distinction between myth and legend. On the one hand, he says, myths are "essentially non-historical tales," by which he refers to narratives about the gods that take place in the *divine world*. On the other hand, legends may "include identifiable and conspicuous historical elements or are historicizing intention." In other words, legends point to events that appear to happen *in this world*. However, it is impossible to maintain such rigid distinction, so Kirk corrects his own statement, adding: "Naturally the distinction is not a hard-and-fast one," and adds an obvious example: "The *Iliad* as a whole can be classified as 'myth' in a very general sense, and finds its way into most surveys of Greek mythology . . . but the *Iliad* is also very different from non-historicizing traditional tales, whether about gods or about Heracles or Perseus."[102] We can add a work from Mesopotamia: *Atraḫasīs* (ca. 1700–1600 BCE). Some scholars classify this narrative as *epic*, because they place the emphasis on the second part of the work which talks about Atrahasis as a heroic figure,[103] in spite of the fact that the section abounds in mythical content. Others classify it as *myth* because they put their focus on the first part of the narrative which mainly talks about the gods at the beginning of creation.[104]

---

101. Xenophon, *Hellenica* v.4.1, in Brownson, *Xenophon: Hellenica*, 453.

102. Kirk, "On Defining Myth," 55. Van Seters concurs: "myth and legend appear so often together, as they do in Homer, that their combination is not a problem" (*Prologue to History*, 25).

103. Lambert and Millard, *Atra-ḫasīs*, 1, 7; Pettinato "Bestrafung des Menschengeschlechts," 166.

104. Renger, "Review," 342.

Likewise, Stith Thompson first declares that "myth has to do with the gods and their actions," but then corrects himself, saying: "This is a minimum definition, for it must be recognized that the word myth is frequently used with a much broader meaning . . . sometimes applied also to the hero tales, whether those hero tales deal with demigods or not."[105] Fritz Graf concurs that it's not possible to sustain a rigid differentiation between myth and legend: "If myth and epic poem are not mutually exclusive categories, then an epic poem is one specific concretization of a myth or of an entire cluster of myths, as is the case with Gilgamesh and the Iliad."[106] Finally, Richard Buxton defines myth as "a narrative about the deeds of gods and heroes and their interrelations with ordinary mortals,"[107] mixing both myth and legend in one single definition. All these definitions blur the boundaries to acknowledge that there is not a solid dividing wall between myth and legend (epic, saga). Myth may refer to the actions of the gods in Heaven or on earth; it could also talk about one god, many gods or divine heroes. Myth can even insert itself in historical narratives.

The gray areas between myth and legend arise partly from the fact that ancient people did not establish firm boundaries between fact and fiction. This distinction was created by the modern world. When Benjamin Foster talks about Mesopotamian literature, he is well aware that it is not always clear whether the stories "were primarily mythological in purpose or whether they were simply narrative strategies for authors in a culture that assigned little literary value to the present and empirically recognizable."[108] Legends may have a historical core or they may totally lack any historical foundation whatsoever, even when the narrative locates them in what it seems to be an earthly milieu. When we encounter these stories, our modern perspective detects a "historicizing" effort on the part of authors who introduce into the narrative details that look like historical information. But this "does not change fancy into fact."[109] It only helps placing a legend or myth in what resembles a somewhat historical narrative.

Here are some biblical examples: Today there is enough scholarly consensus to say that the formation of Israel must have been driven either by an

---

105. Thompson, "Myths and Folktales," 106. For a treatment of the hero legend, see §3.4.

106. Graf, "Myth," 54.

107. Buxton, *Imaginary Greece*, 14. See Burkert, *Structure and History*, 24, who makes a similar case: "There is, by the way, no reason to distinguish myth from saga in the Greek view." And neither should we make the distinction in relation to the Ancient Near East culture.

108. Foster, *Before the Muses*, 42.

109. Van Seters, *Prologue to History*, 25.

internal resettlement of population in Canaan or by a peasant uprising.[110] It was not a military invasion from outside Palestine.[111] Some would also say that the emergence of Israel was assisted by a mixed group coming from Transjordan[112] and a small group of slaves coming from Egypt.[113] In any case, the biblical editors used divine interventions to infuse these narratives with fantastic mythical enhancements like is the case with the story of the Exodus.[114] The story of King David is also an ideological legend with historical and mythological overtones.[115] Historical or legendary narratives may come peppered with strong mythological colors. The Samson Epic starts (Judg 13:3-21) by incorporating a long interaction between Samson's parents and an "envoy of Yahve" (v. 3), who ends his performance with a spectacular *anabasis* through the flames of a sacrifice (vv. 19-20).[116] However, at that time people did not envision the story as a hodgepodge of history, legend and myth. Finally, one of the most pristine examples of how a clear *historical* event could come interwoven with distinct *mythical* threads is Eusebius' report regarding Constantine's victory over Maxentius. We will explore this narrative further in §5.1.

Conclusion

If myth is to be defined as *stories about the gods*, we cannot anymore exempt the god of the Scriptures from this definition. The god in singular must be

110. Ahlström, *History of Ancient Palestine*; Dever, "How to Tell"; Dever, *Who Were the Early Israelites*; Lemche, *Early Israel*; Lemche, *Ancient Israel*; Lemche, *Old Testament*; Mendenhall, "Hebrew Conquest"; Mendenhall, *Tenth Generation*; Mendenhall, "Change and Decay"; Gottwald, *Tribes of Yahweh*; Gottwarld, *Hebrew Bible*; William Dever states that apart from Gottwald's Marxist jargon, his insights were "brilliantly correct" (*Who Were the Early Israelites*, 54).

111. In any case, "there was no real conquest of Palestine in the sense that has usually been understood" (Mendenhall, "Hebrew Conquest," 73). For the conquest model, see several articles and books by Albright, "Archaeology and the Date of the Hebrew Conquest"; "The Israelite Conquest of Canaan"; *Archaeology of Palestine*; *From the Stone Age to Christianity*, and *Archaeology and the Religion of Israel*.

112. Some archaic Bible passages suggest that a pre-mosaic group who worshiped El/Yahve may have come from the southern areas of Seir, Edom, Sinai, Paran, etc. in Transjordan (Deut 33:2-3; Judg 5:4-5; Hab 3:3, 7).

113. See Gottwald, *Hebrew Bible*, 261-76, for an overview of different theories.

114. Ahlström, *History of Ancient Palestine*, and *Who Were the Israelites*; Dever, "How to Tell," and *Who Were the Early Israelites*. Finkelstein and Silberman, *Bible Unearthed*; Hess, *Critical Issues*; Lemche, *Early Israel*; *Ancient Israel* and *Old Testament*; Liverani, *Israel's History*; Soggin, *History of Ancient Israel*.

115. Van Seters, *Biblical Saga of King David*.

116. For a brief analysis of this story, see §2.2.a.5.

incorporated into the genre. The god of Judaic and Christian theology is a mythological figure. Mark Smith defines myth more accurately as:

> narratives about divine beings, but without excluding narratives with only one deity such as Yahweh.[117]

In similar fashion, John van Seters makes room for the god in singular:

> Myth is a traditional story about events in which the god or gods are the primary actors.[118]

Nicholas Wyatt properly insists that Judaism and Christianity did not have a more scientific or historical worldview than other religions, because:

> As soon as divine intent, divine creativity, and divine purpose ... are read into the world of experience, as soon as the certainty of God's presence is perceived in human life, it ceases to be a rational view, in the sense of the historian seeing a chain of events which can be explained in terms of historical causation, the outworking of political strategies or economic cycles, and so forth, and becomes a mythic one. Stories of the beginning and end of the world, and of the resurrection, ascension and second coming of Christ are not in any sense 'historical' narratives, whether past or future in their application. Couched in historiographical form, the narrative of biblical historiography bears the veneer of history, but we know that not only is the facticity of this history largely tendentious, but that introducing Yahweh as the leading character removes it from the cold light of day, and takes it into an interior world of commitment and religious experience.[119]

Therefore, if we make room for a broader definition of myth (which combines myth and legend); and if we accept the fact that all the gods were portrayed as acting in history to guide human affairs; and if we see myth as an extended metaphor, then we should agree with Giovanni Garbini who suggests that from Genesis to Judges the main genre used by the biblical narrative is myth.[120] And we should also consider deeming all language about the gods of theism as metaphorical.

117. Smith, *Origins of Biblical Monotheism*, 23.

118. Van Seters, *Prologue to History* 25.

119. Wyatt, *Mythic Mind*, 171. Biblical studies often suggest that monotheism is not mythological. For example, Robert Alter declares that Psalm 82 could be described "as a poem about the transition from mythology to a monotheistic frame of reference" (*Psalms*, 291). But Alter simply assumes that as soon we talk of only one god, mythology is gone. See §3.3.4.e for an explanation of Psalm 82.

120. Garbini, *Myth and History*, 1–2.

1.3 Excursus: Theomachia

1.3.1 Tišpak Battles against the Sea Dragon

The myth known as *The Slaying of Labbu* shows that the tradition about the *battle among the gods* was a very old theme in the Ancient Near East. The present version comes from *ca.* 1900–1600 BCE[121] and recounts the battle between the god Tišpak[122] and the sea serpent-lion-dragon. Tišpak kills the dreadful serpent-dragon whose "length was fifty leagues; [its height] was one league, its mouth was six cubits, [its tongue] twelve cubits."[123] The name of the serpent was *labbu*, that is, "lion." The mythic beast was also known as the "roaring dragon."[124] The parallelism in Ezekiel 32:2 repeats the equation between lion and dragon: "You are like a lion among the nations, like a dragon in the seas."[125]

---

121. For the text, see Lambert, *Babylonian Creations Myths*, 361–65; Foster, *Before the Muses*, 581–2; Lewis, "CT 13 33–34 and Ezequiel 32," 28–47; and Heidel, *Babylonian Genesis*, 141–43. The narrative shows parallels with the stories about Baal, and with Ezekiel 32:2–8. Two cylinders found in Eshnunna (Sumer) also develop the subject. One cylinder shows two lions battling with a dragon of seven heads. The other shows a god holding two heads cut off from the monster. See Lewis 1996, "CT 13 33–34 and Ezequiel 32," 29.

122. Jacobsen describes Tišpak as "a god who can raise storms and clouds, from which he throws down his cylinder seal to kill. There can be no doubt that such a god is a god of thunderstorms and lightning" ("Chief God," 54). This god is similar to Baal in his battle against Yamm.

123. *Lion-Serpent* i.8–9, in Foster, *Before the Muses*, 581. In Ezekiel 32, the beast is also so huge that his remains cover mountains and valleys (vv. 4–6). According to the narrative about Tišpak, the dead dragon is so big that its blood flows for "three years, three months, one day and night." In Ezekiel 32:6, the blood is so abundant that covers mountains and ravines.

124. Wiggermann, "Tišpak," 118. Cf. Lewis, "CT 13 33–34 and Ezequiel 32," 34.

125. Lewis, "CT 13 33–34 and Ezequiel 32," 40–41, shows that the frequent juxtaposition of lion and dragon/serpent in the Ancient Near East literature signals a synonymous parallelism describing only one mythical monster. Cf. Ps 91:13; Isa 30:6; Amos 5:19

1.3.2 Marduk Shatters Tiamat in Battle[126]

a. Introduction

Enūma Eliš (ca. 1595–1105 BCE) is the story of how Marduk became the supreme god of the Babylonian pantheon.[127] William Hallo correctly states that the central theme of this myth is to narrate how Marduk was rewarded with universal kingship for his heroic actions. This reward included declaring him head of the pantheon (*En. el.* v.77–116; vi.92–120), the construction of Babylon (v.117–56) and its temple (Esagila, vi.39–81), and the proclamation and explanation of Marduk's 50 names (vi.121—vii.144). Therefore, the work should be called "The exaltation of Marduk"—and not "The Creation of the World."[128] In ancient times, it was simply known by the first two words at the beginning of the book: *enūma eliš*, that is, "when on high" (*incipit*).

Marduk was the son of Ea (= Enki) and Damkina. In Sumerian, his name was amar.uda.ak (or ᵈAMAR.UD) which may mean "calf of the storm."[129] He was originally a storm-god.[130] His weapons were lightning, winds and storms (*En. el.* iv.39, 42–47). He rides "the fearful chariot of the

---

126. For *Enūma Eliš*, see the brilliant works of Lambert, *Babylonian Creation Myths*, 3–146; and Talon, *Standard Babylonian Creation Myth*. Both provide the original text, transliteration and translation. Talon also provides a helpful glossary-concordance. See also Lambert, "Mesopotamian Creation Stories," 18–20; Foster, *Before the Muses*, 439–85; Bottéro and Kramer, *Cuando los Dioses*, 618–67; Dalley, *Myths from Mesopotamia*, 233–74; and Heidel, *Babylonian Genesis*, 18–60.

127. There is no consensus regarding the date of composition. Horowitz believes it was written before or during the Kassite period, 1595–1155 BCE (*Mesopotamia Cosmic Geography*, 108). Dalley says it might come from the Kassite or Amorite period, ca. 2000 BCE (*Myths from Mesopotamia*, 229–30). And Lambert thinks that the definitive exaltation of Marduk came during Nebuchadnezzar I, 1126–1105 BCE ("Reign of Nebuchadnezzar"; "Studies in Marduk"; and "Mesopotamian Creation Stories"). See also Sommerfeld, *Aufstieg Marduks*, 175; Heidel, *Babylonian Genesis*, 14; and Speiser, "Creation Epic," 60.

128. Hallo, *World's Oldest Literature*, 559. Similarly Bottéro and Kramer (*Cuando los Dioses*, 616), who name the story "The Glorification of Marduk." Foster begins his discussion of *Enūma Eliš* by saying: "This poem should not be considered 'the' Mesopotamian creation story; rather, it is the individual work of a poet who viewed Babylon as the center of the universe, and Marduk, god of Babylon, as head of the pantheon" (*Before the Muses*, 436). See also Lambert, "Mesopotamian Creation Stories," 17.

129. In the Hebrew Bible, Marduk is called *mərōḏāk* (Jer 50:2) or *bēl* (= "Lord," Isa 46:1; Jer 51:44).

130. Marduk is the "power creating and controlling atmospheric phenomena, lightning, storms, clouds" (Jacobsen, "Battle between Marduk and Tiamat," 106). And see Jacobsen, *Toward the Image*, 35–36.

irresistible storm" (iv.50),¹³¹ and he is in charge of "raising the winds, pouring rain, producing fog and pile up snow" (v.50-51).¹³²

Tiamat is a tragic character. She is a goddess who loves her children, and endures with patience all the noise they make (*En. el.* i.21-25). When Ea kills her husband (Apsu), she does not retaliate (i.55-78). When Marduk amuses himself forming storms inside her, she just bears with the pain (i.105-110). It is only when a group of gods—her children again—blame her for the death of her husband that she becomes a raging threat (i.120-22), accumulating weapons and giving birth to monsters of all types (i.125-46). At the beginning of the story, Tiamat is described as a huge cosmic mass of water (i.1-6),¹³³ but later she appears as a horrific, quadruped monster with head, eyes, nostrils, udder and tail (v.47-66).

b. The conflict

Enūma Eliš is a thriller that tells how a conflict of proportions threatened the very core of the divine world at the beginning of time. Tiamat was determined to avenge her husband's murder by killing the gods. Marduk offers himself to kill Tiamat and save the gods, but with the condition that he'd be crowned king of the universe. The gods accept his conditions, and he is declared king:

> You are Marduk, our avenger,
> We have given you kingship over the sum of the whole universe.¹³⁴

Thorkild Jacobsen points out that the battle between Marduk and Tiamat is "a battle of the elements, of forces in nature, a battle between the thunderstorm and the sea,"¹³⁵ which reminds us of the combat between Baal and Yamm (§1.3.3), and the fight between Yahve and Yām (§1.3.5). Marduk provides himself with a bow, arrows, mace, lightning and fire (iv.35-64). He creates a net and takes hold of the four winds, and seven additional winds (tempest, cyclone, etc.).¹³⁶ He prepares a flood and mounts on "the fear-

---

131. Lambert, *Babylonian Creation Myths*, 89.
132. For a description of Marduk's body and attributes, see *En. el.* i.85-104.
133. The word Tiamat is one of the forms adopted by the Akkadian term *tâmtu*, which points to a huge mass of water: "sea, ocean, lake." See *tâmatu, tiāmtu, tiāmatu*, etc. in "Tâmtu," 150-58.
134. *En. el.* iv.13-14, in Lambert, *Babylonian Creation Myths*, 87.
135. Jacobsen, "Battle between Marduk and Tiamat, 106.
136. Cf. *En. el.* i.23, 109. The psalmist asks against his enemies: "chase them with your tempest and terrify them with your hurricane" (Ps 83:15[16]). Cf. Isa 29:6; 30:30;

ful chariot of the irresistible storm" (iv.50).[137] He harnesses four horses to his chariot: Assassin, Merciless, Crushing and Fast.[138] And then he goes to battle. During the conflict, Marduk uses his net to trap Tiamat and hurls hurricane winds that open her mouth with such force that she is unable to close it again. The winds swell her belly, and then:

> (Marduk) launched his arrow and tore her belly.
> He cut open her entrails and perforated her heart.
> He captured her and extinguished her life.
> He threw down her corpse and stood on it.[139]

Marduk's combat is also connected with the creation of the world. Once Tiamat is shattered, Marduk creates the world from the carcass of the goddess.[140]

1.3.3 The Battle of Baal against Yamm (= Sea)

a. Introduction

The most important gods of the Ancient Near East were weather-gods because they were in charge of the climate conditions that made life possible. People worshiped atmosphere phenomena because water is essential to the production of crops and because the storm is the perfect display of irresistible royal power and violence. Weather-gods were both fertility-gods and warrior-gods. These gods were the rulers of *nature and politics*.[141]

Even under the tutelage of the senior El,[142] Baal (= master, lord, owner) was the most important god of the Siro-Palestine region.[143] Yamm is forced

---

Jer 23:19, etc.

137. Cf. "you make rain-clouds your chariots; you ride on the wings of the wind" (Ps 104:33); "Yahve comes with fire and as a hurricane on his chariots, to discharge his wrath with fury and his rebuke with flames of fire" (Isa 66:15); cf. Zech 6:1–7.

138. In the book of Revelation, we also see four destructive horses (6:1–8).

139. *En. el.* iv.101–4 (cf. Lambert, *Babylonian Creation Myths*, 93).

140. *En. el.* iv.123—v.76 (cf. Lambert, *Babylonian Creation Myths*, 93–103). §1.3.6 talks about Yahve and the battle of creation.

141. For Enlil as a storm-god, see §1.1.4; §1.2.3; §4.2.1. See also Iškur (Adad) and Ninurta in §2.1.1. The storm-god Ningirsu (Ninurta) was Enlil's eldest son, called "the warrior of Enlil" (§4.2.1). Dagan was another important weather god. See Green, *Storm-God*; Schwemer, "Storm-Gods."

142. Baal is known as "the offspring of El" (*Aqhat* 1.17.vi.29, in Parker, "Aqhat," 61). Cf. Pardee, "'Aqhatu Legend," 1:347.

143. Another name for Baal was Hadad (*Baal Cycle, CAT* 1.4.vii.35–39; 1.5.ii.21–23),

to recognize it before the divine assembly: Baal is "the god whom you obey."[144] And Athirat did the same: "Our king is Mightiest Baal, Our ruler, with none above him."[145] He was known as "mightiest Baal" (*aliyn bʻl*).[146] He is also called "rider of the clouds" (*rkb ʻpt*), "Prince, Lord of the earth" (*zbl bʻl arṣ*), "Baal Saphon" (*bʻl ṣpn*), etc.[147]

Baal's sovereignty over life was such that his death would have caused the end of humankind:

> Baal is dead! What is to become of the people?
> The Son of Dagan! What is to become of the multitudes?
> Looking after Baal we shall descend into the Underworld![148]

As a storm-god, Baal is able to say:

> I understand lightning which not even Šamūma[149] knows,
> a matter which mankind does not know,
> which the multitudes of the earth do not understand.[150]

If there is rain, it is Baal's rain:

> A delight to the earth is the rain of Baal,
> and to the fields the rain of the Most High.[151]

Baal was the weather-god whose waters fertilized the earth:

---

taking the name from the Syrian storm-god, and assuming all his powers and functions. For Baal's names, see Day, *Yahwe and the Gods*; Wyatt, "Titles of the Ugarit Storm-God"; Cooper-Pope, "Divine Names."

144. *Baal Cycle*, CAT 1.2.i.18, 34, in Wyatt, *Religious Texts from Ugarit*, 59. Cf. Smith, "Baal Cycle," 129.

145. *Baal Cycle*, CAT 1.4.iv.43–44, in Smith, "Baal Cycle," 128.

146. He's also called "mightiest of warriors" (*aliy qrdm*).

147. The mountain Ṣaphon is located north of Ugarit, and it was "Baal's mountain . . . Mount Saphon, the holy domain" (*Epic of Kirta*, CAT 1.16.i.6–9, in Greenstein, "Kirta," 31). But in Exod 14:2, 9; and Num 33:7, the expression *baʻal ṣepōn* does not refer to a god but a city.

148. *Baal Cycle*, KTU 1.6.i.6–8 (cf. Pardee, "Baʻlu Myth," 1:268; Driver and Gibson, *Canaanite Myths*, 74).

149. Pardee suggests that *šmm* does not refer to the "sky" but to the deity. "The claim is that, although the lightning and thunder appear in heaven, their operation is the work of Baʻlu" ("Baʻlu Myth," 1:251).

150. *Baal Cycle*, CAT 1.3.iii.26–28 (cf. De Moor, *Religious Texts from Ugarit*, 10; Pardee, "Baʻlu Myth," 1:251).

151. *Epic of Kirta*, CAT 1.16.iii.7–8 (cf. Greenstein, "Kirta," 35). Cf. "showers of the rider on the clouds" (*Baal Cycle* CAT 1.3.ii.40, in Driver and Gibson, *Canaanite Myths*, 48).

> So now may Baal enrich with his rain,
>> may he enrich with rich water in a downpour.
> And may he give his voice [= thunder] in the clouds,
>> may he flash to the earth lightning.[152]

And, therefore, Baal is the source of abundance:

> The heavens rain oil,
>> the wadis run with honey...
> For Mightiest Baal lives,
>> the Prince, Lord of the earth is alive.[153]

b. The conflict

The Baal Cycle narrates the fight between Baal (= Lord) and Yamm (= Sea) for the control of the universe. At the beginning, El sides with Yamm and humiliates Baal. The senior god chooses Yamm as king, and commands Kothar to build him a palace.[154] But god Kothar encourages Baal to destroy Yamm, his enemy, in order to become the king of the universe:

> Indeed, I say to you, O Prince Baal,
>> I repeat, O Charioteer of the clouds,[155]
> Now your foe, Baal,
>> now you must smite your foe;
>> now you must destroy your adversary!
> Take your everlasting kingdom,
>> your eternal dominion.[156]

During the battle, Baal fatally strikes Yamm in the head, and:

---

152. *Baal Cycle*, CAT 1.4.v.6–9, in Smith, "Baal Cycle," 129. For the "voice" or lightning of Yahve as a storm-god, see Jer 10:13; Job 37:3; Ps 18:14[15]; 46:7.

153. *Baal Cycle*, KTU 1.6.iii.12–13, 20–21 (cf. Smith, "Baal Cycle," 158).

154. For summaries, see Watson and Wyatt, *Handbook*, 193–95; Green, *Storm-God*, 178–80; Driver and Gibson, *Canaanite Myths*, 2–4; Smith, "Baal Cycle," 81–180.

155. The Hebrew Bible also describes Yahve as a storm-god: "See, Yahve is riding on a swift cloud" (Isa 19:1); or: "He rode on a cherub; he soared upon the wings of the wind" (Ps 18:11[10]). For the resemblance between Psalm 18 and Ugaritic mythology, see Craigie, *Psalms*, 173. Cf. Ps 68:34[33]; Deut 33:26.

156. *Baal Cycle*, CAT 1.2.iv. 7–10, in Wyatt, *Religious Texts from Ugarit*, 65 (cf. De Moor, *Religious Texts from Ugarit*, 39). Ps 74:12 shows that Yahve became king of creation only after defeating Yām (vv. 13–14). See comments below in §1.3.6.

> Yamm [= Sea] collapsed
>   and fell to the earth,
> His joints shook,
>   and his form collapsed.
> Baal dragged and dismembered[157] Yamm,
>   destroyed Nahar [= River], the governor.[158]

And this is how Baal became "Lord of the earth."[159] He did not inherit the kingship, nor was he elected by the gods of the pantheon. In another passage, it is Anat who brags about defeating the enemies of Baal:

> What enemy rises up against Baal?
>   What foe against the Rider of the Clouds?
> Surely I have smitten Yamm, the Beloved of El,
>   surely I exterminated Nahar, the great god.[160]
> Surely I bound Tunnan[161] [= serpent, dragon] and destroyed him.
>   I battled against the Twisty Serpent,
>   the tyrant with Seven Heads.[162]

1.3.4 Mot (= Death) versus Baal

a. Introduction

If our love for life calls for a metaphor that would imagine a life-giving-god like Baal, then death is also a natural force that demands a divinity. Mot is the god of the Underworld and death. All living things die constantly, so Mot is depicted as an extremely hungry god who eats everything: "My

---

157. Marduk cuts up Tiamat in pieces (*En. el.* iv.101-4, 135-38), and Yahve breaks in pieces the heads of Leviathan (Ps 74:14).

158. *Baal Cycle, CAT* 1.2.iv.25-27 (cf. De Moor, *Religious Texts from Ugarit*, 41; Smith, "Baal Cycle," 104).

159. *Baal Cycle, CAT* 1.3.i.2-4.

160. Cf. Hab 3:8-9, 15.

161. Later in §1.3.5, we'll see that Tunnan appears in the Hebrew Bible as Tannīn (Job 7:12).

162. *Baal Cycle, CAT* 1.3.iii.37-40 (cf. Smith, "Baal Cycle," 111). It is not clear whether Tunnan and Serpent are different names referring to Yamm or to his associates. The same tradition is followed in Daniel 7, where we see beasts coming from the sea and one like a son of man. In Revelation 13:1-10, a beast of seven heads rises from the sea.

throat is the throat[163] of the lion in the wasteland... and indeed, indeed, my throat devours flesh,[164] yes indeed, I eat by double handfuls."[165] Responding to Anat, Mot says that he looked everywhere but "there were no humans for me to swallow," until he found Baal and: "I took him as (I would) a lamb in my mouth, he was destroyed as a kid (would be) in my crushing jaws."[166] So Baal is swallowed by death and brought into the Underworld.

The Hebrew Bible shares the same images regarding death:

> Therefore, the underworld [šə'ôl] has opened wide its throat,
> and has opened its mouth beyond measure (Isa 5:14).[167]

While *māwet* (= death) and *šə'ôl* (= underworld) often refer to a place (§3.6), sometimes they are humanized. The Underworld is imagined as having a mouth and a throat, and it's never satiated (Prov 27:20). The personification is clear in the following texts:

> Like sheep they are destined for the Underworld,
> Death (*māwet*) will be their shepherd (Ps 49:15)

> The Underworld (*šə'ôl*) below is excited to meet you when you come;
> it stirs up the dead for you,
> all the leaders of the Underworld (*'ereṣ*).
> He lifts from their thrones
> all those who were kings of the nations (Isa 14:9).

> Death (*māwet*) has climbed in through our windows,
> it has entered into our palaces,
> to cut off the children from the streets
> and the young men from the city squares (Jer 9:20; cf. Isa 28:15, 18 with Hos 13:14).

---

163. Or: "My hunger is the hunger of the lion." The noun *npš* may mean "throat" or "hunger." Cf. "... his throat is empty ... his throat is thirsty" (Isa 29:8). Cf. Ps 107:5, 9 and Koehler, *Hebräisches Lexikon*, 672.

164. Cf. Wyatt, *Religious Text from Ugarit*, 118, note 17.

165. *Baal Cycle*, KTU 1.5.i.14–19, in Pardee, "Ba'lu Myth," 1:264–65.

166. *Baal Cycle*, KTU 1.6.ii.15–23, in Pardee, "Ba'lu Myth," 1:270. Cf. "our bones shall be littered at the mouth of the Underworld" (*šeə'ôl*, Ps 141:7).

167. Habakkuk compares the greed of the arrogant with death, for he "has made his throat as wide as the Underworld, like Death he's insatiable" (Hab 2:5). Cf. Prov 1:12; 27:20.

b. The conflict

Baal sends his divine envoys, Gapn and Ugar, to invite Mot to a party at Baal's newly built palace now that he is the king of the world. But he warns the "gods" not to get too close to Mot for he will eat them. Mot replies with a threatening message that promises the death of Baal who will be swallowed by hungry Death:

> You [Baal] might have destroyed Litan, the Sinuous Snake,
> annihilated the Twisting Serpent,
> the tyrant with Seven Heads.[168]
> But the heavens will overheat and wither,
> because I will tear you to pieces.
> Surely you will descend into the throat of Mot, Son of El,
> into the gullet of the Beloved of El, the Warrior.[169]

Filled with fear, Baal sends the "gods" back to Mot to deliver a message in which Baal pledges to be Mot's slave forever. But ultimately Baal is forced into the Underworld:

> And you [Baal], take your clouds,
> your winds, your thunder-bolts, and your rains . . .
> . . . And descend to the house of seclusion[170] within the underworld (*arṣ*).
> Be counted among the inmates of the underworld (*arṣ*),
> and the gods will know that you are dead.[171]

---

168. These are all references to Yamm who was defeated by Baal.

169. *Baal Cycle, KTU* 1.5.i.1–8 (cf. Pardee, "Ba'lu Myth," 1:265; Smith, "Baal Cycle," 141; Ginsberg, "Poems about Baal and Anath," 138). In the Greek tradition, Zeus battles against Typhon, the monstrous serpent with dragon heads (Hesiod, *Theogony* 820–68, in Most, *Hesiod: Theogony*, 69–73). And Apollodorus of Athens (180–120 BCE) recounts how Perseus rescued Andromeda by fighting and killing the "sea monster" (*thalassiō kētei*, Apollodorus, *Library* ii.4.2–3, in Frazer, *Apollodorus*, 159).

170. The text reads *bthptt*, and we don't need to translate "freedom," (as Smith, "Baal Cycle," 148; De Moor, *Religious Texts from Ugarit*, 78). The meaning is "seclusion" (cf. Pardee, "Ba'lu Myth," 1:267). In 2 Chr 26:21 (= 2 Kgs 15:5), we are told that king Uzziah dwelled *bəbêt haḥopšît* = "in a house of separateness" or confinement (cf. BDB 345), which Gray astutely translates "isolation ward" regarding Baal (*Legacy of Canaan*, 55 note 5; and cf. Koehler, *Hebräisches Lexikon*, 328).

171. *Baal Cycle, KTU* 1.5.v.6–8, 14–17 (cf. Pardee, "Ba'lu Myth," 1:267; Smith, "Baal Cycle," 147–48; Driver and Gibson, *Canaanite Myths*, 72).

Goddess Anat panics for she knows that Baal's death will inevitably trigger the extinction of all life on earth and, therefore, she decides to go into the underworld to rescue him:

> Baal is dead! What is to become of the people?
> The Son of Dagan! what is to become of the multitudes?
> Looking for Baal we shall descend into the Underworld![172]

Anat battles Mot and splits him with her sword, and burns him and grinds him, and rescues her brother Baal from Death. Then Father El has a vision revealing him the good news that Baal has been resurrected:

> In a dream of gracious El, the Benign,
>   in a vision of the Creator of creatures:
> the heavens rain oil,
>   and the wadis run with honey . . .
> For Mightiest Baal lives,
>   the Prince, Lord of the earth, is alive.[173]

1.3.5 Yahve Destroys Yām (= the Sea) in Battle

a. Introduction

Israel inherited the belief that Yahve was a storm-god. Psalm 29 portrays Yahve as the thunderstorm that controls the waters of both fertility and destruction. By "voice" ($qôl$) the poem refers to his terrifying thunder (vv. 3–5, 7–9). And even when the poem does not mention Yām or Baal as his enemies, it is clear that Yahve's overwhelming power required all the gods to praise him (vv. 1–2), for he is the indisputable Lord of the weather (vv. 3, 10):

> ¹ Ascribe Yahve, o gods,[174]
>   ascribe Yahve glory and might.
> ²Ascribe Yahve the glory of his name.
>   Bow down before Yahve in the holiness of his splendor.
> ³The voice of Yahve is upon the waters,

---

172. *Baal Cycle*, KTU 1.6.i.6–8 (cf. Pardee, "Ba'lu Myth," 1:268; De Moor, *Religious Text from Ugarit*, 82).

173. *Baal Cycle*, KTU 1.6.iii.10–13, 20–21 (cf. Pardee, "Ba'lu Myth," 1:271; Driver and Gibson, *Canaanite Myths*, 77–78; Smith, "Baal Cycle," 158).

174. Lit. "sons of the gods" (*bənê'ēlîm*). See §3.3.4.c–e and §3.3.5.

> El of glory thunders,[175]
> Yahve is upon the mighty waters.
> ⁴The voice of Yahve is powerful,
> the voice of Yahve is splendor.
> ⁵The voice of Yahve breaks the cedars,
> Yahve shatters the cedars of Lebanon.
> ⁶He makes Lebanon skip like a calf,
> and Sirion like a young wild ox.
> ⁷The voice of Yahve flashes forth flames of fire.
> ⁸The voice of Yahve gives convulsions to the steppe,
> Yahve convulses the steppe of Kadesh.
> ⁹The voice of Yahve causes the hinds[176] to convulse,
> and strips the forest bare,
> but in his temple all say, "The Glorious One!"
> ¹⁰Yahve has sat enthroned over the flood,
> Yahve has sat enthroned as king forever.
> ¹¹Yahve will give strength to his people!
> Yahve will bless his people with peace! (Ps 29:1–11)

As a weather-god, Yahve is also the god of fertile rain (v. 26), as well as grain and wine (v. 28):

> ²⁶There is none like El, O Jeshurun,
> who rides the heavens to rescue you,
> [who] in his majesty [rides on] the clouds.
> ²⁷A refuge is the ancient Elohe,
> from beneath are the eternal arms.[177]
> He has driven out the enemy before you,

---

175. Cf. "Yahve thunders in the heavens, and Elyon uttered his voice, hailstones and flashes of fire" (Ps 18:13[14]).

176. Instead of following the MT *'ayyālōṯ* (= hinds, cf. LXX *elafous* = deer), it is quite possible to read *'ēlôt* = "oaks" (NRSV, NIV) or "terebinths" (NJB).

177. The first part of v. 27 could be translated in a very different way: "He subdues the ancient gods, shatters the forces of old" (NRSV). This is a very attractive proposal, and might be correct. Instead of the MT "refuge"(*məʻōnāʰ*), the NRSV proposes "he subdues" (*məʻannēʰ*, Piel ptc. from *ʻānā* = to humble oneself). In this way *'ĕlōhê qeḏem* becomes the object of the participle: "He subdues the ancient gods." And instead of "from underneath" (*mittaḥaṯ*) which makes no sense, NRSV proposes amending to "he shatters" (*məhattēṯ*, Piel ptc. from *ḥātat* = to be shattered). See Gaster, "Ancient Eulogy," 60.

and he said: Destroy!

> [28] So Israel has dwelt safely,
> alone resided[178] Jacob,
> in a land of grain and wine,
> with his heavens dripping dew. (Deut 33:26–28)

As a storm-god, Yahve also holds the terrifying destructive power of the storm, which is the main weapon of any warrior-god:

> [10[11]] He rode on a cherub and flew,
> he soared upon the wings of the wind.
> [11[12]] He made darkness his hiding place,
> his pavilion around him
> was the darkness of the waters,
> the dense clouds of dew.
> [12[13]] Out of his brightness before him,
> dense clouds blazed up[179] into hail and coals of fire.
> [13[14]] Yahve thundered from heaven,
> and Elyon gave forth his voice:
> hail and coals of fire.
> [14[15]] He sent out his arrows and scattered them,
> lightning he multiplied and overwhelmed them. (Ps 18:10–14)[180]

b. The conflict

The Hebrew Bible represents Yahve as a warrior-god who defeated Yām and the waters. We already saw (§1.3.3) that in Ugarit, Yamm or his associates were called *litan* or *lôtān* (= twisting, spiral). The Hebrews used the equivalent word *liwyātān* or Leviathan which means "sinuous snake," and represents the sea as a destructive force. At the beginning of the book of Job, the sufferer dreams of powerful sorcerers capable of enchanting and controlling Leviathan.[181] He yearns for them to curse the day he was born:

---

178. The MT reads *ʿēn* (= eye, fountain) which doesn't make any sense. Gaster, "Ancient Eulogy," 61, proposed a simple vocalic change that reads *ʿāz* = dwelt, resided.

179. MT reads *ʿāḇrû* (= they pass through), which could mean "overflow, burst" (Isa 8:9; 23:10). But the parallel passage of 2 Sam 22:13 reads *bāʿărû* (= burn up, blaze up).

180. For Yahve as a storm-warrior god, see Joel 2:11.

181. Sorcery was a fundamental part of ancient culture. A psalm gives expression to the complaint that there are wicked people immune to the enchantments used by the righteous. It happens that the wicked "does not heed the tune of the charmers who are

Let it be cursed by those who curse Yām,[182]
> those who are skilled in inciting Leviathan (Job 3:8).

Later on, Job complains that he is not Yām (= the Sea or primeval waters) nor *tannîn* (= serpent or sea monster) and, therefore, he does not deserve such horrible harassment from Yahve:

> [11]Therefore, I will not restrain my mouth;
> I will speak in the affliction of my spirit,
> and complain in the bitterness of my soul.
> [12]Am I Yām, Am I Tannîn,[183]
> that you set a guard over me? (Job 7:11–12).[184]

Isaiah 27:1 projects the conflict to the future, when the evil embodied in the destructive forces of the Sea shall be defeated:

> On that day, Yahve
> with his inexorable, great and strong sword,
> shall punish Leviathan, the fleeing serpent,
> Leviathan, the sinuous serpent,
> and he shall kill Tannîn who dwells in the sea.

Another passage incorporates the exodus tradition to talk about a new liberation that will bring back the redeemed (Isa 51:10). The author describes the crossing of the Red Sea as a mythical event by using language that recalls the time in which Yahve defeated the primeval waters:

> [9]Awake, awake!
> Clothe yourself with strength, O arm of Yahve.
> Awake, as in the days of old,
> in the generations of ancient times.

---

cunning in binding spells" (Ps 58:5[6]).

182. The parallelism with "Leviathan" demands correcting the MT from *yôm* (= "day" JPS, KJV) to Yām (= Sea). See Gunkel, *Creation and Chaos*, 54; Lipinski, "liwyā*t*an," 7:506; Pope, *Job*, 30. Against the emendation is Day, *God's Conflict with the Dragon*, 61.

183. By means of the upper case, some translations and commentaries correctly identify Yām as a god: "Am I the Sea, or the Dragon . . ." (NRSV, cf. NJB). See Schökel and Sicre, *Job*, 149; Andersen, *Job*, 137; Clines, *Job 1–20*, 157; Habel, *Book of Job*, 152; Pope, *Job*, 56; Rowley, *Book of Job*, 68.

184. Cf. Ps 148:7: "Praise Yahve from the earth, you sea monsters (*tannînîm*) and all the waters of the abyss (*təhōmôt*)." Cf. Gen 1:2; Prov 8:27; Ps 135:6.

> Was it not you who crushed[185] Rahab,
>> who pierced Tannîn?
> ¹⁰Was it not you who dried up Yām,
>> the waters of the primeval abyss (*təhôm*),
> who made in the depths of Yām
>> a way for the redeemed to cross over? (Isa 51:9-10)

Habakkuk 3 portrays Yahve as a warrior-god fighting the same enemy that was destroyed by Baal (§1.3.3). Yahve is presented as a powerful atmospheric-god who makes the earth shudder (vv. 6, 9, 12). He pours destructive waters (v. 10) and uses lightning as his arrows (vv. 9, 11). His enemy is no other than the Nahar/Yamm (= River/Sea) of Ugaritic theology:

> ⁸ Is it against Neharim, O Yahve, that [your anger] burns?
>> Is it against Neharim your anger?
> Is it against Yām your rage,
>> that you mount on your horses,
>> on your chariots of victory? [186]
> ... ¹⁵ You trod upon Yām with your horses,
>> a heap of many waters. (Hab 3:8, 15)[187]

1.3.6 Yahve Defeats Yām as a Precondition of Creation

The Hebrew Bible does not present just one official myth of how the world was created, but provides us with different traditions. One tradition presents the waters as a preexistent impersonal element already present before creation:

> ¹When Elohim began to create heaven and earth,
>> ²while[188] the earth was a formless void,

---

185. The MT reads "cut in pieces" (from *ḥāṣēb*), but Qumran (1QIsa^a col. xlii) reads: "crushed" or "smashed" (from *māḥaṣ*, cf. Job 26:12). Cf. Abegg, *Dead Sea Scrolls*, 356.

186. It is said about Yahve: "you make rain clouds your chariot; you ride on the wings of the wind" (Ps 104:3; cf. Isa 19:1). In his battle against Tiamat, Marduk prepares a flood and then "rode on the chariot of the furious storm that has no equal" (*En. el.* iv.50).

187. See Green, *Storm-God*, 264-66; Roberts, *Hahum, Habakkuk, and Zephaniah*, 128-58; De Moor, *Rise of Yahwism*, 198-206; Smith, *Early Story of God*, 82.

188. In a circumstantial sentence, the *vav* (= and) may be translated according to the idea it introduces ("if," "while," "when," "although," etc.). In Genesis 1:2, the *vav* gives the idea of "while" or "at a moment when" (cf. Driver, *Tense*, §156). In other

and while darkness was over the face of the primeval abyss
and a wind from Elohim was moving over the face of the waters,
³Elohim said . . .[189] (Gen 1:1–3)

In Genesis 1 the god found it necessary to confine the waters: "And Elohim said: Let the waters under the sky gather in just one place" (1:9),[190] but we never hear of a battle between Elohim and the waters. The waters remain only an impersonal force. Genesis 2 presents a different tradition. In this creation story the primeval waters don't play any role. However, other biblical passages adopt a tradition that narrates a battle between Yahve and Yām as a precondition for Yahve's creative activity. The biblical god first needs to defeat the forces of chaos and only then he's able to create a world of diversity, order and beauty. In the book of Job, Bildad composes a hymn to praise Yahve for having established the cosmic order[191] after subjugating the primeval waters:

¹⁰He drew a boundary around the surface of the waters,
at the limit between light and darkness.
¹¹The pillars of heaven tremble,
they were frightened at his rebuke.
¹²By his power he repressed[192] Yām,
by his sagacity he crushed Rahab.[193]

---

words, v. 2 introduces the condition in which the earth was when Elohim began his creation by his powerful fiat in v. 3.

189. Chapter 1 begins with a long sentence. Its main structure is: "When Elohim began to create . . . Elohim said" (1:1, 3). The expression "Elohim said" indicates the start of the creative process discussed in vv. 3–31, until the process reaches its final goal: "Heaven and earth were finished, and everything that is in them" (2:1).

190. Cf. Ps 33:7, and §1.3.6.

191. According to the MT, Job 26:1 introduces a discourse from Job ("Then Job answered," NSRV). But it happens that in all his previous interventions, Job has consistently lashed out against the character of his god (cf. Job 9:5–13; 10:8–13; 12:13–25). This antagonism is contrary to the positive tone of 26:5–14. Therefore, today most scholars think that we should take 25:1–6 and 26:5–14 as one unit, as a poem delivered by Bildad defending the god. See Habel, *Book of Job*, 364–75; Pope, *Job*, 163–67; Rowley, *Book of Job*, 169–74.

192. Most commentaries agree that both the mythic context and the parallelism with *māḥaṣ* (= crushed) suggest that the meaning of *rāḡaʻ* is "repressed," not "stirreth" (ASV) or "divideth" (KJV). See Clines, *Job 21–37*; Habel, *Book of Job*, 364; Pope, *Job*, 166; Rowley, *Book of Job*, 174; Schökel-Sicre, *Job*, 362.

193. Notice that some versions and scholars use the upper case to make clear that the sea is a god: "By his power he stilled the Sea; by his understanding he struck down Rahab" (NRSV, and see Schökel-Sicre, *Job*, 362; Habel, *Book of Job*, 373). The translation with lower case "sea" (NIV) conceals the fact that Yām is a god.

¹³By his wind the heavens glowed,

    his hand pierced the sinuous serpent. (Job 26:10–13)[194]

Later, Job 38 informs that Yahve had to restrain Yām to create the world. In this passage "the Sea is personified as a primordial chaos monster that God had to bring under control as a phase of the creation program."[195] As it happens with other gods, Yām may have been born from a goddess or from the depths of the earth (v. 8). But Yahve soon learned that this violent god needed to be confined, so he locked him up. Then Yahve commanded Yām (v. 11) "in direct speech"[196] to stay within the imposed boundaries:

⁸ I locked up[197] Yām behind doors,

    when he came lashing out[198] from the womb,

⁹ when I made the clouds his blanket

    and thick darkness his swaddling bands,

¹⁰ when I impose limits on him,[199]

    and set doors and bars,[200]

¹¹ and said [to Yām]: This far you may come, and no further;

    here the arrogance of your waves will be broken.[201] (Job 38:8–11)

The next passage comes from Psalm 74 which depicts the mythical concept of the sea as a powerful threat to human life. When the social structures that provide security and meaning are broken, ancient people thought it was because the Primeval Waters had unleashed their devastating force upon the structure of creation. This is why Yahve had to repress, crush and destroy

---

194. While Yām and *ṭannīn* are West Semitic terms, Rahab is an image taken from Babylonian theology. Cf. *rūbu* (= boiling, wrath) and *rubbu* (= waves, breakings). A prayer to Marduk says: "With his flame steep mountains are destroyed! He overwhelmed the expanse of the billowing ocean (*rubbūša*)!" (*Hymn to Marduk* K. 3,351, in King, *Seven Tablets*, 207. Cf. Oshima, *Babylonian Prayers*, 307; "Rubbû," 393).

195. Habel, *Book of Job*, 538.

196. Habel, *Book of Job*, 539.

197. The MT text only reads "he locked up," but the translations usually supply "Who . . . ?" The LXX presents a better option: "I locked up."

198. In Job 40:23, the Jordan River lashes out against the hippopotamus.

199. The MT reads lit. "and I broke (*wā'ešbōr*) on him my boundary." The text is usually amended to read "I set" or "I established" (*wā'āšît*). Other options in Schökel-Sicre, *Job*, 546; Clines, *Job 38–42*, 1054.

200. In *En. el.* iv.139–44, during the process of creation, Marduk assigns guards to Tiamat, and orders the guards "not to let her waters escape."

201. Lit. "And here he will set [*yāšît*] the arrogance of your waves." The text should be amended to *yiššābēr* (Niphal of *šābar*): "here the arrogance of your waves will be broken."

Yām to restore order and life. Psalm 74:13-14 employs the *Chaoskampf* motif to explain Israel's national tragedy. With the fall of Jerusalem (587 BCE) "all that Israel has come to depend on for stability is gone."[202] The enemies of Yahve had destroyed the temple (vv. 4-8) which was the foundation of their social system. The prophetic institution, as bearer of the will of god, was paralyzed (v. 9). The cosmos of wellbeing and meaning exists no more. At this point, the psalmist introduces the myth (vv. 12-14). The passage begins with a reference to the past: "Even so, Elohim is my king from ages past, working salvation on the earth" (v. 12). In other words, in primeval times Yahve became king of creation only after having subdued the forces of destruction (vv. 13-14). It is only after securing his sovereignty that Yahve is able to create order and diversity from a formless mass. Diversity comes in the form of springs, day and night, stars, sun and seasons (vv. 15-17; cf. Ps 104:26).[203] The structure of creation is contrary to the formless and homogeneous mass of primitive chaos. To deal with Israel's horrible national tragedy, the psalmist calls upon the myth because it gives expression to the hope that order and life will finally conquer chaos and death. In this way suffering and destruction acquired meaning within the frame of a mythic narrative. As it happened in the case of Marduk (§1.3.2), the psalm places the *theomachia* as a precondition for Yahve's creative activity. Furthermore, Psalm 74:13-14 portrays Yām as a personal god that Yahve needs to defeat in order to create a structured and diverse world:

> [13]You destroyed[204] Yām with your might,
>   you broke the heads of Tannînîm[205] in the waters,
> [14]you crushed the heads of Leviathan,[206]

---

202. Tanner et al., *Psalms*, 594.

203. The same idea surfaces in Psalm 93, which talks about how the god reigns by affirming the world and subduing the waters. For a treatment of the theme of Yahve versus Chaos, see Seybold, *Introducing the Psalms*, 177-79.

204. The parallelism with "you broke" demands the idea "you destroyed" or "split asunder" (cf. Isa. 24:19, BDB 830; and see Tate, *Psalms 51-100*, 243; Kraus, *Psalms 60-150*, 95), instead of "you divided" (NRSV, KJV, NIV). Also, the translation "sea" in lower case (NRSV, NIV) distorts the mythic meaning of the text. Other passage describes the god El as the one who "trampled the waves of the Sea" (NRSV Job 9:8). The psalmist says to Elohim: "you silence the roaring of the seas" (Ps 65:7; cf. 89:8-9; 106:8-9), and this is possible because "Yahve on high is more majestic than the roaring of many waters, more majestic than the waves of the sea" (Ps 93:4).

205. The term *tannînîm* is an intensive plural referring to the dragon or monster of the waters.

206. We saw above (§1.3.3) how Baal defeated Tunnan, "the tyrant of seven heads." In Mesopotamia, *mušmaḫḫu* was the serpent of seven heads. The storm-god Ninurta is presented as the one "who slew the seven-headed serpent" (Cooper, *Return of Ninurta*,

and gave him as food to a multitude of beasts.[207]

In the above passages we should transliterate "Yam" or translate "Sea," using these terms as proper names (§1.3.5–6). In other words, the biblical Yām appears many times as a personal god. In Ugaritic theology, there is no question that Yamm is a person/monster with personal qualities. He's called "god," and he is able to hear and understand what others are saying. He talks to El and Baal, and sends envoys to deliver his messages, and he wants to be the king of the universe. In the Hebrew Bible, it is clear that Yām is also a personal monster who needs to be subdued, and even killed in the same way that Marduk slayed Tiamat. The biblical Yām is a monster-god to whom Yahve talks: "And said: This far you may come, and no further; here will stop the arrogance of your waves" (Job 38:11). The following passage ascribes clear human attributes to the waters (v.16), and presents Yahve as a warrior-storm-god (vv. 17–18):

> [16] The waters saw you, O Elohim,
>
>   the waters saw you and were afraid,
>
>   the very primeval abyss (*təhōmōṯ*) trembled.
>
> [17] The dark clouds poured down waters,
>
>   the clouds thundered,[208]
>
>   your lightning bolts[209] were shot on every side.
>
> [18] The crash of your thunder was in the whirlwind,
>
>   your lightning lit up the world,
>
>   the earth quivered and shook. (Ps 77:16–18; cf. Ps 104:7)

147; cf. pp. 80–81, 144–45).

207. At the end of v. 14, the MT records a meaningless sentence: "you gave it to a people, to *ṣiyyîm*." We cannot be sure of the meaning of the word *ṣiyyîm* (pl. of *ṣî*). The word seems to have two different roots. One means "ship" (Num 24:24; Isa 33:21; Ezek 30:9; Dan 11:30); the other is usually translated "wild beast" (Isa 13:21; 23:13; 34:14). Regarding Psalm 74:14, we could only guess something like: "to a multitude of beasts" (see Hossfeld and Zenger, *Psalms 51–100*, 240; cf. "wild animals," NJB), or: "to the people of the ships." Some suggest relating the term to *ṣiyyāʰ*, "arid, dry" (see Tate, *Psalms 51–100*, 240), and then guess that the carcass of the monster was given to "the creatures of the wilderness" (NRSV, cf. ASV, JPS, NIV). Cf. LXX: "to the Ethiopian nations." Others even amend the text to read: "you . . . have given him as food to the sharks" (Kraus, *Psalms 60–150*, 96).

208. Lit. "the clouds gave their voice" (cf. v. 18 "the voice of your thunder"). The word *qôl* (= voice) is frequently used for the "thunder-clap." Cf. "I shall call on Yahve, so he may give voices and rain" (1 Sam 12:17; cf. Exod 9:23, 28, 29, 33, 34).

209. The text uses "your arrows" to refer to lightning. Cf. Ps 18:14[15]; 144:6; Hab 3:8, 11; Zech 9:14. Zeus killed Apollos' son, "striking him in the chest with a lightning bolt" (Euripides, *Alcestis* 4; cf. Luschnig and Roisman, *Alcesti*, 15).

1.3.7 Chaos versus Cosmos

Mircea Eliade explains the above mythical perspective about reality, saying:

> What is to become 'our world' must first be 'created,' and every creation has a paradigmatic model—the creation of the universe by the gods . . . [In old times people believed] their labor was only the repetition of a primordial act, the transformation of chaos into cosmos by the divine act of creation. When they tilled the desert soil, they were in fact repeating the act of the gods who had organized chaos by giving it a structure, forms, and norms . . .
>
> [On the contrary,] the *apsū*, the *tehōm* symbolize the chaos of waters, *the preformal modality of cosmic matter*, and, at the same time, the world of death, of all that precede and follows life . . .
>
> [We humans] speak of the chaos, the disorder, the darkness that will overwhelm 'our world.' All these terms express the abolition of an order, a cosmos, an organic structure, and reimmersion in the state of fluidity, of formlessness—in short, of chaos.[210]

The old myths about the creation of the world gave expression to this irreconcilable antagonism between cosmos and chaos. The world begins with a preexistent formless mass, and creation consists in effecting partitions and introducing diversity. *The praise song to the hoe* (1900–1600 BCE) is a myth which talks about the most basic separation in this way:

> In order to make the human seed come forth from the earth,
>> Enlil rushed to separate heaven from the earth,
>> hastened to separate the earth from heaven.[211]

The myth *Bilgames and the Netherworld* also begins the process of creation with a primordial act of separation:

> In those days, in those far-off days,
>> in those nights, in those distant nights,
>> in those years, in those far-off years . . .
> . . . after heaven had been parted from heaven,
>> after earth had been separated from heaven,

---

210. Eliade, *Sacred and the Profane*, 31, 41, 49–50.
211. Cf. Black, *Literature of Ancient Sumer*, 312.

after the name of mankind has been established . . .²¹²

The divisions made on the formless primeval mass are presented as the starting point of creation. Out of the formless mass, two *different* units are created: heaven and earth. This separation creates a space (atmosphere) which allows for the emergence of human life. After the separation, reality is not one homogeneous mass anymore. In Genesis chapter 1, the myth starts with a preexisting formless watery void (1:2), which is followed by a number of separations. Elohim separates light from darkness, and divides the waters to create the atmosphere:

> ⁴ . . . and Elohim separated light from darkness . . .
>
> ⁶ And Elohim said: let there be a dome in the midst of the waters, and let this dome separate the waters from the waters.
>
> ⁷ So Elohim made the dome and in this way he separated the waters which were under the dome from the waters which were above the dome. And it was so.

Humans sense that chaos embodies a relentless threat to their cosmos with sundry misfortunes that may fall upon us in the form of illness, unemployment, natural disaster, national tragedy, loss of a loved one, etc. We yearn to remain in our created and structured world. Eliade adds: "This religious need expresses an unquenchable ontological thirst. Religious man thirsts for *being*. His terror of the chaos that surrounds his inhabited world corresponds to his terror of nothingness."²¹³ Miguel de Unamuno explains his horror of death and nothingness, saying that when he was young:

> I never was made to tremble by descriptions of hellfire, no matter how terrible, for I felt always, that the idea of nothingness was much more terrifying than Hell. Whoever suffers lives, and whoever lives in suffering still loves and hopes . . . And it is better to live in pain than peacefully cease to be at all. The truth is that I could not believe in this atrocious Hell, an eternity of punishment, nor could I imagine a more authentic Hell than that of nothingness and the prospect of it. And I still believe that if we all believed in our salvation from nothingness, we would all be the better for it.²¹⁴

Therefore, some have argued that the impulse to have a religion comes from the fear of death and calamity. David Hume contended that fear and

---

212. *Bilgames and the Netherworld* i.1–10, in George, *Epic of Gilgamesh*, 178–79.
213. Eliade, *Sacred and the Profane*, 64.
214. Unamuno, *Tragic Sense of Life*, 49.

melancholy are emotions that put people on their knees, adding: "The primary religion of mankind arises chiefly from an anxious fear of future events."[215] It is true that metaphorical thinking uses religion to make it easier for people to personify their fears or to imagine some palliative to make life more tolerable. However, we should also take into account that religion has produced so much suffering and horror that maybe its main purpose is not to bring comfort but meaning.[216] We may speculate that the metaphor for the divine is mostly a cognitive instrument to find *meaning* in the universe. In this case, *theomachia* becomes a way of explaining the irrevocable antagonism between life and death, cosmos and chaos. But in the context of myth and values, we can also add this quote: "fairy tales are more than true—not because they tell us that dragons exist but because they tell us that dragons can be beaten" (G. K. Chesterton).

Conclusion

In §1.2.2, we saw that MacKenzie argued that Israelite narratives only portray one single god, while myths are polytheistic. He also claimed that myth occurs only in the divine world, while the biblical stories talk about historical events occurring in this world. The *Theomachia* myth proves his statements wrong. There's absolutely no doubt that the Hebrew Bible contains narratives of Yahve *and other gods*, as well as stories that unfold only *in the divine realm*. The theme that unites all the myths analyzed in §1.3 is the well-known tradition of the battles among the gods. In all these stories the gods are forces of nature that have been humanized (§1.1.4; §1.2.3; §1.3.4.a; §3.1) by means of metaphors.

---

215. Hume, *Natural History of Religion*, 65.

216. In the words of Geertz, "over its career religion probably disturbed men as much as it has cheered them; forced them into a head-on, unblinking confrontation with the fact that they are born to trouble as often as it has enabled them to avoid such a confrontation by projecting them into a sort of infantile fairy-tale world where 'hope cannot fail nor desire deceive' (Malinowski)" ("Religion as a Cultural System," 18).

> *But if horses or oxen or lions had hands*
> *or could draw with their hands*
> *and accomplished such works as men,*
> *horses would draw the figures of the gods*
> *as similar to horses,*
> *and the oxen as similar to oxen.*
>
> —XENOPHANES (CA. 570–475 BCE)[1]

Chapter 2

ANTHROPOMORPHISM

2.1 Definition

2.1.1 Anthropomorphism as a Universal Experience

ANTHROPOMORPHISM IS SIMPLY "THE attribution of human characteristics or behavior to a god, animal or object."[2] Anthropomorphic thinking is so ingrained in our mental processes that it permeates the totality of human life. In the words of David Hume:

> There is a universal tendency among mankind to conceive all beings like themselves, and to transfer to every object, those qualities, with which they are familiarly acquainted, and of which they are intimately conscious. We find human faces in the moon, armies in the clouds; and by a natural propensity,

---

1. Lesher, *Xenophanes of Colophon*, 25.
2. *Oxford English Dictionary*. A distinction is often made between *anthropomorphism* (metaphor pointing to the human body) and *anthropopathism* (metaphor based on the human inner world of thoughts, love, hatred, etc.). The first assigns a human physical form to a god, animal or thing; the latter ascribes them human feelings and passions. The first term is composed by *anthrōpos* (= human being) + *morphē* (= form, figure, body); the second comes from *anthrōpos* + *pathos* (= affection, emotion). We don't employ this distinction in our study. We rather employ *anthropomorphism* to talk about the totality of what is to be human as a metaphor for the divine. However, divine creatures and monsters may be portrayed as having human personality but not human form. They have *pathos* but not *morphē*.

if not corrected by experience and reflection, ascribe malice or good-will to everything that hurts or pleases us. Hence the frequency and beauty of the *prosopopoeia* in poetry; where trees, mountains and streams are personified, and the inanimate parts of nature acquire sentiment and passion. And though these poetical figures and expressions gain not on the belief, they may serve, at least, to prove a certain tendency in the imagination, without which they could neither be beautiful nor natural.[3]

Anthropomorphism inserts itself at every intersection of our lives. Last night I saw a TV commercial in which two dogs were having a conversation. One dog was telling the other about his problems with fleas, mosquitoes and ticks. The other recommended a treatment that would eliminate all parasites. The commercial used an optical illusion to make it look as if the dogs were moving their snouts and actually speaking to each other.[4] In the same way, Genesis 3 depicts a serpent with human skills: it is intelligent (v. 3); and it's able to talk, argue (v. 4), deceive (v. 13) and understand (v. 14). Numbers 22 presents a donkey that is able to see angels, to understand a situation and even talk! (22:22–34). Such portrayals are as real as the dogs in the TV commercial.

Painting personifies everything: Spring is a woman (Élisabeth Louise Vigée Le Brun, 1799); the sun is a young man carrying a bow and an arrow (Anton Raphael Mengs, 1765); Venus is a beautiful young woman surrounded by angels and servants (Charles J. Natoire, 1741); death appears as a hooded man carrying a scythe[5] on his shoulder, ready to snatch away a lumberman (Jean-François Millet, 1859).

Literature abounds in anthropomorphism, especially poetry:

> With my crying the stones soften their natural hardness and break it;
> the trees bend themselves,
> the birds listening to me, when they sing with a different voice,
> they sympathize,
> and my dying singing they discover.[6]

Another example:

> ¡Vae soli! ... it says, angry roaring,

---

3. Hume, *Natural History of Religion*, 29.

4. We can recall the painting *Dogs Playing Poker* by Cassius M. Coolidge (1844–1934 CE). And we all talk about Donald Duck and Mickey Mouse as if they were people.

5. The scythe represents Death performing the human activity of harvesting crops.

6. Garcilaso de la Vega, "Égloga Primera," in Castro, *Biblioteca*, 4.

> the wind, around my house.
> ¡Vae soli! ... howls desperate ...
> And I scream to it (so it understands):
> –"I'm not that alone, winged friend,
> I have my rhymes; they haven't left me;
> with me they live under my tent."⁷

Anthropomorphism also saturates the *lyrics* of our songs. In one of my favorite songs of Frank Sinatra, the summer wind is presented as an individual who comes to touch the lover's hair and to walk with a man who's in love, only to take her away from him at the end of the summer.⁸

Scientists constantly use anthropomorphism. Biologist Lewis Wolpert described how "cells in the developing arm make the decision to become a humerus."⁹ The scientist Jaime Waydo, from the Mars Science Laboratory (NASA), shared with the viewers that all the people who were involved in the "Curiosity" project talked about the rover as if it was a person: "You hear us talk about her as if she's a person because to us, she is."¹⁰

Death is an impersonal occurrence that brings our existence to an end, yet the Apostle Paul addresses death as if it were a person to whom he could talk: "Where, O death, is your victory? Where, O death, is your sting?" ¹¹ Christopher Hitchens, the acclaimed atheist philosopher, was quite aware that these expressions are only metaphorical but he wasn't exempt from using them:

> When I described my tumor in my esophagus as "a blind, emotionless alien," I suppose that even I couldn't help awarding it some of the qualities of a living thing. This at least I know to be a mistake: an instance of that pathetic fallacy (angry cloud, proud mountain, presumptuous little Beaujolais) by which we ascribe animated qualities to inanimate phenomena. To exist, a cancer needs a living organism. Its whole malice—there I go again—lies in the fact that the "best" it can do is do die with its host.¹²

---

7. "Fidelidad," Amado Nervo. This quote was suggested to me by Alfredo Tépox.

8. See *Summer Wind*, music by Heinz Meier, lyrics for the English version by Johnny Mercer.

9. Wolpert, *Unnatural Nature of Science*, 137. Charles J. Chaplin (1825–1891 CE) painted science as a young beautiful woman reading a book.

10. "Ultimate Mars Challenge."

11. 1 Cor 15:55. Cf. Acts 2:24; Rom 6:9; 1 Cor 15:26.

12. Hitchens, *Mortality*, 11.

2.1.2. Cognitive Medium[13]

Some have described anthropomorphism as the remnant of an infantile stage in the evolution of humankind.[14] That is not correct. Of course that if we take it *literally* it provides an erroneous view of reality, but in no way should it be considered primitive thinking because no one has ever been exempt of using it, not even the modern individual. Anthropomorphism is a universal cognitive tool. After all, we all know that dogs don't talk; the wind is not a fickle friend; spring is not a woman; death is not a person; and the stones are incapable of showing empathy. We also know that god is not an old man (Michelangelo) and nonetheless we cannot avoid using metaphors all the time.

Neuropsychologist Richard Gregory explains that all perception "involves betting on odds." All perception is an interpretation of phenomena based on mental models through which we attempt to understand the world in search of meaning and information. The accumulation of these "perceptual hypotheses (perceptions) confers immense survival benefits."[15] In this process, humankind itself stands as the main cognitive model because our most immediate experience is the experience of our own body. Therefore, our point of view tends to be anthropocentric and teleological, like in the expression quoted above: "cells make the decision to become a humerus." And if it's true that "man is the measure of all things" (Protagoras), it should come as no surprise that we imagine natural phenomena as having human traits. This is why the most universal metaphors are the ones coming directly from our bodily experience. Here are a few examples:

---

13. See §1.1.5 where we described the cognitive use of metaphor.

14. As many others, Sigmund Freud said that "Animism, the first conception of the world which man succeeded in evolving, was therefore psychological. It did not yet require any science to establish it, for science sets in only after we have realized that we do not know the world and that we must therefore seek means of getting to know it. But animism was natural and self-evident to primitive man; he knew how the things of the world were constituted, and as man conceived himself to be. We are therefore prepared to find that primitive man transferred the structural relations of his own psyche to the outer world" (*Totem and Taboo*, 150). Jean Piaget also argued that children believe in the man in the sky until they are eight years old (Piaget, *Child's Conception of the World*, 288). But the truth is that no one is able to avoid personifying natural phenomena, even if it is only figuratively.

15. Gregory, *Eye and Brian*, 187, 246. See also Lawson and McCauley, *Rethinking Religion*; Malinowski, *Magic, Science and Religion*; Morris, *Anthropological Studies of Religion*; Watts, *Psychology, Religion and Spirituality*.

Our bodily experience as main source of metaphors

Metaphor	Meaning
He didn't *see* what I wanted to say	He did not understand
She *fell behind* in her payments	Her payments are overdue
His mind was *wandering* all the time	He was unable to pay attention
Get *off my back*!	Stop harassing me!
The species is *at the edge* of extinction	Extinction is imminent
We are *moving ahead* with the project	We are making progress
Don't force your views *down his throat*	Don't force him to agree with you
I was left *in the dark*	I was not informed
She's *pushing* a deal that won't work	She's imposing, promoting
He's got both *feet on the ground*	He's a realistic person
It was an *uphill* battle until we sold the house	It's been very difficult
I'm *warming up* to her	I'm beginning to like her
You're *going too fast*. I can't *follow* your argument.	You talk too fast. I can't understand

2.1.3 Theistic Definition

In chapter one, we defined *myth* as a metaphor extended into a narrative. Now we need to show that the most fundamental metaphor employed in imagining the gods of theism is *anthropomorphism*. Philip Clayton gives a good definition of *religious* anthropomorphism:

> Theism is the belief in the existence of a supernatural force or forces, understood to have a personal nature. The term is often used synonymously with *monotheism*. Taken generically, however, theism should include a broad variety of metaphysical positions that are opposed to atheism: polytheism (the belief in many gods), monotheism (the belief in a single god), deism (the belief in a creator God who does not have any subsequent influence upon the world), and panentheism (the belief that the world is within God, although God is also more than the world). Theism contrasts with nonpersonal understandings of ultimate

reality, such as the law of karma or the principle of emptiness in Buddhism.[16]

We are all familiar with the famous fresco painted by Michelangelo, *The Creation of Adam* (Sistine Chapel, 1510 CE). The painting portrays the god of Christianity as an old man. But long before Michelangelo, glyptic art represented the gods in the likeness of human beings. From the vast amount of material (seals, bullae, stelae, statues, amulets, etc.), let's look at a few examples. A serpentine cylinder seal shows Ea (Enki) in the form of a bearded *man* seated on his throne, wearing a horned crown with a flowing stream of water and fish around him.[17] A seal has Ninurta carved into *human* form, "carrying in one hand a plough and in the other hand a lion-head club," showing that Mesopotamia understood this weather-god to be a god of both fertility and war.[18] A basalt stela from Arslan Tash (Syria) represents the storm-god Adad (Iškur) as a *man* riding on a bull (symbol of power and fertility). He carries a bow in his back and in his hands he wields lightning bolts as his arrows (stela AO 13092, Louvre Museum). Other seals represent Adad as a *man* standing upon two mountains, mounted upright upon a bull or seated on a dragon and wielding a three-tongued fork of lightning.[19] A white limestone bas-relief from Ugarit (ca. 1700–1500) portrays Baal as a bearded *man* with curly locks standing on top of mountains (stele AO 15775, Louvre Museum). He wears a pointed helmet with two horns, and he is dressed with a short kilt with horizontal lines fastened with a belt and tassel. He also carries a sword on his belt. As a warrior-god, Baal is shown with his right arm up brandishing a mace, and as a fertility-god his extended left arm is holding a spear which he thrusts into the ground—the top of the spear sprouts into a plant. In front of Baal stands a small man with a long garment who may be a king or a priest praising Baal.[20] These and

---

16. Clayton, "Theism," 880. Clayton's definition really improves on those explanations that incorrectly confuse *theism* with *monotheism* (like the misleading definition found in Bertocci, "Theism," 9102). Werblowsky correctly states that the "ultimate, residual anthropomorphism ... is the theistic notion of God as personal, in contrast to an impersonal conception of the divine" ("Anthropomorphism," 317). So any god who is conceived as personal is part of theism, whether Yahve, Marduk, Enlil, etc.

17. British Museum, seal number 103317, ca. 2250. See Budge, *Amulets and Superstitions*, 88–90.

18. Frankfort, *Cylinder Seals*, 146. A cylinder seal represents Ninurta as a bearded *human* warrior with a horned crown on his head and stars floating around it. The warrior-god wears a striated open robe over a fringed kilt. He is armed with a sword and a sickle, while aiming an arrow at a winged lion (British Museum, seal number 119426).

19. Frankfort, *Cylinder Seals*, 124, 163, 174. Another god is shown riding a chariot pulled by a winged lion. See Weber, *Altorientalisch Siegelbilder*, 62 (figure 298).

20. Cornelius, *Iconography of the Canaanite Gods*, 134–36, and plate 32 BR1. And

many other images of the gods were taken from our human world: thrones, crowns, ploughs, clubs, bulls, lightning, mountains, helmets, kilts, chariots, etc. And most important, all the gods are portrayed as human beings.

Myth is highly anthropomorphic and, therefore, demands the production of a *narrative*, because human beings move, talk, work, etc. But there is another element added to the mix. When we ascribe human attributes to the gods, we also enhance their human traits to make the gods fantastically powerful. Those who have seen the movies of Thor (Chris Hemsworth) and Superman (Christopher Reeve) have an idea of how people imagined the gods.[21] For example, like any other human being Enki had the capability of knowing things, but his knowledge was also tremendously enhanced. A story narrates that when goddess Inana went to visit him, he already knew why she was coming:

> On that day, he who has all knowledge,
> who knows the divine powers in heaven and earth,
> who from his own dwelling already knows the intentions of the gods,
> Enki, the king of the Abzu,
> who, even before the holy Inana had approach within six miles from the temple of Eridug, knew what her intentions were.[22]

Anthropomorphism is about conceptualizing the divine realm (*target domain*) in terms of our human world (*source domain*).[23] In other words, multitudes of individual metaphors taken from the human domain are used to construct the conceptual metaphor GOD IS (SUPER) HUMAN.[24]

On the basis of this fundamental metaphor, the gods are envisioned as *personal* and as having a human body. Additionally, the gods of theism feel, think, will, love, hate, etc. The axis of all theistic beliefs rests on this anthropomorphic way of thinking about the gods. As Herbert Spencer remarks:

> It is now generally admitted that a more or less idealized humanity is the form which every conception of a personal God

---

see Schaeffer, "Les de Minet-el de Ras Shamra," 96.

21. Some anthropologists correctly call the gods "superhuman beings" (Spiro, "Religion" 91–92), or "superhuman agents" (Lawson and McCauley, *Rethinking Religion*, 46, 53, 61).

22. *Transference of the Arts of Civilization from Eridug to Unug*, B.6–15. For the text, see ETCSL; Farber, "Inanna and Enki," 290; Kramer and Maier, *Myths of Enki*, 58.

23. See §1.1.2 (fourth point) for an explanation of both target and source domains.

24. Humans have this "universal tendency to form religious concepts and ideas and, on a more basic level, to experience the divine . . . in the categories and shapes most readily available to human thinking—namely, the human ones" (Werbloswky, "Anthropomorphism," 388).

must take. Anthropomorphism is an inevitable result of the laws of thought. We cannot take a step towards constructing an idea of God without the ascription of human attributes. We cannot even speak of a divine will without assimilating the divine nature to our own; for we know nothing of volition save as a property of our own minds.[25]

2.2 The Body of Yahve and the Gods[26]

In this section we discuss the actual data regarding the anthropomorphic images that are used to portray the gods of theism. Subsequently we'll show how Plato chastised this way of describing the gods as too demeaning (§2.3). His influence started a refinement that ended creating many distortions in biblical interpretation. For if the church defines god as "almighty, eternal, immense, incomprehensible, infinite . . . who, as being one, sole, absolutely simple[27] and immutable spiritual substance, is to be declared as really and essentially distinct from the world,"[28] and if, at the same time, we declare that this definition comes from the Scriptures, we generate tremendous problems. It happens that countless portions of the Scriptures are completely alien to such a definition. The new platonic theology led many interpreters to twist the meaning of the biblical text to accommodate its content to the doctrine of the church.

Let's first examine the human images used to describe the gods. We may repeat *ad nauseam* that god is essentially different from this world, but the truth is that, in the Ancient Near East and the Mediterranean, the

25. Spencer, *Illustrations of Universal Progress*, 442.

26. See Fretheim, *Suffering of God*; Knafl, *Forming God*; Smith, *How Human Is God?*; Sommer, *Bodies of God*. Though the divine is imagined in a variety of ways, our concern here lies only on the humanized god. A discussion of other manifestations is found in Sommer, *Bodies of God*. Cf. fire (Exod 3:2), cloud (Exod 16:10; Deut 31:15), glory (Lev 9:23; Num 16:42), etc. But even in these cases, anthropomorphism is still dominant. Yahve appears in the fire, but *talks* from the fire (Exod 3:4–9), and says he's been able to gather information *by seeing and hearing* (3:7). As a bodily being, he also comes down from heaven (3:8).

27. Humans are multipart creatures (organs, members, cells, molecules, atoms, etc.), and we are subject to changes and moods. By contrast, the god of classical theology is a "simple substance." His being is not complex; it has no parts or divisions. We are even told that we cannot find in god any distinction between essence and attributes. God lacks potentiality or movement. See Bavinck, *Reformed Dogmatics*, 118–31; Heppe, *Reformed Dogmatics* 63; Sennet, *Analytic Theist*, 228–49; Wolterstoff, *Inquiring about God*, 91–111.

28. "Dogmatic Decrees of the Vatican Council," section I (1870 CE), in Schaff, *Creeds*, 2:239.

human body and any other human characteristic were openly employed as a way of understanding the gods, whether biblical or not. Homer describes Zeus as having eyebrows and hair:

> The Son of Cronos spoke, and gave his approval by bowing his dark eyebrows; his divine locks waved on the King's immortal head.[29]

The god of the Hebrew Bible is also represented with bodily human characteristics:

> ... and one who was ancient of days[30] sat,
> whose garments were white as snow,
> and the hair of his head was like pure wool (Dan 7:9, cf. vv. 13, 22).

Ugarit portrays El as a humanized god:

> You are great, O El, so very wise;
> The gray hair of your beard instructs you,
> [Your] soft b[eard] that comes down to your chest.[31]

In the fable of Judges 9:13, the vine responds to the trees, saying: "Should I stop producing my wine that cheers gods[32] and humans, to go and sway over the trees?" This fable shows that the gods were imagined as people who could enjoy some glasses of wine.[33] The new platonic theology, however, insisted in defining god as invisible (Col 1:15; 1 Tim 1:17), claiming that nobody has ever seen him (John 1:18; 1 John 4:20). This contradicts many biblical accounts. A prophet declared: "I saw Adonay sitting on a throne" (Isa 6:1). And we are told that Moses, Aaron, Nadab, Abihu and the elders—lots of people!—"saw the Elohe of Israel" (Exod 24:9-11). Here the mythographer reports that all these men enjoyed a good dinner with their god in the mythic mountain where they "beheld Elohim, and ate and drank" (24:11). Later on, Zechariah's first vision (1:7-17) talks about several divine beings

---

29. Homer, *Iliad* i.528-30 (cf. Murray, *Iliad 1-12*, 53).

30. Similarly, in Ugarit the god El is called "Father of years" (*Baal Cycle*, KTU 1.6.i.36; cf. 1.3.v.8). See Cross, *Canaanite Myth and Hebrew Epic*, 15-16.

31. *Baal Cycle*, CAT 1.4.v.3-5 (cf. Smith, "Baal Cycle," 129).

32. We have translated *'ĕlōhîm* as plural: "gods" (NJB, NRSV, NIV) but it could also be singular: "god" (LXX, ASV, JPS; Butler, *Judges*, 227).

33. In the *Epic of Aqhat*, Lady Danatay gives "food and wine" to the god Kothar. See §2.2.4.a.4). See also *Baal Cycle*, CAT 1.3.i.15-17; 1.4.vi.53-54. See *En. el.* iii.133-36, where the gods drink beer during a joyful celebration. In the myth *Enki and Ninmaḥ*, we are told that "Enki and Ninmaḥ were drinking beer and their heart became cheerful" (i.52).

who appeared in human form. One was a "man" (*'îš*) riding on a red horse, and there were other additional riders (vv. 8-11). The leader of the group is called "man" (vv. 8, 10), "lord" (*'ădōnî*, v. 9), "messenger" (*mal'āk*, v. 9) and "messenger of Yahve" (*mal'āk yhwh*, vv. 11, 12; cf. Zech 3:1-5). At the very beginning of the famous work *Atraḥasīs* (ca. 1700-1600 BCE), we find these words: "When the gods were like human beings." This story claims that there was a time when a group of proletarian gods lived like men, in the sense that they were subjected to forced labor in this world.

People believed that the gods could visit us "in human form" (Acts 14:11). Joshua 5:13-15 reports that Joshua "saw a man standing before him with a drawn sword in his hand" (v. 13), ready for war. The man identifies himself as the "commander of the army of Yahve" (v. 14).[34] Joshua worships him and asks him what he wants. As in Exodus 3:5, the commander orders Joshua to remove his sandals because he was on holy ground. Unexpectedly, we are told that the man is really a god: "Yahve said to Joshua..." (Josh 6:2). In Babylon, a seer had a similar experience, and then reported the vision to King Ashurbanipal (668-627 BCE), saying:

> [The goddess] Ishtar, who dwells in Arbela, came in. Right and left quivers were hanging from her. She held the bow in her hand (and) a sharp sword was drawn to do battle. You [= Ashurbanipal] were standing in front of her and she spoke to you like the mother who bore you. Ishtar called unto you, she who is exalted among the gods, giving you the following instructions...[35]

As in the case of Joshua, the goddess of war appeared in human form, armed with quivers, a bow and a sharp sword (cf. Josh 5:13). She comes to instruct Ashurbanipal on how to win a battle (cf. Josh 6:2-5). It would be dishonest to argue that the story of Joshua reports a "historical" event while the story about Ishtar conveys a myth. On the contrary, we are dealing with two mythical narratives that use anthropomorphic language to talk about the gods.

Aristotle admitted that "men portray the appearance[36] [of the gods] to be like their own."[37] So it should come as no surprise that the Hebrew Bible

---

34. In Dan 8:11, the expression "commander of the army" (*śar-haṣṣābā'*) refers to the god of Israel, and here in Joshua it may also point at Yahve as a warrior god. In favor of this is the fact that Joshua's experience (Josh 5:15) resembles that of Moses.

35. Pfeiffer, "Oracular Dream concerning Ashurbanipal," vv. 54-59.

36. By "appearance" the word *eidos* means human form and figure. See §4.1.1 for the full quote.

37. Aristotle, *Politics* i.1252b27. Cf. "men imagine the gods in human form" (Rackham, *Aristotle Politics*, 9).

describes Yahve as having a body similar to that of humans.[38] Sometimes Yahve's body is represented as having an identical complexion as the human body; to the point that those who encounter the divinity may think he's just a man.[39] Something similar happens with Clark Kent, who looks like a normal person until he shows that he's really Superman.[40] Other texts present the body of Yahve as having a size and power beyond what is found in humans or its composition seems to be different from the human body.[41] Finally, the god assumes what it seems to be a cosmic body.[42]

In §1.1.5, we said that metaphors can affect how we perceive the world. Metaphor has the power to materialize itself in such a way that our brains may perceive a metaphor as real, as a literal description of reality. An obvious example is the statement "this is my body" (Mark 14:22). For Protestants this is a metaphorical expression made real only by the Spirit, but for Catholics the statement is materialized to the point that the bread and the wine "are substantially changed into the true, proper and life-giving flesh and blood of Jesus Christ."[43] In the same way, the passages about the visits of the gods that we'll soon examine (§2.2.1–5), do not give any indication that their anthropomorphisms were merely poetic. The mythographers thought the gods had human form.

In approaching this type of passages, Benjamin Sommer invites us to ask ourselves:

> Did these ancient authors mean precisely what they said, or did they use anthropomorphic language for other reasons—for example, because they were attempting to appeal to an unsophisticated audience, because they used physical terms to describe something nonphysical that was otherwise difficult to explain, or because they were merely resorting to old, fossilized expressions that no longer meant something to them? In the absence of any statements telling us that these many verses are mere figures of speech, I think that a likely answer must be that the

---

38. The following threefold description of Yahve's body is taken from Smith, *How Human Is God?*, 6–7.

39. Cf. Gen 2–3; 18–19; 32:24–29[25–30].

40. Cf. Judg 13:6, where we are told that the man from god had an imposing appearance. See §2.2.4.a.5.

41. Cf. Exod 24: 33–34; Isa 6:1–5.

42. Cf. 1 Kgs 8:27; Ps 139:7–12; Isa 66:1; Jer 23:23–24; Ezek 1:26–28.

43. Denzinger, *Magisterio*, 132. Or: "in this sacrament, the bread verily transubstantiates into the body, and the wine in to the blood of our Lord Jesus Christ" (169).

ancient who talk about God's body really do think that God has a body.⁴⁴

Anne Knafl adds that, in many cases, "anthropomorphism, unlike figures of speech, goes beyond esthetics and seeks to make a statement about reality ... The anthropomorphism of a deity (or animal, or natural force) reveals an author's (and culture's) conception of the nature of the deity."⁴⁵ And to the question of whether there is an essential continuity between god and his human form, Terence Fretheim correctly concludes that "it is probable that Israel did not conceive of God in terms of formlessness, but rather that *the human form of divine appearances constituted an enfleshment which bore essential continuities with the form which God was believed to have.*"⁴⁶ Finally, when Jacob Neusner writes about anthropomorphism in the Hebrew Bible, he uses the concept of "incarnation," which he defines as "the representation of God in the flesh, as corporeal, consubstantial in emotion and virtue with human beings, and sharing in the modes and means of actions carried out by mortals."⁴⁷ Neusner correctly denies that the incarnation is a doctrine unique to Christianity for it was already part of Judaism.⁴⁸ To be fair, the truth is that not only in Judaism but in all of the Ancient Near East and the Mediterranean the gods were incarnate gods. Therefore, in many cases metaphor is not a mere rhetorical dressing. Metaphor can materialize itself in such a way that it affirms the bodily form of the divine. We should now move on to comment on some biblical passages that portray Yahve as incarnate, as having a body like humans do.

2.2.1 Genesis 3:8–13: The God Who Walks through the Garden

⁸ Then they heard the sound of the steps⁴⁹ of Yahve Elohim,

---

44. Sommer, *Bodies of God*, 8–9.
45. Knafl, *Forming God*, 43–4.
46. Fretheim, *Suffering of God*, 105 (italics original).
47. Neusner, *Incarnation of God*, 12.
48. For examples, see Neusner *Incarnation of God*, 15–18.
49. The text could be interpreted as saying: "They heard the voice of the Lord" (KJV, cf. ASV, JPS), but Yahve does not speak until v. 9, when he calls to Adam. It is better to interpret: "They heard the sound of Yahve" (*wayyišməʿû ʾet-qôl yhwh*, in which the genitive is subjective: the sound made by Yahve), which is a shorter way of saying: They heard the sound made by Yahve's feet or footsteps. The word *qôl* has this same meaning in other texts: "When Ahijah heard the sound of her feet" (*ʾet-qôl raglêʸhā*, 1 Kgs 14:6); or: "the sound of the feet" (*qôl raglê*, 2 Kgs 6:32; cf. 1 Kgs 14:6; 2 Sam 5:24). Cassuto translates "the sound of His walking" (*Genesis*, 152, cf. NVI). See Koehler, *Hebräisches Lexikon*, 1013; Delitzsch, *Genesis*, 157; Driver, *Genesis*, 46; Gunkel, *Genesis*, 19; Skinner,

who was walking⁵⁰ in the garden during the breeze of the day. And the man and his wife hid themselves⁵¹ from the presence of Yahve Elohim among the trees of the garden.⁵²

⁹ Yahve Elohim called to the man, and said: Where are you?

¹⁰ He responded: I heard the sound of your steps⁵³ in the garden, and I was afraid because I'm naked, so I hid myself.

¹¹ And [Yahve] said: Who taught you that you are naked? Have you eaten from the tree of which I commanded you not to eat?

¹² The man answered: The woman whom you gave me, she gave me [the fruit] from the tree, and I ate.

¹³ Yahve Elohim said to the woman: What is this that you have done?⁵⁴ The woman answered: The serpent deceived me, and I ate.

When examining this story, we should avoid disfiguring it with prejudices coming from later Christian dogma. A god may be called "Almighty" (*upermenēs*),⁵⁵ but the truth is that the gods were also portrayed in very human fashion. Susan Niditch points out that in trying to explain the story of the fall,

> Modern scholars try to make sense of what they consider to be an all-powerful, all-knowing deity who appears to fear human's possible acquisition of knowledge and immortality, who has to deal with humans on the loose, who has tricky snakes sneaking around his back, and who must adjust in a totally ad hoc way to the events around him. Not unlike all the great heads of pantheons such as Odin or Zeus, he is a powerful creator god—more powerful than all other forces—but he can be tricked, becoming subject to the wiles of those whom he has created, such as

---

Genesis, 77; Speiser, *Genesis*, 24; Westermann, *Genesis 1–11*, 182, 254.

50. As usual, a verb of perception ("they heard") is able to carry two complements: a direct object (lit. "the sound," cf. Gen 6:2) and a secondary complement (circumstantial ptc. *mithallēk* = "walking").

51. See Ges. § 145f for a verb in singular with a plural subject.

52. Cf. "The man and his woman hid themselves among the trees of the garden, so the Lord God would not see them" (PER).

53. Again, the text does not say: "I heard thy voice" (ASV, KJV), but: "I heard the sound of you" (NJB, cf. 3:8). The idea is: "I heard your steps," or: "I heard you walking" (NLT).

54. The idea seems to be: How could you have done such an atrocity!? (cf. Gen 12:18). Or maybe: "Confess, what have you done?" (Gunkel, *Genesis*, 19).

55. See Homer, *Iliad* ii.116, 350, 403. Cf. Gen 17:1.

Loki, Prometheus, the snake, Adam and Eve. He is, in short, a parent.[56]

If we idealized Yahve as a god who is invisible, omniscient and essentially different from the world, it is impossible to experience the dramatic force of Genesis 3:7–13. In the words of Hermann Gunkel: "The narrative does not report that Yahweh knew or saw it all, rather that strolling in the Garden, he accidentally discovered the transgression."[57] The drama of the story only comes to life when we imagine a god who possesses the limitations and advantages of a physical body. He seems to be a god who has *legs and feet*; a god who went for a walk to refresh his *body* at a time when he would have enjoyed a breeze. The suspense of the narrative reaches its climax in vv. 8–13, when the mythographer reports that Adam and Eve heard the steps of the god who "was walking in the garden" (Gen 3:8). The couple realized that he was approaching, and they were thrown into a state of panic.

Yahve does not know where Adam is, so he calls him: "Where are you?" (3:9).[58] Adam and Eve were hiding from the god, and we ruin the story when we insist that humans cannot hide from an omniscient god. Note that this god is able to *speak out loud*, which takes for granted that he has an articulatory system that allows him to talk (lips, tongue, teeth, vocal chords, etc.). It seems the god was also equipped with an auditory system that transmitted sound waves to his brain for Yahve was able to hear and understand when Adam answered: "I heard the sound of your steps in the garden, and I was afraid because I'm naked, so I hid myself" (3:10). This god could learn something he did not know, for he's surprised that Adam knew he was naked. Yahve infers that Adam must have eaten from the tree of knowledge, so he demands more information to confirm his guess: "Who taught you that you are naked? Have you eaten from the tree of which I commanded you not to eat?" (3:11).[59] Adam accuses his wife, and the god reprimands her: "What is this that you have done?"(3:13). She defends

---

56. Niditch, *Folklore*, 42.

57. Gunkel, *Genesis*, 18. Cf. Gen 18:20–21, where Yahve needs to walk down to the valley to look at the situation. See §2.2.4.c.

58. Cassuto, *Genesis*, 155; Speiser, *Genesis*, 24; and Wenham, *Genesis*, 76, argue that Yahve knew where Adam was hiding, so the questions are rhetorical. This is a modern prejudice. It's better to recognize that "the question expresses ignorance" (Skinner, *Genesis*, 77), that the "statement presumes he does not know where the man is" (Gunkel, *Genesis*, 19).

59. A modern prejudice drives Wenham to argue that the questions are rhetorical, because according to him we are not dealing with an "ignorant inquirer" but an "all-knowing detective" (*Genesis*, 77). A real omniscient god doesn't need to be "a detective"(!).

herself accusing the serpent. As it happens with other gods of the Ancient Near East, Yahve acts like a human being. And it is precisely this representation which allows the mythographer to write a story that evolves in such a dramatic way within a space-time structure completely alien to any immutable and omniscient divine nature. In fact, these attributes would have made it impossible to write a narrative that unfolds in this world.

2.2.2 Genesis 6:1–4: The Gods Get Married and Procreate[60]

¹When the human race began to multiply on the face of the earth, and daughters were born to them, ²the gods[61] saw that the daughters of the human race were beautiful; and they took[62] wives for themselves, anyone they chose . . .

⁴ . . . the gods copulated[63] with the daughters of the human race, and they gave birth [children] for them . . .

Although this passage is saturated with problems, one thing is pretty clear: the literal expression "sons of the gods" (bᵊnê-hā'ĕlōhîm, vv. 1, 4) simply means "gods." The phrase belongs to a common idiom:

The expression *sons of* as a common idiom

Idiom	Meaning
sons of the gods	= gods ('ēlîm, Pss 29:1; 89:6[7]; Deut 32:8 = 4QDeutʲ; 'ĕlōhîm, Gen 6:2, 4; Job 1:6; 2:1; Job 38:7; cf. Wis 5:5). See §3.3.4.c–e; §3.3.5.
sons of the prophets	= prophets (1 Kgs 20:35; 2 Kgs 2:3, 5, 15; 4:1, 38; Amos 7:14, etc.).
sons of Adam	= human beings (Gen 6:2, 4; Num 23:19; Deut 32:8; 1 Sam 26:19; 2 Sam 7:14; Job 25:6; Pss 11:4; 14:2; 80:17[18], etc.).
sons of the priests	= priests (1 Chr 9:30).
son of the perfumers	= perfumer (Neh 3:8).

---

60. Later on (§2.4), we'll provide a closer analysis of Genesis 6:1–2.

61. Lit. "the sons of the elohim" (bᵊnê-hā 'ĕlōhîm, cf. v. 4). LXX *hoi huioi tou theou* = "the sons of god" (cf. NRSV, NIV). More correctly, Aquila: *hoi huioi tōn theōn* = "the sons of the gods" ("divine beings," TJPS).

62. The verb *lāqaḥ* carries the meaning of "take in marriage" + prep. *lᵊ* (= "for themselves"). Cf. Gen 4:19; 11:29; 12:19.

63. The impf. *yāḇō'û* (= lit. "they went," cf. NRSV) in the sense of having sexual relations (cf. Gen 16:2; 30:3; 38:8; Judg 16:1, etc.).

sons of the Levites	= Levites (Neh. 12:23).
sons of the exiles	= exiles (Ezra 4:1).

Gesenius confirms that the word *ben* (= son) was used to "denote membership of a guild or society (or of a tribe, or any definite class)," adding that the expression *bənê-hā'ĕlōhîm* means "beings of the class *'ĕlōhîm* or *'ēlîm*" [= gods].[64]

Genesis 6:1–4 claims that the gods were capable of love and sex.[65] In the light of Ancient Near East and Mediterranean literature, we could safely assume that these gods have genitals allowing them to procreate.[66] This is another case of anthropomorphism. The separation between the divine and human realms was not as absolute as it was later conceived by platonic theology. For example, we can mention an exquisite story in which Ištar (Venus) tries to seduce the mortal king Gilgameš. The goddess is described in strong anthropomorphic terms as a woman who's in love and wants to get married:

> (Gilgamesh) washed his locks,
>   He tied them up with a suitable ribbon
> And he [throw]
>   his curls over his back.
> He took off his dirty clothes
>   to put on new ones,
> Wrapping himself in a wide cloak
>   which he girded with a sash.
> Having [the King] put on
>   his crown,
> Princess Ishtar was fascinated
>   by the beauty of Gilgamesh:[67]

---

64. Ges. § 128v. Brevard Childs also admits that: "the *bənê-' ĕlōhîm* are individuals of the class 'god'" (*Myth and Reality*, 51). And more recently: "the 'marriage of angels' (6:1–4) originally concerned divine creatures (*bənê'ĕlōhîm*) who had intercourse with earthly women to produce a mixed species" (Childs, *Biblical Theology*, 120).

65. Later on (§3.4.1 and §4.3.3), we will explore the popular concept of gods having sex with humans to produce the heroes and kings of ancient times.

66. Let's remember that Cronos castrated Uranus. He "cut the genitals" of his father (Hesiod, *Theo.* 180–81; cf. Most, *Theogony*, 17).

67. Lit. the text says: "upon Gilgameš' beauty, princess Ištar put the eyes" (*ana du-un-qí ša* ᵈ*Gilgāmeš īnī ittaši rubūtu* ᵈ*Ištar*), which sounds closer to what Genesis says about the gods seeing that the women were beautiful. See "Našû," 104; Parpola, *Epic of Gilgamesh*, 91; George, *Epic of Gilgamesh*, 48.

> "Come, Gilgamesh *(she said to him)*
> marry me!
> Offer me
> your voluptuousness.
> Be my husband,
> I will be your wife."[68]

2.2.3 Genesis 6:5–7: The God Who Repents

Anthropomorphism also incorporates the inner life of the gods, their emotions, thoughts, will, etc. (cf. Neh 9:17; Ps 103:8–9). Numbers 23:19 may say that "El is no human being that he should lie; nor a son of Adam that he should change his mind,"[69] but the truth is that all gods changed their minds:

> [5] When Yahve realized that the wickedness of humankind [was] great on earth, and that every intention of the thoughts of their hearts [was] only evil every day, [6] Yahve regretted having made humankind on the earth, and it caused hurt to his heart. [7] Therefore, Yahve said: I will exterminate from the earth the human beings I created: humankind together with animals, reptiles and birds of the sky, because I regret having made them.

The anthropomorphic images of this passage portray a god who regrets having created humankind. This is a humanized god. Other biblical texts present god's repentance as conditional. For example, Jeremiah says that "perhaps" the people of Judah will turn from their sins and "obey" their god (Jer 26:3). If that happens, the god may repent from punishing them. But even in these cases, the idea of an omniscient and omnipotent god does not tally with a deity that participates in the contingencies of the world, because a conditional repentance means that Yahve has to wait to see the outcome of a situation to change his mind about punishing or blessing his people.[70] However, in Genesis 6:5–7 god's regret is definitive. The text is charged with feelings of irreversible disappointment. God is brokenhearted: "it caused hurt to his heart." There is nothing the god could do to change the situation. The experiment of creation has failed. If we impose into the situation the

---

68. *Gilg.* vi.1–9, in Bottéro, *Epopeya de Gilgamesh*, 118. In a myth mentioned in §1.2.1, goddess Inana is described as a human being who needs new sheets for her bed.

69. We already saw that Yahve is capable of deceiving (§1.1.3).

70. Cf. Jer 18:8–10. Central to the plot of Jonah's tale is the concept of a god who changes his mind (Jon 3:9, 10; 4:2).

element of omniscience, we simply ruin the narrative. If the god knew what would happen, how is it possible for him to regret it? Why did he begin a project knowing it was set to failure? Why was an omnipotent god not able to achieve his purpose? All these musings have no place in a story whose drama must be taken seriously. In the unfolding of an earthly narrative nobody knows everything. Yahve wasn't able to predict what would happen, and he grieves the outcome. Anthropomorphism encompasses the plans, emotions and thoughts of the gods.

2.2.4 Genesis 18–19: Divine Visits

a. Cultural background

A well respected ancient tradition imagined the gods visiting people. When Paul healed a crippled man, the crowd shouted: "the gods have descended to us in human form!" (Acts 14:11; cf. 28:1). The myth aimed at encouraging people to be hospitable towards outsiders by promising the host great rewards. To accomplish this goal, the situation demanded that the gods should appear disguised as human beings. A proverb discloses the *raison d'etre* behind this tradition:

> Do not forget to show hospitality to foreigners,[71] for by doing so some gave shelter to angels [= gods] without knowing it. (Heb 13:2)[72]

Shepherd of Hermas also promotes hospitality by declaring that those who entertain strangers[73] will live among the gods or angels:

> Bishops and hospitable people[74] who joyfully always received the servants of God in their homes, without hypocrisy, and the bishops who ceaselessly sheltered the destitute and the widow by their assistance, always behaving with holiness; all these shall always be sheltered by the Lord. Therefore, those who have done

---

71. Lit. "Do not forget of hospitality."

72. Harold Attridge says that this genre "involves a common folkloristic motif that would be familiar in a Greco-Roman audience" during the apostolic age (*Hebrews*, 386). We should also remember that Zeus was called the "hospitable" (Homer, *Odyssey* ix.269–70; xiv.389), and that: "all strangers and beggars belong to Zeus" (*Odyssey* xiv.55–6). On the basis of Genesis 18, the Babylonian Talmud (*Sabbath* 127.a, in Rodkinson, *Babylonian Talmud*, 277) avers that "hospitality is a greater merit than to receive the Shekhina" (= god's presence).

73. See §2.2.4 for the tradition about entertaining strangers and its rewards.

74. Lit. *filoxenoi* = "lovers of the alien and stranger." Cf. 1 Tim 3:2; 1 Pet 4:9.

these things are distinguished before the Lord, and their place is already with the angels, if they continue serving the Lord unto the end.[75]

Homer (*ca.* 850) reports that Odysseus disguised himself as a beggar in order to attend one of the revelries of Penelope's suitors. Antinous, the vilest of them, insulted him and threw a footstool at him. In the presence of so much nastiness, one of the young men reprimanded Antinous, saying:

> Antinous, it wasn't right for you to strike the unfortunate vagabond. Cursed man you are. What if perchance he be some god come down from heaven? Because it happens that the gods, in the guise of strangers from afar and adopting many appearances, visit the cities to inspect the arrogant violence or the good order of people.[76]

The function of the myth was to encourage hospitality. At that time people did not have the motels and restaurants we enjoy today through the arteries and highways that connect our cities. The march on foot or donkey meant long and exhausting journeys that would last for days or even weeks through inhospitable and desolate places. The preservation of human life and the functioning of the social system depended on the hospitality of people. A way of securing that practice was to promise divine rewards.[77]

This type of story is usually comprised by three elements: the arrival and welcome of the stranger which is a god(s) in disguise; the showing of hospitality to the outsider; and the divine reward for that hospitality. The myth percolated into the Christian tradition. A Christian legend tells that, when the holy family fled to Egypt (cf. Matt 2:13–15), a man named Dysmas offered them hospitality and protection. When the host saw Mary, he confessed that she was indeed *theotokos*, and invited the holy family to come into his house. The man asked his wife to entertain them while he went hunting. The reward for the hospitality came when the wife prepared a bath

---

75. *Shepherd of Hermas*, Similitude ix.27.2–3 (cf. Lake, *Apostolic Fathers*, 285).

76. Homer, *Odyssey* xvii.483–487 (cf. Murray, *Odyssey*, 12–24, 189–90). Cf. Plato, *Sophist* 216a–b, in Fowler, *Theaetetus, Sophist*, 265.

77. These visits were connected with the belief that each city had a patron god who visited the city in order to repay its inhabitants with punishments or rewards. The myth *Enki and the World Order* relates the story of Enki traveling in his barge visiting several cities as the giver of abundance and destinies (See Black, *Literature of Ancient Sumer*, 215–44; Kramer, *Sumerians*, 171–73). He visits Sumer, Ur, Meluha, Dilmun, and even the nomads of Mardu. The gods were also in charge of setting boundaries between city states as well as the irrigation channels. The gods were the owners of the lands, and placed their kings as their representatives. See Cooper, *Sumerian and Akkadian Royal Inscriptions*.

for Mary to bathe her child, Jesus. Then with the same water, the wife bathed her own child who was afflicted with leprosy, and the child was instantly healed. When the husband came back, he praised Mary for the miracle.[78] Let's now consider some other myths or stories about the gods.

1) The legend of Falernus

Silius Italicus (*ca.* 28–103 CE) says that, in primordial times, there was neither vines nor wine. People only drank the pure water of a spring. During one of his journeys, the god Bacchus[79] stopped in a city. Falernus welcomed him without knowing he was a god. His generosity was greatly rewarded:

Arrival and welcome

> When Lyaeus was on his way to the shore of Calpe and the setting sun, a lucky foot and a lucky hour brought him hither as guest; nor did the god disdain to enter the cottage and pass beneath its humble roof. The smoke-grimed door welcomed a willing guest.

Hospitality

> The meal was set, in the fashion of that simple age, in the front of the hearth; nor was the happy host aware that he was entertaining a god . . .

Reward and revelation

> . . . Pleased by the old man's willing service, Bacchus decreed that his liquor should not be lacking. Suddenly a miracle was seen: to pay the poor man for his hospitality, the beechen cups foamed with the juice of the grape; a common milk-pail ran red with wine; and the sweet moisture of fragrant clusters sweated in the hollow oaken bowl. "Take my gift," said Bacchus; "As yet it is strange to you, but hereafter it will spread abroad the name of Falernus, the vine-dresser"; and the god was no longer disguised. Straightway ivy crowned his brows that glowed and flushed; his locks flowed down over his shoulder; a beaker hung down from his right hand; and a vine-plant, falling from his green thyrsus, clothed the festive board with the leaves of Nysa.[80]

78. This legend comes from the fourteenth century CE. For the text, see Bilby, "Hospitality of Dymas," 39–40.

79. Also known by the name Lyaeus or Dionysus, the god of wine.

80. Silius Italicus, *Punica* vii.170–74, in Duff, *Silius Italicus*, 349. Note that even

2) The hospitality of Hyrieus

Ovidius Naso (43 BCE—17 CE) reports that once Jupiter (Zeus), Poseidon and Mercury were traveling together. It was already late, when the old Hyrieus saw them passing by, so he invited them into his humble abode, saying "my door is open to the foreigner." The gods "concealed their divine nature"[81] and entered the humble cottage. When the host served them wine, Poseidon was the first to drink, and then he said: "Pour out some more, that Jupiter, in his turn, may drink." When the old man realized that they were gods, he turned pale. Then he sacrificed the ox he used to till the soil, and prepared it for them. The gods had a feast. In gratitude, Jupiter asked the old man: "if you desire anything, ask for it, and it will be yours." Hyrieus was a widower with no children, so he said he wanted to have a son. The gods covered the hide of the ox with dirt, and after ten months had passed, a baby boy was born without the participation of a woman.[82] The old man named the boy Urion.[83]

3) Goddess Athene visits Telemachus

Athene descended from the Olympus to visit Odysseus' son. She appeared "in the likeness of a stranger" (*eidomenē xeinō*).[84] We are told that for the occasion she took the human form of Mentes, king of the Taphian islands. The reader should notice the diligence with which Telemachus entertains the goddess, which resembles the attentiveness shown by Abraham (§2.2.4.b) when he welcomed the gods who visited him:

> . . . he went straight to the outer door; for in his heart he felt it a shame that a stranger should stand long at the gates . . . So, drawing near . . . he said: 'Hail, stranger; in our house you'll be treated kindly. After you've eaten, you shall tell me what it is that you need.' . . . He led Athene and sat her on a chair, spreading on it a linen cloth (it was a beautiful chair richly wrought), and below her feet was a footstool . . . Then a handmaid brought water for the hands in a beautiful pitcher of gold, and poured

---

when Bacchus is "no longer disguised," he still looks like a man.

81. Ovidus Nason, *Fasti* vi.505, in Frazer, *Ovid's Fasti*, 297.

82. This way of creating a human being is as weird as forming Adam from dust or Eve from Adam's rib.

83. Ovid, *Fasti* vi.505–35. Note that, as in the case of Abraham (§2.2.4.b), the gods gave Hyrieus the gift of a son in reward for his hospitality.

84. Homer, *Odyssey* i.105, in Murray, *Odyssey*, 21.

it over a silver basin for them to wash, and beside them drew up a polished table. And the respected housekeeper brought and set before them bread, and with it dainties in abundance, giving freely of her store. And a carver lifted up and placed before them platters of all sorts of meats, and set by them golden goblets, while a herald continually walked to and fro pouring them wine.[85]

4) God Kothar[86] visits Daniel

This story is part of the *Epic of Aqhat*. The legend reports that King Daniel and his wife couldn't have children. The king offered many sacrifices to the gods until Baal had mercy and interceded before El, head of the Pantheon. El issued the following decree: "In kissing his wife, conception! In embracing her, pregnancy."[87] So with the help of the goddess of fertility, the couple was able to procreate a son whom they named Aqhat. Later the myth mentions that the god Kothar brought Daniel a bow and arrows as a gift for his son Aqhat. The story goes like this:

Arrival and welcome

> [...] I will bring the bow,
> > I will convey there many arrows.
>
> Then, on the seventh day,
> > Daniel, man of Rapiu,
> > the hero, man of the Harnemite,
>
> gets up and sits by the gateway,
> > among the chiefs on the threshing floor.
>
> [Daniel] Takes care of the case of the widow,
> > defends the need of the orphan.
>
> Raising his eyes, he sees
> > a thousand yards off,
> > ten thousand furlongs off.
>
> He observes the coming of Kothar,
> > observes the march of Khasis.

---

85. Homer, *Odyssey* i.118–43.

86. Kothar is the god of craftsmanship with residence in Memphis, Egypt. He makes furniture, bows, and palaces. His full name was Kothar-wa-Khasis, "skillful and wise." Baal was able to defeat Yamm with his help. See §1.3.3.

87. *Aqhat*, CAT 1.17.i.39–40 (cf. Parker, "Aqhat," 54).

Here he was bringing the bow,
    he was bringing many arrows.

The wife prepares a banquet for the god

Then Daniel, the man of Rapiu,
    the hero, man of Harnemite,
Calls out aloud to his wife:
"Listen, Lady Danatay,
    prepare a lamb from the flock.
For the relish of Kothar-wa-Hasis,
    for the hunger of Hayyan, the crafter.
Give the gods food and wine,
    serve and honor them,
    the lords of Memphis, allotted by El."
Lady Danatay listened,
    and she prepared a lamb from the flock,
for the relish of Kothar-wa-Hasis,
    for the hunger of Hayyan, the crafter.

Divine gift

After Kothar-wa-Hasis arrive,
    They hand Daniel the bow,
    On his lap they lay the arrows.

Hospitality: The god is entertained

Then Lady Danatay
    gave the gods food and wine,
    served and honored them,
    the lords of Memphis, allotted by El.

The god leaves

Kothar left for his tent,
    Hayyan left for his dwelling.[88]

The mythographer describes Kothar in very human terms. Daniel is sitting at the gate of the city. When he lifts his eyes, he sees the god walking towards him carrying the gifts. He asks his wife to prepare dinner, and the god

---

88. *Aqhat*, CAT 1.17.v.2–33 (cf. Parker, "Aqhat," 58; Pardee, "'Aqhatu Legend," 1:346).

delivers the presents. Then the god eats, drinks, and goes away. This legend is similar to the story about the three gods who visited Abraham.

5) The Visit of a Man-God

Judges 13:1–25 conveys an adaptation of the well-known legend of the extraordinary birth of a hero (§3.4; §4.3.3). The background for the visit is established at the beginning of the narrative, when the mythographer informs us that Manoah's wife "was barren and had borne no children" (13:2).[89] Once the need for a miracle is established, the reader is informed that a god intervened immediately: "The envoy of Yahve appeared to the woman" (13:3) to promise her that she shall have a son (Samson) who from the womb shall be consecrated to Elohim and who shall deliver Israel from the Philistines (13:3–5). The woman runs to share the news with her husband:

> A man of Elohim[90] visited me, and his appearance was like that
> of an envoy of Yahve, that is, imposing.[91] I didn't ask him where
> he came from, nor did he tell me his name; but he said to me:
> You shall conceive ... (13:6–7)

Following the usual format of the genre, the story-teller hides the identity of the god because it is expected for people to be hospitable to strangers without knowing their true identity. This is why the wife thought the god was a prophet, despite his imposing physical appearance.[92] Believing the messenger was a man, Manoah prays to Yahve asking him to send the "man of Elohim" again, so he could receive instructions about what to do with his son (13:8). Yahve responds sending again the "envoy of Elohim". After the visit, the woman runs to the husband, and says: "the man who visited me

---

89. In similar fashion, Yahve visits Abraham (Gen 18) to assure him the birth of a son, in spite Sarah's infertility (Gen 11:30; 16:2). In the story of Aqhat, Daniel wasn't able to procreate, as was also the case with old Hyrieus.

90. The expression "a man of Elohim" is always used of a human prophet. Cf. Deut 33:1; Josh 14:6; 1 Sam 2:27; 9:6, 10; 1 Kgs 12:22; 13:1, 4–8, 11, 12, 14, etc.

91. Or: "awe-inspiring" (NRSV), "awesome" (NIV).

92. We disagree with Niditch, who argues that Manoah's wife "immediately recognized that the messenger is not mere mortal" (*Judges*, 145). It seems that the expression "imposing" only means that the prophet had an impressive physique, not that he was divine. Note that through the whole narrative both the wife (13:6, 10) and Manoah (13:8, 11) always refer to the visitor as a man. Only the narrator knows he's a god (13:3, 9, 13, 15–18, 20). In §3.4.1, we'll see how goddess Aphrodite fell in love with Anchises because "in his physical structure [*demas*] he was like the immortal gods." Aphrodite makes a comparison that does not pretend to assert that Anchises was really a god but that his body was, you know, "divine."

the other day has appeared to me" (13:10). Manoah got up and followed his wife. He "approached the man," and asked him: "Are you the man who spoke to this woman?" (13:11). The question develops into a dialogue between Manoah and "the envoy of Yahve" (13:12-14). The host offers the man the required hospitality (13:15), but the god refuses to eat with Manoah. We are told in plain terms "that Manoah wasn't aware that he was the envoy of Yahve" (13:16). The host offers a sacrifice to Yahve, and suddenly the god ascends through the flames of the fire. Only then does the couple realize that the visitor was a god: "And they fell on their faces to the ground" (13:20). This legend shows how human were the gods of ancient times.

b. Yahve visits Abraham: Genesis 18:1-16

Imitating the old tradition of "the visits of the gods," the mythographer fabricates a story about Yahve. The story follows the structure of the genre: arrival of the strangers and welcome; display of hospitality; and finally the reward for the hospitality.

Welcome

> ¹ Yahve appeared to him [Abraham] by the oaks of Mamre, while he sat at the entrance of his tent during the hottest time of the day.
> ² He [Abraham] lifted up his eyes and saw three men standing[93] by him.
> When he saw [them], he ran from the tent entrance to meet them, bowing to the ground.
> ³ He said: "my lords,[94] if I have found favor in your sight, I beseech you don't pass by your servant. ⁴ Let some water be brought, and wash

---

93. When Yahve talked to Jacob in Bethel, it is said that the god "stood by him" (*niṣṣāḇ ʿālāyw*, Gen 28:13), which points to a bodily god. In 1 Samuel 3:10, "Yahve came and stood [*wayyityaṣṣaḇ*] there and called" Samuel. Amos describes Adonay "standing by a wall" (Amos 7:7) or "standing beside the altar" (9:1).

94. The alternative interpretations for Genesis 18:3 are as follows: 1. The MT reads ʾăḏōnāy (with long vowel), a form generally used to address Yahve. It is the "Lord" in upper case (cf. Gen 15:2, 8; 18:27, 31), and this is the translation used here by the KJV and some scholars (Sailhamer, *Genesis*, 185-7; Waltke, *Genesis*, 267). This would mean that already at v. 3 Abraham recognized that the visitor was Yahve. 2. However, most interpreters today believe that the genre requires the host not to know that he was entertaining a god (cf. Heb 13:2). Therefore, the text is modified to read ʾăḏōnî, that is, "my lord" with lower case (Baldwin, *Genesis*, 69; Blenkinsopp, *Abraham*, 119; Gunkel, *Genesis*, 193; Hamilton, *Genesis 18-50*, 3; Hartley, *Genesis* 178; von Rad, *Genesis*, 203; NRSV, JPS, ASV, NIV, NJB). This rhymes perfectly with the use of the 2nd pers. sing. used in v. 3: "your sight," "don't pass," "your servant." 3. Finally, we could also correct the

your feet and rest under the tree. ⁵Let me bring a piece of bread, that you may strengthen yourselves, and then you may proceed [with your journey], since you have visited your servant for this purpose."

[The men] responded:⁹⁵ "Do as you have said."

Hospitality

⁶ Then Abraham hurried into the tent where Sarah was, and said: "Quickly, take three measures of fine flour, knead it and bake some bread."

⁷ Abraham ran to the herd, took a tender and selected calf, and gave it to the servant, who hastened to prepare it.

⁸ Then he took curd, milk and the calf which had been prepared, and set [them] before them, standing by them under the tree while they ate.

Divine reward

⁹ They asked:⁹⁶ "Where is Sarah, your wife?"

[Abraham] responded: "There, in the tent."

¹⁰ And [Yahve] said: "Certainly, I will return to you next year,⁹⁷ and your wife Sarah shall have a son."

(Sarah was listening at the tent entrance behind him. ¹¹ Abraham and Sarah were old, advanced in age, and Sarah has ceased menstruating.)⁹⁸

---

text to read *ăḏōnay* = "lords" in plural (Skinner, *Genesis*, 299s; Westermann, *Genesis* 12-36, 273; TJPS; cf. 19:2). The context favors this reading. The plural is consistently used in vv. 2, 4, 5, 8, 9, and the ST reads the whole v. 3 as plural, too: "my lords, if I have found favor in your [pl.] sight, I beseech you [pl.] don't pass by your [pl.] servant." (Tsedaka, *Samaritan Version*, 37). We should also note that in Genesis 19:18, the MT is surely wrong in using the same vocative with long vowel (*ăḏōnāy* = "Lord" with upper case). This would require the translation: "Lot reply to them: No, Lord, please" (LXX, KJV), but the plural "them" seems to point to "lords" (NRSV, NIV, cf. 19:2 "my lords"). I personally prefer the reading of the Samaritan Text, but whether we read "my lord" (lower case) or "my lords," both readings would establish that in v. 3, Abraham did not recognize Yahve yet.

95. The LXX uses the singular: "he answered" (*eipan*).
96. The LXX uses the singular: "he asked him" (*eipen*).
97. The expression *kā'ēṯ ḥayyāʰ* (lit. "at a living time") is explained by the Akkadian *balāṭu* (= life, vigor), which is used to talk about the coming year: "he will return the silver next year" (*ina palāṭ uttêršu*, "Balaṭu," 51). See Koehler, *Hebräisches Lexikon*, 852. Cf. "I survived to the next year," in Lambert, *Babylonian Wisdom*, 39.
98. The parenthesis is meant to provide background (vv. 10b-11) for the coming dialogue in vv. 12-15, and to assure the reader that the birth of the child will be a miracle.

¹² Sarah laughed to herself, thinking: "Shall I have pleasure now that I'm worn out, and my husband is also old?"

¹³ Yahve said to Abraham: "Why did Sarah laugh, thinking 'Shall I indeed bear a child now that I'm old'? ¹⁴ Is there anything too difficult for Yahve?⁹⁹ At the set time, I will return to you next year, and Sarah shall have a son."

¹⁵ But Sarah lied, saying: "I did not laugh" (for she was afraid).

And [Yahve] said: "Don't [deny it], you laughed."

The gods depart

¹⁶ Then the men rose up and looked towards Sodom. Abraham went with them to send them off.

1) Welcome and hospitality: Genesis 18:1–8

It is very easy to detect the acute similarities between the present story and the myths examined above (§2.2.4.a). It is clear that this narrative belongs to the same genre, and that the mythographer adapted the tradition to fit his purpose.¹⁰⁰ This is achieved by beginning the story with the words "Yahve appeared to him" (v. 1). But the word "appeared" creates an incongruence. It makes us anticipate the unmistaken manifestation of the divine (theophany).¹⁰¹ Yet we only get a worldly narrative that talks about three "men" who can be seen and identified as such (v. 2). In the words of Claus Westermann, the gods meet Abraham in an "earthly, every day, utterly secular life without any element of theophany."¹⁰² Abraham offers them the refreshments that every tired traveler longs for: water for their feet, and shade from the relentless sunlight (vv. 4–5). The patriarch brings them bread, meat, curd and milk; and the men eat and rest (vv. 6–7). Then at the end of the story, we are told that the "men rose up" and left (v. 16). These gods have been totally humanized.

In later Greco-Roman times, theology started to shift from bodily gods to gods whose nature was exclusively spiritual. Therefore, Philo's Platonism forced him to distort the present story. He argued that Abraham thought he was visited by prophets or angels "who had changed from their

---

99. LXX reads "for god."

100. The story of 2 Kgs 4:8–17 could be another adaptation of the motif. It contains similar traits, and it is the only other text in the Hebrew Bible that uses the enigmatic expression *kāʿēṯ ḥayyāʰ* (see the footnote to Gen 18:10 above).

101. Cf. Exod 3:2; 33:7–11; Num 14:10; Isa 6:1–4, etc.

102. Westermann, *Genesis 12–36*, 275.

spiritual and soul-like essence into a human appearance" (*anthrōpomorphon idean*),[103] adding that:

> What a portent that those who did not drink and did not eat presented the appearance of drinking and eating ... And the most portentous thing was that these incorporeal beings took the appearance of a body in human form.[104]

But the myth describes the gods in very human terms, just as it was done in Ancient Near East and Mediterranean literature. Consequently, Esther Hamori correctly explains that there is no indication that "the term *ʾănāšîm* [= men] is intended metaphorically: the men accept Abraham's invitation to sit, wash their feet, and rest, and then share a meal with him."[105] This is a case in which metaphorical thinking has materialized to the point that the metaphor is taken as real.[106]

The anthropomorphic nature of the passage is so strong that it's impossible to pinpoint exactly when Abraham realized that the visitors were gods. We might think that we have found evidence of this recognition in the assiduous way in which the patriarch welcomes the strangers. However, the warm reception is not really a clue in that direction. The diligent hospitality provided by Abraham was only the standard protocol on how to treat a stranger; apart from the fact that these stories always overplay this aspect of the encounter.[107] As Terence Fretheim says, from the point of view of the editor, Yahve appeared to Abraham (v. 1), but from Abraham's perspective, there were only three men in front of him.[108] Interpreters generally admit that, at the beginning, Abraham did not know that these men were gods.[109] And everything depends on how we understand the vocative of verse 3. It does not matter whether we translate "my lord" (*ʾăḏōnî*) or "my lords" (*ʾăḏōnay*). In both cases the sense should be that the travelers were thought to be just men (cf. the footnote to v. 3 above).

103. Philo, *De Abrahamo* i.113 (cf. Colson, *Philo*, 6:59).

104. Philo, *De Abrahamo* i.118.

105. Hamori, *When Gods Were Men*, 10.

106. In the appearances of Genesis 12:1-3, 7 and 17:1, 9, 15, Yahve talks with Abraham as if he was a man conversing with a friend.

107. "Abraham's treatment of the men includes nothing to indicate whether he recognizes their supernatural nature. The bowing, foot-washing, and offer of refreshment in the shade and a meal are all standard aspects of meticulous hospitality" (Walton, *Genesis*, 452; see Fretheim, *Genesis*, 462-63). See above (§2.2.4.a.3) in connection with Telemachus' hospitality.

108. Fretheim, *Genesis*, 462-63.

109. Blenkinsopp, *Abraham*, 118; Brueggemann, *Theology*, 166; Fretheim, *Genesis*, 462-63; Hamilton, *Genesis*, 4; Towner, *Genesis*, 169.

A clue may be found at the moment the text changes the verbs into singular (vv. 10–15), and the narrator uses the words "Yahve said" (v. 13). However, it can still be argued that this knowledge is the prerogative of the narrator and that nothing in Genesis 18:1–16 clearly states that Abraham knew they were gods. The story even ends saying that "the men" (v. 16) left as they had arrived, in incognito.[110] One thing is certain though, the subsequent monologue of the god, in 18:17–21, seems to clearly establish that it is Yahve speaking. And verses 23–33 indicate without a doubt that Abraham was conscious of the fact that he was talking to Yahve. But what is so surprising is how comfortable Abraham feels in god's presence, as if he was talking with another human being. If somewhere during the encounter Abraham became aware that these men were gods, he is portrayed as believing these gods had real human bodies.

2) Divine Reward and the Departure of the Gods: Genesis 18:9–16

This section talks about the divine reward that will put an end to the couple's sad situation of not having children. Theologically, this announcement can only be given by Yahve himself. So the verbs are changed to singular: "And [Yahve] said: Certainly, I will return to you next year . . . Yahve said to Abraham . . . Is there anything too difficult for Yahve? At the set time, I will return to you next year . . ."

The narrative might also suggest that the men had special powers. They know that the wife's name is Sarah (v. 9). The main character knows that the couple is childless and he is able to predict they will have a son (v. 10). Even when Sarah "laughed to herself," one of the men knew she did (v. 12–13). The peak of the story comes when vv. 13–14 mention Yahve by name, and avers that nothing is too difficult for him. The birth of a son will surely be a miracle.

Conclusion

None of the stories examined in §2.2.4 are historical narratives. They are all fictional. The tales are based on a tradition about gods who reward those who are hospitable to the stranger. The reader should note that all these stories are told as occurring here on earth, and not in a divine world (§1.2.2). The *stories of the gods* frequently describe them intervening in our reality

---

110. See the arguments of Gunkel, *Genesis*, 198.

(§1.2.3). The tale about Abraham must have been an independent tale about how Abraham's good deeds obtained for him the reward of a son. Later the story was inserted into the larger saga of the life of the patriarch. This insertion may elucidate why the text does not provide a hint about how Abraham reacted to Yahve's promise, and it may also explain why the story does not provide an ending informing us of the important detail of how the promise was fulfilled.[111] An independent story was cropped in order to be attached to the following Sodom narrative as a kind of introduction to it.

c. The visit of the gods: Genesis 18:17—19:25

1) Abraham's intercession: 18:17-33

When Abraham departs with the men, Yahve informs him that he's heading to destroy Sodom (vv. 17-20), adding that he needs to go there to see the situation first hand:

> [21] I must descend[112] to see whether they really have done according to the outcry that has come to me, and if [they have] not, I will know.
> [22] Then [two of] the men turned away from there, walking towards Sodom, while Abraham stood before Yahve (vv. 21-22).

The description is tremendously anthropomorphic. Yahve needs to descend to Sodom to confirm whether the rumor is true. The other two men did not disappear flying but they seem to have left on foot (*wayyēlkû*). Abraham is left standing "before" Yahve, and they enter into a dialogue which shows clearly that Abraham knows he's talking with a god (vv. 23-32). The section ends by saying that "Yahve went his way (*wayyēlek*) . . . and Abraham returned to his place" (v. 33).

2) Destruction: Genesis 19:1-25

The narrative begins informing the reader that "the two divine envoys" finally arrived in Sodom during the evening (19:1), but Lot does not have the advantage of this information.

---

111. See the above cases of Falernus and Hyrieus, in §2.2.4.a.1 and 2, where the stories reach a final resolution.

112. While in Genesis 11:5, 7 Yahve comes down from Heaven (cf. Exod 3:8; Ps 18:10; 144:5; Isa 64:1-2), in the present case it seems that Yahve walks down to the Arabah valley to see whether the situation is as bad as he's been informed.

Welcoming the strangers

¹ The two envoys arrived at Sodom in the evening, and Lot was sitting at the gate of Sodom. When Lot saw [them], he stood up to meet them and bowed with his face on the ground. ² He said: "My lords, please come into your servant's house to pass the night and wash your feet. Then you can rise early in the morning and go your way." They replied: "No, we shall pass the night in the city square." ³ But he insisted so much, that they turned into his house with him. He prepared a feast for them, and baked bread, and they ate.

The threat of violence against the guests

⁴ But before they lay down, the men of the city, the men of Sodom, surrounded the house, young and old, all the people without exception. ⁵ And calling out to Lot, they said, "Where are the men who came to you tonight? Bring them out to us, that we may have sex with them.[113]

Lot tries to protect his guests

⁶ Lot came out to them at the door and, having shut the door behind him, ⁷ said, "Please, my brothers, do not act wickedly. ⁸ Look, I have two daughters who are virgins.[114] Let me bring them out to you, and do to them as you please, but do nothing to these[115] men since they are now under the protection of my roof."

The gods intervene

⁹ But they reply, "Out of the way!" And they said: "This fellow [= Lot] came here as a foreigner, and now he wants to play the judge! We shall harm you more than them." Then they pushed hard against the man, Lot, and drew near to breaking down the door. ¹⁰ But the men [inside] reached out their hands and pulled Lot back into the house with them, and shut the door. ¹¹ And they struck with blinding light[116] the men who were at the door

---

113. Lit. "that we may know them." Cf. Gen 4:1, 17, 24; 19:8.
114. Lit. "who have not known man."
115. The expression *hā ʾēl* is only a variant of *hā ʾēlleʰ* = these.
116. The "Heb. *sanwērīm* is a loanword based on Akk. *šunwurum*, an adjectival form with superlative or 'elative' force: 'having extraordinary brightness'" (Speiser, *Genesis*, 139). See Sarna, *Genesis*, 136.

of the house, both small and great alike, so that they tried in vain to find the door.

Just like Abraham before (Gen 18:1–8), Lot offers the two men the standard hospitality due strangers. These humanized gods were able to enter into Lot's house because their height was like that of any other men. They have feet to wash and can eat like the rest of us (19:1–3). Then the mob demands that Lot must let "the men" out so they can have sexual relations with them (v. 5). Lot offers his own daughters to prevent the crowd from assaulting "these men" (vv. 6–8). But when the crowd is about to break into the house, "the men reached out with their hands, and pulled Lot back into the house" (v. 10). These gods have hands! Up to verse 11, the divine men looked and have been acting like any other human being, but the blindness they inflict on the crowd is a clear indication that they were supermen. At this juncture, "the men" (v. 12) devise a retreat plan to take Lot and his family out of the city, before the coming destruction (vv. 12–14). The "envoys" forced them out of the city (vv. 15–17) and from Heaven Yahve destroys the cities (vv. 24–25).

2.2.5 Genesis 32:22–31[23–32]: A God Fights with Jacob

[22] That same night, [Jacob] got up and took his two wives and his two maids[117] and his eleven children, and crossed the ford of Jabbok.

[23] He took them and made them cross the stream along with all his possessions.

[24] Jacob was left behind alone. And a man wrestled[118] with him until daybreak.

[25] When [the man] saw that he wasn't able to overpower him, he struck his femur's joint, and the joint of Jacob's femur was dislocated in his wrestling with him.

[26] Then [the man] said: Let me go for the day is breaking!

But [Jacob] answered him: I will not let you go, unless you bless me!

[27] [The man] asked him: What's your name? And he responded: Jacob.

[28] [The man] said: Your name will no longer be Jacob but Israel, for you have contended with ʾĕlōhîm and with men, and have prevailed.

---

117. Or: "concubines."

118. The verb ʾābaq (= to wrestle) occurs only here (vv. 25, 26) in the Hebrew Bible, and it might have been chosen to indicate that the struggle was connected to the ford. The relationship is suggested by the assonance between yēʾābēq (= he wrestled) and yabbōq (= Jabbok). This gives force to the proposal that the god fighting with Jacob was the god of the ford. See Delitzsch, *Genesis*, 204–5.

²⁹ Jacob asked him: Tell me your name.

But he replied: Why do you ask my name? And there he blessed him.

³⁰ So Jacob called the place Peniel, for he said I've seen ʾĕlōhîm face to face, and yet my life was spared.[119]

³¹ The sun rose upon him as he passed Penuel, limping because of the femur.

Behind the present story there might have been a legend which only spoke of a traveler who was attacked by the guarding spirit of a ford. The editor adapted the legend to complement Jacob's saga on the basis of the journey motif (vv. 22-23, 31). The identity of the ʾĕlōhîm wrestling with Jacob is not clear,[120] but whatever his identity might have been we have a narrative in front of us that describes a god in anthropomorphic terms. We are told that by some shallow water, during the night, a "man" (ʾîš), who's never identified, physically attacked Jacob and "wrestled" with him until daybreak (v. 24[25]). As Hermann Gunkel points out, the passage has nothing to do with a spiritual fight or wrestling in prayer.[121] It is rather a physical struggle that ends hurting Jacob's femur (v. 25[26]). When the man realized that he wasn't able to overcome Jacob, he asked him to let him go, arguing that the day was already breaking (v. 26[27]).[122] It seems that the words about

---

119. Or: "and I survived."

120. We ask ourselves who the divine agent might have been. The original story might have talked about the encounter of a Canaanite god and Jacob (Brueggemann, *Genesis*, 266) or talked about the guardian spirit of a ford (Gunkel, *Genesis*, 352-53; Westermann, *Genesis 12-36*, 515-17). The latter proposal might be correct, having the following in its favor: "The folkloric character of this haunting episode becomes especially clear at this point. The notion of a night spirit that loses its power or is not permitted to go about in daylight is common to many folk traditions, as is the troll or guardian figure who blocks access to a ford or bridge. This temporal limitation of activity suggests that the 'man' is certainly not God himself and probably not an angel in the ordinary sense" (Alter, *Genesis*, 181). To secure that no one will imagine that this humanized being was God, *Targum Jonathan* (in Etheridge, *Targum Onkelos*, 272) changes the wording of the narrative, and declares that "an angel" whose name was Michael "contended with him in the likeness of a man." Then when the "angel" asks Jacob to let him go, the Targum states that the reason given was "the hour cometh when the angels on high offer praise to the Lord of the world." And at the end of the story, Jacob exclaims: "I have seen the Angels of the Lord face to face" (see Friedman, *Commentary on the Torah*, 112). Hosea also felt the need to change the narrative, saying that Jacob rather "strove with a divine envoy (*malʾāk*) and prevailed" (Hos 12:4[5]). These traditions may be trying to avoid the implication that Yahve has a body.

121. Gunkel, *Genesis*, 349.

122. Let's recall the time when Jupiter (= Zeus) told his wife: "Why do you hold me? It is time to go: I wish to depart from the city before dawn" (Titus Maccius Plautus, *Amphitryon or Jupiter in Disguise* i.3, in Riley, *Comedies*, 25).

the sunrise made Jacob aware that he was before a divine agent. It was the type of god that needed to go away before the sunlight arrives, but it was also a deity who had a physical body that Jacob held clutching. As he was a god, Jacob astutely asks him for a blessing. Since the god doesn't know who Jacob is, he asks his name in order to change his identity and destiny (vv. 27–28[28–29]). From that moment on, Jacob becomes Israel (= the one who strives with El) "for you have contended with ʾĕlōhîm" (v. 28). Jacob's perspective is shown in the way he names the place. He called it pənîʾēl, that is, "the face of El," exclaiming: "I've seen ʾĕlōhîm face to face" (v. 31).

2.3 Anthropomorphism as a Problem

In chapter 1, we described a scene in which Yahve appears as a human-like king holding a meeting with the members of his council (§1.1.3). Then we discussed some versions of the *Theomachia* myth in which gods fight with each other in order to become kings of the universe (§1.3). We also mentioned that, as rulers of the universe, the gods controlled both nature and history (§1.1.3; §1.1.4; §1.2.3). In ruling the universe, the gods not only established or destroyed kingdoms, but they also controlled the lives of individuals as shown in the story of *Ludlul bēl nēmeqi* (§1.2.3). The gods acted in the same way as humans do, and glyptic art even portrays them as human beings (§1.2.3). In the present chapter, we have examined several stories which describe the gods as having human form. We saw a god walking through a garden and arguing with Adam and Eve. The same god regretted having created humankind. We saw gods who procreated; humanized gods who visited Abraham and Lot; and a god who fought with Jacob. We could easily add more stories about humanized gods, like the one in Exodus 4:24–26. This myth maintains that during the night Yahve himself attacked Moses.[123] The supposedly omnipotent god "tried to kill" Moses. But his wife ran to circumcise their son and then touched Moses' genitals[124] with their son's foreskin. The child's blood protected Moses from the angry god. Only then the god "withdrew from him."

2.3.1 New Beginnings: The Input of the Greeks

But with time this mythical perspective started to fade. Ionia started to explain the world without recurring to stories about the "deeds of the gods."

---

123. The LXX softens the text by saying it was really "the angel of the Lord."
124. The lit. expression "Moses' feet" is a euphemism for his genitals.

Ionia established itself as the cradle of rational philosophy. Mervin Perry explains it this way:

> By giving to nature a rational rather than a mythical foundation and by holding that theories should be grounded in evidence and that one should be able to defend them logically, the early Greek philosophers pushed thought in a new direction. This new approach allowed a critical analysis of theories, whereas myths, accepted unconditionally on faith and authority, did not promote discussion and questioning.[125]

Hecateus of Miletus (550–476 BCE) is considered the first secular geographer and historian[126] who laid down his secular approach at the beginning of his work:

> I transcribe [*graphō*] what follows [*tade*] according to the criteria of verisimilitude [*hōs moi dokei alēthea einai*]; the stories [*logoi*] of the Greeks are many and often, it seems to me, laughable.[127]

Jordi Pàmias explains that with Hecateus emerges for the first time the contrast between mythography (*muthos*) and historiography (*logos*). The mythical stories were not taken *literally* anymore. The new perspective strove to examine reality by means of more objective criteria such as likelihood and plausibility. Myth was subordinated to *logos* (reason) to the point that *muthos* became equivalent to fictitious, while *logos* pointed to real events.[128] Later Thucydides (460–395 BCE) and Polybius (200–118 BCE) introduced the secular study of history. These historians attempted to interpret facts without resorting to divine intervention. Polybius still allowed crediting the gods for things whose causes were yet not known, like plagues and natural

---

125. Perry, *Western Civilization*, 75. The Ionic School produced a good number of leading characters, like Thales of Miletus (620–546 BCE), who had a tremendous impact in the study of mathematics, geometry, astronomy and philosophy. He omitted the gods in his speculation about cosmology (see Freely, *Flame of Miletus*; O'Grady, *Thales of Miletus*. The work of Wöhrle, *Milesians* provides a fantastic bilingual edition of the texts). Anaximander (610–546 BCE) and Anaximenes (585–528 BCE) also took the *via naturalis* to explain the functioning and origin of the world (see Krebs, *Groundbreaking*, 41–59). Pythagoras (570–495 BCE) proposed a naturalist cosmological model, in which the earth appeared as a sphere and as the center of the universe with the sun and the planets revolving around it. See Loeb Classical Library vols. 526–527, 529–530. See also Copleston, *History of Philosophy*; Graham, *Explaining the Cosmos*; Guthrie, *History of Greek Philosophy*; Kirk, *Presocratic Philosophers*.

126. See Freely, *Flame of Miletus*, 9–10; Pàmias, "Reception of Greek Myth," 42.

127. Quoted in Calame, *Poetic Speech*, 92.

128. Pàmias, "Reception of Greek Myth," 42, 47–48.

disasters. But regarding the causes of public events, he preferred to discard the gods, fate or chance as an explanation:

> But as for matters whose efficient and final cause we can discover, I think we should not assign them to divine action (*to theion poieisthai*).[129]

All these efforts were baby-steps towards rational inquiry, and we cannot compare them to the results produced by modern science and historiography. Moreover, these new perspectives did not stop others from bringing the mythical configuration into their narratives. Historians like Herodotus (*ca.* 484–425 BCE) and Dionysius (*ca.* 60 BCE—7 CE) still kept combining both perspectives.

2.3.2 The Effects of Platonism

The anthropomorphic descriptions of the divine also started to become unacceptable. The Ancient Near East started reducing the number of gods and began to use clear henotheistic concepts.[130] A monotheistic tendency also started to become more popular. For example, the varied and dominant ways in which *Enūma Eliš* (*ca.* 1595–1105 BCE) talks about the absolute power of Marduk, forces Wilfred Lambert to declare that in that myth "his supremacy was verging on monotheism."[131] Later on, in the Persian period, the god Ahuramazda was conceived as the only supreme god.[132] In the pre-Socratic age (*ca.* 600 BCE) it was undeserving to picture the gods in human form. The trend acquired a definite character with Plato (428–348 BCE) who protested against excessively humanizing the gods. This refinement won many supporters and finally ended up influencing the way classical theology defines god and interprets the Scriptures.

a. The gods as idealized human beings

When addressing the issue of the education of children, Plato insists in what he thought was the only right way of teaching about gods, heroes, demons (lesser gods) and the life hereafter. He underlined the need for stories that

---

129. Polybius, *Historiae* 37.17.4, in Büttner-Wobst, *Polybius Historiae*, 458.

130. See Bottéro, *Religion in Ancient Mesopotamia*, 44–47. Hruša, *Ancient Mesopotamian Religion*, 34–35.

131. Lambert, "Reign of Nebuchadnezzar I," 5.

132. Shaked, "Iranian Influence on Judaism," 315–16.

would promote virtues and civility, and rejected any story that would disfigure the gods as dissolute. He says distortions are produced:

> Whenever a person awfully portrays[133] in his story the nature of gods and heroes, as it happens when the painting of an artist in nothing reflects those whose likeness[134] he was trying to portray.[135]

Plato argues that the function of myth should be instilling in people a sociable and constructive character for the wellbeing of society. Consequently, he protests against any myth that would portray the gods as cruel and bellicose, like the story in which Uranus (= Heaven) locked up his own children in Tartarus, or when one of his sons (Cronus) avenged his mother castrating Uranus. In his *Laws*, Plato attacks the way Homer represented the gods. He argues that theft and robbery are uncivilized, and that the gods never had such practices:

> Let no man, therefore, be deluded concerning this or persuaded either by poets or by any perverse myth-mongers into the belief that, when a person steals or forcibly robs, he is doing nothing shameful, but just what the gods themselves do. That is both unlikely and untrue; and whoever acts thus unlawfully is neither a god at all nor a child of the gods.[136]

Plato was convinced that immoral stories encourage the youth to commit crimes because they will think that they are following "the example of the first and greatest of the gods."[137] So instead of representing the gods killing each other, we should use their stories to teach that it is impious to quarrel with one another. Myth should be an instrument for teaching values and goodness. The same criticism came from Xenophanes (*ca.* 580–475 BCE) before him:

> Homer and Hesiod have ascribed unto the Gods all that is reproach and blame in the world of men, stealing and adultery and deceit.[138]

---

133. The verb used here is *eikathoō* = "to represent by an image, to depict with similar features." Cf. Xenophon, who talks about the "portrait (*eikasas*) of a woman" (Xenophon, *Oeconomicus Convivum* x.1, in Marchant, *Xenophontis Opera*, vol. 2).

134. *homoia* = similarity, resemblance, nature.

135. Plato, *Republic* ii.377e (cf. Emlyn-Jones and Preddy, *Plato Republic*, 197).

136. Plato, *Laws* xii.941b, in Bury, *Plato Laws*, 475.

137. Plato, *Republic* ii.378b (cf. Emlyn-Jones and Preddy, *Plato Republic*, 199).

138. Xenophanes, *Curfrag.tlg-0267.11*, in Edmonds, *Elegy and Iambus*, 200.

Plato demands that the *stories of the gods* should teach virtues like courage in the face of death and suffering (particularly in war). Myth should foster courage and, therefore, we should avoid representing gods or heroes bemoaning over pain and defeat. So he condemns Homer for presenting Achilles, "a son of a goddess" (*theas paida*), complaining and defeated.[139] Then he adds:

> And all the more we ask [the poets] not to portray the gods as complaining... But if they do represent the gods in this way, at least let them not have the gall to portray such a questionable image of the Supreme God [= Zeus].[140]

Plato also wanted to foster truth and self-control, which led him to reject the stories that depicted the gods as liars or ruled by passions, like the story which talks about how Zeus got so aroused that he wasn't able to reach his chamber but copulated with Hera right on the floor.[141] We should not teach the youth that:

> the gods bring about evil or that our heroes are not better than men for, as we said, such statements are illicit and false, as we have already shown that it is impossible for evil to originate with the gods ... Besides, such assertions are pernicious for those who hear them, for they will make every man to become indulgent with his own misdeeds if he's convinced that the relatives of the gods do and have done such things... For these reasons, we should put an end to those stories (*muthous*), lest they foster in our youth a strong inclination towards vileness...[142]

If someone would have asked Plato: What's the standard for doing theology? Or "What are the models regarding theology?" (*hoi tupoi peri theologias*), he would have said: "Whether you write epic, lyric or tragedy, you should represent the god as who he really is."[143] And if we ask about god's character, Plato would answered that a god is good and that nothing evil comes from him or her, because "god is not the cause of everything but only the cause of those things which are good, not those which are bad."[144] Plato condemns the stories that portray Zeus as "the dispenser of good and evil,"[145] as well as

---

139. Plato, *Republic* iii.388a.
140. Plato, *Republic* iii.388b–c.
141. Plato, *Republic* iii.390c.
142. Plato, *Republic* iii.391d–392a.
143. Plato, *Republic* ii.379a.
144. Plato, *Republic* ii.379b.
145. Plato, *Republic* ii.379e. Plato would have opposed the monistic passage of

the cause of quarrels and calamities. God only bestows what is good. And then Plato sets the norm for doing theology:

> ... this would be one of the norms and models (*nomōn kai tupōn*) regarding the gods, which orators and poets should follow: that a god is not the cause of everything but only of what is good.[146]

Conclusion

We should make clear that Plato did not completely abandon the use of anthropomorphism. Plato was only opposed to the kind of humanizing that would portray the gods as having physical bodies or would accuse them of evil deeds and intentions. He wanted the gods to be models of honesty, kindness, loyalty, courage, truth, self-control and goodness, *which are all human qualities*. So Plato was not against all anthropomorphism. He was interested in assigning the gods the best human qualities and behavior, rejecting any description that would make them cruel, vicious, unhinged, etc. In this way, Plato created a god that was an idealized-non-physical version of the human being, a metaphor for human values. Even Platonism still uses anthropomorphism.

b. God as transcendent

Plato also pleaded in favor of a transcendent concept of god and fought against the idea that a god could change his appearance or become visible adopting different earthly shapes. This is a direct attack against stories like the "visits of the gods" (§2.2.4). According to Plato, the gods were simple, immutable and perfect beings. Therefore, we should not allow any poet to tell us that "the gods, in the likeness of strangers, assume all kinds of appearances when visiting the cities," or that "some gods go about at night in the likeness of strangers and adopt all sorts of appearances."[147] And he ties it all up by saying:

Isaiah 45:7, which according to 1QIsa^a 45.7 reads: "I form light and create darkness, I make goodness [*tôḇ*] and create evil" (Abegg, *Dead Sea Scrolls*, 344). Texts like Job 30:26 and Isaiah 5:20 seem to support Qumran's reading. The MT reads instead: "I form light and create darkness; I make well-being [*šālôm*] and create misery." The Babylonian Talmud (*b. Berakoth* fol.11a) also reworks the text to produce a morning blessing, saying "I make peace and create all things" (Cohen, *Babylonian Talmud*, 70).

146. Plato, *Republic* ii.380c.
147. Plato, *Republic* ii.381d.

Therefore, god is absolutely simple and truthful in word and deed, and he does not change or deceive others by means of apparitions, stories or a procession of signs, whether in a waking or sleeping state.[148]

c. Divinization of humankind

It is important to note that the new ideas were more ambitious. In antiquity all people were thought to be mere mortals who after death went to the Underworld (§3.6). The stories of Homer and Gilgameš reminded people of their transience. Mesopotamia used the term *šīmtu* to refer both to "destiny" and "death."[149] In similar fashion, the Greeks used *moira* to talk about death as the "destiny" or "portion" of humankind.[150] Only the gods were immortal.

The new theology opened the door to the idea that human beings could reach *theōsis* (= deification), and become divine and immortal. However, immortality involved a program of ethical transformation. It was an immortality achieved through the cultivation of philosophy and virtues. In order to reach deification humans were required to imitate the gods. And if it was true that we can achieve a divine state by imitating the gods, the gods had to be worthy of being imitated. The old stories representing the gods committing "adultery and deceit" had to be reformulated.[151] The image of god was moved away from anything physical to the realm of ethics and good behavior. To be like god was to be righteous. In advising Theodorus, Socrates tells him that evil will always be present on earth because it has no place among the gods, and:

> Therefore, we ought to try to escape from this earth to the abode of the gods, as quickly as we can. This escape is the likeness of a god, as much as possible. And the likeness [of a god] is to become righteous, pure and prudent ... God is in no way or manner unrighteous but perfectly righteous; and there is nothing

---

148. Plato, *Republic* ii.382e.
149. See "Šīmtu," 11–19.
150. Cf. "the cruel fate [*moira*] of pitiless death shall strike him down" (Homer, *Odyssey* ii.100, in Murray, *Odyssey 1–12*, 53); "While he yet lived he was always gentle to all, but now death and fate [*thanatos kai moira*] have seized him" (*Iliad* xvii.672; cf. Murray, *Iliad 13–24*, 279).
151. See Dillon, *Middle Platonists*; Jaeger, *Theology of Early Greek Philosophers*; Kingsley, *Ancient Philosophy*; Kingsley, *Reality*; Lenz, "Deification of the Philosopher"; O'Meara, *Platonopolis*; Sedley, "Ideal of Godlikeness"; Zimmermann and Markantonatos, *Crisis on Stage*.

more similar[152] to him than those of us who become completely righteous.[153]

2.3.3 Hellenization

Alexander the Great (356–323 BCE) was able to build an empire starting from the Indus River, and moving westward to what today is Pakistan, Afghanistan, Iran (Persia), Iraq (Babylonia), Egypt, Palestine, Syria, Turkey, Greece, Albania, Macedonia, Kosovo and Bulgaria. His extensive empire created an international culture (*oikoumenē*) that adopted Greek as its *lingua franca*. This "new world" was Hellenized, and its influence reached the Roman Empire. Hellenism was a mixture of Babylonian, Persian and Greek ideas.

The transcendentalism of Classical Greek Philosophy (*ca.* 470–320 BCE) was welcomed in the Hellenistic Period (*ca.* 340 BCE).[154] Up to this point, the myths and legends of the Ancient Near East and the Mediterranean have been considered sacred, but the new wave questioned their validity. By no means this eliminated the old theologies which coexisted with the new trends. But a new way of thinking was gaining steam. Diogenes Laertius (*ca.* 180–240 CE) shares a myth that exemplifies the reaction against the old theology. He says that when Pythagoras descended to Hades, he saw:

> Hesiod's soul bound fast to a brazen pillar and screaming, and Homer's soul hung on a tree with serpents writhing about it, this being their punishment for what they had said about the gods.[155]

In the words of Renaud Gagné:

> Other critics of Homer and Hesiod, such as Xenophanes (DK B 14-16) or Empedokles (DK B 27-9), contested the anthropomorphism of epic in its depiction of divine bodies, and offered alternatives that emphasized the god's non-human form . . . The

---

152. The term *homoioteron* may give the idea of "equal" or "alike."

153. Plato, *Theaetetus* 176a–c (cf. Fowler, *Theaetetus, Sophist*, 127–28). See § 2.3.2.c; and §3.4.2–3 for the expectation that humans may become like gods or angels.

154. Among other texts, Siegert ("Early Jewish Interpretation," 132), quotes a passage where Plato reinterprets a text from the *Iliad* (viii.18–22) to make it say something more appropriate. See also Plato, *Theaetetus* 153c–d, in Fowler, *Theaetetus, Sophist*. For the platonic negative theology, see Carabine, *Unknown God*. For Hellenistic philosophers, see Kristeller, *Greek Philosophers*; Long, *Hellenistic Philosophy*.

155. Diogenes Laertius, *Lives* viii.21, in Hicks, *Diogenes Laertius*, 339.

authority of the early poets was the great rival that had to be supplanted.[156]

Stoicism (350 BCE) protected the new transcendence of the divine by proposing an intermediary agent between god and the world. Middle Platonism (90 BCE) also insisted that god does not have direct contact with the world but that he directs the world through a second god or demiurge. This mediator was the *logos*. Material reality was created by the *logos* who is the universal *reason* infusing unity, harmony and rationality into the world. This *logos* was also part of the human being and the fountain of virtue. The philosopher Numenius of Apamea (*ca.* 150–200 CE) sympathized with Judaism and had a strong influence on Eusebius, Clement and Origen. By means of the allegorical method, Numenius was able to create a theological blend that allowed him to say: "What else is Plato than a Moses who (speaks Greek, or) reveals Greek tendencies?"[157] According to Numenius, matter was created by a mediator god, and salvation consisted in the soul ascending through the planetary spheres (Pythagoras) to reach the Heavens. Those who fail becoming virtuous in this life are punished in a region located between the moon and the earth, to later reincarnate into a new body.[158]

Hellenism infused these platonic concepts of god into Jewish culture, forcing new interpretations of the older traditions. In other words, god was ascribed a transcendence that required him the use of intermediary beings to interact with the world.[159] Apocalyptic literature widely displays angels as mediators between god and the world, and in the war between good and evil.[160] A similar role was given to *Sophia* who became an intermediary god

---

156. Gagné, "Literary Evidence," 83.

157. Numenius, *peri tagathou* i.xiii, in Guthrie, *Numenius of Apamea*, 2–3. See Cook, *Interpretation of the Old Testament*, 36; Lamberton, *Homer the Theologian*, 54–56.

158. See Dillon, *Middle Platonists*; Goodenough, *By Light, Light*; Long and Sedley, *Hellenistic Philosophers*; Long, *Hellenistic Philosophy*.

159. Regarding the influence of Hellenism on Judaism, see Barlett, *Jews in the Hellenistic and Roman Cities*; Bickerman, *Jews in the Greek Age*; Collins and Sterling, *Hellenism in the Land of Israel*; Feldman, *Jews and Gentile*; Grabbe, *Judaistic Religion in the Second Temple*; Gruen, *Heritage of Hellenism*; Hays and Mandell, *Jewish People in Classical Antiquiety*; Hengel, *Judaims and Hellenism*; Levine, *Judaism and Hellenism*; Schürer, *Historia del Pueblo Judío*; Tcherikover, *Hellenistic Civilization and the Jews*.

160. See Newsome, *Greeks, Romans, Jews*. Walter Eichrodt observes correctly that in ancient Israel, the idea of angels governing the world was a marginal concept "because it was paralyzed by the belief in God's direct exercise of his power," but during the Persian and Hellenistic eras the angels' involvement in the world blossomed unhindered. "It is clear that as the transcendent character of God becomes more acute, it thrives an angelology that entails a darkening of the idea of God" (*Teología* 2:204).

who lives in Heaven but who also emanates from god and fills the universe and, especially, Israel:

> [1] Wisdom praises herself,
> and glorifies herself in the midst of her people.
> [2] In the assembly of the Most High she opens her mouth,
> and in the presence of his hosts she boasts:
> [3] I came forth from the mouth of the Most High,
> and like a mist I covered the earth.
> [4] I dwelt in the Highest,
> and my throne was upon the pillar of the cloud.
> [5] I alone compassed the dome of Heaven
> and walked the depths of the abyss.
> [6] Over the waves of the sea, over all the earth
> and over all peoples and nations, I have great dominion.
> [7] Among all of them I sought for rest
> and for an inheritance where to live.
> [8] Then the creator of the universe commanded me,
> the one who created me established my residence.
> He said: dwell in Jacob,
> Israel will be your inheritance.
> [9] Before the ages, in the beginning, he created me,
> and I shall not cease to be forever. (Sir 24:1–9)[161]

Aristobulus of Alexandria (*ca.* 181–124 BCE) is a clear example of how a Jewish philosopher could harmonize his religion with Greek philosophy. Aristobulus wrestles with the anthropomorphic problem produced by biblical passages that talk about the hands, arms, face and feet of god. He maintains that we should "grasp an adequate concept of God and not fall in a way of thinking that is mythic and human" (*muthōdes kai anthrōpinon*). Therefore, by "hands" we should understand "God's power." When the biblical text says that god descended onto a mountain (Exod 19:11), Aristobulus argued that this descent was not literal, because "God is everywhere." He argued that Plato's philosophy only mimicked the Jewish law which he carefully studied. He also claimed that Pythagoras took many Jewish doctrines into his system.[162]

---

161. Cf. Prov 8:22–31; Wis 7:22–27; 7:30—8:1.

162. Aristobulus is quoted by Eusebius in his *Praeparatio Evangelica* viii.10, in Migne, *Patrologiae Graecae*, 21:636–37. See Charlesworth, *Pseudepigrapha*, 2:837–39.

ANTHROPOMORPHISM

As Aristobulus' successor, Philo of Alexandria (25 BCE—50 CE) passed down platonic definitions of god: "God is not a composite being, nor is he made up of many parts, but he has no mixture with anything else."[163] Henry Chadwick reminds us that the idea of the *logos* was generated by Platonism in its belief that "a remote transcendent God requires a second, metaphysically inferior aspect of himself to face towards the lower world."[164] Philo sustained that the invisible and unknowable god can only be known through the *logos* who is his "image," as well as the creator of the world:

> The logos [= reason] is the image of God (*eikōn theou*),
> by whom all the world was fabricated.[165]

God also rules the world through the *logos*: "He has appointed as ruler his upright logos and firstborn son, who is to receive the charge of this sacred company as viceroy of the great king."[166] Philo recounts all the titles of the *logos*: "His firstborn logos, the eldest [son] of the angels, as the great archangel who has many names, for he's called the beginning,[167] the name of God and the logos, the man according to the image of God, the one who guards, Israel."[168]

This *logos* is "neither uncreated[169] like god, nor created as you, but he's between these two extremities." [170] God "employs the logos as a minister of his gifts, by whose agency he also made the world."[171] It is the *logos* who "holds all things together and who binds all of its parts."[172] As a mediator,

---

163. Philo, *Legum Allegoriarum* ii.2. See Runia, who discusses the use of Plato by Philo (Runia, *Philo of Alexandria*, 71–522).

164. Chadwick, "Philo and the Beginnings of Christian Thought," 145.

165. Philo, *De specialibus legibus* i.81 (cf. Cohn and Wendland, *Philonis Alexandrini Opera*, 5:21).

166. Philo, *De agricultura* i.51 (cf. Colson and Whitaker, *Philo*, 3:135).

167. Or: authority, dominion.

168. Philo, *De confusione linguarum* i.146 (cf. Colson and Whitaker, *Philo*, 4:89–91).

169. *Agenetos*, "uncreated, unoriginated."

170. Philo, *Quis rerum divinarum heres sit* i.206 (cf. Colson and Whitaker, *Philo*, 4:385).

171. Philo, *Quod deus sit immutabilis* i.57 (cf. Colson and Whitaker, *Philo*, 3:39). Cf. "The logos is the shadow of God, whom he used as an instrument when he was creating the cosmos. And this shadow, as a model, is the archetype of other things" (*Legum allegoriarum* iii.96; cf. Colson and Whitaker, *Philo*, 4:365).

172. Philo, *De fuga et inventione* i.112 (cf. Colson and Whitaker, *Philo*, 5:71). Cf. "If there is anything in some place that is consolidated, it has been bound together by the logos, for the logos is glue and chain, filling all things with his essence. And the logos, who bonds and fastens everything together, is properly full of himself, having no need whatsoever of anything else" (*Quis rerum divinarum heres sit* i.188).

the *logos* is the "High Priest," he is "the Idea of ideas,"[173] according to which God shaped the cosmos. The Idea is incorporeal and discerned only by the intellect."[174] As High Priest, "the logos pleads on behalf of the mortal race before the immortal [god]."[175] The *logos* is "the heavenly and incorruptible food of the soul."[176]

These platonic ideas had a tremendous influence on Christianity. The first chapter of the Gospel of John makes it clear that the transcendent god who "no one has ever seen" makes himself known through his "only son" (1:18). This son is no other than the *logos*,[177] the divine reason who created the world and who is life and light (1:1–10).[178] A passage from Colossians presents Christ as a secondary god who acts as an intermediary between god and the world. God has lost most of his anthropomorphic representations, so now the "invisible" god is portrayed as creating and running the world through a demiurge. The following passage is a clear exposition of Hellenistic theology. Its author has only replaced the *logos* with Christ:

> [15] ... who [= Christ] is the image of the invisible God,[179]
>
> > the firstborn of all creation,
>
> [16] for by him all things were created,[180]
>
> > in heaven and on earth:

---

173. The term *idea* refers to platonic forms or archetypes. Colson and Whitaker translate: "the original principle behind all principles" (*Philo*, 4:191).

174. Philo, *De migratione Abrahami* i.102–3 (cf. Colson and Whitaker, *Philo*, 4:191).

175. Philo, *Quis rerum divinarum heres sit* i.205.

176. *Quis rerum divinarum heres sit* i.79. What feeds the soul is "the word of God and the divine logos" (*De fuga et inventione* i.137).

177. The term *logos* is often translated by "Word" (NRSV, NIV) but its Hellenistic meaning here is "Reason." It is also argued that John took his *logos* from Proverbs 8:1–36, but this is quite improbable. Judaism knew well the doctrine of *sophia*. The term *sophia* was the Jewish version of the divine *logos* (cf. Wis 7:21–28, etc.). Therefore, it is hard to imagine why John did not use the actual word *sophia* if he took it from Proverbs. It is more probable that John imported his *logos* from Philo or Hellenistic Judaism where these concepts were popular (see Bultmann, *Gospel of John*, 21; Bury, *Fourth Gospel*, 5–9; Dodd, *Interpretation*, 263–65; Harris, *Prologue*, 199; Scott, *Fourth Gospel*, 145–47).

178. Philo explains that "the invisible and intelligible light has come into being as the image of the divine logos ... As soon as the intelligible light came into being, darkness retreated" (*De opificio mundi* i.31, 35; cf. Colson and Whitaker, *Philo*, 1:25–27).

179. According to Hellenistic Judaism, the importance of the doctrine of the *logos* lies in the fact that, as the image of God, the *logos* was able to "bridge the otherwise unbridgeable gulf between the invisible world and God on the one side and visible creation and humanity on the other" (Dunn, *Colossians*, 88).

180. Or: "in him everything was created."

> whether visible or invisible,
> whether thrones, lordships,
> authorities or powers.
>
> All things were created by him and for him.
>
> ¹⁷ And he himself is before all things,
> and by him all things hold together.
>
> ¹⁸ He is the head of the body, the church.
>
> He is the beginning,
> the firstborn [risen] from the dead,
> so that in everything[181] he might be the first ... (Col 1:15–18).[182]

Philo's ideas had such an influence on Christianity that David Runia gives him the title of "Church Father *honoris causa*."[183] In similar fashion, Henry Chadwick asserts that "the history of Christian philosophy begins not with a Christian but with a Jew, Philo of Alexandria."[184] In his *Confessions*, St. Augustine shared with us that there was a time when he thought god had "a luminous and immense body" (*corpus lucidum et immensum*).[185] But later in chapter 7, he recounts how he changed his mind by reading platonic writings. Thomas Aquinas, too, was influenced by Aristotle and Plato, and we cannot fail to mention the tremendous influence that Maimonides (1135–1204 CE) had on Aquinas and, therefore, on classical theology.

2.3.4 The Confession of the Church and the Distortion of the Biblical Text

This type of theological refinement ended fostering a transcendent-nonphysical image of the deity. Christian theology imagined god to be *increatus, immensus, aeternus, omnipotens*.[186] The Catholic Church confessed:

181. Or: "among all."

182. Colossians shares with Philo's *logos* that Christ is the image of god, that he is the firstborn and creator, and that in him the whole cosmos finds unity.

183. Runia, *Philo in Early Christian Literature*, 3. Runia documents the influence of platonic philosophy on Paul, Hebrews, John, Clement of Rome, Ignatius of Antioch, etc. See also Berchman, *From Philo to Origen*; Engberg-Pedersen, *Paul and the Stoics*; Rasimus, *Stoicism in Early Christianity*; Tomasino, *Judaism before Jesus*; VanderKam and Adler, *Jewish Apocalyptic*; Seland, *Strangers in the Light*.

184. Chadwick, "Philo and the Beginnings of Christian Thought," 137.

185. Augustine, *Confessionum* iv.16.31, in Migne, *Patrologiae Graecae*, 22:706. Cf. the translations: "a physical being of great size and splendor" (Wills, *Saint Augustine Confessions*, 80); "an immense brilliant body" (Ryan, *Confessions*, 71).

186. *Athanasian Creed*, in Schaff, *Creeds*, 2:66–67.

> that there is one true and living God, Creator and Lord of heaven and earth, almighty, eternal, immense, incomprehensible, infinite in intelligence, in will, and in all perfection, who, as being one, sole, absolutely simple and immutable spiritual substance, is to be declared as really and essentially distinct form the world, of supreme beatitude in and from himself, and ineffably exalted above all things which exist, or are conceivable, except himself.[187]

Lutherans agreed that this god is:

> eternal, without body, indivisible [without parts], of infinite power, wisdom, goodness, the Creator and Preserver of all things, visible and invisible.[188]

Calvinist theology played along by saying that god is:

> one only simple and spiritual Being . . . eternal, incomprehensible, invisible, immutable, infinite, almighty, perfectly wise, just, good, and the overflowing fountain of all good.[189]

In his *Ekdosis tēs Orthodoxou pisteōs*, the theologian John of Damascus (675–749 CE) wrote that god:

> has neither beginning nor end, is eternal and perpetual, uncreated, unchangeable (impassible), invariable, simple, not composed, incorporeal, invisible, impalpable, uncircumscribed, incomprehensible, unavailable . . .[190]

The following table shows that most of these terms are nowhere to be found in the Scriptures in reference to god:

Most platonic attributes for god do not come from the Bible

word	translation	LXX	Christian Bible
anarchos	without beginning (no *archē*)	0x	0x
ateleutētos	without end, endless (no *teleia*)	0x	0x
aiōnios	eternal	12x[191]	1x (Rom 16:26)

---

187. "Dogmatic Decrees of the Vatican Council," section I (1870 CE), in Schaff, *Creeds*, 2:239.

188. *Augsburg Confession* (1530 CE) i.1, in Schaff, *Creeds*, 3:7.

189. *Confessio Belgica* (1619 CE), in Schaff, *Creeds*, 3:383–84. See *Westminster Confession*, article II, in Schaff, *Creeds*, 3:606.

190. Kornaros and Lakamaridēs, *Iōannou tou Damaskenou*, 2.

191. The LXX talks about the "everlasting God" in Gen 21:33 (MT "everlasting

aidios	perpetual	0x	0x
aktistos	uncreated	0x	0x
atreptos	unchangeable, immutable / impassible, indifferent[192]	0x	0x
analloiōtos	invariable, immutable[193]	0x	0x
aploos	simple, not composed or mixed	0x	0x
asunthetos	not composed	0x	0x
asōmatos	without a body, incorporeal[194]	0x	0x
aoratos	invisible	0x	4x (Rom 1:20; Col 1:15; 1 Tim 1:17; Heb 11:27)
anafēs	impalpable, intangible[195]	0x	0x
aperigraptos	uncircumscribed, unlimited	0x	0x
aperinoētos	incomprehensible, inconceivable[196]	0x	0x
akatalēptos	unavailable, ungraspable	0x	0x

The above list shows that this vocabulary does not originate in the Scriptures but comes from Platonic Judaism. It maintains that god "does not have the form of a man (*anthropōmorphos*) but is unchangeable and immutable" (*atrepton kai ametablēton*).[197] Let's remember that Aristotle proposed a god

---

El"), Isa 26:4 (MT "eternal rock") and 40:28 (MT "eternal Elohe"). It also uses the term *aiōnios* twice in Job (33:12; 34:17), but the MT lacks the Hebrew equivalent ('ôlām). Most occurrences happen in Hellenistic times (2 Macc 1:25; 3 Macc 6:12; 7:16; Bar 4:8, 10, etc.). Yahve is said to be an eternal god (Ps 90:2) but his eternity was conceived as everlasting in terms of immortality, not as an existence outside time.

192. Cf. "For we know that God . . . is remote from these affections of pain and pleasure" (Plato, *Epinomis* 985a, in Lamb, *Plato*, 12:463).

193. Josephus also expressed the belief in a god who is "unbegotten and invariable (*analloiōtos*) through all time perpetual (*aidios*), superior to all mortal concepts of beauty and, although we know him by his power, unknown to us regarding his essence" (Josephus, *Contra Apionem* ii.167; cf. Thackeray. *Josephus*, I:359).

194. The Bible never says god is *asōmatos*. But during the Hellenistic era (*ca.* 100 or 125 CE) we find a legend claiming that on one occasion Isaac ran to greet god, and "fell at the feet of the bodiless one, and the bodiless one blessed him" (*T. Ab.* A iii.6). Yes, the "feet" of the bodiless one!

195. Cf. "For reason is not able to understand completely the one who is untouchable and impalpable (*anafēs*)" (Philo, *Legatio ad Gaium* i.6).

196. A later work (*ca.* 100 or 130 CE) talks about the "unborn and incomprehensible (*aperinoētos*)" god (4 Bar 9:6). Cf. "to the unknown god" (*agnōstōs deō*, Acts 17:23).

197. Philo, *De mutatuione nominum* i.54 (cf. Colson and Whitaker, *Philo*, 5:169). In §2.3.2.b, we already saw that Plato claimed that the gods can't change: "It is impossible even for a god to have the desire of changing himself, but being the best and finest

who is an "eternal and immovable (*aidios kai akinētos*) substance separated from sensible things ... [and that] he can have no magnitude but is impartible and indivisible (*amerēs kai adiairetos*)."[198] According to Aristotle, god is "the unmoved (*akinētos*) mover ... who remains in a simple form (*aplōs*) and invariable."[199] Following these leads, Philo repeats that "the Existing Being, who moves and changes all things, is himself unchangeable (*akinētos*) and immoveable (*atreptos*)."[200] These were the authorities driving Hellenistic Judaism into claiming concepts such as:

> God is alone and a single being, not a composite (*sunkrina*) but a single nature (*aploos*), while each of us and all other creatures are made of many parts. For instance, I myself am made of many parts ... but God is not a composite being made of many parts, nor is he mixed (*amigēs*) with anything else.[201]

> For he who imagines that God has a quality (*poiotēs*) or that he's not one, or that he's not uncreated and imperishable, or that he's not unchangeable (*atreptos*),[202] injures himself not God ... For we must conceive him without qualities (*apoios*), imperishable and unchangeable (*atreptos*).[203]

> Therefore, the soul that loves God and seeks to know the Existent Being according to his essence, is trying to enter into what is formless and invisible. The greatest benefit out of this quest would be to understand that God is in his being inaccessible (*akatalēptos*) to all creatures and to understand that he's invisible (*aoratos*).[204]

Saint Augustine placed the same ideas at the center of his concept of god and the Trinity:

> These [platonic] philosophers, who deserve to be famously exalted in glory over the rest, saw that god does not have a material

---

possible, they always remain in their own shape" (Plato, *Republic* ii.381c).

198. Aristotle, *Metaphysics* xii.1073a (cf. Tredennick, *Metaphysics*, 151).

199. Aristotle, *Physics* viii.6 (cf. Wicksteed and Cornford, *Aristotle: Physics*, 341–43).

200. Philo, *De posteritate Caini* i.28 (cf. Colson and Whitaker, *Philo*, 2:345).

201. Philo, *Legum allegoriarum* ii.2. Or: "For God ... who is the ruler and lord of all things, ever One, permanent, motionless, himself unto himself, and different from everything." (Philo, *De opificio mundi* i.100).

202. Cf. "Therefore, it is necessary that every creature should undergo change, for this is peculiar to them, as it is for God to be unchangeable" (Philo, *Legum allegoriarum* ii.33).

203. Philo, *Legum allegoriarum* i.51.

204. Philo, *De posteritate Caini* i.15.

body . . . they observed that anything that is mutable (*mutabile*) is not the almighty God . . . Starting with this immutability and simplicity (*incommutabilitatem et simplicitatem*), they understood that all things must have been made by Him . . . That which admits more or less [that is, degrees of comparison] without a doubt is mutable . . . Since the philosophers saw that body and mind can be more or less perfect . . . they realized that there is an Existence in which the first unchangeable form resides and, therefore, that it does not admit any degree of comparison,[205] rightly believing that there was the first principle of all things, which had not been made by anything and by whom all things were made.[206]

We need to underline here that it's not our intention to advocate on behalf of the old anthropomorphic theology (§2.2), nor it is our intention to defend the church's platonic theology.[207] We only want to emphasize that if biblical interpretation is going to remain a *grammatical-historical* enterprise, it should put aside the innovations of Christian Dogmatics in order to understand that the god of the Scriptures is an intensely humanized god, especially in the Hebrew Bible. It is a god who rejoices, loves and sings (Zeph 3:17); a person who moans like a woman in childbirth (Isa 42:14); a god who can get tired of a situation (Isa 1:14; Mal 2:17); a god who can explode in rage: "Even the priests . . . must sanctify themselves, to avoid Yahve bursting out against them" (Exod 19:22; cf. 19:24).

When humans experience injustice, sickness or misfortunes, we are left asking "why is this happening to me?" Sometimes not even the biblical god is able to figure out why people act the way they do. In the following two passages, Yahve is unable to grasp why Israel keeps leaving him:

---

205. Cf. "Therefore, the Existent is eternal and firm, ever equable, or identical; and it neither arose nor passed away, nor increased nor diminished; never did it become more or less, and it entails no spatial or other kind of motion" (Numenius, *Numenii Fragmenta* 2.xix, in Guthrie, *Numenius of Apamea*, 19).

206. Augustine, *De civitate dei* viii.6, in Dombart and Kalb, *Civitate*, 329. Cf. "For there is a Good and only he is simple (*simplex*) and, therefore, unchangeable (*incommutabile*). All things were created by this Good, but they are not simple and, therefore, they are changeable" (*Civitate* xi.10). Augustine elaborates these ideas in *De Trinitate*, books v–vii. See vi.v.7, where he says that "God is supreme simplicity" (*summa simplicitas*). Then in xv.v.7–8, he declares that all the attributes of god are identical to each other for god is a simple being. Thomas Aquinas also placed god's simplicity as a fundamental element of his theology (*Summa Theologica*, i.Q. 3).

207. The church's Platonism still retains an anthropomorphic idea of god, for it allows thinking about god as an idealized human being, a symbol of human virtues like love, kindness, justice, etc. (§2.3.2.a).

Why do you litigate against me?
You have all rebelled against me, says Yahve. (Jer 2:29)

⁴ Say to them: Thus says Yahve:
If people fall, do they not get up again?
If someone goes away, does he not come back?
⁵ Why then have this people[208] turned away in perpetual apostasy?
They have held fast to deceit,
they have refused to come back. (Jer 8:4–5)[209]

The book of Proverbs warns us against frequenting people "given to rage" (*baʿal ʾāp*), for we run the risk of becoming like them (Prov 22:24–25). It warns that a person "given to rage" (*baʿal ḥēmāʰ*) will commit many transgressions (Prov 29:22).[210] The exact same idiom is used to describe Yahve:

Yahve is a jealous and vindictive El,
   Yahve is vindictive and given to rage[211] (*baʿal ḥēmāʰ*, Nah 1:2a; cf. Isa 63:6)

Exodus 32 describes the humanized god who was later rejected by Platonism:

⁷ Then Yahve said to Moses: Go and come down [from the mountain] because your people, whom you brought up from Egypt, have corrupted [their way].[212]
⁸ They have quickly turned aside from the way that I commanded them. They have made for themselves a metal calf,[213] and they have bowed down to it and sacrificed to it. They have said: Israel, this is your Elohim,[214] who brought you out of Egypt.

---

208. The MT registers the word *yərûšālaim* (= "Jerusalem," ASV, JPS), which seems to be an explanatory gloss.

209. See Fretheim, *Suffering of God*, 114–16.

210. The idiom *baʿal ḥēmāʰ* means "possessor of rage," the one who has rage as an attribute or trait. Ecclesiasticus (Sirach) 8:16 gives the following advice: "Do not pick a fight with the quick-tempered" (NRSV).

211. Roberts translates: "lord of a violent temper" (*Nahum, Habakkuk, and Zephaniah*, 42).

212. The Piel verb *šiḥēṯ*, is not reflexive ("have corrupted themselves," ASV) but transitive, implying a direct object. See Propp, *Exodus 19–40*, 553.

213. Cf. "they . . . have made themselves an idol cast in the shape of a calf" (NIV).

214. The MT contains words in plural: "these are your gods" (*ʾēlleʰ ʾĕlōheʸḵā*; also the LXX, *houtoi hoi theoi sou*; cf. NRSV, NIV). But Dozeman correctly explains that the plural is an intentional mistake intended to provide background for Rehoboam's idolatry (*Exodus*, 685–87). Note that the narrative of 1 Kings 12 talks about two calves, one in Dan, the other in Bethel. And this is why the king used the plural "gods" in his

⁹ So Yahve said to Moses: I saw this people [down there], and, behold, it is a stubborn people!²¹⁵

¹⁰ Now, leave me alone,²¹⁶ so that my wrath may rage²¹⁷ against them and I may exterminate them.

¹¹ Then Moses appeased Yahve his Eloha,²¹⁸ saying: Yahve, Why does your wrath is raging against your people whom you brought out of Egypt with great power and a mighty hand?

¹² Why should the Egyptians say: For destruction he brought them out [of Egypt], to kill them in the mountains and to exterminate them from the face of the earth?²¹⁹ Desist from your burning wrath and repent²²⁰ from the destruction against your people.

¹³ Remember your servants Abraham, Isaac and Israel, to whom you swore by your very self, saying: I will multiply your descendants like the stars of heaven; and all this land that I have spoken of, I will give to your descendants, and they will inherit it forever.

¹⁴ Then Yahve repented from the destruction he said would inflict on his people.

This passage portrays a god who participates in the flux of space-time. There are things that take him by surprise. Yahve looked down from the mythic mountain (Exod 31:18), and voilà he saw his people committing idolatry (32:9). They had crafted a golden calf to represent and worship their god (vv. 1–8). This is also a god who can pass from a state of calm to a state of uncontrollable anger, and it is this anger which led him to decide to

---

address: "O Israel, here are your gods who brought you out of Egypt" (v. 28). In Exodus 32:8, the editor sacrifices the obvious singular meaning provided by the context (one calf and one god), to secure that the reader is reminded of the sin of the monarchy and, therefore, understands the Exodus story as the original sin of Israel. Israel was contaminated with idolatry from the very beginning. Cf. Nehemiah 9:17–18, which correctly amends Exodus to the singular: "This is your god who brought you up out of Egypt."

215. The construction *rāʾîtî . . . wəhinnēʰ* conveys this meaning: "I saw" the people down there, and it was that sight which produced the "behold!" The element of surprise is brought about by seeing. See Andersen, *Sentence in Biblical Hebrew*, 94–95.

216. Or: "do not interfere."

217. We have here the usual impv. (*hannîḥāʰ* = "leave me alone") followed by a jussive of purpose: *wəyiḥar* = "so it may burn." See Davidson, *Hebrew Syntax*, 90.

218. Cf. "Moses tried to pacify Yahweh" (NJB).

219. The questions in vv. 11–12 are only rhetorical, establishing the reasons for Moses' petition (see Ges. § 150c.). In the affirmative, the idea would be: After the great liberation that you provided for your people, you cannot now be filled with wrath against them, and you cannot let the Egyptians accuse you of evil intent either.

220. LXX softens to "be merciful."

exterminate his people. His decision starts a quarrel between Moses and Yahve—a dispute that pretty much looks like two men arguing face to face in a heated debate. As exterminating the people would have entailed having to start from scratch, Yahve tries to win Moses using flattery. God will form a new people out of him (v. 10). But Moses tries to pacify the furious god by asking him to ponder the consequences of acting on impulse. First, the god should consider that all the power he displayed in bringing the people out of Egypt will end in nothing (v. 11). Second, the god should also consider his reputation, what would people say about him! (v. 12). In forcing him to assess the situation without being driven by his emotions, Moses insists that he must control his wrath. Only then would he change his mind (v.12). He adds that the god should also consider the promises made to the forefathers. These are commitments that cannot be abandoned in a moment of rage (v. 13). With good arguments and rebukes, Moses succeeds in calming the god: "Desist from your burning wrath and repent," this is the only way to come out from a bad decision.[221]

There is no doubt that societies evolve and cultures change. The church is free to move into a transcendent view of her god, but since these views are a later development, it is important to underline two methodological imperatives: First, church doctrinal formulations about god's transcendence do not necessarily harmonize with each and every description that the Scriptures provide regarding the divine world (§2.2). Second, again and again we should be on guard against the way Bible interpreters deal with the Scriptures, for too often they approach the sacred text from an anachronistic perspective based on later Christian Dogmatics. This perspective leads interpreters to deny old anthropomorphic descriptions. Every time we use our Christian theology to engage the Scriptures, we run the risk of abandoning the *integrity of the grammatical-historical research*. The reasonable thing to do would be to admit that faith has evolved and that today we do not believe in some of the descriptions of god found in the Scriptures. But it is not honest to twist the meaning of a biblical text to accommodate its content to the newer theology regarding who god is or "what really happened." This is not *historical research*. The doctrine of *progressive revelation* is really an artificial way of coping with the evolution of human thought. We

---

221. However, the editors also added a different tradition. As punishment for the golden calf, Moses orchestrates a massacre which kills three thousand people. And the Levites who executed the slaughter were rewarded with the gift of priesthood! (Exod 32:25–29). We are also told that Yahve insists that he will anyhow take revenge in the future (Exod 32:30–35). So much for repenting! For a description of how evil, genocidal, and tribal the god of the Scriptures can be, see Nelson-Pallmeyer, *Jesus against Christianity*.

see this development already in the Scriptures, as well as in the church today when she tries to accommodate her beliefs to new ways of thinking.

2.3.5 Between Silence and Metaphor

If the platonic view of god is true; if it is true that god is above anything we can imagine; if it is true that god is indescribable, unknowable and incomprehensible; then there is nothing we can say about him. For if god is simple and essentially different from the world, we cannot know anything about him. There is no physical place where to localize god. It is a god who is outside the universe, a god who is separated from nature and who is not explicable in terms of the laws of physics. This generates agnostic pronouncements like the one found in 1 Timothy 6:16 which in Hellenistic style describes god as the one "who dwells in inaccessible light."[222] Aquinas also said:

> Now, because we cannot know what God is, but rather what He is not, we have no means for considering how God is, but rather how He is not.[223]

Saint Augustine agrees:

> If you understood, then it is not God. If you were able to understand, then you understood something else than of God. If you were able to understand, even partially, then you deceive yourself with your own thoughts.[224]

David Hume was absolutely right when he concluded that there is not much of a difference between theism and atheism. For if we proclaim the "mysterious, incomprehensible nature of the deity," and if it is true that god's being "has no manner of likeness or resemblance to human creatures," then how those "who maintain the absolute incomprehensibility of the deity, differ from sceptics or atheists, who assert, that the first cause of all is unknown and unintelligible?"[225]

---

222. See Dibelius and Conzelmann, *Pastoral Epistles*, 90; Towner, *Letters to Timothy and Titus*, 421.

223. *Summa Theologica*, i.Q. 3.

224. Augustine, *Sermon* 52, vi.16, in Migne, *Patrologiae Graecae*, 38:360. John Calvin wrote: "His essence, indeed, is incomprehensible, utterly transcending all human thought" (*Institutes* i.v.1; cf. i.xiv.1; i.xvii.1–2).

225. Hume, *Dialogues*, 35. Both Schleiermacher (*Über die Religion*) and Otto (*Das Heilege*) took refuge in an unmediated experience of god with no rational content. Tillich (*Systematic Theology*) talked only about the "ground of being."

When we face such a quagmire, the only recourse remaining is to take refuge in metaphor. It is only through metaphor that we can say something about god, in spite of the fact that *at the second we talk about god, we only talk about ourselves*, and theology ends being an *imitatio homini*. When we talk about the god of theism, we are forced to talk anthropomorphically. The confessions and theologians may say that god is simple, incomprehensible, infinite, invisible and immutable, but they also ascribe god the qualities of an idealized human being. For example, a confession describes the transcendent god as "infinite in being and perfection, a most pure spirit, invisible, without body parts," etc. but then it describes god in human terms: god is "most loving, gracious, merciful, long-suffering, abundant in goodness and truth."[226] At the end god is an ideal, a symbol of human virtues.

Christian practice insists on talking about god or Jesus as if he were that "invisible friend" whom believers know intimately, a posture which rhymes with the old metaphors of the Hebrew Bible:

> Yahve used to speak to Moses face to face,
> as one speaks[227] to a friend. (Exod 33:11; cf. Num 12:8)

The same warm anthropomorphism is attributed to Enki in relation to his devotee:

> There was one man named Atra-ḫasīs,
>   his god was ᵈEnki.
> He used to talk with his god,
>   and his god talked to him.[228]

The idea of a transcendent god cannot sustain religion in the way that it is understood by Christian experience. Metaphor helps out providing images that help evoke the unimaginable god. Herman Bavinck explains that if we want to have a Christian religion:

> We need a God who is like us, whom we may picture as a person, and who cares for his children like a father. True, such a religious view is always vulnerable to criticism on the part of science. It is not the highest and the most truthful, but we cannot do better.[229]

---

226. *Westminster Confession*, ii.i.

227. The impf. *yəḏabbēr* is frequentative. See Davidson, *Hebrew Syntax*, 66; Driver, *Tenses*, 38.

228. *Atra.* i.364–67.

229. Bavinck, *Reformed Dogmatics*, 45.

It doesn't matter how much we may refine our language about god, the truth is that theism finds it impossible to talk about god without the use of anthropomorphism. As Bavinck said, "Scriptures does not just contain a few scattered anthropomorphisms but is anthropomorphic through and through."[230] So Bavinck criticizes those:

> distinguishing between a concrete representation and an abstract concept [of God]. Plato already started it, Neoplatonism and Gnosticism continued the process, and Hegel reintroduced the distinction. But it makes no difference. Even the most advanced speculation and the most searching philosophy still has to think and speak about God. Though they throw out all concrete representations and only retain pure and abstract concepts, they will never transcend the necessity of thinking and speaking in human, creaturely terms or come close to the infinite One himself. Even the most abstract names—such as existence, substance, the Absolute, the One, the Spirit, Reason—are and remain anthropomorphisms. As humans we have only two alternatives: either absolute silence or human thought and speech about God; either agnosticism (i.e., theoretical atheism) or anthropomorphism.[231]

In fact, Christians usually describe their religious experience as a relationship with a living person whom they somehow experience in everyday life. But that person is "imaginary" or grasped only "by faith." This indicates that we are using metaphorical language in the style of the following passage which describes a god in terms of a father:

> When Israel was a child, I loved him;
> and out of Egypt I called my son . . .
> It was I who taught Ephraim how to walk,
> the one who took him up in my arms . . . (Hos 11:1–2)

The fact that we need a god who is like us does not mean that this god exists except figuratively. In order to be real, this god would need to have a body; it would need to be part of creation, living within the constraints of space-time. Otherwise, we wonder about the difference between the "personal relationship" Christians have with Jesus and the relationship John Nash (Russell Crowe) had with his three imaginary friends in the movie *A Beautiful Mind* (2001). When some religions—like Judaism, Christianity and Islam—insist incorrigibly on establishing humankind as the fundamental

---

230. Bavinck, *Reformed Dogmatics*, 99.
231. Bavinck, *Reformed Dogmatics*, 105.

metaphor by which they understand their god, a problem surfaces regarding the question of how we justify that persistence except by taking refuge in the anthropocentric character of our own cognitive mechanisms.

However, not everyone is happy with the transcendent god who "is but one eternal living and true God, incorporeal, impartible and impassive" (*incorporeus, impartibilis, impassibilis*).²³² Some theologians will deny that god is simple;²³³ others have limited god's omniscience, omnipotence and independence.²³⁴ Jürgen Moltmann has denied that god is simple, perfect and self-sufficient. According to him, god's unity is not in his essence but in the relationship which is sustained by the persons of the Trinity. God is not independent from historical reality, and this produces an eschatology which portrays god as not perfect until he becomes perfect with the world. Moltmann also underlines god's suffering on the cross.²³⁵ Wolfhart Pannenberg believes that when god created the world, he made himself dependent on the contingencies and imperfections of this world. God's redeeming actions bring perfection to himself in the eschatological fulfillment of the created world.²³⁶ In these theologies, anthropomorphism is understood as the way god incarnates in the world to move it to a situation of perfection and justice.

2.3.6 Grammatical-Historical Interpretation

Be as it may, the only thing we want to underline here is this: The dogma of a transcendent god is in conflict with the many descriptions of god we find in the Scriptures. Let's go back to the story of Adam and Eve in the Garden (examined in §2.2.1). If Adam and Eve did not hear Yahve's footsteps because he doesn't have feet or legs; if they were not able to hide because god knows everything; if the questions raised by the god were only rhetorical

---

232. *Thirty-Nine Articles of the Church of England*, article I, in Schaff, *Creeds*, 3:487.

233. "We believe that this attribute [of simplicity] has not real biblical basis and has in fact worked to defeat the resources of a full-fledged trinitarianism" (Plantinga, *Introduction to Christian Theology*, 104; see further 125, 132–34, 303). See Cooper, *Idea of God*, 72–83; Morris, *Our Idea of God*, 113–18; Smith, *Oneness and Simplicity of God*; Wierenga, *Nature of God*, 173.

234. See Boyd, *God of the Possible*; Boyd, *Crucifixion of the Warrior God*; Cobb, *Process Theology*; Hartshorne, *Divine Relativity*; Hartshorne, *Natural Theology*; Hartshorne, *Omnipotence*; Whitehead, *Process and Reality*.

235. Moltmann, *Church*.

236. Pannenberg, *Systematic Theology*, vol. 1. See Jüngel, who argues: "in his self-determination God comes to himself precisely in coming to man . . . God comes from God; but he does not wish to come to himself without us. God comes to himself but with man" (*God's Being*, 37).

because god is omniscient; if god really did not talk to them because he doesn't have a mouth, then what happened in the Garden? Nothing! God's transcendence leaves us without god, while mythology imagines a story using concepts borrowed from human experience in order to invent a narrative that is capable of describing something that happens in this world.

Platonic theology denies god any human emotion, form or representation. Therefore, in dealing with Genesis 6:6–7 (see §2.2.3), Philo of Alexandria condemned those who concluded "that the Existent is controlled by rage and wrath, when he's not susceptible to any passion whatsoever."[237] According to Philo, Moses used these words only to admonish people who would not be corrected otherwise. If god is represented as a man it is only "for the instruction of the many."[238] He argues that there are two types of people, those who serve the soul and those who serve the body. The first ones have no problem with the incorporeal nature of god and won't compare him "to any form of created beings."[239] But other people get attached to bodily things, so he objects:

> For what are we to say? If God employs organic parts, then he has feet to walk? But whither will he walk since he fills everything? To whom will he go, when no one is equal in honor to him? And for what purpose is he to walk? It cannot be because he's preoccupied for his health as we do. We have hands to give and receive, but he receives nothing from anyone. Since he owns everything, he has no needs. And when he gives, he employs the logos as the minister of his gifts, by whom he also made the cosmos.[240]

Platonism was embraced by the reformers, so when Calvin found that Genesis 6:6 declares that god repented, he tried to convinced us that the omniscient and omnipotent god is not capable of such a thing. Calvin argues that this language is only an accommodation to our limited capacities:

> The repentance which is here ascribed to God does not properly belong to him, but has reference to our understanding of him. For since we cannot comprehend him as he is, it is necessary that, for our sake, he should, in a certain sense, transform himself. That repentance cannot take place in God, easily appears

---

237. Philo, *Quod deus sit immutabilis* i.52.
238. Philo, *Quod deus sit immutabilis* i.54.
239. Philo, *Quod deus sit immutabilis* i.55.
240. Philo, *Quod deus sit immutabilis* i.57. Note how the platonic God maintains his distance from the world by using the *logos* as mediator and creator. Cf. John 1:1–10.

from this single consideration, that nothing happens which is by him unexpected or unforeseen.[241]

Calvin's explanation is just more anthropomorphism. For all we know, it is humans who adapt the way they communicate so others may understand. Whether we imagine god as a nurse, teacher or parent who needs to explain to children complex matters in uncomplicated language, we are simply using one anthropomorphism (a parent) to explain another anthropomorphism (god's repentance).[242] Instead we should admit that in antiquity people described their gods as having real bodily and psychologically human attributes.

2.4 Case Study: The Interpretation of Genesis 6:1–4

In §2.2.1–5, we studied five passages in which the gods are portrayed in human form. Then we established that these representations collide with the transcended concepts of god that later surfaced under Plato's influence (§2.3.1–2). For the present study, we have chosen to return to Genesis 6:1–2 (§2.2.2) because it is a passage that tests our *academic integrity*. The fundamental question here is: Are we going to remain within the grammatical-historical method or give in to theological prejudice?[243] This biblical passage forces us to recognize that *honesty* is the first prerequisite to Bible study. We reject the idea that to understand, first we need to give assent to the faith of the church (*credo ut intelligan*, Anselm). There is no reason why we should treat the biblical text differently than we treat the *Epic of Gilgameš*.

However, we are not interested in analyzing each and every aspect of Genesis 6:1–4. The ramifications and problems of this passage are so many that to deal with them it would require a long discussion which we have no interest in pursuing here. We will only concentrate in the identity of the "sons of the gods." The text says:

> ¹ When the human race began to multiply on the face of the earth, and daughters were born to them, ² the gods[244] saw that

---

241. Calvin, *Genesis*, 248–49.

242. Calvin uses metaphors to explain metaphors: "For who is so devoid of intellect as not to understand that God, in so speaking, lisps with us as nurses are wont to do with little children? Such modes of expression, therefore, do not so much express what kind of a being God is, as accommodate the knowledge of him to our feebleness. In doing so, he must, of course, stoop far below his proper height" (*Institutes* i.xiii.1).

243. In §3.7 we'll take Psalm 82 as a case study, which is very interesting for it involves John 10:35 in the conversation.

244. Lit. "the sons of the elohim" (*bənê-hā'ĕlōhîm*). Most versions translate "sons

the daughters of the human race were beautiful, and took wives for themselves ... (6:1-2).

2.4.1 The Sons of the ʾĕlōhîm = Gods

Though the interpretation of Genesis 6:3-4 remains a puzzle, the meaning and structure of vv. 1-2 is fairly clear: the gods saw the beauty of human-women and married them. The scantiness of these two verses invites interpreters to read between the lines what is really not in the text. Many speculate that the gods committed the sin of crossing the boundaries that separate the divine world from the human world, but this inference simply takes for granted that it was wrong to cross those boundaries. The truth is that, in ancient times, the breach between divine and human did not have the absolute character that it acquired later on. Others speculate that the sin of the gods was lust, for we read that the gods "saw" that the women were "beautiful" (v. 2). It is obvious that this seeing produced a desire that prompted the gods to marry but we don't need to find evil intent. The truth is that nothing in vv. 1-2 says anything about whether the actions of the gods were good or bad. The verses are merely descriptive. In the words of Walter Brueggemann: "The first two verses seem clear enough about the interaction of the world of God and human creatures. There is not criticism implied."[245] While the context of passages like Genesis 3:6 and 2 Samuel 11:2 clearly assert that there was malicious intent, Genesis 6:2 remains silent. Most of what is read into Genesis 6:1-4 comes from the book of 1 Enoch (see §2.4.2.a).

Be as it may, one thing is indisputable: the expression *bǝnê-hāʾĕlōhîm* (lit. "sons of the gods," vv. 1, 4) simply means "gods" (see our discussion in §2.2.2). Later (§3.3.4.c) we shall see that the Hebrew Bible uses this and other similar expressions to talk about the gods of the heavenly pantheon. In Ugarit, the gods were also referred to as "the sons of El," and in the Greco-Roman world they were described as "the sons of Zeus." So Herbert Haag resolves:

> There can be no doubt that in this fragment of a mythical narrative [Genesis 6:1-2] the author of the original oral or written tradition was thinking in gods, especially in light of the Ugaritic

---

of God" (NRSV, ASV, NIV, NJB), but the idiom requires "sons of the gods," or simply "gods" (§2.2.2).

245. Brueggemann, *Genesis*, 71.

parallels (where *ben* is often used to denote membership in a group).²⁴⁶

William Albright also makes it clear that the expression:

> meant simply "gods" in Canaanite, as is clear from numerous passages in Ugaritic literature, illustrated by many parallel Semitic expressions. In Gen 6:1ff., for example, we have an original myth in which the (astral) gods had intercourse with mortal women who gave birth to heroes.²⁴⁷

2.4.2 Angels

To soften the expression "gods," many interpreters today prefer to understand the text in terms of *angels*, which really are a class of lower gods subordinated to Yahve (§3.2).²⁴⁸ This interpretation still retains the mythical meaning of the text, but the use of the term "angels" makes it more palatable.

a. Early Judaism

Second Temple Judaism (*ca.* 530 BCE—70 CE) took the expression "sons of the elohim" as a reference to the angels of the Lord. *First Enoch* (250-200 BCE) may be the first attempt to domesticate the gods²⁴⁹ by placing them under a class of angels known as *watchmen* or *guardians*.²⁵⁰ While Genesis

---

246. Haag, "Ben," 157. Thus too Alter, *Genesis*, 26; Speiser, *Genesis*, 45; Westermann, *Genesis 1-11*, 371; Xeravits talks about "divine beings" ("Son of God," 1248).

247. Albright, *From the Stone Age*, 226. Again, *banê-hā'ĕlōhîm* "is a term for divine beings which, according to OT belief, resemble Yahweh in essence and power but are subordinate to him" (Gunkel, *Genesis*, 56). Brueggemann explains that the expression "refers to lesser gods in a polytheistic understanding of the world" (*Genesis*, 71).

248. Thus Arnold, *Genesis*, 89; Bennett, *Genesis*, 133; Brett, *Genesis*, 40; Cassuto, *Genesis* 291; Driver, *Genesis*, 82; Fretheim, *Genesis*, 382; Goldingay, *Old Testament Theology* 725; Longman, *Genesis*, 115; Provan, *Genesis*, 110; Routledge, *Old Testament Theology*, 121; Sarna, *Genesis*, 45; Skinner, *Genesis*, 139-41; Towner, *Genesis*, 78; Von Rad, *Genesis*, 113; Wenham, *Genesis 1-15*, 140.

249. The story of the sexual sin of the angels is narrated mainly in *1 Enoch* 6-11 and 12-16.

250. The term used is *'îr* = awake, vigilant. The Greek employs an adjective used as a noun, *egrēgoros* = awake, attentive. In *1 Enoch*, the term *vigilant* mostly refers to the angels who sinned, but it can also signal good angels, as in *1 En.* 12:2-3; 20:1-8 (cf. Dan 4:13[10], 23[20]; pl. in Dan 4:17[14]). Cf. *Jub.* 4:15, 22; 7:21; 10:5; *T. Reu.* 5:6-7; *T. Naph.*3:5; and the Dead Sea Scrolls (CD 2:18; 1QapGen 2:1, 16; 4Q534.1ii+2, 15).

6:1–2 narrates the event with very few words, *1 Enoch* and Qumran deliver many details:[251]

The gods get married and have children

1 (*Ethiopian Apocalypse of*) Enoch

6 ¹In those days, when the children of man had multiplied, it happened that there were born unto them handsome and beautiful daughters. ²And the angels, the children of heaven, saw them and desire them; and they said to one another, "Come, let us choose wives for ourselves from among the daughters of man and beget us children"
...

7 ¹And they took wives, and everyone (respectively) chose one woman for himself, and they began to go unto them. And they taught them magical medicine, incantations, the cutting of roots, and taught them (about) plants. ²And the women became pregnant and gave birth to great giants whose heights were three hundreds...

9 8 [The angels] went in unto the daughters of the people on the earth; and they lay together with them—with those women—and defiled themselves, and revealed to them every (kind of) sin. ⁹ As for the women, they gave birth to giants to the degree that the whole earth was filled with blood and oppression.

4Q201 frag. 1, col. 3 (4QEnoc^a, or: 4QEn^{a}ar)

Th[ey and th]eir [ch]iefs [all took for themselves] ¹⁴women, from all they chose, and [they began to penetrate them, to be defiled by them]

¹⁵ and to teach them sorcery, [incantations and the cutting of roots and to explain herbs.] ¹⁶ They became pregnant by them and gave [birth to giants, some three thousand cubits tall who] were born upon the earth...

4Q201 frag. 1, col. 4

²² [They have gone to the daughters of men of the earth and have slept with those women] becoming defiled [by them].

Jubilees (ca. 150 BCE) transmits the same tradition:

> And when the children of men began to multiply on the surface of the earth and daughters were born to them, that the angels of the Lord saw in a certain year of that jubilee that they were good to look at. And they took wives for themselves from all of those

---

251. García, *Dead Sea Scrolls*, 403 (cf. Vermes, *Dead Sea Scrolls*, 546; Wise, *Dead Sea Scrolls*, 282; *1 En.* 6:1–2; 7:1–2; 9:8–9, in Isaac, "Ethiopic Apocalypse of Enoch," 15–6). For 4Q201 frag. 1, col. 4, we use García's reconstructed text, in *Dead Sea Scrolls Translated*, 248.

whom they chose. And they bore children for them; and they were the giants.[252]

Philo of Alexandria (25 BCE—50 CE) gives this account:

> When the angels of God (*hoi angeloi tou theou*) saw the daughters of men that they were beautiful, they took to themselves wives from all those whom they chose. Those whom the philosophers call demons,[253] Moses usually calls angels. They are souls flying in the air.[254]

b. Church fathers

Ante-Nicene Fathers did not have any problem recognizing that Genesis 6 talks about angels. Justin Martyr (100-165 CE) says that angels "were made captive by their love for women, and they beget sons who were called demons."[255] Athenagoras (133-190 CE) says that some angels "fell in the lust (*epithumian*) for virgins, and they were defeated by the flesh . . . Therefore, from these owners of virgins were born those who are called giants."[256]

---

252. *Jub.* 5:1, in Wintermute, "Jubilees," 64.

253. The term *demon* here refers to patron gods who control cities and the lives of people.

254. Philo, *De gigantibus* i.6 (cf. Colson and Whitaker, *Philo*, 2:449). Josephus similarly says: "many angels of god, coming together with women, procreated violent sons, despisers of all that was good, because they trusted their own power" (Josephus, *Antiquitatum Judaicarum* i.73, in Niese, *Flavii Iosephi Opera*, 1:17).

255. Justin, *Apologia secunda pro Christianis* v.88, in Migne, *Patrologiae Graecae*, 6:452 (cf. Gildersleeve, *Apologies*, 71-72; Ruiz, *Padres Apologetas*, 265). In another place, he says "in antiquity, some vile demons, making their appearance, committed adultery with women" (*Apologia prima pro Christianis* v.48, in Migne, *Patrologiae Graecae*, 6:336).

256. Athenagoras, *Legatio pro Christianis* xxiv.40, in Migne, *Patrologiae Graecae*, 6:948 (cf. March, *Athenagoras*, 38; Ruiz, *Padres Apologetas*, 689). Clement of Alexandria (150-215 CE) taught that the mind "is led astray by pleasure . . . An example of this for you is the angels who forsook the beauty of God for perishable beauty and fell as far as heaven is from the earth" (*Christ the educator* 3.2.14, in Wood, *Clement of Alexandria*, 210). Tertullian (160-220 CE) said that Scriptures testify that: "From some angels, that fell by their own free will, came a breeding of wicked demons, condemned long ago by God together with the authors of their breed" (*Apologeticus adversus gentes pro Christianis* xxii.2, in Migne, *Patrologiae Latina*, 1:405, 407; cf. Donaldson, *Tertullianus*, 96-97).

c. Objection based on Matthew 22:30

Some have objected that Matthew 22:30 establishes that angels do not marry: "for in the resurrections they neither marry nor are given in marriage, but are like the angels in Heaven." This objection is made null by merely saying that Jesus is referring to obedient angels who stay put in Heaven (Judas 6). Tremper Longman III correctly argues:

> ... no Israelite/Jewish reader would have thought of angels as incapable of sexual intercourse. Yes, they are spiritual beings, but they are capable of taking on human appearance (see Gen 18-19; Mark 16:5). The opposite idea is not a biblical one, but one produced by a faulty view on angels developed during the Middle Ages when Christian thinkers were influence by a neo-Platonic philosophy that radically separated the spiritual from the physical.[257]

If Longman is correct, then we need to reflect a bit on the meaning of Matthew 22:30. Early Judaism (*ca.* 530 BCE—70 CE) taught that the righteous will live in Heaven, and that they will be like angels. For example, in talking about the punishment of the wicked and the reward of the righteous, Qumran declares that the righteous will become "glorious angels."[258] *Second Baruch* adds that the righteous will be transformed "into the splendor of the angels ... For they will live in the heights of that world and they will be like the angels, and be equal to the stars."[259]

However, the same writers who argue for the heavenly life of the righteous can also say that the angels had sexual intercourse with women. After having said that some angels came down from Heaven to procreate with mortal women (6-11 and 12-16), *1 Enoch* avers that the heavenly life of the righteous will be like that of the angels (*1 En.* 37-71, 92-105). So Jesus could perfectly be saying that in the resurrection, the righteous will be "like the angels in Heaven," that is, like the angels who obediently remained in Heaven doing god's will.

---

257. Longman, *Genesis*, 114.

258. 4Q511, frag. 35. See Wise, *Dead Sea Scrolls*, 529; Vermes, *Dead Sea Scrolls*, 453.

259. *2 Bar.* 51:5, 10, in Klijn, "2 Baruch," 638 (cf. 2 Esd 7:97-98, 125). *Shepherd of Hermas* also declares that bishops and hospitable people "already have a place with the angels" (*Similitude* ix.27.3). As we shall see later in §3.1, we should note that *2 Baruch* asserts that the angels are stars in Heaven.

2.4.3 The Sons of Seth and the Daughters of Cain

When interpreting Genesis 6:1–4, theologians love to eliminate the mythological component in order to construct an interpretation that is in agreement with Plato. For example, Augustine (354–430 CE) was willing to accept the "verified" rumor that there are incubi and devils who sexually assault women, but "I cannot accept," he said, "that the holy angels of God could have fallen in this way at that time." Therefore, he concludes that the "sons of God" from Genesis "were not gods or God's angels but they were really men" who marry "the daughters who live according to the flesh. In other words, the sons of Seth marry the daughters of Cain."[260] The key concept here is "I cannot accept." The Scriptures must submit to platonic theology.

In favor of this misleading interpretation, it has been argued that the Hebrew Bible uses the term "son" to refer to a spiritual filiation with god. Israel is called "my son, my firstborn" (Exod 4:22), "my son" (4:23; Hos 11:1), "sons" (Deut 14:1; 32:5, cf. v. 20; Isa 1:2, 4; 30:1, 9; etc.). Accordingly, we are asked to take the expression "sons of the elohim" as a spiritual expression pointing to the sons of Seth, the "godly sons" who got marry with the daughters of Cain, the daughters of the rest of humanity.[261] These unions were wrong because the Scriptures condemn the marriage of godly people with pagans who do not worship the true god. The spiritual interpretation aims to understand the text in this way: "When the human race in general (*hā'ādām*) began to multiply and daughters were born to them, the sons of Seth saw that the daughters of (only the Cainite) humanity (*hā'ādām*) were beautiful and married them."

The problem with this proposal is, first, the use of anachronistic language. The use of the word "son" in a spiritual sense appears for the first time in the later context of Yahve's election and covenant with Israel. This meaning of the word is absent before that era, which forces us to *conclude* that it is not appropriate to apply it to the world before the flood.[262] Second, it is

---

260. *De Civitate Dei* xv.23, in Dombart, *Civitate*, 108–10 (cf. Dods, *City of God*, 92–94). Calvin also denied that the text talks about gods/angels procreating: "That ancient figment, concerning the intercourse of angels with women, is abundantly refuted by its own absurdity; and it is surprising that learned men should formerly have been fascinated by ravings so gross and prodigious" (*Genesis*, 238). Consequently, Calvin also defended the idea that "sons of the elohim" refers to the descendants of Seth mating with the daughters of Cain.

261. Thus Aalders, *Genesis*, 153; Green, *Genesis*, 51–52; Keil, *Genesis*, 127–29; Mathews, *Genesis 1–11*, 323; Reno, *Genesis*, 114; Sailhamer, *Genesis*, 113.

262. In Gen 4:17, 25, 26; 5:3, 28, the term "son" is consistently used for literal descendants. The metaphorical meaning shows up for the first time in Exod 4:22 with the formation of Israel. Luther even imports the idea of spiritual children from the

also anachronistic to argue that the sons of Seth should not have married the daughters of Cain. This prohibition also comes from a later context in the life of Israel (Exod 24:16). John Walton recognizes that "it is difficult to extrapolate the warnings against elect Israel intermarrying and apply them to a group (Sethites) that has not been designated as elect and has not even been identified as ethnically isolated."[263] Third, this interpretation cannot explain how sexual intercourse between mere mortals (the sons of Seth and the daughters of Cain) was capable of producing the heroes of old (Gen 6:4). The procreation of heroes only agrees with the fact that, in antiquity, the heroes were the product of the sexual intercourse between gods and humans (§3.4). Fourth, the technical expression "the sons of the gods" (*bənê-hāʾĕlōhîm*) is never used to refer to Israel or to the righteous, but to divine beings (§3.3.4.c). Finally, the text registers only one single circumstantial sentence:

> Protasis: When the human race (*hāʾāḏām*) began to multiply... and daughters were born to them,
>
> Apodosis: the gods saw that the daughters of the [just mentioned] human race (*hāʾāḏām*) were beautiful, and took wives for themselves...

The protasis provides the setting within which the actions of the gods took place. It is in the context of humankind having daughters (Gen 6:1) that the gods accomplished their actions (v. 2). Humankind had daughters, and the gods married the daughters of the human race *just mentioned*. In other words, the term "human race" has the same meaning in both verses and, therefore, includes all humanity. The daughters mentioned in v. 2 are not the daughters of Cain but the daughters of all humankind. Both the technical expression *bənê-hāʾĕlōhîm* and the grammatical structure of the sentence also indicate clearly that the "sons of the elohim" are not part of humanity but act upon it. There is a contrast between gods (*bənê-hāʾĕlōhîm*) and humans (*hāʾāḏām*).

2.4.4 Kings, Nobles, Aristocrats

Targum Onkelos reads:

Christian Bible: "Moses designates as sons of God those people who had the promise of the blessed Seed. It is a term of the New Testament and designates the believers, who call God Father and whom God, in turn, calls sons" (in Pelikan, *Luther's Works*, 2:270).

263. Walton, *Genesis*, 293.

> And it was when the sons of men had begun to multiply upon the earth, and daughters were born to them, that the sons of the mighty (*benê rabrəbayyāʾ*) saw the daughters of men that they were beautiful...[264]

According to this interpretation, the expression *bənê-hāʾĕlōhîm* refers to rulers or powerful men. Meredith Kline tried to give traction to this meaning by arguing that "sons of the elohim" (Gen 6:1-4) refers to tyrants kings who are condemned for practicing polygamy.[265] As we shall see, there is no doubt that kings were thought to be gods or sons of the gods (§4.3.3). However, the king is always referred to as a god or son of a god individually. Kings are never collectively called *bənê-hāʾĕlōhîm* (= sons of the gods). Finally, the Hebrew Bible does not condemn polygamy.

2.4.5 Kings Possessed by Demons

Finally, some have tried to mix the angels' interpretation (§2.4.2) with the kings' interpretation (§2.4.4), producing fanciful explanations whose only purpose is to dodge the idea of angels/gods having *direct* sexual relations with mortal women. Allen Ross argues:

> In the Old Testament, the expression "sons of God" primarily refers to angels... but since spirit beings such as angels cannot cohabit with mortal flesh (Matt 22:30), "sons of God" cannot merely refer to angelic spirits in this passage. If angelic spirits possessed certain powerful people, the despots of the ancient world, they would be able to cohabit with humans and claim the lofty title, "sons of God" as well... Thus, it may be that "sons of God" here denotes fallen angels who invaded or possessed human life... The "sons of God" would be powerful leaders, people who became military conquerors or rulers over the whole world, who were enabled to do this because of the spirit forces within them.[266]

---

264. Cf. Etheridge, *Targum*, 46. Symmachus also translates "the sons of the powerful" (or: "rulers," *hoi huioi dunasteuontōn*).

265. Kline, "Divine Kingship," 196-98. Kline's study imposes to the book of Genesis a philosophical concept regarding the kingdom of god, even bringing Jesus Christ into the argument. But this terminology about kings and kingdoms is nowhere to be found in the text, and this intromission allows him to convert the "sons of the elohim" into sacred kings supposedly present in Cain's genealogy (p. 199) and who failed as a dynasty (p. 200).

266. Ross, *Genesis*, 68.

2.4.6 Prejudices Distorting Biblical Interpretation

The interpretations of §2.4.3–5 are clearly desperate attempts to make the Hebrew Bible say what it doesn't say. Those who reject the idea of gods procreating with mortal women are led by *doctrinal preconceptions* about what angels can or cannot do. We just saw how Ross starts with the presumption that angels cannot have sexual relations with humans because they are "spirit beings." This *theological prejudice* forces him to invent that the text is talking instead about kings possessed by fallen angels, even though the text neither says nor implies such a thing. Bruce Waltke also rejects the idea that angels can have intercourse with women, because according to him:

> ... angels do not marry (Matt 22:30; Mark 12:25). It is one thing for angels to eat and drink (see Gen 19:1–3), but quite another to marry and reproduce.[267]

Waltke cannot accept that angels were able to have sexual relations. But if a myth portrays gods eating and drinking (Gen 18:5–8), why we cannot accept the fact that other myths talk about gods getting married and having kids? (§3.4.1 and §4.3.3). Aquinas (1225–1274 CE) is the poster child for how theological prejudice fabricates fancy interpretations. He starts with the *presupposition* that the angels are disembodied, spiritual beings. So he feels the need to speculate on how it is possible for angels to interact with our reality. Every time the angels take human form, this is what happens: "... the angels assume bodies of air, condensing it by the Divine power in so far as is needful for forming the assumed body."[268] According to him, this means that the bodies assumed by angels are not alive: "through their assumed bodies they appear to be living men, although they are really not."[269] The angels do not really act through the organs of those bodies. Angels really don't see, talk or eat through their bodies, but everything is figurative. Even when Aquinas quotes favorably Augustine's idea that the "sons of the elohim" were the sons of Seth, he also suggests that Genesis 6:1–2 could be a case in which demons stole human semen to impregnate women:

> Still if some are occasionally begotten from demons, it is not from the seed of such demons, nor from their assumed bodies, but from the seed of men taken for that purpose ... so that the person born is not the child of a demon, but of a man.[270]

---

267. Waltke, *Genesis*, 116.
268. Aquinas, *Summa Theologica*, i.Q. 51.1–3.
269. Aquinas, *Summa Theologica*, i.Q. 51.3, *ad.* 1.
270. Aquinas, *Summa Theologica*, Q. 51.3, *ad.* 6.

All these fanciful inventions are aimed at neutralizing the anthropomorphic descriptions that we find in the Scriptures in order to maintain the "spiritual" nature of the angels. The theological system subordinates the Scriptures to creeds and confessions. But in ancient times people did not have a platonic concept of the gods. It would be more honest to say that the Scriptures contain old-fashioned or mistaken theological concepts. We could also recognize that we cannot expect a book compiled through a period of a thousand years to contain a single and systematized concept of the divine. It comes as no surprise that the interpretation of §2.4.3 (Seth and Cain) is the one favored among conservative systematic theologians.[271]

Some Christian denominations even demand all their officials to sign a document stating that the underwriters uphold that the creeds and confessions of their church agree fully with the Word of God. No one seems to be aware that these creeds and confessions appeared later in history, and that in many cases they do not project biblical content. When someone signs such a document, that person is *promising academic dishonesty*. To trust these scholars is like trusting scientists or politicians sold to the interests of corporations. No historical investigation should be subjected to the creed of a church. Orthodoxy freezes everything in the imaginary time of dogma, and in so doing it renounces the *historical method*. Scriptures are removed from their own time and culture, and its content does not register any historical evolution anymore. When historical research is called into the discussion it is only to confirm dogma. The creeds anticipate the results.

Another taboo that prevents people from accepting the mythic meaning of Genesis 6:1–2 is that such recognition would place them in the uncomfortable position of having to defend "with a poker face" that we are dealing with a "historical" fact that happened in the reality of space-time. A better option would be to simply recognize that Genesis 6:1–2 is myth; it is an imaginary story. Waltke cannot tolerate such a thing because, according to him, "the inspired narrator regarded it as history."(!)[272] Therefore, the meaning has to be twisted to fit the dogma. Waltke claims that "the best solution is to combine the 'angelic' interpretation with the 'divine king' view. The tyrants were demon possessed"[273] (§2.4.5). Waltke feels that it is more credible to believe in demons that somehow controlled kings than to believe that angels can procreate with mortal women. He bets in favor of the possibility that the mythology he himself is creating would be more

---

271. See Akin, *Theology of the Church*, 310; Berkhof, *Systematic Theology*, 314; Erickson, *Christian Theology*, 412; Grudem, *Systematic Theology*, 414; Turretin, *Institutes*, 153.

272. Waltke, *Genesis*, 115.

273. Waltke, *Genesis*, 117.

palatable to modern man and surely in accord with Christian doctrine. It's true that all these ideas are fanciful, but my point here is that the defenders of orthodoxy always brag about how they are the defenders of the infallible Bible, while at the same time they subjugate the Scriptures under their own theological system.

As long as scholars keep resisting the fact that the Scriptures contain mythology, interpreters will argue that the meaning of a passage is ambiguous or they will try to twist it. Today we should recognize that Genesis 6 is not registering a historical fact but a fictional story. For a historian this conclusion does not arise first and foremost from some "materialism that tends to doubt the existence of spirits, good or ill,"[274] but from the fact that all the cultures of the Ancient Near East and the Mediterranean shared the same mythical world. Myths about sexual relations between gods and humans were a common thread among Sumerians, Babylonians, Hittites, Egyptians, Greeks, Romans, etc. Christians would need to substantiate why the mythical tradition from Genesis is a historical fact while the rest are myths. As we have stated, a narrative is not a myth because of the number of gods present in it or because it describes an event as occurring in Heaven (§1.2.2), but because all these stories are extended metaphors (§1.1.1–3).

2.4.7 Presuppositions and Research

Some scholars would contend that the denial of the historicity of the Bible results from interpreters influenced by the presupposition that miracles cannot happen and that god cannot intervene in the historical process. They argue that these presuppositions contaminate all the research.[275] We agree that all scholars have presuppositions. But when a historian detects legendary-mythical elements in a biblical story it is not because of a bias against god or the Bible. It is rather a *conclusion* arising from having scrutinized both the text and the culture in which the biblical text originated. The myths we find in the Scriptures are not floating in a cultural void but are adaptations of myths shared or borrowed from surrounding cultures that Christians later disparaged as pagan. The present study shows example after example of this usufruct. In antiquity there was an abundance of stories of gods procreating with humans (§2.2.2; §3.4.1; §4.3.3) or visiting humans for the purpose of reward or punishment (§2.2.4). We find the same stories in the Scriptures. We shall also demonstrate the pagan origin of the fundamental metaphor by which the Scriptures envision its god as a cosmic king

---

274. Wenham, *Genesis 1–11*, 140.
275. See Stein, *Synoptic Gospels*, 217, 218 n. 64.

(§4), as well as the metaphor of a warrior-god who protects the territory of his king (§4.3.4). It is not honest to despise pagan myths as fictional stories and then pretend that the same stories in the Scriptures are "historical."

A story can be classified as myth not because it contains more than one god (polytheism) or because it occurs in Heaven (§1.2.2), but because it is a *metaphorical narrative*. And the pivotal metaphor of theism is anthropomorphism: Zeus has eyebrows and hair; Yahve is old, has hair and wears clothing; El has a beard and gray hair (§2.2). Another story portrays Yahve visiting Abraham in the form of a man who rests, eats, drinks and talks (§2.2.4.b). The biblical god appeared to Joshua with a sword in his "hand" ready to go to war like a human general (Josh 5:13–15), in almost exactly the same way that goddess Ištar appeared to another seer (§2.2). Later we shall see Yahve personally removing the wheels of Egyptian chariots (Exod 14:15–25, §4.3.4.c), and Apollo throwing deadly arrows at the enemies of his priest (§4.3.4.d). In these and many other myths, *the gods are imagined as people with human bodies*. How can we regard the biblical stories as historical and the pagan myths as fanciful stories? This is not about presuppositions but about *honesty and evidence*.

Chapter 5 will show that the only reason Matthew could have claimed that a young man suffered from a "disease given by the Moon" (Matt 17:15, in §5.7.2) was because a thousand years before Mesopotamia began talking about the Moon afflicting people with epilepsy (§5.7.1). When we study the Gospels in light of the culture in which they were immersed, we are forced to conclude *a posteriori* that the sacred text shares the same mythic perspective. Both pagans and Christians talk in the same way, they all share the same fundamental metaphors to talk about the gods.

If we look for presuppositions that contaminate historical investigation, we insist on two colossal obstacles to the study of the Scriptures. One is the *a priori* belief in the *infallibility of the church*:

> To be right in everything, we ought always to hold that the white which we see, is black, if the Church so decides it, believing that between Christ our Lord, the husband, and the Church, his wife, there is the same Spirit which governs and directs us for the salvation of our souls. Because by the same Spirit and our Lord Who gave the Ten Commandments, our holy Mother the Church, is directed and governed.[276]

The other is the toxic prejudice of the *infallibility of the Scriptures*:

---

276. Rule 13 of Loyola's *Rules for Right Thinking*, in Caldwell, *Sources of Western Society*, 231.

Not only is Scripture inspired and authoritative, it is also inerrant and infallible. By this we mean that it is without error in the original manuscripts. It is inerrant in all that it affirms, whether in historical, scientific, moral, or doctrinal matters. Inerrancy extends to all of Scripture and is not limited to certain teachings of Scriptures.[277]

On the basis of an infallible Bible, a famous Christian apologist comes with this irrational proposal:

> Should a conflict arise between the witness of the Holy Spirit to the fundamental truth of the Christian faith and beliefs based on argument and evidence, then it is the former which must take precedence over the latter, not vice versa.[278]

According to this defender of the faith, Christian dogma wins over "evidence." This statement is not only meaningless but dangerous, for once we have accepted its premises *anything can be perceived as truthful*. Any denial of reality or ethics becomes acceptable. Any call to commit atrocities is not only warranted but necessary "in the name of god." If a person accepts that 2 + 2 = 5 because the Bible or a church says so, then evidence, facts and reason are of no consequence. We become victims of ideas that resist all rational criticism; and we are left at the mercy of mirage and illusion, deception and prejudice.

Let's look at Mark 2:25–26. It claims that when David and his companions where hungry, "he entered the house of God, when Abiathar was high priest, and ate the consecrated bread." But 1 Samuel 21:1–8 maintains that during this episode the high priest in office was Ahimelech. An impartial commentator would recognize that "the reference to Abiathar in Mark 2:26 is obviously a mistake."[279] But William Hendriksen seeks to solve the problem guided by the unwarranted premise of an inerrant Bible:

> . . . in our attempt to solve the problem room must be left for any solution that does not ascribe error to the original author

---

277. Thiessen, *Systematic Theology*, 63. Cf. "Being wholly and verbally God-given, Scripture is without error or fault in all its teachings, no less in what it states about God's acts in creation, about the events of world history, and about its own literary origins under God, than in its witness to God's saving grace in individual lives" ("Chicago Statement on Biblical Inerrancy," 1978). Or: "The inerrancy of Scriptures means that Scripture in the original manuscripts does not affirm anything which is contrary to fact" (Grudem, *Systematic Theology*, 91).

278. Craig, *Reasonable Faith*, 48.

279. Corney, "Abiathar," 7. Matthew and Luke avoided the problem by simple deleting the problematic reference to Abiathar.

... [for] in writing their books divinely inspired authors did not commit errors.[280]

Once people enjoy the privilege, security and identity that come with the so-called inerrancy of Scripture, dogma vitiates the way we process data. Instead of evaluating the evidence independently, dogma anticipates the conclusion and directs our thinking. We shun any information causing cognitive dissonance in order to avoid the disintegration of our world.[281]

---

280. Hendriksen, *Gospel of Mark*, 107.

281. See Festinger, *Cognitive Dissonance*; Kunda, "Case for Motivated Reasoning"; Köneke, *Psychology of Self-Insight*; Westen, "Neural Bases of Motivated Reasoning." We see the same problem in the debate about global warming. An Internet article from Yale University correctly underlines the fact that climate change is based on cumulative evidence, that is, things like "increased water vapor to increasing sea levels, from moisture and rainfall to measurements of the cryosphere, of snow ice, and of the heat content of the planet's oceans." Then the article quotes University of Michigan emeritus professor Henry Pollack, saying: "Ice asks no questions, presents no arguments, reads no newspapers, listens to no debates. It's not burdened by ideology and carries no political baggage. As it passes the threshold from solid to liquid, it just melts" (Sinclair, "It's the Data").

> *We shall not cease from exploration*
> *and the end of all our exploring*
> *will be to arrive where we started,*
> *and know the place for the first time.*
>
> —T. S. ELIOT, *FOUR QUARTETS*, 59

Chapter 3

DIVINE WORLD

3.1 Divine World: Personal and Impersonal

IN THE FIRST CHAPTER, we defined myth as a metaphor extended into a story. We also pointed out that the accumulation of mythical stories and expressions helped create a *conceptual metaphor*, that is, a concept of god. In chapter two, we claimed that any form of theism needs to imagine the gods as if they were *people* who think and act as we do. We visualize the gods as even having human bodies (§2.2).[1] In chapter four, we will use monarchy as a case study to provide definite evidence for what has been said in chapters 1 and 2. But before we do that, we need to talk a bit more about the divine world in general.

When Silvio Rodriguez sang "I see a light that hesitates, and promises to leave us in the dark,"[2] he was giving *light* human qualities. And this raises the question: What is theism portraying as human beings? In the case of the gods, it is often the *impersonal* forces of the universe. For example, the Sumerian word An means "sky," but it also refers to the personal god An, head of the Sumerian pantheon. Plato described time, sun, moon and

---

1. The title song of the TV series *Joan of Arcadia* (2003) summarized its message this way: "What if God was one of us, Just a slob like one of us, Just a stranger on the bus, Tryin' to make his way home?" (Joan Osborne, "One of Us," 1995). The program presents an exquisite humanized god immersing himself in the life of people.

2. "Óleo de Mujer con Sobrero" (1978).

stars as gods.³ In Ugarit, the stars were the gods who comprised the divine council:

> [ ] which the gods do not know,
> [ ] the assembly of the stars (*pḫr kbbm*),
> [ ] the circle of those in the heavens.⁴

In Mesopotamia, Utu (or Šamaš) was the Sun god, but he is also portrayed as a *person* acting as the guarantor of justice in human society. A Babylonian psalm describes him as the one:

> Who lightens the darkness . . .
> Your rays grasp secrets unceasingly . . .
> Illuminator, dispeller of darkness of the *vault* of the heavens . . .
> Regularly and without cease you traverse the heavens . . .
> [. . .] you blaze abroad the judgements on the criminal and law-breaker . . .
> A circumspect judge who pronounces just verdicts . . .⁵

However, this is not the whole story, because some gods are not forces of nature. If we consider Enki (or Ea), for example, we find that even though he is the god of the subterranean waters (Apsu), he is never identified with the waters. Enki is the most human god, the god of creation, culture, art and civilization,⁶ always protecting humankind and involved in its destiny. His name means "lord of the earth" (ᵈen-ki).

The polarity between the personal and impersonal character of the gods creates ambiguities. In 1 Kings 22:19-22, the personal element is clearly present (§1.1.3). The heavenly "stars" are depicted standing (*'ōmēḏ*, v. 19)⁷ in front of Yahve in a meeting of the heavenly council, as if they were people. Yahve asks them who will go and deceive Ahab, and the star-gods propose several ideas (v. 20). Other texts declare that the stars can be punished (Isa 24:21) or that they are Yahve's "ministers who do his will" (Ps 103:21). The stars are able to bow down in worship with their "faces" to the ground (Neh 9:6), just like people do (Deut 4:19; Isa 44:15, 17). Revelation 1:20 maintains

---

3. Plato, *Timaeus* 39–40, in Bury, *Timaeus*, 76–77.
4. *Baal Fathers a Bull*, *CAT* 1.10.i.3–4, in Parker, "Baal Fathers a Bull," 182.
5. *The Šamaš Hymn* i.2, 9, 17, 27, 58, 101, in Lambert, *Babylonian Wisdom*, 127–30.
6. Nudimmud was another name for Enki. According to Jacobsen it means "maker of images" as the god of craftsmanship (*Treasures*, 111).
7. Here we find the same ptc. *'ōmēḏ* employed to describe Abraham "standing" by the three gods who visited him (Gen 18:8) or when he was "standing" in front of Yahve (Gen 18:22). Cf. §2.2.4.c.

that "the seven stars" are angels. When all the host of Heaven, the sun, the moon and the stars are invited to praise Yahve, we again detect this ambiguity of a psalmist who addresses people who, at the same time, are impersonal elements of nature (Ps 148:1–3). In Joshua 10:12, the sun and the moon act as soldiers of Yahve's army. They stop their course around the earth (geocentric cosmology) in order to grant Israel a crushing victory over her enemies. Joshua speaks to them as if they were people who would understand and act accordingly.[8] And Judges 5:8 claims that "the stars fought from heaven, from their courses they fought against Sisera." These are all personal gods who engage in warfare against the enemies of Israel.

Job 38:6–7 is quite illuminating. As personal gods, the clamor and shouts of the stars are very real. Notice that verse 7 contains a synonymous parallelism that leaves no doubt that by "stars" the psalmist means "gods":

[6]Where are its bases embedded?
    Who laid its cornerstone,
[7]when the morning stars clamored together,
    when all the gods[9] shouted with praise?

To the north of Israel, Ugarit also talked about the gods as the "assembly of the stars."[10] And the same equivalence between stars and gods that we just found in Job 38:7, repeats itself in this Ugaritic text:

He pres[ents] a meal for the gods,
into the heavens he sends incense,
[to the] stars (he sends) the incense of Harnemite.[11]

It is interesting that 1 Enoch first presents the gods as the "sons of Heaven" (= gods) who came down to the earth to have sex with women.[12] But later in the book the same incident is described by saying that "a star fell from Heaven," and that Enoch saw "many stars descend and cast themselves down from Heaven" to procreate with women.[13] The stars had some sort of

8. See Taylor, *Yahweh and the Sun*, 111, 139.

9. The lit. idiom "sons of elohim" means "gods." See §2.2.2; §3.3.4.c; §3.3.5.

10. *Baal Fathers a Bull*, CAT 1.10.i.3–4, in Parker, "Baal Fathers a Bull," 182. See §3.3.4.a.

11. *Aqhat*, CAT 1.19.iv.22–25 (cf. Parker, "Aqhat," 76). See Driver and Gibson, *Canaanite Myths*, 120. And cf. "Raise an offering to the Lady Sun, thanks to the immovable stars" (*Birth of the Gracious Gods* 1.23.54, in Lewis, "Birth," 212).

12. *1 En.* 6:1–7, in Nickelsburg and VanderKam, *1 Enoch*, 23–24. Cf. Gen 6:1ff.

13. *1 En.* 86:1–6, in Nickelsburg and VanderKam, *1 Enoch*, 120–21. Today we find a bit laughable that Enoch would say that stars fell down to earth, when the volume of a star is larger than our planet. Inside our sun we could fit about 1.3 million earths.

human body whose size, shape and constitution enabled them to procreate with human women.

In the previous chapter, we mentioned the irresistible human tendency to personify everything (§2.1). We talked about dogs chatting, the wind as a fickle friend, stones that show empathy, and a god who looks like an old man. Even when we know that these expressions are not meant to be taken *literally*, we find it natural to humanize everything, as the following examples show:

- The flowers are *begging* for water
- Oreo is milk's *favorite* cookie
- That piece of pie *is calling* my name
- Opportunity *is knocking* at her door

So it may be true that the gods only exist metaphorically as a way of talking about the glory and mystery of the Universe. How many times do we say: "Life is so unfair," when *fairness* is a human trait that cannot be ascribed to *life*. Metaphor may be a way of referring to our orderly ("laws" of nature) and arbitrary (chance) Universe. The metaphorical nature of the theistic narratives makes it feasible to argue with Levi-Strauss that "religion consists in a *humanization of natural laws* . . . The anthropomorphism of nature."[14] Freud also described religion as "the humanization of nature,"[15] adding that we humanize the elements of nature to feel in our own world, in order to calm our anxiety, for if the universe is personal maybe we could "apply the same methods used within society. One can try to conjure them up, placate them, bribe them—and through such influence rob them of some of their power."[16] Even today in a time when humans prefer to dominate their environment via science and technology, we still humanize nature, whether we trust *by faith* that there is a personal force/god behind life or whether we simply admit it is the way our brains works.

3.2 Hierarchies of the Divine World

We are not interested in presenting a comprehensive catalogue of divine beings. We only want to mention some specifics which are relevant to our discussion. When the Scriptures use the term "gods" (§3.3.5), it employs a *nomen naturae* pointing to their divine nature. However, the Scriptures

---

14. Levi-Strauss, *Savage Mind*, 221.
15. Freud, *Future of an Illusion*, 20.
16. Freud, *Future of an Illusion*, 20–21.

often avoid making their divine character explicit and prefer using a *nomen officii* that only describes a particular function of the gods. To this end, the favorite term is *mal'ak* or *angelos*, that is, "envoy, messenger." The terms do not entail that the only function of the gods is to carry messages.

Monarchy (§4.1.1) became the main *source domain* (§1.1.2-3) for theistic concepts, providing a multitude of expressions that were used to create the conceptual metaphor YAHVE IS KING. The divine world was divided into several hierarchies imitating earthly monarchy:

First, there was a chief god who was the king and head of the pantheon (An, Marduk, El, Yahve, Zeus, etc.). For example, Psalm 95:3 describes Yahve in his role of king of the gods:

> For Yahve is great El
> and great king above all gods (*kol-'ĕlōhîm*, see §4.2.3).

Second, in the Ancient Near East and the Mediterranean, there were other adjacent gods with much autonomy. These gods were not just angels of the main god, but they also had their own devotees, stories and purposes (Enlil, Enki, Inana, etc.; Baal, Yamm, Athene, Hera, Apollo, Hermes, etc.). Although Israel mostly eliminates this tier, Christianity brings it back by introducing Jesus and the Spirit as gods in their own right.

Third, there were minor gods acting as servants and envoys of the most important gods. For example, Sumerian mythology portrays An as a king who employs a whole array of minor gods acting as cooks, gardeners, counselors, etc.[17]

In Ugarit, Baal had "seven assistants and eight attendants,"[18] and we also find the god Kothar-wa-Hasis (expert craftsman, sorcerer, builder, etc.)[19] who also functions as an envoy of the gods. The importance of this figure is seen when "a throne is set up and he is seated at the right hand of Mightiest Baal."[20] The gods Gapn and Ugar were also angels who are clearly designated as "gods" (*ilm*). When Mot (= Death) sends a threatening warning to Baal, we are told that the two "gods depart" (*tbʿ ilm*) to Baal's mountain to deliver the message.[21] In Job 4:18, the parallelism identifies the

---

17. Bottéro, *Religion in Ancient Mesopotamia*, 51.

18. *Baal Cycle, KTU* 1.5.v.8 (cf. Smith, "Baal Cycle," 147). For other attendants of the house of Baal, see Smith, *Origins of Biblical Monotheism*, 56; Miller, *Divine Warrior*, 18-19.

19. Kothar made gifts for Athira (*Baal Cycle, CAT* 1.4.i.23-6), weapons for Baal (1.2.iv.11-14), and a house for Baal (1.4.v-vi), etc.

20. *Baal Cycle, CAT* 1.4.v.46-7, in Smith, "Baal Cycle," 131.

21. *Baal Cycle, KTU* 1.5.i.9, in Smith, "Baal Cycle," 141. Cf. *Baal Cycle, CAT* 1.3.iii.32. They are also called "divine servants" (cf. *CAT* 1.3.iv.32; 1.4.viii.15).

messenger-gods as servants: "He doesn't even trust his servants, and in his messengers he finds faults."

In Israel, Yahve is the supreme god of his pantheon, but he has neither wife nor children. The removal of wife and offspring eliminates an element capable of producing the well-known family conflicts, and eliminates the independence seen in the gods of the surrounding cultures (tier 2 above). This fact discolors Yahve's life and impoverishes his relationships and interactions. Yahve is limited to pursue Israel as his only source for a love-relationship. Later, Christianity adds two other gods into the mix, Jesus and the Spirit.

The Hebrew Bible provides us with at least one passage that talks about goddesses or feminine angels. The book was written in the Persian period:

> I looked up and, behold, I saw two women coming forth with the wind in their wings; their wings were like the wings of a stork. (Zech 5:9)

The story talks about two winged goddesses carrying a receptacle containing the goddess Iniquity. The receptacle is a symbol of the guilt of the land (5:6), [22] while the goddess inside the receptacle is the wickedness that produced that guilt (5:8). The personification of iniquity makes it possible to remove her from the land, so she's taken to Shinar (Mesopotamia) where she can have her own temple (5:11).

To summarize, "Yahweh was envisioned seated on a throne in his temple or palace surrounded by a nameless host of divine beings who rendered service to the enthroned deity (1 Kgs 22:19; Isa 6:1–4). Yahweh took counsel with them and commissioned them with tasks. They sat as a court to judge a case and pronounce a verdict. The gods went from the assembly to accompany Yahweh into battle. In all of this activity, the members of the divine assembly had no autonomy or independence apart from the word and action of Yahweh." [23] Thus the role of the gods is servitude, as stated in this psalm:

> Bless Yahve, you his envoys,
>
> mighty warriors who execute his orders,
>
> obedient to his spoken word (Ps 103:20).

---

22. In Zechariah 5:6, the MT reads *ênām* (= "their appearance," ASV; or: "their eye," Vg., TJPS, JPS), but Zech 3:4, 9 seems to suggest that we should read *'ăwōnām* (from *'ăwōn* = guilt, offense) = "their guilt," as it is also suggested by the translation of the LXX *adikia autōn* = "their injustice." Cf. NRSV: "This is their iniquity" (cf. NJB).

23. Miller, *Religion of Ancient Israel*, 26–27.

The predominant henotheism of the Hebrew Bible becomes more monotheistic in later texts, as shown in Second Isaiah 43:10-11; 44:6, 8; 45:5-7, 14, 18, 21; 46:9. But even in such cases, we still find that the god of Israel is "Yahve of hosts" (44:6), an expression that points again to the star-gods who comprise his army.[24] So texts like Second Isaiah 44:6, 8; 45:21 still admit the existence of gods who act as servants of Yahve. However, their subordination is such that the prophet can add "besides me there is no elohim" (44:6).

In the period of the Second Temple (*ca.* 530 BCE—70 CE), Persian theology introduced an innovative development. Its dualistic perspective talked about gods who became independent and who contested the sovereignty of the only one god. These gods became rebels. The new trend tried "to deal with the problem of evil and the fact that the reality of human sin and divine judgment could not alone carry the moral burden of accounting for all the evil that happened."[25] The new theology claims that sin has an angelic or supernatural origin. Sin is not solely a human product.

3.3 Divine Assembly

Metaphorical reasoning allowed humans to conceive gods as if they were kings (§4.1-2), and it also brought them together into divine assemblies replicating the council of an earthly king (anthropomorphism). The cultural background creating these images starts at the beginning of the agricultural revolution when the villages of Mesopotamia were governed by *patres familias* who formed assemblies (unkin, Sum.; *puḫrum*, Akk.). Thorkild Jacobsen points out that these assemblies only met in situations of internal crisis, war or when an individual had violated the social order. In these cases, an *ad hoc* governor was named to impose corrective measures or a warrior was asked to protect the village from an external threat.[26]

But with the rise of the monarchy and the complexity of urban life, the political power shifted to the crown. Each city still had its own assembly, as the following example shows: "King Ur-Ninurta ordered its case accepted for trial in the assembly of Nippur."[27] A document from the First Babylonian Dynasty (1800-1500 BCE) talks about a murder case in which "the council of Nippur" issued a verdict.[28] The city was ruled by a council, a governor

---

24. Cf. Ps 82:1, 6; 89:8; 95:3, etc. And see §3.3.4.c-e, and §3.3.5.
25. Miller, *Religion of Ancient Israel*, 28.
26. Jacobsen, *Toward the Image*, 137-39. See Postgate, *Early Mesopotamia*, 80-82.
27. "Puhru," 488.
28. Chiera, *Sumerian Epics and Myths*, 172-73. A text from Ur III (2112-2004

and a director of the temple (*sanga*). The king of a region or league lived in the capital city.

The story of *Gilgameš and Agga*[29] narrates the conflict that arose between Agga (king of Kiš) and Gilgameš (king of Uruk). The crisis started when Agga sent messengers to Gilgameš demanding forced labor from the people of Uruk. Gilgameš warned the "elders of the city"[30] about the impending threat, and proposed waging war against Agga, but "the convened assembly of the elders of the city" recommended submitting to the aggressor. In the face of the assembly's rejection, Gilgameš sought help from goddess Inana and the warriors of the city. In the end, they managed to capture and defeat Agga.

The *Epic of Gilgameš* reports that the legendary king feared dying without having achieved "eternal fame." So he suggested to his friend Enkidu that they could gain such fame by going up to the Cedar Forest to kill the formidable Humbaba (or Huwawa), the guardian of the forest. Gilgameš summons the council of the city and says: "Listen to me, elders of walled Uruk," and then reveals his plans to them.[31]

3.3.1 Mesopotamia

Replicating earthly reality, the head of a pantheon was a king-god who was assisted by an assembly of gods or elders. *Atraḫasīs* (*ca.* 1700–1600 BCE) refers to the divine assembly (*puḫru*) as the "assembly of all the gods."[32] Later in the story, goddess Nintu laments having decided the extermination of humankind "in the assembly of the gods."[33] The *Bilingual Story of Creation*

BCE) relates a trial in which "the assembly imposed a divorce arrangement" ("Puhru," 487). The epic of Lugalbanda mentions "the wise elders of the city" (*Lugalbanda in the Mountain Cave* i.433, in Black, *Literature of Ancient Sumer*, 20).

29. The story comes from manuscripts *ca.* 1800 BCE, but describes a situation that might have occurred *ca.* 2600. For transliteration and/or translation, see Kramer, "Gilgamesh and Agga," 7–13; and Kramer, "Gilgamesh and Agga," 44–47. Revised translation in Kramer, *Sumerians*, 183–90. See also Cooper, "Gilgamesh and Akka," 235–38. Jacobsen, *Harps that Once*, 345–55. Katz, *Gilgamesh and Akka*, 40–45.

30. Lit. ab-ba-iri^{ki} = fathers of the city.

31. *Gilg.* ii.171–300. See George, *Epic of Gilgamesh*, 21–22; Foster, *Gilgamesh*, 20–22.

32. *Atra.* i.122 (cf. Lambert and Millard, *Atra-ḫasīs*, 51).

33. *Atra.* III.iii.36. In *The Lament over the Destruction of Sumer and Ur* i.364–5 (*ca.* 2000 BCE), we find these words about the gods: "The judgment of the assembly cannot be turned back, The word of An and Enlil knows no overturning" (in Michalowski, *Lament*, 59).

(*ca.* 1000 BCE) reports that having created the universe, "the gods held an assembly" to decide what else to do.³⁴

3.3.2 Egypt

During the reigns of Intef II and III, a funerary stela requests on behalf of Tjetji, the treasurer (2070 BCE), that:

> He may cross the firmament, travers the sky,
> Ascend to the great god . . .
> May he reach the council of the gods.³⁵

3.3.3 Mediterranean

Coming to the Greek tradition, Homer relates the occasion when "the gods were sitting in assembly (*thōkonde*). Among them was Zeus, who thunders on high, whose might is supreme."³⁶ In the *Iliad*, we are told that "Father Zeus drove his wheeled chariot and his horses from Ida to Olympus, and came to the assembly of the gods" (*theōn thōkous*).³⁷

3.3.4 Syro-Palestinian Region

a. The divine assembly

In Ugarit, the divine governing body was called "the assembly of the sons of El" (or: "of the gods").³⁸ A parallelism of three members identifies the gods in terms of the divine assembly (*pḫr*):

> [ ] which the gods do not know,
> [ ] the assembly of the stars (*pḫr kbbm*),
> [ ] the circle of those in the heavens.³⁹

---

34. *Bilingual Story of Creation* i.7–20, in Pettinato, *Das altorientalische Menschenbild*, 74–81.
35. *Stela of the Treasurer Tjetji* 17–20, in Lichtheim, *Ancient Egyptian Literature*, I:93.
36. Homer, *Odyssey* v.3 (cf. Murray, *Odyssey 1–12*, 183).
37. Homer, *Iliad* viii.438 (cf. Murray, *Iliad 1–12*, 383).
38. *Baal Cycle*, CAT 1.4.iii.14 (cf. Smith, "Baal Cycle," 124). Cf. Job 1:6; 2:1; 38:7; Ps 29:1; 89:7.
39. *Baal Fathers a Bull*, CAT 1.10.i.3–4, in Parker, "Baal Fathers a Bull,"182.

Isaiah presents a tyrant king[40] with dreams of divinity, saying:

> [13] To heaven I will ascend;
> higher than the stars of El,
> I will raise my throne.
> I will take my sit on the mountain where the gods assemble,[41]
> on the heights of [mount] Zaphon.[42]
> [14] I will ascend above the highest clouds,
> I will become like Elyon (Isa 14:13-14).

First Isaiah has adapted here an exquisite piece of Canaanite mythology. The stars are the gods of El's pantheon (v. 13), they comprise "the assembly of the stars" (see *CAT* 1.10.i.3-4). And the place where they hold their meetings is none other than Baal's mountain (v. 14). The Qumran community also mentions the "council of the gods" (*sôḏ ʾēlîm*)[43] who assist the Jewish god. The *War Scroll*, which deals with the battle of the end of the times, mentions the so-called "angels" by using the expression "assembly of the gods"(*ăḏat ʾēlîm*).[44] In other words, the angels are recognized as gods.

b. The saints or holy ones (qeḏōšîm)

The gods who form the divine council are called "saints" or "holy ones." The expression is not used in a moral sense, but it refers to the fact that the gods are part of a realm apart from this world. An old inscription (tenth century

---

40. Roberts (*First Isaiah*, 207) suggests that the king might be the Assyrian king Sargon II (765-705 BCE). He crushed all uprisings in Syria and Palestine. He destroyed the kingdom of Samaria (710 BCE), and then demolished Hamath, in Syria. He also gained control of Urartu, Elam, Babylon, Persia and Palestine. But it is impossible to identify the tyrant with any certainty.

41. Lit. "the mountain of the meeting" (*har-môʿēḏ*), but Watts correctly points out that the function of the construct chain is to indicate the place where the gods meet (*Isaiah 1-33*, 206). The word *môʿēḏ* (= meeting) also occurs in the Ugaritic phrase *pḫr mʿd*, translated "the assembled council" (*Cycle of Baal* 1.2.i.14, 20, 31, etc., in Smith, "Baal Cycle," 98-100, 212) or "assembled body" (Ginsberg, "Poems about Baal," 130).

42. The phrase *bəyarkəṯê ṣāpôn* should not be translated "in the uttermost parts of the north" (JPS). The meaning is "on the heights of Zaphon" (NRSV), which is almost identical with the Ugaritic "on the summit of Sapan" (*Baal Cycle*, *CAT* 1.3.i.22, in Smith, "Baal Cycle," 106, cf. 114, 127, etc.). In the *Epic of Kirta*, Kirta's son tells his father: "Father, Baal's mountain will weep for you, Mount Saphon, the holy mountain" (*CAT* 1.16.i.6-8; cf. Greenstein, "Kirta," 31).

43. 4Q181; 4Q511, in Wise, *Dead Sea Scrolls*, 270, 527.

44. 1QM 1.10, in Lohse, *Die Texte aus Qumran*, 180. C. Dupont-Sommer, *Essene Writings*, 171; Wise, *Dead Sea Scrolls*, 148.

BCE) talks about a temple restored by king Yeḥimilk. The inscription records a prayer, asking:

> May Baal Šamēn and Baal of Byblos and the assembly of the holy [qdšm] gods of Byblos lengthen the days of Yeḥimilk . . . because [he is] a loyal king and an upright king before the holy [qdšm] gods of Byblos.[45]

An inscription of the Phoenician king Eshmunazar II of Sidon (ca. 500 BCE) talks about "holy gods" (h'lnm hqdšm).[46] Notice also the parallelism in this text from Ugarit:

> Daniel [gave] the gods . . .
> he gave [the gods] to eat;
> [gave the son]s of the holy ones [to drink].[47]

In a synonymous parallelism, Baal complains:

> As for me, I have no house like the gods,
>   nor a court like the holy ones (qdš).[48]

The Hebrew Bible also refers to the gods as the holy ones:

> Heaven praises your wonders, Yahve,
> and your faithfulness in the convocation of the holy ones (qədōšîm) . . .
> El is astonishing in the council of the holy ones (qədōšîm, Ps 89: 5[6], 7[8]).

Daniel is described as a prophet endowed with "the spirit of the holy gods" (rûaḥ-'ĕlāhîn qaddîšîn, Dan 4:8[5]; 5:11), and we are told that "the holy ones of Elyon shall receive the kingdom" (Dan 7:18). Hosea declares that "Judah still walks[49] with El and is faithful to the holy ones" (pl. qədôšîm,

---

45. *Inscription of Yehimilk* KAI 4, in Green, "I Undertook Great Works", 91.

46. *Inscription of Eshmun-'azar*, in *Corpus Inscriptionum Semiticarum* i.3, line 9; in Cooke, *Text-Book of North Semitic Inscriptions*, 30. See Rosenthal, "Eshmun'azar of Sidon," 662.

47. *Aqhat*, CAT 1.17.i.6–8 (cf. Driver and Gibson, *Canaanite Myths*, 103; Parker, "Aqhat," 52).

48. *Baal Cycle*, CAT 1.2.iii.19–20, in Smith, "Baal Cycle," 97. We find the same thing with the Phoenicians; see Smith and Pitard, *Baal Cycle*, 62.

49. We keep the reading of the MT, which uses the word *rād*, which may derive from *rûd* = roam, wander. The LXX came up with a weird translation: "Now God knows them and they shall be called God's holy people." Inspired by the LXX, Horst has changed *rād* to *yədā'ām*: "But Judah knows God and they are called holy people" (*Die Zwölf kleinen Propheten*, 44).

11:12[12:1]).⁵⁰ In apocalyptic style, Zechariah 14:5 announces: "Then Yahve, my Eloah, will come, and all his holy ones with him." And Jude 14 repeats that "the Lord is coming with tens of thousands of his holy ones (*hagiais*)." The Qumran community also talks about the gods as "the community of your holy ones";⁵¹ or as "the holy ones of El."⁵²

c. The sons of El (*ʾēlîm*, etc.)

We already established that the formula "sons of the gods," and other similar expressions, means "gods" (§2.2.2; §2.4.1). In Ugarit, the divine assembly was comprised by the "sons of El," who was the head of the pantheon:

> May it [the holocaust] ascend to the Father of the sons of El,
> > may it go up to the family of the sons of El,
> > may it go up to the assembly of the sons of El.⁵³

When Baal presents his complaints against Yamm, he says:

> The Beloved came up and insulted me,
> > he arose and spat upon me,
> > in the midst of the ass[emb]ly of the sons of El.⁵⁴

The same description is found in the Hebrew Bible when it talks about the divine council:

> One day the sons of the gods came to present themselves before Yahve, and the prosecutor came among them (Job 1:6; cf. 2:1).

---

50. The MT actually reads *wǝ'im-qǝdôšîm neʾĕmān*, that is, Judah "is faithful to the holy ones" (cf. Smith, *Origins of Biblical Monotheism*, 141). But some want to believe that *qǝdôšîm* is a plural of majesty referring to god, so they translate: "the Holy One" (NRSV, NIV, NLT). See Horst, *Die Zwölf kleinen Propheten*, 44; Schökel and Sicre, *Profetas*, 913.

51. 1QM 12.7. Cf. 1QM 10.11; 15.14; 18.2, etc.

52. 11Q13.9, in García and Tigchelaar, *Dead Sea Scrolls*, 2:1206.

53. *Atonement Ritual*, KTU 1.40 (= CTA 32). Wyatt translates dynamically: "may go up to the Father of the gods, to the pantheon of the gods, to the assembly of the gods" (Wyatt, *Religious Texts from Ugarit*, 345). Cf. De Moore, *Rise of Yahwism*, 340.

54. *Baal Cycle*, CAT 1.4.iii.12–14, in Wyatt, *Religious Texts from Ugarit*, 95–96. Yamm sends messengers (*mlkm*) to the "gathered council" of the gods (*Baal Cycle*, CAT 1.2.i.13–14; cf. Smith, "Baal Cycle," 98). And wishes are expressed that king Kirta may be exalted as a divine hero in the Underworld, among the "assembly of Ditan," (*Epic of Kirta*, CAT 1.15.iii.2–4, 13–15; cf. Driver and Gibson, *Canaanite Myths*, 91–92; Greenstein, "Kirta," 25).

Sons of the gods (*ʾēlîm*),⁵⁵ ascribe to Yahve,
ascribe to Yahve glory and power (Ps 29:1).

11Q13 also describes the gods as the sons of El:

> ⁹ [And Melchizedek] will judge the holy ones of El (*qəḏôšē ʾēl*) with his power, executing judgment ... ¹⁴ To his aid shall come all the sons of El (*bənê ʾēl*).⁵⁶

d. Psalm 89

This hymn deserves separate treatment. By a chain of metaphorical expressions, verses 5-8[6-9] depict a clear mythic scene in which Yahve appears as a cosmic ruler together with his council:

> ⁵ Heaven praises your wonders, Yahve,
>   and your faithfulness in the convocation of the holy ones (*qəḏōšîm*);⁵⁷
> ⁶ For who in the clouds is comparable to Yahve,
>   or is like Yahve among the gods?⁵⁸
> ⁷ El is astonishing in the council of the holy ones (*qəḏōšîm*),
>   great and dreaded⁵⁹ upon all those around him.⁶⁰
> ⁸ Oh Yahve, Elohim of hosts,

---

55. Some versions wrongly translate: "sons of the mighty" (= "powerful men," ASV), or "O ye mighty" (KJV), while others soften to "heavenly beings" (NRSV, NIV, NLT).

56. See García and Tigchelaar, *Dead Sea Scrolls*, 1:1206. For an analysis of this text, see §3.7.1.

57. We just saw that in Ugarit the gods were also called "the holy ones," just as in the Hebrew Bible (Job 5:1; 15:15; Dan 8:13, etc.). Oesterley correctly notes that the convocation mentioned in the text "refers to the gathering of all the gods in council, just as in the Babylonian myth all the gods assembled to decide how best they might be able to meet and overcome their enemy Tiamat. Late Jewish monotheistic teaching explained that the 'gods' were ministers of Yahweh, and wholly subordinated to him" (*Psalms*, 400).

58. The form *ʾēlîm* (= gods) is the plural of *ʾēl* (= god), and cannot be confused with Elohim. Therefore, the expression *biḇnê ʾēlîm* clearly means "among the sons of the gods" or just "gods" (See Oesterley, *Psalms*, 398; Dahood, *Psalms 51-100*, 308). Cf. "Who is like you among the gods" (*bāʾēlîm*, Exod 15:11); "God of gods" (*ʾēl ʾēlîm*, Dan 11:36; 1QM 14:16). See BDB 42; Koehler, *Hebräisches Lexicon*, 47.

59. The MT reads the adv. *rabbāʰ* = "and exceedingly" (cf. "greatly feared," NIV), but we follow the suggestion of the LXX that translates "great and fearsome" (*megas kai phoberos*, cf. NRSV, NJB), understanding the text to say *rab hûʾ* (= "great is he").

60. Schökel and Carniti translate "fearsome to all his court" (*Salmos II*, 1140), expressing clearly the identity of those who surround Yahve.

> who is like you, O mighty Yah,
> with your faithful around you?[61]

The passage depicts a mythic scene in Heaven in which the king-god rules in the midst of a senate comprised by other gods. This surely complies with MacKenzie's arbitrary rule that a myth must feature at least two gods and talk about an event in Heaven (§1.2.2). But there is no monotheism here. The text admits the existence of other gods even when they are consigned to the position of an advisory council. Just as in Ugarit, this psalm calls the gods "saints" (or "holy ones," *qəḏōšîm*, vv. 5[6], 7[8]). They are identified as "sons of the gods" (*bənê ʾēlîm*, v. 6[7]). It is important to mention that in verse 6[7] some versions distort the meaning of the text by translating "sons of the mighty" (KJV, NAS) or "sons of might" (JPS). The passage is not referring to human rulers or powerful people.

e. Psalm 82[62]

This is another psalm that merits a more detailed analysis. Samuel Terrien designates it with the title "The death of the gods."[63] This is because Elohim pronounces capital punishment against the gods for threatening the human social order. Today people would find the story a bit off-the-wall, so Beth Tanner feels the need to warn us that:

> Psalm 82 places the modern reader in a very unfamiliar world. Modern thinking holds to a monotheistic theology, meaning there is only one god and the gods of others simply do not exist. Ancient Israel did not have the same definition of monotheism. Indeed, for them not only did other gods exist, but those gods were active in the world. This psalm gives us a window on the assembly of the gods, a place where the gods are gathered to make decisions about the world. This council is part of the greater Ancient Near Eastern mythology and would be a familiar image to ancient Israelites.[64]

---

61. With Dahood (*Psalms 51–100*, 308), we take the abstract *wǝʾĕmûnāṯḵā səḇîḇôṯeʸḵā* (lit. "your faithfulness around you") as concrete "your faithful around you," following what the former verse suggests by "all those around him."

62. At the end of the chapter, we will use this psalm as a case study (§3.7).

63. Terrien, *Psalms*, 586.

64. De Claissé-Walford, *Psalms*, 641. Clifford warns in similar fashion: "The vivid mythology in the psalm may surprise readers who assume that mythology characterizes Canaanite religious literature, whereas history characterizes biblical literature. It is a mistake, however, to make a dichotomous distinction between history and myth in

Let's take a look at Psalm 82:

Prophetic vision: Elohim opens proceedings against the gods

> ¹Elohim stands up in the assembly of El,⁶⁵
> > in the midst of the gods he renders verdict.

Elohim recriminates the gods

> ²How long will you judge unjustly
> > and will take the side of the wicked?

Duties neglected by the gods

> ³Do justice to the weak and the orphan,
> > maintain the rights of the poor and destitute.
> ⁴Rescue the week and the indigent,
> > deliver them from the hand [= power] of the wicked.

Cause of their sin

> ⁵They have neither knowledge nor understanding,
> > they wander in darkness,
> > while all the foundations of the earth are shaken.⁶⁶

Sentence against the gods

> ⁶Therefore, I declare: even when you are gods,
> > sons of Elyon, all of you,
> ⁷you shall die like mere mortals,
> > and fall like every other ruler.

The seer who saw the heavenly vision makes a request

> ⁸Rise up, Elohim, judge the earth,
> > for all the nations belong to you.

---

the Ancient East and to suppose that biblical writers did not employ the language and imagery of the day for their God" (*Psalms 73–150*, 64).

65. Some versions paraphrase v. 1 by saying "divine council" (NRSV) or "divine assembly" (NJB, cf. NIV), but the text talks about "the assembly of El" (*'ăḏaṯ-'ēl*). The *Epic of Kirta* uses a similar expression to talk about a "company of gods" (*'dt ilm*, CAT 1.15. ii.7, 11). Other similar expressions were "assembly of the stars" (§3.3.4.a) or "assembly of the sons of El" (§3.3.4.c)

66. We understand this verse as a further accusation against the gods, but Oesterley (*Psalms*, 374) may be right when argues that it rather refers to the desperate situation of the poor.

A vision gives a prophet access into the divine council. He has the privilege of witnessing the moment when Elohim "stands up" (anthropomorphism) to begin court proceedings. Then the supreme god himself addresses the defendants (vv. 2–7).[67] This psalm certifies that the gods are not just the gods of nature, detached from history (§1.2.3). The psalm reflects the standard idea of the Ancient Near East that the gods ruled the world. Each city had a patron god or goddess. Justice in society was the responsibility of kings and gods. Deuteronomy 4:19 cautions Israel not to worship the astral gods, for they were not allotted to Israel but "to all the peoples under heaven" (cf. Deut 29:29). Daniel 10:13, 20–21 and 12:1 talk about the patron gods of Persia, Greece and Israel.

Deuteronomy 32:8–9 adopts the same theology. It claims that at the beginning of the world ("the days of old," v. 7),[68] the supreme god Elyon appointed gods to rule over the nations. Again, it is important to grasp that in this passage *'elyôn* (or Most High) does not refer to Yahve, but to the head of the Canaanite pantheon (cf. Gen 14:17–20). In this story Yahve is presented as one of the "sons of the gods," and had not yet been elevated to the position of supreme god. So it is Elyon who assigns Yahve the role of guardian of Israel, as he assigns other gods the supervision of the nations:[69]

> [8] When Elyon apportioned the nations their heritance,
>   when he dispersed humankind,
> he established the boundaries of the peoples
>   according to the number of the gods.[70]
> [9] And the portion that fell on Yahve was his people,
>   Jacob was the territory allotted to him.

---

67. Thus Gunkel, *Salmos*, 376; Gerstenberger, *Psalms*, 113; Schökel and Carniti, *Salmos II*, 1076; Tate, *Psalms 51–100*, 334. However, Goldingay, *Psalms 42–89*, 563, believes that it is the prophet who speaks in vv. 2–7.

68. Lundbom notes that Deut 32:7–14 provides a story about the origin of Israel. First, the mythographer talks about the beginning of the world in ancient times (vv. 7–9), reaching "back into the pre-Israelite mythic past when the Most High gave to each nation its inheritance" (Lundbom, *Deuteronomy*, 876). Second, it describes how the Hebrew god took care of his people in the desert (vv. 10–12). And finally, it narrates how the god gave them the Promised Land (vv. 13–14).

69. See Blenkinsopp, *Treasures*, 73–74; Gaster, *Myth*, 318; Zobel, "'elyôn," 11:128. For the development of the concept of the god of Israel, see Cross, *Cannanite Myth and Hebrew Epic*; Eissfeldt, "El and Yahweh"; Smith, *Origins of Biblical Monotheism* and *Early History of God*.

70. Lit. "the sons of the gods." We follow here the reading of column xii of 4QDeut[j] (or: 4Q37), where we find *banê 'ēlîm*. See Abegg, *Dead Sea Scrolls*, 191.

Note: Let's pause for a moment to show how a tradition is subject to change according to the theological taste of its handlers. Following the MT, the NIV reads "sons of Israel" (Deut 32:8). But the DSS contain what is, without a doubt, the original reading: "the sons of the gods" (*banê ʾēlîm*, 4QDeut^j or 4Q37).[71] The LXX also uses a similar expression: "angels of god" (*aggelōn theou*). But a faction of Judaism found unbearable the phrase "sons of the gods." This discomfort is reflected in the MT, which reads "sons of Israel." The editorial change aims to avoid the theological quagmire of having Elyon placing the gods in charge of the nations (v. 8) and Yahve in charge of only Israel (v. 9).

In tune with the theology of Deuteronomy 32:8–9, Greek mythology proposed that the gods were in charge of securing justice in society. Hesiod (*ca.* 700 BCE) relates that, once the Golden Race died, their members "became, by the will of Supreme Zeus, good gods upon the earth; the guardians (*fulakes*) of mortal human beings; and who watch (*fulassousin*) judicial sentences and merciless deeds. Dressed in haze[72] they roam through all the earth."[73] Then Hesiod issues a warning to the kings, saying that:

> Among humankind there are immortals (= gods) nearby, watching all those who wrong one another with false verdicts and who don't care about the vengeance of the gods. Thirty thousand upon the abundant earth are Zeus' immortals, the guards of human beings; and who guard judicial sentences and merciless deeds. Dressed in haze they roam through all the earth.[74]

Psalm 82 adopts the same theology: "The charge against the gods is not that they are idols or nonexistent but that they have failed to put down wickedness and bring justice."[75] If we ask why the poor suffered, this psalm argues that it is because the gods were corrupt. Therefore, they were condemned

---

71. Translations like "sons of god" (RSV) or "children of god" (NJB) are misleading. They may give the impression that "god" refers to Yahve. The DSS do not use the singular "god" but the plural "gods" (*ʾēlîm*, cf. "gods," NRSV). The majority of modern commentators also prefer the DSS reading. See Lundbom, *Deuteronomy*, 849; Pakkala, *God's Word Omitted*, 186; Christensen, *Deuteronomy*, 790; Crawford, "Textual Criticism," 319; Fox, *Five Books of Moses*, 1002; Mayes, *Deuteronomy*, 384; McConville, *Deuteronomy*, 444; Nelson, *Deuteronomy*, 363; Von Rad, *Deuteronomy*, 192; Work, *Deuteronomy*, 283.

72. Or: "clad in invisibility."

73. Hesiod, *Works and Days* 122–24 (cf. Most, *Hesiod*, 97).

74. Hesiod, *Works and Days* 249–54.

75. Mays, *Psalms*, 269. This situation reminds us of the episode when Yahve issued his verdict against the gods of Egypt: "I will execute judgment on all the gods of Egypt" (Exod 12:12).

to die, and Elohim takes their place in order to secure justice in the world (even when life teaches us every day that nothing really changed with this new cosmic government. The world continued to be overwhelmed by abuse and violence.).[76]

3.3.5 Summary of the Terminology Used to Refer to the Gods in the Hebrew Bible

In reviewing the following expressions, we should remind ourselves that the Hebrew Bible does not use these terms to "mean 'angels'—a typical gloss put on it by a later insistence on a panbiblical monotheism—but 'gods.'"[77] Let's review the main expressions used to talk about the divine council:

Hebrew Bible terms used to refer to the gods

Hebrew term	Meaning
ʾabbîrîm	= hero, brave (Ps 78:25; cf. Ps 103:20)
ʾĕlōhîm	= gods (Exod 12:12; 15:11; 18:11; 20:3; Pss 82:1, 6; 86:8; 96:5; 138:1)
ʾēlīm	= gods (Exod 15:11; cf. sing. "You shall not worship another El," Exod 34:14. Cf. Ps 44:20[21])
ʾĕlôᵃh	= god (2 Chr 32:15; Dan 11:37; Hab 1:11)
bənê ʿelyôn	= sons of Elyon or Most High (Ps 82:6)[78]
bənê ʾēlîm	= sons of the gods = "gods" (Pss 29:1; 89:6[7]; Deut 32:8 = 4QDeutʲ)
bənê-hāʾĕlōhîm	= sons of the gods = "gods" (Gen 6:2, 4; Job 1:6; 2:1; bənê ʾĕlōhîm Job 38:7; cf. Wis 5:5)
ʿădat-ʾēl	= assembly of El (Ps 82:1; cf. 1QM1.10)
qədôšîm	= holy ones, saints (Hos 11:12[12:1])
ʾĕlāhîn qaddîšîn	= holy gods (Dan 4:8, 9, 18[5, 6, 15]; 5:11)
qəhal qədôšîm	= convocation of the saints or holy ones (Ps 89:5[6]; cf. Wis 5:5)
sôd-qədôšîm	= council of the saints (Ps 89:7[8]). Cf. Job 5:1; 15:15; Dan 4:17[14]; Zech 14:5

---

76. In Isa 24:21, both gods ("the host of heaven") and their kings are punished.

77. Wyatt, "Titles of the Ugaritic Storm-God," 407 n. 21, who is referring specifically to the following texts: Gen 6:1, 2; Job 2:1; 38:7; Ps 21:1; 89:7[8].

78. Baal is also called Most High: "Look to the earth for Baal's rain; to the field, for the Most High's rain." *Epic of Kirta*, CAT 1.16.iii.7–8, in Greenstein, "Kirta," 35.

3.4 The Hero

3.4.1 God or Demigod by Birth

Heroes merit a separate treatment. Kings were part of this group for they were heroes par excellence.[79] The Greek word *hērōs* means "equal to the gods, divinity, patron god of a city." Kings and heroes received titles like *antitheos* = "equal to the gods, divine,"[80] *theoeikelos* = "godlike,"[81] *diogenēs* = "sprung from Zeus,"[82] *theoeidēs* = "akin to the gods."[83] When Socrates (*ca.* 470–399 BCE) was asked about the meaning of the word "hero," he responded:

> They [i.e., the heroes] were born
> when a god made love (*erasthentos*) with a mortal woman,
> or a mortal man made love with a goddess.[84]

Homer (*ca.* 850 BCE) illustrates Socrates' definition with an exquisite story that narrates how goddess Aphrodite (= Venus) fell in love with the mortal Anchises, whose forms were like those of the "immortal gods."[85] When he saw Aphrodite, he also fell in love with her. She deceived him saying that she was only a woman that wanted to be his wife and have children. And then:

> ... by the will of the gods and Fortune,[86] he laid with her, a mortal man with an immortal goddess, not clearly knowing what he was doing.[87]

When Anchises realized that his lover was a goddess, he was filled with terror. But she calmed him down, and promised him that their union would result in the birth of a hero:

---

79. This section should be read together with §4.3.3.

80. Cf. Homer, *Iliad* v.663. Pindar talks about the "divine heroes" (*hērōes antitheoi*), in *Pythian* i.53; iv.58 (cf. Sandys, *Pindar*, 161, 205).

81. Heroes like Achilles (*Iliad* i.131; xix.155) and Telemachus (*Odyssey* iii.416) are referred to as "godlike."

82. Achilles is called *diogenēs* in *Iliad* i.489; as well as Odysseus in *Odyssey* ii.352.

83. *Iliad* iii.16, 27, 30; xxiv.217; *Odyssey* xiv.173.

84. Plato, *Cratylus* 398d, in Burnet, *Platonis Opera*, vol. I (cf. Jowett, *Dialogues of Plato*, 341).

85. Homer, *Hymn 5 to Aphrodite* 55, in Evelyn-White, *Homeric Hymns*, 411. This implies that the gods looked like human beings of great beauty and strength.

86. Goddess *Aisa* (= Fortune) allotted people their destinies. See Homer, *Iliad* xx.127; *Odyssey* vii.197.

87. Homer, *Hymn 5 to Aphrodite* 165 (cf. in Evelyn-White, *Homeric Hymns*, 417).

> You are loved by the gods, and you shall have a dear son who shall reign among the Trojans, and so the children's children after him, being born continually. His name shall be Aeneas.[88]

Born of a human father and a divine mother, Aeneas grew to be one of the heroes of the Trojan War. The legend says that, after the fall of Troy, Aeneas escaped to Italy where he became the progenitor of the Romans through his son Ascanius. As part of the *gens Iulia*, Julius Caesar claimed to be the descended of the legendary Aeneas.

Genesis mentions heroes born from marriages between gods and mortal women: "these were the heroes of old, famous warriors" (Gen 6:4).[89] Diodorus Siculos (90–30 BCE) relates that the mother of Hercules (or Heracles) was a mortal woman (Alcmene) and his father a god (Zeus).[90] Achilles, the central figure of the Trojan War, had goddess Thetis as his mother and the mortal Peleus as his father.[91] The historian and philosopher, Lucius Flavius Arrianus (ca. 86–160 CE) ends his work about Alexander the Great (*The Anabasis of Alexander*), mentioning the divinity of the conquistador:

> Therefore, it seems to me that a man totally unlike any other human being could not have been born without divine agency (*exō tou theiou*). And this is said to have been revealed after Alexander's death by oracle responses, by the apparitions (*fasmata*) that presented themselves to various people, and by the dreams which were seen by different individuals. It is also shown by the honors paid to him by men up to the present time, and by the remembrance which is still held of him as someone more than human. Even at the present time, after so long a time, the nation of the Macedonians receive oracular responses in his honor . . . For this reason, I undertook the task of writing this history not without God's inspiration.[92]

---

88. Homer, *Hymn 5 to Aphrodite* 195–98. In the *Iliad* (ii.821), Aeneas is described as the one "whom Aphrodite conceived to Anchises among the mountainsides of Ida, a goddess copulating with a mortal."

89. The Ugaritic Daniel is called "Daniel, man of Rapiu, the hero, the man of Harnemite" (*Aqhat*, CAT 1.17.v.4–5, in Parker, "Aqhat," 58), but he's not referred to as having a divine birth.

90. Diodorus, *Bibliotheca Historica* iv.9.1, in Bekker, *Diodori*, 409 (cf. Oldfather, *Diodorus*, 369–70). In fact, the idea of a god impregnating a mortal woman is very old. See §3.4.1; §4.3.3.

91. Hesiod, *Theo.* 240–45 (in Most, *Hesiod*, 23) presents Thetis as the goddess of the sea. In one occasion, she says to Achilles: "I gave birth to you in the palace" (*Iliad* i.418). Ovid (43 BCE–17 CE) relates how Proteus prophesied that Thetis would be the mother of a man who would achieve great marvels (Ovid, *Metamorphoses* xi.221–24).

92. Flavius Arrianus, *Anabasis Alexandri* vii.30.2–3, in Roos, *Flavii Arriani*, 333.

3.4.2 Divinization at Death

In older times, Heaven was a place reserved only for the gods (§3.5). However, the legends recount that Alexander the Great, Moses, Hercules, Julius Caesar, Caesar Augustus, Jesus and other heroes, all ascended to Heaven. These ascensions to the divine world were extraordinary events, for the rule was that at death all mortals descended to the Underworld (§3.6). The old theology taught that to go up to Heaven to become a god was reserved only for very special people. It was this exceptional experience that allowed Elijah and Moses to show up during Jesus' transfiguration (Mark 9:1–8). Those who died couldn't come back to this world in a bodily manner. Only those who were transposed to Heaven had this privilege.

Pseudo-Callisthenes (third century BCE) talks about the divinization of Alexander the Great. Instead of saying that he was begotten by a god (§3.4.1), he asserts that his divinization occurred at the moment of his death:

> ... a dark mist crossed the sky and a bolt of lightning was seen to fall from heaven into the sea and with it a great Eagle. And the bronze statue of Aramazd in Babylon quivered; and the lightning ascended into heaven and the eagle went with it, taking with it a radiant star.[93] And when the star disappeared in the sky, Alexander too had shut his eyes.[94]

According to Diodorus Siculos (90–30 BCE), the gods promised Hercules the gift of "immortality" (*athanasia*),[95] which he obtained in a very peculiar way. It happened that Nessus tried to rape Deianeira his wife. So Hercules shot a poisoned arrow right into Nessus' heart, killing him. While he was dying, Nessus told Deianeira that the blood of his heart was a magic potion that would secure her Hercules' eternal love, knowing that the poisoned blood would kill Hercules. Deianeira was jealous of Iole whom Hercules loved, and in desperation placed the blood on his tunic. Hercules got fatally sick. When Deianeira realized what she had done, she took her own life (Greek tragedy!). Hercules then consulted Apollos about how to get well but the god answered him that he needed to be cremated on a pyre. "Having lost all hope, Hercules climbed on to a pyre and asked each one of those present to come up and place a torch on the pyre." Philoctetes was the only one who dared set it on fire, and:

---

93. Jesus is also called: "the bright morning star" (Rev 22:16).

94. Pseudo-Callisthenes, *Romance of Alexander the Great* 281, in Wolohojian, *Romance*, 157. See Polybius, *Histories* xii.23.4–5, in Büttner-Wobst, *Polybius Historiae*, 206.

95. Diodorus, *Bibliotheca Historica* iv.10.7, in Bekker, *Diodori*, 411.

> Immediately, a bolt fell from the sky and the pyre was completely consumed. Later, when the friends of Iolaus came to gather Hercules' bones, they weren't able to find even a single bone anywhere. Therefore, they believed that, according to the words of the oracle, he [Hercules] had left men to go to the gods (*ex anthrōpōn eis theous methestasthai*).[96]

It is important to note that it was not only Hercules' soul that ascended to Heaven. His friends couldn't find "a single bone" because the hero ascended in body and soul, purified and transformed by fire, in order to be immortalized. Hesiod adds that Hercules "is today a god, escaping all evil, and he lives with those who have their mansions in the Olympus, those who are immortal and have no years."[97]

Early Judaism applied the divinized-hero tradition to Moses. Ecclesiasticus (or Ben Sirach) 45:2 maintains that the Jewish god created Moses "equal in glory to the holy ones," which means "he gave him the glory of the gods."[98] Philo of Alexandria (25 BCE—50 CE) argues that Moses was one of the people to whom the Jewish god enabled:

> to soar above all species and genus, having placed them beside himself, as he said to Moses: 'stand here with me.' [Deut 5:31]. So when Moses was about to die . . . 'by means of the word' [*rēmatos*, Deut 34:5] of the supreme Cause, he was transferred (from this world) . . . Therefore, understand that God considers the righteous as having the same value as the world, having created everything and having elevated to himself the perfect man from earthly material by the logos.[99]

And Philo adds that this god gave Moses the power to "rule over the passions of the soul" and that he "appointed him to be a god" (*eis theon echeirotonei*, cf. Exod 7:1).[100] Philo even says that Moses "was named god and king of the whole nation" of Israel (*holou tou ethnous theos kai basileus*).[101] Moses' depiction as a divine person is elaborated in this way:

> But God is not susceptible of subtraction or addition, inasmuch as he is complete and entirely equal to himself. For which reason we are also told 'that no one knows of his grave' [Deut 34:6]

---

96. Diodorus, *Bibliotheca Historica* iv.38.1–5, in Bekker, *Diodori*, 456–57.
97. Hesiod, *Catalogue of Women* xxii.25–27, in Most, *Hesiod*, 77.
98. The expression "the holy ones" refers to the gods (§3.3.4.b).
99. Philo, *De sacrificiis Abelis et Caini* i. 8 (cf. Colson and Whitaker, *Philo*, 2:99).
100. Philo, *De sacrificiis Abelis et Caini* i. 9.
101. Philo, *De vita Mosis* i.158 (cf. Colson, *Philo*, 6:357).

for who could be competent to contemplate the migration of a perfect soul to the Being? Nor do I expect that the soul [of Moses], while awaiting this event, was conscious of its own improvement, for at that time it was becoming divine.[102]

Philo describes Moses' ascension to Heaven with these words:

> Afterwards, when [Moses] was about to begin his migration to heaven, leaving this mortal life to become immortal (*apathanatidsesthai*), having been summoned by the Father, who transformed him—having previously been a double being composed of soul and body—into a simple nature, transforming him wholly and entirely into a beaming mind . . . In fact, when [Moses] was being taken away and stood at the very line of departure, ready to direct his journey flying to heaven . . . he prophesied . . . Such was the life and such was the death of the king, lawgiver, high priest, and prophet, Moses, as it is recorded in the sacred scriptures.[103]

After his tragic death, Julius Caesar (100–44 BCE) was divinized, and a temple was built in his honor (*Aedes Divi Iuli*). The historian Gaius Suetonius (*ca.* 69–126 CE) describes his apotheosis in this way:

> He died when he was fifty-six years old, and was ranked amongst the gods, not only by a formal decree, but by the conviction of the people. For during the first games which Augustus, his heir, consecrated to his memory, a comet (*stella crinita*) glowed continuously for seven days, rising always about the eleventh hour; and it was believed to be the soul of Caesar, now received into heaven. This is why a star was placed on his statue on top of his statue.[104]

When dealing with Caesar Augustus (Gaius Octavius), the historian Dio Cassius (155–235 CE) mentions that because of all his noble deeds the emperor became a god:

> Therefore, it was for all of this that you . . . made him a *hērōa* [= demigod] and declared him to be immortal (*athanaton*). Hence

---

102. Philo, *De sacrificiis Abelis et Caini* i. 9–10.

103. Philo, *De vita Mosis* ii.288–92. Note though that the Hebrew Bible never mentions anywhere that Moses ascended to Heaven.

104. Suetonius, *Divus Julius* lxxxviii.1–4, in Ihm, *Suetonii*, 47. See Dio Cassius, who says that a comet appeared in the sky, and the majority of the people believe it meant that Caesar "had become immortal and had been received into the number of the stars," that is, the gods (*Historiae Romanae* xlv.6.7, in Cary, *Dio's Roman History*, 4:419).

it is appropriate also that we should not lament because of him but ... we should glorify his soul as that of a god (*hōs kai theou*) forever.[105]

Moreover, when Augustus died, the senator Numerius Atticus "swore that he had seen Augustus ascending to heaven (*es ton ouranon anionta*) in the same way the tradition talks about Proculus and Romulus."[106] Suetonius adds that a member of the praetorium swore upon oath "that he saw his cremated image ascending to heaven."[107] In the same way as we have been told regarding Jesus, the "eye witnesses" here testify that they saw the emperor ascending to Heaven.

Written during the Hellenistic period, the *Book of Wisdom* did not limit divinization to kings and heroes but it also mentioned the glorious end of the righteous in general. It first depicts the wicked plotting to kill the righteous (2:12–20), and talks about the premature death of the righteous, which provokes the derision on the part of the wicked who live longer lives (4:7–18). But in the Day of Judgment, the wicked are forced to recognize their mistake (5:1–5), and they are astonished at the vindication of the righteous which occurs when he is promoted to divine life:

> How did he come to be counted
> among the gods,[108]
> and to have his lot
> among the holy ones? (5:5)[109]

Finally, Christianity borrowed the three known mechanisms of divinization and applied them to the historical Jesus. First, it was argued that he became a divine king when his mother got pregnant by a god (§3.4.1 and 4.3.3.e).

---

105. Dio Cassius, *Historiae Romanae* lvi.41.9 (cf. Cary, *Dio's Roman History*, 7:97).

106. Dio Cassius, *Historiae Romanae* lvi.46.2 (cf. Cary, *Dio's Roman History*, 7:105). Titus Livius (59 BCE–17 CE) says that when Romulus attended a muster in Campus Martius, "suddenly rose a storm with thundering clouds and a thick cloud surrounded him, hiding him from the sight of the assembly; and from that moment Romulus disappeared from earth." After the storm was over, the soldiers "saw that the royal throne was empty," and they believed what the senators were saying, that Romulus "had been caught up on high in the blast." Therefore, "all hailed Romulus as a god and a son of god, the King and Father of the Roman city and with prayers implored his favor ..." (Titus Livius, *History of Rome* i.16.1–3; cf. Foster, *History of Rome*, I:57–9).

107. Suetonius, *Divus Augustus* c.4, in Ihm, *Suetonii*, 116.

108. Lit. *huioi zeou* = "the sons of god" = "gods." See §3.3.4.c.

109. The parallel expressions "sons of god" and "holy ones" point to the gods who comprise the heavenly court. See §3.3.4.b–c and Nickelsburg, *Resurrection, Immortality, and Eternal Life*, 81. For the divinization of mankind as a Hellenistic and Christian project, see §2.3.1.c (and the *Shepherd of Hermas*, similitude ix.27.2–3).

Second, the legend avers that Jesus was the *logos*, the secondary god of Hellenism, who came into the world to become a man (John 1:1–10, §2.3.3). And third, another tradition states that he was made into a god after his death (§3.4.2). It is important to clarify here that Greeks and Romans cremated their dead, while Semites buried them. This explains why Hercules and Augustus were divinized by fire, while Jesus became god at his resurrection from a grave. Finally, although Jesus' resurrection is a mythological construct, there is no doubt he was a real human being.[110] The Jesus myth only compels us to recognize that in that time the life and deeds of a holy man were usually narrated "in the form of a legend,"[111] and heroes were described as divine.

3.5 Heaven

In ancient times, the universe was thought to be divided into three realms: "heaven and earth and underworld" (Phil 2:10). In this section we will focus on Heaven. The bodily character of the gods compelled mythographers to assign them a habitat. A body needs a place, and that place was described anthropomorphically: it was a city or a palace in Heaven or on a mountain. Their residence was also described geographically: Heaven is up there. Of course, this representation comes from a cosmology we no longer accept *literally*. If we use telescopes or satellites to look at the skies, we won't be able to find the gods described in the old myths.

3.5.1 Mesopotamia and Egypt

Enūma Eliš (ca. 1595–1105 BCE) declares that, at the very beginning of the world, Marduk built a temple in Heaven for the Babylonian trinity:

> The great temple of Ešarra, that he built, (is in) heaven,
> where he made Anu, Enlil and Ea dwell in their sanctuaries.[112]

---

110. "Of course the doubt as to whether Jesus really existed is unfounded and not worth of refutation. No sane person can doubt that Jesus stands as the founder behind the historical movement whose first distinct stage is represented by the oldest Palestinian community" (Bultmann, *Jesus and the Word*, 13).

111. Dibelius, *Formgeschichte*, 106. "The Christ who is proclaimed is not the historical Jesus, but the Christ of the faith and the cult. Therefore, in the foreground of the proclamation of Christ stands the death and resurrection of Jesus Christ as the saving acts which are known by faith" (Bultmann, *Historia de la Tradición*, 432).

112. *En. el.* iv.145–6 (cf. Foster, *Before the Muses*, 462).

Then Marduk built the city of Babylon so the gods could have a place to live when visiting from Heaven:

> When you descend from heaven for the [assembly],
>> here you'll find your resting place, before the assembly.
>
> I shall call its name [Baby]lon,
>> the houses of the great gods.[113]

As a copy of our earthly reality, Heaven is depicted as a walled city. When Marduk created Heaven, "he opened gates on both sides (of Heaven), and put strong bolts left and right."[114] Ašur answers the prayer of a supplicant, saying: "I have heard your cry of distress, and I will descend from the gate of heaven."[115] Another prayer says: "Šamaš, you have opened the locks of the gates of Heaven. You have gone up by the staircase of pure lapis lazuli."[116] An Egyptian inscription dedicated to Nebneteru (ca. 1550 BCE), also mentions the walled city of Heaven with its gates: "(the god Amun) He granted my office of door-opener of heaven, He appointed me intimate of the palace."[117]

3.5.2 Mediterranean

Since the residence of the gods is in Heaven, they are called *ouraniōnoi* = "heavenly."[118] Homer (*ca.* 800–701 BCE) informs us that Heaven is Zeus' residence:

---

113. *En. el.* v.127–29 (cf. Lambert, *Babylonian Creation Myths*, 99).

114. *En. el.* v.9, 10.

115. Cf. "Abullu," 87. The text uses the expression KA.GAL *šame* (= gate of Heaven), borrowing the Sumerian term ka-gal (= big gate). Its Akkadian equivalent is *abullu* (= "gate" of a town or building; see *Gilg.* xi.221, in Foster, *Gilgamesh*, 91). For example, *Erra and Ishum* iv.13 talks about "the gate of the city of Babylon" (see Foster, *Before the Muses*, 902; Dalley, *Myths from Mesopotamia*, 303).

116. *Babylonian Prayer* HSM 7494, in Heimpel "Sun at Night" 133. Cf. "Utu, when you emerge from the interior of pure heaven . . . when you open the big gate of pure heaven" (*Fourth Prayer of the Household*, in Heimpel, "Sun at Night," 130). Enlil gives god Emeš the task of closing "the gates of heaven" (Vanstiphout, "Debate between Summer and Winter," i.9; see Bottéro-Kramer, *Cuando los Dioses*, 493–94).

117. *Inscription of Nebneteru*, left side 5–8, in Lichtheim, *Ancient Egypt Literature*, 3:22.

118. Homer, *Iliad* i.570; v.373; Hesiod, *Theo.* 461, 919.

Zeus, the most noble, the greatest, covered with dark clouds,[119] who dwells in heaven.[120]

During the war against the Titans, we are told that: "Zeus did not hold his power anymore but his breast was filled with strength and he manifested his full force. He immediately marched from Heaven and the Olympus, relentlessly throwing lightning bolts."[121] The *Iliad* describes an exquisite scene in the divine world:

> The immortal gods came to the Olympus, all at once, and Zeus led the way. [Goddess] Thetis did not forget the charge she received from her son [Achilles], but early in the morning rose up from the waves of the sea, and mounted up to great heaven and Olympus.[122]

The Greek tradition also takes up the metaphor of Heaven as a walled-gated city:

> Athene, daughter of Zeus . . . put on the tunic of Zeus that gathers the clouds, and arrayed herself in armor for the painful war . . . Then she stepped on the fiery chariot and grasped her heavy, huge and strong spear . . . Then Hera [Zeus' wife] swiftly touched the horses with the whip, and by their own impulse the gates of heaven opened on their hinges, grinding the gates of heaven (*pulai ouranou*), the gates that are kept by the Hours, to whom great heaven and Olympus have been entrusted in order to open or shut the thick cloud.[123]

3.5.3 Syro-Palestinian Region

In Ugarit, king Kirta is told:

> Lift up your hands to heaven,
> and sacrifice to the bull El, your father.[124]

---

119. Coming down from his temple in Heaven, Yahve is portrayed as "covered in a canopy of darkness, gathering waters and thick clouds" (2 Sam 22:12).
120. Homer, *Iliad* ii.410.
121. Hesiod, *Theo.* 687.
122. Homer, *Iliad* i.493-95.
123. Homer, *Iliad* v.735-37.
124. *Epic of Kirta*, CAT 1.14.ii.22-24 (cf. Greenstein, "Kirta," 14). See Driver and Gibson, *Canaanite Myths*, 84.

The Ugaritic king Daniel "pres[ents] a meal for the gods, into the heavens he sends incense, [to the] stars the Harnenites's incense."[125] We are told that the gods are "the circle of those in the heavens."[126]

In Israel, Yahve's "holy dwelling" is in Heaven (Deut 26:15; 2 Chr 30:27, etc.). Yahve also descends (Gen 11:5), talks (Exod 20:22), punishes (Gen 19:24) or battles (Josh 10:11) "from Heaven." Yahve opens the gates of his celestial city to drop down manna like rain (Ps 78:23–24). Heaven itself contains a palace or temple for the king-god (Ps 11:4; Isa 6:1; 63:15). *First Enoch* describes Enoch going through all the gates of the Heavens (chapters 17–36). *Second Enoch* relates that Enoch toured the Heavens, until he arrived to the "seventh heaven."[127] *Third Baruch* says:

> And the powerful angel took me and led me to the fifth heaven. And he showed me large gates . . . , and they were closed. And I said, "Lord, will these gates open so that we can enter through them?" And the angel said to me: "It is not possible to enter through them until Michael, the holder of the keys of the kingdom, comes." And the angel said to me, "Wait and you will see the glory of God."[128]

3.5.4 Christian Bible

In the same way that Zeus is the "god of heaven,"[129] the Christian god is the "god of heaven" (Rev 11:13; 16:11). When we pray, we say "our Father in heaven" (Matt 6:9),[130] where he has a throne (Matt 5:34; 23:22; cf. Heb 8:1) and a temple (Rev 11:19). Just as all the other gods, this god lets his voice be heard "from heaven" (Matt 3:17). The book of Hebrews exploits the mythical concept of a temple in Heaven. Jesus is described as the perfect king and high priest who "went into heaven" (Heb 4:14) and "sat at the right hand of the throne of the Majesty in heaven" (8:1). There he's acting as *leitourgos* of the "true" sanctuary and tabernacle (8:2), which is not "earthly" (9:1) or "handmade, that is, from this creation" (9:11; cf. 9:23). Therefore,

---

125. *Aqhat*, CAT 1.19.iv.22–25, in Parker, "Aqhat," 76. See Driver and Gibson, *Canaanite Myths*, 120.

126. *Baal Fathers a Bull*, CAT 1.10.i.3–4.

127. *2 En.* 20:1, in Andersen, "2 Enoch," 134.

128. *3 Bar.* 11:1–2, in Gaylor, "3 Baruch," 675. The Apostle Paul claims that he was taken to the "third heaven" (2 Cor 12:2).

129. Hesiod, *Theo.* 71.

130. Cf. Matt 5:16, 45; 7:11, etc.

metaphorically "Christ ... entered into heaven itself" (9:24) to remove sin by his own sacrifice. All of this is mythology.

3.6 Underworld[131]

Although a god could punish someone with death, the Ancient Near East did not teach that the Underworld was a place of punishment nor did it know the doctrine that in the hereafter there are separate places for the righteous and the wicked. Neither was it acquainted with Hell as a place of punishment. As opposed to Heaven above, the Underworld was a place under the ground; a place where all humans went after death. This is why the Hebrew Bible sometimes employs the word ʾereṣ (= earth, ground, soil, land) to refer to the Underworld:

> ... all of them have been handed over to Death,
>
> to the underworld (ʾereṣ) below (Ezek 31:14. Cf. Exod 15:12; Ps 63:9[10]).[132]

We find the same picture in Ugarit. The Underworld is conceived of as located under the "earth" (arṣ). When Baal sends his emissaries to Mot (= Death), he instructs them using the language employed to describe those who die:

> Then descend to the house of seclusion within the earth (arṣ),
>
> you must be counted among those who go down into the earth (arṣ).[133]

The *Epic of Gilgameš* reveals that the king's adventures brought him to the mythic mountains, which were so high that they touched the Heavens and so deep that they reached into the Underworld (*arallû*):

> To Mashu's twin mountains he came,
>
> > which daily guard the rising [sun,]
>
> whose tops [support] the fabric of heaven,
>
> > whose base reaches down to the Netherworld.[134]

---

131. See §1.3.4.a.

132. During the Second Temple period, Josephus used the word *chthōn* (= earth, ground, land) to say that the Pharisees believed that "under the ground (*hupo chthonos*) there will be rewards or punishments" (Josephus, *Antiquitatum Judaicarum* xviii.14).

133. Or: "within the underworld ... into the underworld." *Baal Cycle*, CAT 1.4.viii.7 (cf. Pardee, "Baʿlu Myth," 1:267. And see Wyatt, *Religious Texts from Ugarit*, 112; De Moor, *Religious Texts from Ugarit*, 66; Driver and Gibson, *Canaanite Myths*, 66. Akkadian also used *erṣetu* (= "earth") for the underworld. Cf. *Gilg.* xii.83f.

134. *Gilg.* ix.38-41, in George, *Epic of Gilgamesh*, 71. The same contrast between

In Israel, the Underworld or Sheol (*šəʾôl*) was also conceived as located under the ground. The Hebrew Bible talks about the "underworld below" (*šəʾôl*, Isa 14:9), or "the depths of the underworld" (*šəʾôl*, Ps 86:13; Prov 9:18). The psalmist prays that his enemies "go down alive to the underworld" (*šəʾôl*, Ps 55:15[16]).

The Greeks used the term *chthonios* = "underworld," as opposed to *hupatos* = "highest, uppermost." For example, a Chorus-Leader gives a farewell to Alcestis, saying: "May Hermes of the Underworld (*chthonios*) and Hades receive you kindly."[135] Both the Greeks and the LXX employed the word *haidēs*[136] (or *hadēs*) to refer to the "underworld, grave, death." For example, the divine king Theseus "went down to the underworld" (*eis haidou kateisi*) looking for Persephone.[137] Apollos sees Death coming to take the wife of Admetus: "Ah, I see that Death ... is nearby to take her down to the House of Hades (*eis hadou domous*)."[138] And Herodotus relates that King Rhampsinitus "went down alive to what the Greeks called Hades" (*thōon katabēnai ... es ton ... haidēn*).[139]

Moving back to Mesopotamia, *Ištar's Descent and Resurrection* conveys a famous description of the Underworld:

> To the Netherworld (*kurnugê*), the Land of no Return,
> Ištar (Venus), the daughter of Sîn, set her mind.
> Indeed, the daughter of Sîn set her mind
> to the dark house, the dwelling of Irkalla,
> to the house which none leaves who enters,
> to the road where traffic is one-way,
> to the house, whose dwellers thirst for light,
> where dust is their food, clay their bread.

---

up and down, between Heaven and Underworld, can be seen in a threat that Erra pronounced by saying: "I shall shake the netherworld and make heaven tremble" (*Erra and Ishum* iv.123, as is quoted in "Irkallu," 178; cf. Dalley, *Myths from Mesopotamia*, 308). A lament says: "Who knows the will of the gods in heaven? Who understand the plans of the underworld gods?" (*Ludlul* ii.36–37, in Lambert, *Babylonian Wisdom*, 41; cf. Annus and Lenzi, *Ludlul*, 35).

135. Euripides, *Alcestis* 743, in Laushning and Roisman, *Alcestis*, 37.

136. The term *haidēs* seems to be comprised by privative *a* + *idein* (= to see), giving the primary sense of the "unseen, secret." For example, in *Phaedo* 79a, Plato talks about two kinds of existences, "one visible and the other invisible" (*to men horaton, to de aides*).

137. Apollodorus, *Epitome* E1.23, in Frazer, *Apollodorus*, I:153.

138. Euripides, *Elcestis* 25, in Luschnig and Roisman, *Alcestis*, 16.

139. Herodotus, *Histories* ii.122.1, in Godley, *Herodotus*, 423.

They see no light, they dwell in darkness,
clothed like birds in garments of feather.
Over the door and the bolt dust has settled,
over the door beam a deathly silence has sunk.
When Ištar arrived at the gate of the Netherworld (*kurnugê*),
she opened her mouth and said
uttered a word to the gatekeeper:
"Hey, gatekeeper, open your gate!
Open your gate for me that I may enter!"[140]

The Hebrew Bible inherits the same view. The netherworld is a murky place from which there's no escape:

Only a few years will pass
before I take the path of no return! (Job 16:22).

⁹As a cloud fades and vanishes,
so is the one who descends to the underworld (*šəʾôl*),
never to come up again.
¹⁰He will never return to his house,
nor his place will know him any more (Job 7:9–10).[141]

This is because the place is locked behind doors and bolts; and this is why "the prisoner"[142] and the dead are alike . . . man is incarcerated."[143] The concept was already present in Sumer. One incantation says: "The messenger, the son of the fates, came forth from the gate (ká-gal) of the Earth-Of-No-Return."[144] We just saw above that when Ištar arrived at the gate of the

---

140. *Descent of Ištar* i.1–15. We use here the Akkadian version of the Middle Babylonian Period (*ca.* 1600–1155 BCE) as it is found in Lapinkivi, *Ištar's Descent*, 29 (see also Dalley, *Myths from Mesopotamia*, 155; Foster, *Before the Muses*, 499). A longer Sumerian version comes from the Ur III period (*ca.* 2112–2002 BCE). The Sumerian version has been labeled *The Descent of Inana to the Netherworld*, and it can be found in Black, *Literature of Ancient Sumer*, 65–76; Jacobsen, *Harps that Once*, 205–35.

141. The person trapped in the Underworld lives in "the most profound darkness" (Ps 88:6[7]). Cf. "Are your wonders known in the darkness?" (Ps 88:12[13]). Job asks for a just a little relief "before I go, and never return, to the land of darkness and shadows" (Job 10:21).

142. *šalālu* means "to take prisoner or captive" (see "Šalāhu," 196).

143. *Gilg.* x.321, 323, following Lambert, "Theology of Death," 55.

144. Paul, "Gates of the Netherworld," 165.

Underworld, she said to the gatekeeper: "Hey, gatekeeper, open your gate! Open your gate for me that I may enter!"[145]

The Hebrew Bible also mentions "the gates of death ... the gates of darkness" (Job 38:17).[146] The *Book of Wisdom* records a prayer to the god, saying: "For you have the power over life and death; you make mortals descend to the gates of the underworld (*hadēs*) and back again" (16:13).[147] 1QH 3.16–18 shows the netherworld opening its gates to let the wicked come in, and then it closes them behind them.[148] The Greeks also talked about the "gates of Hades,"[149] which as we have seen it was imagined like a house. Penelope asked a goddess whether Odysseus was alive or whether he was "already dead and in the House of Hades" (*ein Aidao domoisi*).[150]

Persian influence brought new ideas into the theological discourse. Jesus' time was a multi-faceted period in which we find different views competing for cultural space. For example, Josephus explains that most Pharisees still believed that the souls of all people went "under the earth" (*hupo chthonos*), even when some people were now embracing the new idea that in such a place there were "rewards and punishments" according to how people lived their lives here on earth. New also was the idea that while the wicked remain in an everlasting prison, the righteous will rise again.[151] Josephus adds that he personally believed that the souls of the righteous depart to "a most holy place in heaven" to later be resurrected with pure bodies, while the unrighteous go to "a darkest place in the underworld" (*hadēs*).[152] In Jesus' time, it became popular to believe that good people went to Heaven (Matt 5:12; Luke 23:43; 2 Cor 5:1; Col 1:5; 1 Pet 1:4) and bad people to *hadēs* (Luke 16:23, 26).

---

145. *Descent of Ištar* i.15.

146. The afflicted asks his god: "Be merciful to me, Yahve, see the affliction I suffer from those who hate me; you are the one who lifts me up from the gates of Death" (Ps 9:13[14]). During his illness, Hezekiah wailed on the fact that after his death he will go to the netherworld: "... in the prime of my days, I must go. To the gates of the underworld [*šəʾôl*] I'm consigned for the rest of my years" (Isa 38:10). Cf. "the doors of Hades" (*hadou*, Matt 16:18). These doors even have a key (Rev 1:18).

147. In *Psalms of Solomon* 16:2, we read: "my soul was almost thrown into death (*zanaton*), to the gates of the underworld (*hadou*)." Cf. "I cried out ... imploring ... to the Ruler ... to have mercy on those at the gates of the underworld" (3 Macc 5:51).

148. See Lohse, *Die Texte aus Qumran*, 120; Wise, *Dead Sea Scrolls*, 182.

149. Homer, *Iliad* v.646.

150. Homer, *Odyssey* iv.834, in Murray, *Odyssey*, 181.

151. Josephus, *Antiquitates Judaicae* xviii.14.

152. Josephus, *De Bello Judaico* iii.374–75. Cf. "And you, Capernaum, will you be exalted to heaven? No, you will be brought down to the underworld" (*hadou*, Matt 11:23).

While the Hebrew Bible mostly maintained a monist view of the universe, the Persians introduced a stronger cosmic dualism. They made popular what we call today *apocalyptic theology*. Gregory Riley helps summarize the new approach: "Foremost, God gained an enemy in the devil, and these two were seen to be locked in a bitter and protracted battle for survival that involved all creation. The Persians taught of righteous angels and wicked demons, the judgment of the dead, heaven and hell, the resurrection, eternal life, and an eschatology of the coming end of the world."[153] Since the time of Alexander the Great and the Persians, military and political fluctuations brought change to culture and theology.[154]

3.7 Excursus on Psalm 82

In §2.4, we used Genesis 6:1–4 to illustrate how theological prejudice blurs grammatical-historical investigation. We close this chapter with an additional example. The fact that John 10:35 is involved makes it more interesting. We already presented (§3.3.4.e) what today is the standard interpretation of this psalm, so now let's review other alternatives.

3.7.1 Angels

In approaching Psalm 82, the Qumran community used the preferred method of rabbinical Judaism, which was to take a text out of its original context, and arbitrarily apply it to anything they wanted to teach. We refer here to the manuscript 11Q13 which links various biblical texts to create a new story based on the year of jubilee (Lev 25:8–55).[155] The compilation of texts aims at assigning Melchizedek the task of executing judgment in the day of the eschatological jubilee.[156] To that end the mythographer lumps to-

---

153. Riley, *One Jesus, Many Christs*, 26. For this new cosmic dualism found in the Christian Bible, see Brown, *New Testament Studies*; Collins, *Apocalyptic Imagination*; Jackson, *Zoroastrian Studies*; Lange and Meyers, *Light against Darkness*; Murphy, *Apocalypticism*; Martin, *New Testament History and Literature*; Nickelsburg, *Resurrection, Immortality and Eternal Life* and *Jewish Literature*; Schwarz, *Eschatology*. Special attention should be given to *1 Enoch* and the Dead Sea Scrolls.

154. Among the apocalyptic literature, see *Book of Daniel 7–12, 1 Enoch, 2 Enoch, Jubilees, Sibylline Oracles, 4 Esdras, 2 Baruch, 3 Baruch, Testament of Abraham, Testament of Levi*, and several Qumran writings, like *Rule of War*.

155. We depend here on the study by Fitzmyer, "Further Light on Melchizedek," 25–41.

156. 11Q13 mentions the captives of "the last times" to whom liberation is announced, quoting Isa 61:1 and 52:7.

gether Psalm 7:7–9[8–10] and Psalm 82:1–2, to underline the role of judge played by Melchizedek. The gods of Psalm 82 become evil angels who are judged by Melchizedek. This new reading retains a mythical vein, but creates a new story, different from the original trust of the psalm:

> [9] [And Melchizedek] will judge with his power the holy ones of El,[157] executing judgment, as it is written [10]about him in the songs of David, who said: "Elohim has taken his place in the assembly of El; in the midst of the gods he judges" [Ps 82:1]. And about him [= Melchizedek] he said: "and above it [= assembly] [11]take your throne on high, that El[158] may judge the peoples" [Ps 7:7–9]. And said: "How long will you judge unjustly and show partiality to the wicked?" [Ps 82:2]. [12]Its interpretation concerns Belial and the spirits of his lot, who rebelled by turning away from the commandments of god. [13]But Melchizedek will carry out the vengeance of god's judgment from the hand of Belial and from the hand of all the spirits of his lot. [14]To his aid come all the sons of El.[159]

3.7.2 Judges

The rabbinical method could, of course, even change the wording of the original passage. In the present case, the change is aimed at making the text talk about human tribunals, not gods. Compare the different renditions:[160]

Two different renditions of Psalm 82

Masoretic Text: Psalm 82	Targum on the Psalms
[1]Elohim stands up in the assembly of El, in the midst of the gods he pronounces judgment …	[1]As for God, his Shekinah dwells in the assembly of the righteous who are mighty in the Law; he judges among the judges of truth …
[6]I declare: even when you are gods, sons of Elyon, all of you …	[6] I said: You are reckoned as like the angels, and like *the angels of the height*, all of you …

---

157. The expression "the holy ones of El" (*qəḏôšē ʾēl*) refers to the gods who form the divine assembly. See above §3.3.4.b.

158. Ps 7:7 reads "Yahve," but 11Q13.11 uses "El" (*ʾēl*), in order to apply the text to Melchizedek, who is taking god's place in executing judgment.

159. See García and Tigchelaar, *Dead Sea Scrolls*, 2:1206–8; Vermes, *Dead Sea Scrolls* 532.

160. For the Targum, see Stec, *Targum of Psalms*, 160

Note the changes that the Targum has introduced into the text. It reads "righteous" instead of "El," and "judges" instead of "gods" (v. 1). Then it uses "angels" to compare human judges with angels (v. 6). This purge is theologically motivated. Luis Schökel and Cecilia Carniti detect this tendentious development: "The Psalm was not removed or corrected [in the Hebrew Bible], and they kept praying it. But the identification of the ʾlhym [= gods] was changed. It is not gods anymore but judges."[161] In similar fashion, the *Babylonian Talmud* used Psalm 82 to require judges to do justice by reminding them that god will punish those who give false witness "because it is written: 'God stands in the congregation of God; in the midst of the judges gives judgment.'"[162]

Today the overwhelming majority of interpreters recognize that Psalm 82 talks about gods,[163] but it should not come as a surprise that some have tried to distort its meaning in order to alter the theology of the psalm. Following the tradition of the Talmud, some have argued that the "gods" mentioned in the psalm are human judges. But if the psalm was referring to human beings, it would be impossible to explain how it is that vv. 6-7 say they will die like any other mortal. If the psalm talks about human judges, how else would they die other than like mortals?[164] It has been argued that the "assembly of God" (v. 1) refers to Israel,[165] even when the focus of the psalm is not Israel but all the earth (vv. 5, 8) and all the nations (v. 8). We should add that the Hebrew Bible never makes the judges of Israel responsible for the justice of the nations.

---

161. Schökel and Carniti, *Salmos II*, 1080.

162. *Sanhedrin* i.9, in Rodkinson, *Babylonian Talmud*, 11. Cf. Danby, *Tractate Sanhedrin*, 30.

163. See the long list: Anderson, *Psalms*, 591; Broyles, *Psalms*, 335; Clifford, *Psalms*, 635; Dahood, *Psalms 51-100*, 268; Eichrodt, *Teología*, 2:203; Goldingay, *Psalms 42-89*, 558; Hossfeld and Zenger, *Psalms 51-100*, 328; Kraus, *Psalms 60-150*, 153; Longman, *Psalms*, 305; Mays, *Psalms*, 268; McCann, *Psalms*, 1005; Mowinckel, *Psalms in Israel*, 57, 150; Schökel and Carniti, *Salmos II*, 1073; Tanner et al., *Psalms*, 641; Tate, *Psalms 51-100*, 328.;Vangemeren, *Psalms*, 623; Weiser, *Psalms*, 556, etc.

164. Kraus correctly argues that the interpretation that finds here human judges or aristocrats "has been proved out of the question by religion-historical research, especially by texts discovered in Ras Shamra [Ugarit]. The Syrian-Canaanite mythology thinks of the heavenly world as populated by innumerable 'divine essences'" (*Psalms 60-150*, 155).

165. See Perowne, *Psalms*, 101; Delitzsch, *Psalms*, 400.

3.7.3 Israel [166]

A further interpretation uses the method of taking a text out of its original context in order to create a new story. Here the scene is transferred to Mount Sinai, where the god is portrayed as giving his people eternal life by means of his law. The gift of immortality protected them from the Angel of Death. According to this myth, Psalm 82:6 addresses Israel:

> Another explanation of "Behold I send and angel" [Exod 32:20; 33:2], it is written, "I said: ye are godlike beings, and all of you sons of the Most High" [Ps 82:6]. When Israel stood at Sinai and received the Torah, the Holy One, blessed be He, said to the Angel of Death, "Thou has power over all the heathen but not over this people, for they are my portion, and just as I live forever, so will my children be eternal, as it says, 'When the Most High gave to the nations their inheritance . . . for the portion of the Lord is his people, Jacob the lot of his inheritance.'" [Deut 32:8–9].[167]

Then the story adds that the gift of immortality was taken from them when Israel sinned by making a golden calf. Therefore, the god said to Israel: "I said ye are gods [immortals] and all of you the children of the Most High, now that you have spoilt your deeds, ye shall indeed die like mortals."[168] And this was how Israel lost her immortality.

3.7.4 The Gospel of John

Finally, John also uses the rabbinic method to interpret Psalm 82, saying:

> [33]The Jews answered: We are not going to stone you for a good work [you might have done], but for blasphemy, because you make yourself God even though you are[169] [just] a man.
>
> [34] Jesus answered: Is it not written in your law, "I said you are gods"?
>
> [35] Since[170] he called them "gods," that is, them to whom the Word of God came (and the Scripture cannot be abolished),

---

166. We follow here the study by Ackerman, "Rabbinic Interpretation of Psalm 82," 186–91.

167. *Midrash Rabbah* Exod 32:7, in Ackerman, "Rabbinic Interpretation of Psalm 82," 186–87.

168. *Avodah Zarah* 5a.

169. The ptc. *ōn* is concessive.

170. Here the conj. *ei* assumes a causal meaning. See BDAG 219; Moule, *Idiom-Book*, 35.

[36] to whom the Father consecrated and sent into the world you say "you are blaspheming" because I said "I am God's Son"? (John 10:33–36)

First, verse 33 creates a contrast between man and god, and Jesus is threatened with stoning for making himself divine. In his answer, Jesus points to an occasion when simple men were called "gods" (v. 34) and, therefore, his adversaries should not be surprised that Jesus does the same. If this is correct, John is using the rabbinic method of taking a text out of its original context.[171] Psalm 82 now refers to human beings who were called gods. Second, who were the people called "gods"? Jesus says that they are those "to whom the Word of God came" (v. 35). The LXX uses similar expressions when the word of god came to a prophet,[172] but the Hebrew Bible never calls the prophets gods. So maybe John refers to Israel (§3.7.3),[173] even when the passage is too meager to allow a positive identification. If Israel is what John meant in quoting the psalm, then vv. 34–36 would be *a minore ad maius* argument intended to protect Jesus from the accusation of blasphemy. The idea would be that god called Israel "gods" when they received his word at Sinai and, therefore, there is no justification in condemning Jesus because he maintains that he is the son of god.[174] Be as it may, it is ironic that a passage that distorts the original meaning of Psalm 82 argues that "the Scripture cannot be abolished" (v. 35).

171. Schnackenburg admits that like "other proofs from Scripture used by the rabbis, here the original meaning of the quote in its Old Testament context does not matters" (*Evangelio de Juan*, 385). In similar fashion, Bultmann says that the quote is used "without any regard for the original meaning and context of the verse. In the psalm those addressed are divine beings (the gods of the nations) (*Gospel of John*, 389). See O'Day, *Gospel of John*, 677; Von Wahlde, *Gospel and Letters of John*, 475.

172. In the LXX, the expression "the word of god" (*logos tou zeou*) occurs only once in Jer 1:2. The LXX clearly prefers the expression "word of the Lord" (*logos kuriou* + *pros* + addressee; cf. 2 Sam 24:11; 1 Kgs 12:22; 13:20; 16:1; Hos 1:1; Mic 1:1; Joel 1:1; Jonah 1:1; Zeph 1:1; Hag 1:1; Zech 1:1, etc.). It also employs *rēma kuriou* + *pros* + addressee (cf. Gen 15:1; 1 Sam 15:10; 2 Sam 7:4; 1 Kgs 17:2, 8; 18:1; 19:9; 2 Kgs 20:4, etc.). The Hebrew Bible uses "word of god" only twice (*dəḇar hā ʾĕlōhîm*, 1 Kgs 12:22; 1 Chr 26:32), preferring "the word of Yahve" (*dəḇar yhwh*, Isa 1:10; Jer 1:2, etc.).

173. In favor of Israel, see Barrett, *Gospel according to St. John*, 384; Carson, *Gospel according to St. John*, 398; Köstenberger, *John*, 315; Kruse, *John*, 2003:240; Schnackenburg, *Evangelio de Juan*, 386; Von Wahlde, *Gospel and the Letters of John*, 474.

174. Other interpreters believe that John 10:34 calls "gods" the judges of Israel (§3.7.2), and incorrectly maintain that this is also the meaning of Psalm 82. See Meyer, *Hand-Book to the Gospel of John*, 331; Malina and Rohrbaugh, *Gospel of John*, 188; Plummer, *Gospel according to St. John*, 227; Whitacre, *John*, 273.

> *In our investigations,*
> *do we search for quietude, peace, happiness?*
> *No, we only search for the truth,*
> *it does not matter how deterrent and unsightly . . .*
> *If you strive for calm and happiness, then believe.*
> *If you want to be a disciple of the truth, do research.*
>
> —FRIEDRICH NIETZSCHE,
> LETTER TO HIS SISTER ELISABETH, JUNE 11, 1865[1]

Chapter 4

CASE STUDY: MONARCHY

4.1 The Myth of the King-God: Background

4.1.1 Metaphorical Foundation

IN CHAPTER ONE, WE proposed that myth is a literary genre by which we tell stories about the gods. The combination of all these stories creates a conceptual metaphor, that is, a concept of god. Here metaphor is the all-embracing concept. Then in chapters two and three, we argued that the fundamental metaphor of theism is *anthropomorphism,* which is a type of metaphor. In the present chapter we move a step further by showing that the central anthropomorphism of theism is the *king-metaphor.*

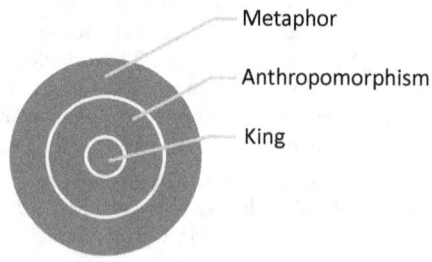

Metaphorical basis of myth

---

1. Colli and Montinare, *Nietzsche Briefwechsel,* 60.

In antiquity, the gods were represented *as if* they were kings (§1.1.3; §2.1). This metaphor was the product of social conditioning: Monarchy was almost the only system of government known at the time. Its overwhelming presence affected all areas of life. Monarchy provided a host of images and linguistic expressions that made possible the construction of a mental representation of the divine. The accumulation of all these metaphors created the conceptual metaphor GOD IS KING. The abstract and unknown divine world (*target domain*) was understood in terms of the concrete experience of the earthly monarchy (*source domain*, cf. §1.1.2):

> [19] Yahve has set his throne in heaven,
> and his royal power rules over all.[2]
> [20] Praise Yahve, O you his envoys,
> his powerful heroes[3] who carry out his word,
> obedient to his spoken word.
> [21] Praise Yahve, all you his hosts [= gods],
> his servants who fulfill his will.
> [22] Praise Yahve, everything he has created,[4]
> in all the places of his dominion.
> Praise Yahve, my soul (Ps 103:19–22).

Let's describe how *monarchy* (anthropomorphism) has functioned in the theological discourse and in the formation of a worldview. Jean Bottéro explains how humans felt the need to portray the supernatural order using our earthly reality as a model and, therefore, invented a parallel universe of gods.[5] The world of the gods was a replica of the world of the Ancient Near East. This "could be easily certified by carefully looking at the secular documents of the time, which reveal that all [the divine functions] were borrowed from the organization of the state and the king's palace."[6] The divine world "was transformed into a supernatural replica of the earthly political authority. In the same way as it was with that human authority, the world of the gods also had a supreme authority, a god and his descendants."[7] Aristotle also recognized that by representing the gods in human form, theology was mimicking earthly reality. One particular form of humanizing the

---

2. Cf. "And his rule is over the universe" (Kraus, *Psalms 60–150*, 289).
3. Or: "warriors," "mighty valiants."
4. Lit. "all his works." Cf. Ps 145:9; Dan 9:14.
5. Bottéro, *Religion in Ancient Mesopotamia*, 44.
6. Bottéro, *Religion in Ancient Mesopotamia*, 51.
7. Bottéro, *Religion in Ancient Mesopotamia*, 51.

gods was to create the concept of a king-god. The idea was a metaphorical concept fruit of the imagination:

> ... all people speak of the gods as ruled by a king, because the gods too are or were, in old times, under the rule of a king. Because as men describe the appearance[8] [of the gods] like their own, so they also imagine their way of life to be like their own.[9]

4.1.2 Historical Development[10]

This particular anthropomorphic construct of the divine may have started taking a more definite shape in Mesopotamia in the so-called Neolithic Period (10000–6000 BCE). During this time, humans embraced the new enterprise of agriculture which was then exported to Europe via the Danube and the Mediterranean. The Ancient Near East provided the climate conditions for wild spelt, emmer and barley to grow. Before this humans had moved around as nomads hunting and collecting, but the new discovered tool of agriculture supplied the means to control the production and availability of provisions. Agriculture had an irreversible impact on human life. Suddenly the soil acquired a value it had never had before. Land became *property*, something people needed to own in order to control its production, because farming required tending the land on a year-round basis. Agriculture forced a *settled* way of life, which led to the creation of the city and civilization (Ubaid I, *ca.* 5300–4000 BCE).[11] People were now capable to store grain which turned into a most coveted commodity.

It is in this period that we see the emergence of monarchy, armies and walled cities for the protection of the new wealth created by agriculture. City people now lived close to each other which provided the possibility of distributing responsibilities. A new bureaucracy oversaw the labor of

---

8. The word *eidos* (= appearance) indicates that the human figure becomes the model used to represent the gods.

9. *hōsper de kai [tōn theōn] ta eidē heautois aphomoiousin hoi anthrōpoi, huotō kai tous bious tōn theōn.* Aristotle, *Politics* 1252b.27 (cf. Rackham, *Aristotle Politics*, 9).

10. For the historical development of the period, see Chavalas, *Ancient Near East*; Kuhrt, *Ancient Near East*; Maisels, *Emergence of Civilization*; Mellaart, *Neolithic of the Near East*; Nissen, *Early History of the Ancient Near East*; Oates and Oates, *Rise of Civilization*; Roux, *Ancient Iraq*; Snell, *Life in the Ancient Near East* and *Companion to the Ancient Near East*; Van de Mieroop, *History of the Ancient Near East*.

11. For a description of the Mesopotamian urban life, see Leick, *Babylonians*; Van de Mieroop, *Ancient Mesopotamian City*; Westenholz, "Sumerian City." Most probably, the oldest city of Sumer was Eridu (Tell Abu Shahrein).

scribes, soldiers, craftsmen, merchants, etc.[12] Thordkild Jacobsen indicates that the main function of the king was to act as warrior and judge, but soon *metaphorical thinking* made possible the use of the same images to represent the gods:

> The king, awesome and majestic in his power over men, was alike the defender against outside foes and the righter of wrongs among his people. The new concept ... was early applied to the gods and it profoundly influenced the religious outlook.[13]

The king was seen as warrior, shepherd, protector, legislator, judge, husbandman and provider, and the same images were applied to the gods. The king was powerful, feared and majestic, and so were the gods. An inscription describes king Damīq-Ilišu (*ca.* 1816 BCE) as a mighty shepherd, provider and priest:

> Damīq-Ilišu, constant (attendant) of Nippur, shepherd,
>   favourite of the god An,
> who heeds the god Enlil,
>   prince beloved of the heart of the goddess Ninisina,
> farmer who piles up the produce (of the land) in granaries,
>   true provider of the shrine Egalmah,
> mighty king, king of Isin,
>   king of the land of Sumer and Akkad,
> suitable for the office of *en* priest
>   befitting the goddess Inana.[14]

Psalm 45:2–6[3–7] talks about the glory of the warrior king:

> ²You are the most handsome of men,
>   grace has been poured upon your lips;
>   therefore, Elohim has blessed you forever.
> ³Gird your sword on your thigh, O warrior,
>   (in) your glory and majesty, prosper.
> ⁴Ride for truth, humility and justice,[15]

---

12. See Jacobsen, *Toward the Image*, 132–56.

13. Jacobsen, *Toward the Image*, 43.

14. Inscription of *Damiq-ilīšu* E4.1.15, in Frayne, *Old Babylonian Period*, 103. Cf. 2 Sam 5:2; Ps 78:70–72.

15. The Hebrew text in vv. 3–4[4–5] shows several problems. One is that v. 3[4] ends with the words *wahădārekā* (= "and your majesty"), and the next verse begins with exactly the same words: *wahădārkā* (= "and your majesty"). If this is a case of

and your right hand will show you tremendous deeds.
⁵Your arrows (are) sharp,
the peoples submit to you,
the enemies of the king flinch.¹⁶
⁶Your throne, O Elohim, endures for ever and ever,
scepter of equity is your royal scepter.

4.1.3 Mesopotamia: Where Writing and Theology Began

Let's pause for a moment to examine an important detail shaping the way theology developed in the Ancient Near East. Sumerian civil and mercantile activities grew in complexity. This created the need for a system that would be able to store information. The problem with audible language is that as soon as a person pronounces a word, it disappears forever. The solution came in the form of a new technology. Sumer invented the first writing system of the world: cuneiform.¹⁷ It is impossible to overstate the impact of this invention. Peter Daniels correctly defines prehistory as the "absence of writing."¹⁸ In other words, it is the invention of writing what provides the technology to register contracts, lists, poems, theology, history, etc. Written on tablets of clay, the documents were almost indestructible. We could

---

dittography, we are authorized to delete the second occurrence. And if we follow the parallelism as it is shown in *Biblia Hebraica Stuttgartensia*, the sense would then be: "(in) your glory and majesty push forward" (vv. 3b–4[4b–5]). For other suggestions, see Dahood, *Psalms 1–50*, 271; Kraus, *Psalms 1–59*, 451.

16. The MT contains a reading that makes no sense; lit. it reads: "your sharp arrows the peoples under you fall in the heart of the enemies of the king." Instead of *yippelû bəlēḇ* (= "they fall in the heart"), an option would be to read *yippōl lēḇ* ("the heart falls"), which gives the following result: "the heart of the enemies of the king fall"; that is, the enemies are frightened.

17. In spite of Schmandt-Besserat's proposal (in *Before Writing*), today the consensus is still that writing originated out of pictograms that developed into cuneiform (first was archaic Sumerian 3500–2600 BCE). Later Canaan created the lineal script during the Intermediate (2000–1525 BCE) and Late (1525–1200 BCE) Bronze Age. We can confidently say that the invention of the lineal or phonetic script was "the most significant direct contribution of the Canaanites to the world" (Pitard, "Canaanite Literature," 261–62). Borrowing from the Phoenicians, the Greeks (*ca.* 800 BCE) invented their effective writing system. Then immigrants from Euboea took a version of their Greek alphabet to the Italian Peninsula, where it was adapted to form the Latin alphabet, which was embraced by the European Languages. See Bottéro, *Mesopotamia*; Coulmas, *Writing Systems*; Driver, *Semitic Writing*; Glassner, *Invention of Cuneiform*; Michalowski, "Tokenism"; Sayce, *Elementary Grammar*.

18. Daniels, "First Civilizations," 19.

confidently say that the title of the book *History Begins at Sumer* (1981) by Samuel Kramer testifies to this fact.

Babylon and Assyria used this new technology to write their own language, that is, Akkadian (*ca.* 2600–2500 BCE).[19] The fame and political supremacy of these powers made Akkadian the international language of literature, politics and trade in all the Ancient Near East. Cuneiform gave Mesopotamia the luxury of becoming the first culture to put their mythology in writing, setting the theological agenda for the whole Ancient Near East, and thus influencing Israel and Greco-Roman cultures.

During the Akkadian Classical Period (*ca.* 1900–1600 BCE), Mesopotamia produced works like *Hammurabi Code, Atra-ḫasīs*, and the main parts of the *Epic of Gilgameš*, as well as chronicles about kings, hymns, laws, prayers, laments, songs of love, enchantments, etc.[20] During the Kassite period (*ca.* 1600–1155 BCE), we see the arrival of other important works, like *Ludlul bēl nēmeqi* (§1.2.2), *Enūma Eliš* (§1.3.2), *Anzu, The Myth of King Etana*, etc., and also the longer version of *Gilgameš*.

The international character of the Akkadian language and theology impacted both the Syro-Palestine region and the Mediterranean. Canaan (Palestine) was comprised by a conglomerate of small independent kingdoms that shared a similar culture. This culture extended to Syria (Ugarit). During the Late Bronze Age (*ca.* 1550–1200 BCE), this area came under the power of Egypt. Nonetheless, in the very capital city of Pharaoh Akhenaten (or Amenhotep IV, *ca.* 1364–1347 BCE), a place known today as el-'Amarna, archaeologists found 382 tablets written in Akkadian. Most of these documents were letters about political affairs sent by vassal kings to Pharaoh or his officials. There were also letters written in Akkadian that were sent to Egypt by other political entities like Babylon, Assyria, Mitanni, etc.[21] In Ugarit, archaeologists found many letters written in Akkadian. Ugaritic scribes were also busy producing lists of Akkadian (and Sumerian) words as a tool to learn the international language. The language of Babylon and Assyria was the language of politics and trade.

The area also displays the presence of Mesopotamian literature. In Amarna, archaeologists found works like *Adapa and the South Wind*; and

---

19. This adaptation of cuneiform is known as Akkadian (*akkadûm*) because the technique acquired great fame during the Akkade empire (or *Agade*, in Sum.), under the key figures of Sargon I (*ca.* 2296–2240 BCE) and his grandchild, the powerful Narām-Sîn (*ca.* 2213–2176 BCE).

20. See Foster, *Before the Muses*; Wasserman, *Style and Form in Old-Babylonian*.

21. The standard introduction and translation of these letters can be found in Moran, *Amarna Letters*.

Nergal and Ereškigal.[22] Ugarit furnishes parts of *Atra-ḫasīs* (RS 22.421), and possible references to *Gilgameš* (RS 22.219 and 22.398),[23] and tablets with the practice of students who wrote in Akkadian *The Poem of the Righteous Sufferer* (or *Ludlul bēl nēmeqi*, RS 25.460), *The poem of the Early Rulers* (RS 25.130), and *Admonitions of Šūpē-awīlin to his son* (RS 22.439).[24] Emar (Tell Meskene, Syria) was an important Amorite city. An excavation (1973) brought to light many documents in Akkadian, among which was *The Epic of Gilgameš*.[25] Even the DSS mention Gilgameš in one of the fragments of *The Book of Giants*.[26]

Wayne Horowitz and Takayoshi Oshima have catalogued ninety-one objects found in Canaan, the majority of which were written in Akkadian—plus other documents written in alphabetic cuneiform and Sumerian. These objects come from twenty-eight different places in Canaan, covering from the Intermediate Bronze Age to the first Millennium BCE, and representing a variety of objects and literary genres. In Megiddo (Tell al-Mutasallim), a tablet was found containing thirty-eight verses from *Gilgameš* (Late Bronze Age).[27] All this reveals that Israel lived in a cultural biosphere whose dominant theology emerged in Mesopotamia long before Israel appeared in history. In addition, Israel literally lived in Babylon during captivity. This all substantiates that history and theology began at Sumer.

4.2 The Myth: The Gods Are (like) Kings

The conceptual metaphor GOD IS KING was the foundational myth of the old theology (§1.1.3), and it has shaped the Christian view of god. Ancient Near East and Mediterranean literature is saturated with individual expressions and stories that together form this conceptual metaphor. We now proceed to share some examples. While reviewing the material, the reader should keep in mind that Israel was not the first in creating the mythic idea of a *king-god*, or the concepts of Heaven (§3.5) and its divine assembly (§3.3).

---

22. See Dalley, *Myths from Mesopotamia*, 178–88; Foster, *Before the Muses*, 525–30; Izre'el, *Amarna Scholarly Tablets*, 43–46; Izre'el, *Adapa and the South Wind*; Kilmer, "Fugal Features of Atraḫasis," 127–39.

23. George, *Babylonian Gilgamesh Epic*, 99, 121, 138.

24. For the literary presence of Mesopotamia in Ugarit, see Lambert, "Interchange of Ideas," 311–16; Mack-Fisher, "Survey and Reading Guide" 67–80; Rowe, "Scribes, Sages and Seers," 95–101; Van der Toorn, "Cuneiform Documents," 97–103.

25. Chavalas, *Emar*, 13–15; George, *Babylonian Gilgamesh Epic*, 326–29.

26. Cf. Wise 2005:290–2.

27. Goetze and Levy, "Fragment on the Gilgamesh Epic"; George, *Babylonian Gilgamesh Epic*, 339; Horowitz and Oshima, *Cuneiform Canaan*, 102–5.

Israel only adapted the theological images she found in the world around her. Israel did not live in a vacuum. When Israel showed up in history, Mesopotamia and Egypt had already set the theological agenda for more than a thousand years.

4.2.1 Mesopotamia

It is essential to notice that *anthropomorphism* is the primary cognitive mechanism allowing ancient people to imagine celestial beings behaving *as if* they were part of a monarchy. *Atra-ḫasīs* (*ca.* 1700–1600 BCE) describes Anu (or An), head of the Sumerian pantheon, as the "king of heaven."[28] *The Laws of Hammurabi* depict him as "the august god Anu, king of the Anunnaku deities."[29] *Enūma Eliš* (*ca.* 1595–1105 BCE) gives Marduk the title of "king of the gods of heaven and earth," that is, of the whole universe (merismos).[30] Marduk obtained absolute power after the divine council granted his demands: "When I speak, let it be me who ordains the destinies instead of you. Let nothing that I decide be altered, nor what I say be revoked or changed."[31] What a Calvinist god! When the gods declared him Lord of the universe, they hailed: "Marduk is King!"[32]

In the famous *Gudea Cylinder* A (*ca.* 2125 BCE), god Ninĝirsu (= Ninurta) describes himself as a royal and indomitable god:

> I am [god] Ninĝirsu who has turned back the fierce waters,[33]
>> the great warrior of Enlil's realm, a lord without opponent.
>
> My house the E-ninnu, a crown, is bigger than the mountains;
>> my weapon the Šar-ur subdues all the lands.
>
> No country can bear my fierce stare,
>> nobody escapes my outstretched arms.
>
> Because of his great love, my father who begot me,
>> called me King, Enlil's flood,
>
> whose fierce stare is never lifted from the mountains,
>> Ninĝirsu, warrior of Enlil,

---

28. *Atra.* i.101.
29. *Laws of Hammurabi* i.1–5, in Roth, *Law Collections*, 76.
30. *En. el.* v.113.
31. *En. el.* ii.160–62.
32. *En. el.* iv.28.
33. For the mythic tradition of the gods battling the waters of chaos, see §1.3.

and endowed me with fifty powers.[34]

It is no surprise that Enlil was also represented in all his royal majesty:

> You are Lord! You are King!
> > Enlil, you are Lord! You are King!
>
> Nunamnir, you are Lord! You are King!
> > You are supreme Lord, you are powerful Lord!
>
> Lord who makes flax grow,
> > Lord who makes barley grow.
>
> You are Lord of heaven,[35] Lord Plenty, Lord of the earth!
> > You are Lord of the earth, Lord Plenty, Lord of heaven![36]
>
> Enlil in heaven, Enlil is King!
> > Lord whose utterances cannot be altered at all!
> > His primordial utterances will not be changed![37]

4.2.2 Egypt

Amen-Re (sun god) was the chief deity of Egypt. An inscription (*ca.* 660 BCE) portrays him as "King of the gods."[38] Another inscription (*ca.* 1280 BCE) represents him as the universal Lord of thrones:

> May your city-god act for you,
> Amen-Re, Lord of Thrones-of-the-Two-Lands,
> Sole god, truly benign, whose glory endures,
> Lord of all in heaven and earth.[39]

4.2.3 Syro-Palestinian Region

In Ugarit (*ca.* 1350–1315 BCE), Baal is described as a mighty king:

---

34. *Gudea Cylinder* A:241–53, in ETCSL t.2.1.7. Cf. Jacobsen, *Harps that Once*, 400.

35. Cf. "god of heaven" (Dan 2:18, 19; Rev 11:13). Cyrus declared: "Yahve, Elohim of heaven, has given me all the kingdoms of the earth" (Ezra 1:2).

36. Cf. "Yahve, Elohim of heaven and Elohim of earth" (Gen 24:3).

37. *Enlil and Ninlil* i.143–54, in Black, *Literature of Ancient Sumer*, 106.

38. *Inscription of Djedkhonsefankh* 1–5, in Lichtheim, *Ancient Egypt Literature*, 3:14.

39. *Inscription of Nebneteru*, right side 5–7, in Lichtheim, *Ancient Egyptian Literature*, 3:20. The god Apis Osiris is called: "King of Gods, Lord of eternity, ruler of everlastingness" (*Stela of Taimhotep* 1–3, in Lichtheim, *Ancient Egyptian Literature*, 3:60).

> Our king is mighty Baal,
>> Our ruler, with none above him.
> All of us will bring him a gift,
>> All of us will bring him a cup.[40]

Israel shared the same theology:

> For great El is Yahve,
>> and a great king above all the gods (Ps 95:3).

Isaiah 6:1 presents Adonay as a king:

> I saw Adonay sitting on a throne, high and elevated;
> the hem of his robe filled the temple.[41]

The Hebrew Bible also shares the mythic concept of a council of gods (§3.3) who are ruled by a supreme god (henotheism). Repeatedly Yahve appears as king of his pantheon:

> ⁶For who in the clouds is comparable to Yahve,
>> or who is like Yahve among the gods?[42]
> ⁷El is astonishing in the council of the holy ones,
>> great and dreaded upon all those around him (Ps 89:6–7[7–8]).

> For Yahve is a great El,
>> king above all the gods (Ps 95:3).

> Bow down before him, you all gods (Ps 97:7).

> For I know that Yahve is great,
>> our Adon is above all gods (Ps 135:5).

4.2.4 Mediterranean

Aristotle recognized Zeus as the king of the gods:

> ... it was not the original forces—Night, Heaven, Chaos or Ocean—but Zeus who was king and ruler.[43]

---

40. *Baal Cycle*, CAT 1.3.v.32–5, in Smith, "Baal Cycle," 117.

41. Cf. Ps 11:4 saying: "Yahve is in his holy temple; Yahve, his throne is in heaven." Cf. Ps 5:3; 10:16; 47:3, 8; 48:3[4]; 103:19; Ezek 1:26, etc.

42. The lit. expression "sons of the gods" (*ʾēlîm*) means simply "gods." See §2.2.2; §2.4.1; §3.3.4.c;

43. Aristotle, *Metaphysics* 1091b.4–5, in Tredennick, *Aristotle Metaphysics*, 287.

Homer (*ca.* 800–701 BCE) describes Zeus as "Master of gods and men."[44] And Hesiod calls him "king in heaven, the one who holds the thunder and the blazing thunderbolt himself,"[45] and adds that after defeating Typhon, the gods:

> urged the visionary Zeus to become King and to rule over the immortals (= gods); and he divided their honor well for them. Zeus, king of the gods ... (*theōn basileus*).[46]

4.3 Myth and Empire

4.3.1 Empires

The ideology of the earthly empire began in the form of a league of cities under an authoritarian and expansionist leader who exercised control over a region from his capital city (cf. Ubaid period, 5000–4000 BCE). The city of Uruk had that function (4000–3000 BCE). Gilgameš (*ca.* 2700 BCE) became the most famous of the old kings whose life was wrapped in legend. But it was Sargon the Great (2340–2284 BCE) the one who built the first empire. Benjamin Foster defines the Agade empire this way: "'Empire' is used here in its conventional sense of supreme and extensive political dominion, presided over by dynastic rulers, who claimed extraordinary, even superhuman or divine powers. It was an entity put together and maintained by force, with provinces administered by officials sent out from the capital in the heartland."[47] Sargon declared himself "king of the universe."[48] The following table provides a sketch of the main empires of the time:

---

44. Homer, *Iliad* ii.669 (cf. Murray, *Iliad*, 111).

45. Hesiod, *Theo.* 71 (cf. Most, *Hesiod*, 9).

46. Hesiod, *Theo.* 881–86. The historian geographer Pausanias (*ca.* 110–180 CE) argued that Zeus not only "reigns in heaven" (*en ouranō basileuein*) but that he also rules "under the earth," adding that Zeus is god "in the sea," too, and, therefore, king in the three realms that comprise the universe (*Descriptio Graeciae* 2.24.4, in Schubart, *Pausaniae*, 157). Other gods are also called kings or masters: "the Lord [*anax*] Apollo, son of Zeus" (Homer, *Iliad* vii.23), "Lord [*anax*] Poseidon" (Homer, *Iliad* xx.68).

47. Foster, *Age of Agade*, 83.

48. *King of Battle* i.18, in Westenholz, *Legends of the Kings of Akkade*, 115.

CASE STUDY: MONARCHY

Main empires in the Ancient Near East and the Mediterranean

King	Empire
Eanatum (*ca.* 2450 BCE).	Sumerian king from the city state of Lagaš.
Sargon the Great (*ca.* 2340–2284 BCE) and Narām-Sîn (*ca.* 2260–2223 BCE).	Sargon was a Semitic king who established the first empire: The Akkadian Empire. He was able to control Mesopotamia and part of the Syro-Palestinian region.
Ur-Nammu (*ca.* 2112–2095 BCE) and Šulgi (*ca.* 2094–2047 BCE).	The Ur III period saw the return of Sumer to power. This was a Neo-Sumerian empire, Mesopotamia.
Hammurabi (*ca.* 1792–1750).	Amorite king. Old Babylonian Empire, Mesopotamia.
Saushtatar (*ca.* 1440 BCE) and Shuttarna II (*ca.* 1400 BCE).	Mitanni Empire, (1600–1300 BCE), northeast off Syria.
Ahmose I (*ca.* 1552–1525 BCE), Thutmose III (*ca.* 1490–1436 BCE) and Ramses II (*ca.* 1290–1224 BCE).	Egyptian empire that controlled Palestine.
Šuppiluliuma I (*ca.* 1344–1322 BCE).	Hittite empire, northeast off Palestine.
Tukulti-Ninurta I (*ca.* 1244–1208 BCE) and Tiglath-Pileser I (*ca.* 1114–1076 BCE).	Middle Assyrian Empire.
Tiglath-Pileser III (*ca.* 744–727 BCE), Sennacherib (705–681 BCE), Esarhaddon (*ca.* 681–669 BCE) and Ashurbanipal (*ca.* 669–627 BCE).	Neo-Assyrian Empire (934–610 BCE).
Nabopolassar (*ca.* 626–605 BCE) and Nebuchadnezzar II (*ca.* 604–562 BCE).	Neo-Babylonian Empire (626–539 BCE).
Cyrus I (620–590 BCE), Darius I (522–486 BCE) and Xerxes I (486–465).	Achaemenid Empire (550–330 BCE) that controlled the entire Ancient Near East and Asia Minor.
Alexander the Great (356–323 BCE).	Macedonian Greek Empire.
Seleucus I Nicator (358–281 BCE), and Antiochus III the Great (241–187 BCE) and Antiochus IV Epiphanes (175–164 BCE).	Hellenistic or Seleucid Empire (312–63 BCE).
Ptolmy I Soter (305–282 BCE), Ptolemy IV (221–204 BCE), Ptolemy V (204–181 BCE).	Ptolemaic Empire (305–30 BCE)
Caesar Augustus (63 BCE—14 CE)	Rome.

4.3.2 The Gods as Imperialistic Warrior-Kings

Created in the image of earthly kings, the gods of the Ancient Near East were imagined as warriors with universal dominion. The god Šamaš is described as the one "who rules over all that exists," and who is "the ruler over the princes of the entire earth."[49] Enlil is "the king of all lands."[50] The Assyrian god Ašur is portrayed as the one "who directs the entire universe."[51] The *Sumerian Flood Story* talks about "An, Enlil, Enki (and) Ninhursag, the gods of the universe."[52] In the Mediterranean, Zeus is depicted as the god "who thunders on high, whose might is supreme."[53] The Hebrew Bible joins the choir, saying that Yahve is the king who is "mighty in battle" (Ps 24:8). Exodus 15 turns what may have been a historical event into a complete mythical story: "Yahve is a warrior" (Exod 15:3), his "right hand" shatters the enemies (15:6–7). Since Yahve is a storm-god, at the "blast of his nostrils" (15:8) and the blowing of his "wind" (or: breath," 15:10) the waters washed away the enemy. He personally destroyed his enemies with brutal cruelty (15:4–10, 15–16), and sent them to the Underworld[54] (15:12). Because Yahve is a mighty warrior-storm-god, we know the answer to the following rhetorical questions:

> Who is like you, Yahve, among the gods (ʾēlīm)?
> Who is like you, majestic among the holy ones,[55]
> awe-inspiring of praises,
> worker of wonders? (15:11)

The gods were described as despotic deities, hungry for power and dominion. A prayer states that Ištar is a warrior-goddess: "You are the lady of the ladies, the goddess of warfare, the lady of battle and the counsellor of the gods, your fathers!"[56] This way of conceptualizing the gods derives from

---

49. "Kullatu," 504.
50. *Enlil and Ninlil* i. 134, in Jacobsen, *Harps that Once*, 179 (cf. p. 472).
51. "Kullatu," 506.
52. *Sumerian Flood Story* iii.143–5, in Civil, "Sumerian Flood," 143.
53. Homer, *Odyssey* v.3, in Murray, *Odyssey*, 183.
54. The text uses the word "earth" (*ereṣ*) to say: "the Underworld swallowed them." See §3.6.
55. Both the LXX (that reads *desoxasmenos en hagiois* = "glorified among the holy ones") and the parallelism with "gods" clearly indicate that we should read *qədōšīm* instead of *qōdeš* (= "holiness," MT). See §3.3.4.b.
56. *Assurbanipal's War against Teumman, King of Elam* i.37–38, in Nissinen, *Prophets and Prophecy*, 147.

CASE STUDY: MONARCHY

the empire-building aspirations of the *earthly* monarchies. Sargon the Great (2340–2284 BCE) talked about his military expansionism:

> Thus says King Sargon, King of Agade,
> > city of great streets and squares,
> the mighty king who speaks with the gods,
> > whose strength the Storm God gave him:
> I captured territory from where the sun rises
> > to where the sun sets.[57]

It is written about the Assyrian king Tukulti-Ninurta I (*ca.* 1244–1208 BCE):

> Your exalted power has been set over the whole world,
> > the seas and the mountains.
> With the wrath of your scepter
> > you have made to submit all regions, in all quarters.
> You spread the might of your land to territories beyond count,
> > you established (their) boundaries.[58]

Psalm 72 affirms that the only relationship the king of Israel can have with other nations is for them to be either vassals or enemies:

> [8]May he have dominion from sea to sea,
> > from the Euphrates to the ends of the earth.
> [9]May his adversaries bow down before him,[59]
> > and his enemies bite the dust.
> [10]May the kings of Tarshish and the isles render him tribute,
> > may the kings of Sheba and Seba bring him gifts.
> [11]May all kings fall down before him,
> > may all the nations give him service.

---

57. Sargon, *Lord of the Lies* i.1–4, in Foster, *Before the Muses*, 72. Sargon was thought to be "king of the universe" (*Sargon, King of battle* i.17, in Foster, *Before the Muses*, 340).

58. *Tukulti-Ninurta Epic* v. (= A rev.) 16–8, in Foster, *Before the Muses*, 312.

59. The MT reading is corrupt: *ṣiyyîm* (= wild beasts). The NIV conjectures "desert tribes." Following the LXX (*Aithiopes*) and Vg. (*Aethiopes*), it may be guessed: "the Ethiopians." The parallel expression "his enemies" rather suggests that the original text might have been *ṣārāyw* = "his adversaries" (cf. Ps 89:23[24]).

4.3.3 The Myth of the Divine-Human King as Foundation of Despotic Power[60]

The earthly monarchy supplied the images with which a divine world was constructed. At the same time, the divine realm thus created was used to legitimize the power of the earthly king. This was a *quid pro quo* in which both worlds (one real, the other imaginary) supported each other. The following Sumerian statement sets the foundation:

> After the kingship descended from heaven,
> the kingship was in Eridug.[61]

This foundation asserts unequivocally that at the very beginning of the world monarchy was not something humans invented. It descended from Heaven and inserted itself in Sumer's oldest city. This is the foundational myth of Sumerian theology which sets the theological agenda for the rest of time until the Enlightenment threw it to the trash. Once humans created the gods to the image of their kings, the gods returned the favor by sending the monarchy down to earth. The gods are imagined as *if they were* kings and, at the same time, the earthly kings *became gods*. The government's legitimacy was founded on the claim that the earthly king was a son of a god.[62] Let's quote Socrates again:

> They [= heroes and kings] were born when
> a god made love with a mortal,
> or a mortal made love with a goddess.[63]

a. Mesopotamia

The city of Lagaš gave us the famous *Stele of the Vultures*, which clearly proclaims that king Eanatum (*ca.* 2450 BCE) was procreated by a god:

---

60. This section should be read with our treatment of legendary heroes in §3.4.

61. *Sumeria King List* i.1–2, in ETCSL 2.1.1. Cf. Jacobsen, *Sumerian King List*, 71. The latest edition of this list ends with the king Sin-magir (*ca.* 1827–1817 BCE), Isin Dynasty, but the document started to be assembled in the middle of the Bronze Age (3300–1200 BCE). See Rowton, "Sumerian King List," 200; Postgate, *Early Mesopotamia*, 20–25; Steinkeller, "Ur III Manuscript of the Sumerian King List," 267–86.

62. It's especially in Egypt, where the king was regarded as god himself. In Mesopotamia, the concept is intermittent, but at least we know the king was always regarded as a "son of god." It is pointless to try to determine the ontological degree of such a concept.

63. See §3.4.

(the god) Ninĝirsu implanted semen for Eanatum in the womb.[64]

The stele adds that Ninhursag, goddess of maternity, breast-fed the king. The first king to declare himself god was Narām-Sîn (ca. 2213–2176 BCE), grandchild of Sargon the Great. Several inscriptions describe him as "god of Agade."[65] A seal used by one of his officers says:

> Naram-Sin,
> the strong male,
> god of Agade,
> king of the four quarters (= all the earth).[66]

A six feet tall stele, carved in limestone, commemorates Narām-Sîn's victory over his enemies.[67] At the very center of the stele, the king's height excels over all the people surrounding him. The king is shown climbing the mountain towards the gods who are depicted with astral symbols at the very top of the stele. Nāram-Sîn is wearing a bull-horned tiara which was the tiara worn by the gods.[68] An inscription engraved in a copper figure relates how the citizens of Agade asked the gods for the divinization of the king and the construction of a temple to worship him:

> Naram-Sin the mighty, King of Agade,
> when the four quarters of the earth
> attacked him together,
> through the love Ishtar bore him,
> he was victorious in nine campaigns . . .
> Because he defended Agade in this crisis,
> his city asked of Ishtar in Eannaki,
> of Enlil in Nippur,

---

64. *Vulture Stele of Eannatum* iv.9–12. Cf. Cooper, *Sumerian and Akkadian Royal Inscriptions*, 34; Stol, *Birth in Babylonia and the Bible*, 83–84. For images of the stele, see the Louvre Museum's website at https://www.louvre.fr/en/oeuvre-notices/stele-vultures.

65. Radau, *Early Babylonian History*, 165.

66. Kuhrt, *Ancient Near East*, 51.

67. For a great photo of the stele, see the Louvre Museum's website at https://www.louvre.fr/en/oeuvre-notices/victory-stele-naram-sin. See Ascalone, *Mesopotamia*, 30. The *Apotheosis of Washington* (1865), located in the U.S. Capitol, shows George Washington ascending into the heavens in glory together with the goddesses of liberty and victory. The cult of the hero!

68. A hymn describes Inana "crowned with great horns" (*Hymn to Inanna as Warrior, Star and Bride*, i.18, in Jacobsen, *Harps that Once*, 113).

> of Dagan in Tuttul,
> of Ninhursag in Kesh,
> of Enki in Eridu,
> of Sin in Ur,
> of Shamash in Sippar,
> of Nergal in Cutha,
> that he [= Narām-Sîn] be god of their city,
> and built a temple in Agade ...[69]

The kings of the Ur III Dynasty (*ca.* 2119, Isin, Larsa and Babylon) referred to themselves using divine titles.[70] Ur-Nammu (2112–2095 BCE) is portrayed as "son born of the goddess Ninsun."[71] A song pictures Enlil impregnating a priestess so that she may give birth to king Šulgi (2094–2047 BCE):

> The *en* priestess gave birth to the trustworthy man from his [= Enlil's] semen placed in the womb. Enlil, the powerful shepherd, caused a young man to emerge: a royal child, one who is perfectly fitted for the throne-dais, Šulgi the king.[72]

A famous lament (*ca.* 1500–1300 BCE) describes the king of Babylon as:

> The King, the flesh of the gods, the sun of his people.[73]

The expression "flesh of the gods" (*šīr ilī*) asserts that the very substance of the king was divine. We are told about king Gilgameš (*ca.* 2700 BCE) that "two-thirds of him were divine, and one-third of him was human,"[74] for he was procreated by the demigod Lugalbanda and the goddess Ninsuna. The epic relates that occasion when Gilgameš marched against a terrifying pair of scorpion-people:

> The scorpion-man called to his mate:
> 'He who has come to us, flesh of the gods is his body.'

---

69. *Naram-Sin inscription* i.1–8, in Foster, *Before the Muses*, 63.

70. See Kuhrt, *Ancient Near East*, 51; Ascalone, *Mesopotamia*, 107.

71. *Laws of Ur-Nammu* A.i.32, in Roth, *Law Collections*, 15. At the entrance of the palace of king Lipit-Eštar (*ca.* 1934 BCE), there is an inscription describing him as "son of the god Enlil" (*Lipit-Eštar* E4.1.5.3, i.28, in Frayne, *Old Babylonian Period*, 51).

72. *Adab to Enlil for Šulgi* i.19, in ETCSL 2.4.2.07. Another poem describes Šulgi with these words: "I, the king, was a hero already in the womb; I, Šulgi, was born to be a mighty man ... I am a respected one, the god of all the lands" (*Praise Poem of Šulgi* A i.6, in ETCSL 2.4.2.01).

73. *Ludlul* i.55, in Annus and Lenzi, *Ludlul bēl nēmeqi*, 32. Cf. Lambert, *Babylonian Wisdom*, 33.

74. *Gilg.* i.50, in Foster, *Gilgamesh*, 4–5.

The scorpion's mate answered him:
'Two-thirds of him is god, and one third human.'[75]

An epic about the Assyrian king, Tukulti-Ninurta I (1244–1208 BCE), portrays him as created by the gods:

> By the fiat of the lord [= Enlil] of the world,
> he was cast sublimely form the womb of the gods.
> It is he [= the king] who is the eternal image of Enlil ...
> ... the lord of the world appointed him to lead the troops,
> he praised him with his own lips,
> Enlil exalted him as if he were his own father,
> right after his firstborn son (= god Ninurta).[76]

b. Egypt

In a stela, the supreme god Amen-Re says to king Thutmose III (1490–1436 BCE):

> I give you protection, my son, my beloved,
> Horus, Strong-Bull-arisen-in-Thebes,
> Whom I begot in my divine body, Thutmose, everlasting ...[77]

The Egyptian Ptolemaic Dynasty (305–30 BCE) propagandized the divinity of their pharaohs. Ptolemy I (reign 305–282) was called *megistos theos sōter* (= greatest god savior). Ptolemy IV (reign 221–204) was called *theos filopatōr*, and similarly he and his wife Arsinoe III were called "father-loving gods." Ptolemy V (reign 204–181 BCE), also claimed divinity calling himself *theos epiphanes eucharistos* (= gracious god manifest).[78]

c. Syro-Palestinian region

In Ugarit, King Keret was believed to be the son of El. Therefore, his son was bewildered by the king's imminent death:

---

75. *Gilg.* ix.48, in George, *Epic of Gilgamesh*, 71. Cf. *Gilg.* x.7.

76. *Tukulti-Ninurta Epic* i.(= A obv.)18–20, in Foster, *Before the Muses*, 301–2.

77. *Poetical Steal of Thutmose III*, epilogue 3–5, in Lichtheim, *Ancient Egyptian Literature*, 2:38. Cf. "I have begotten you" (Ps 2:7); or "this is my beloved son" (Matt 3:17; 17:5).

78. Hölbl, *History of the Ptolemaic Empire*, 169–70.

> How could it be said
>> that Keret is the son of El,
>> offspring of the Wise and Holy One?
> Do the gods die?
>> Does the offspring of the Wise One not live?[79]

The Hellenistic king Antiochus IV (reign 175–164 BCE) was called God Manifest (*theos epifanēs*).[80] Second Maccabees informs that Antiochus thought that he could "walk on the sea" (5:21) and "that he could command (*epitassein*) the waves of the sea" (9:8).[81]

Perpetuating imperial theology, the king of Israel was thought to be the son of Yahve:

> I will announce the decree of Yahve.
> He said to me: "You are my son,
> I myself have begotten you today." (Ps 2:7)

This verse reveals one of the central tenets of the theology of Judah. During the coronation ceremony, the king was declared son of god. In this psalm, the god takes the role of a king issuing a decree (*hōq*) which institutes the king of Israel as his son (adoptionism).[82] The promise of divine filiation is the foundation of the covenant between Yahve and David. The key promise for this covenant was:

> I shall be his father, and he shall be my son. (2 Sam 7:14; 1 Chr 22:11)

Or:

> It is your son Solomon who shall build my house and my courts,
> for I have chosen him as my son, and I will be his father. (1 Chr 28:6)

Psalm 89:26, 27 [27, 28] gives expression to a reciprocal relationship between father and son:

---

79. *Epic of Kirta*, CAT 1.16.i.22–23, in Wyatt, *Religious Texts from Ugarit*, 222. In Ugarit, Ebla and Mari, Kings were divine, and when they died people worshipped and offered them sacrifices. See Schmidt, *Israel's Beneficent Dead*, 14–131.

80. Habicht, *Hellenistic Monarchies*, 191–92. Josephus also says that Antiochus was called "the god" (*Antiquitates Judaicae* xii.125).

81. Cf. "Who then is this, that can even command (*epitassei*) the winds and the water, and they obey him?" (Luke 8:25).

82. For the concept of regal law as coronation protocol, see Von Rad, *Teología*, 191–93; Noth, *Estudios sobre el Antiguo Testamento*, 159–61.

> ²⁶He shall call upon me: "You are my Father,
>   my El, and the Rock of my salvation."
> ²⁷On my side: "I will make him my firstborn,
>   Elyon of the kings of the earth."⁸³

The most astonishing text is Psalm 45:6[7], where the earthly king is called nothing less than Elohim:

> Your throne, O Elohim, is forever and ever.
> *kisʾăḵā ʾĕlōhîm ʿôlām waʿed*.⁸⁴

d. Mediterranean

Earthly kings were called *diotrefēs* = "raised" or "nurtured by Zeus":

> Great is the spirit⁸⁵ of kings nurtured by Zeus,
>   for their honor is from Zeus; and Zeus, the counselor, loves them.⁸⁶

It is important to mention the theology regarding Emperor Augustus who ruled in the time of Jesus. The senator and historian Cassius Dio (155–235 CE) sustained that Augustus was the son of Apollo. He reports that Julius Caesar wanted him to be his successor because:

> ... he was influenced largely by Attia's emphatic pronouncement, which said that he [Augustus] had been engendered by Apollo (*ek tou apollōnos auton kekuēkenai*); for she said that she had intercourse with a serpent one time when she was sleeping in the temple. This caused her to bear a son at the end of the designated time. Before he was born, she saw in a dream her entrails lifted to the Heavens and spreading out over all the earth; and that same night Octavius thought that the sun rose form her womb. Hardly had the child been born when Nigidius Figulus prophesied (*emanteusato*) immediately that [the boy] would have absolute power. This man could distinguish more accurately than his contemporaries the order of the firmament

---

83. The earthly king is the *ʿelyôn* (= Almighty) of all kings, in the same way Yahve is Elyon of all the other gods (Ps 82:6). The rest of the kings can only aspire to be the servants of the king of Israel.

84. The same reading is found in the LXX: "Your throne, o God, is forever and ever" (*ho thronos sou ho theos eis ton aiōna tou aiōnos*); also Vg.: *sedis tua Deus in saeculum saeculi*. Cf. NRSV, NIV.

85. Or: "terrible is the anger."

86. Homer, *Iliad* ii.196; cf. i.176; ii.98, 445.

and the differences between the stars, what they accomplish by themselves or together, by their conjunctions and by their intervals ... In this occasion he [= Nigidius] met Octavius ... and cried out: "you have begotten an emperor (*despotēn*)."[87]

e. Jesus: another king who was son of a god

In §4.3.3.c, we saw that Israel inherited the Mesopotamian ideology that made her king the son of Yahveh. It should come as no surprise that the Christian Bible took advantage of such a well-established metaphor: "Rabbi, you are the son of god, you are the king of Israel" (John 1:49), or: "Jesus is the Messiah, the son of god" (John 20:31; cf. 11:27). The Gospel of Luke first employs dynasty-claims to turn Jesus into a son of god. He informs the reader that the child to be born belongs to "the house of David" (Luke 1:27; cf. v. 32). This claim allows Gabriel to tell Mary that Jesus will be "son of the Most High," and that he will enjoy an eternal kingdom (Luke 1:31–33). The adoptionist theology of the Hebrew Bible provided sufficient license to declare that Jesus was the son of god because he was part of David's dynasty.

But then Luke steers the conversation away from the royal dynasty argument into a supernatural birth by divine impregnation. To this end, Luke places an obtuse question on Mary's lips. She asks the angel: "how can this be since I am a virgin?" (1:34). Gabriel could have simply responded "as I just told you, Joseph belongs to David's dynasty and, therefore, when Joseph gets you pregnant, the child will be the son of the Most High." Instead, the angel introduces the typical "getting pregnant by a god" mythology:

> holy spirit will come upon you,
> and the power of the Most High will overshadow you.
> Therefore, the holy (child) to be born[88] will be called son of god. (Luke 1:35)

---

87. Cassius, *Historiae Romanae* xlv.1.2–5 (cf. Cary, *Dio's History of Rome*, 4:407–9). Suetonius (69–122 CE) confirmed that Attia got pregnant in Apollo's temple by a serpent, and that "after the tenth month, Augustus was born and was, therefore, regarded as the son of Apollo. Before giving birth, Attia dreamed that her entrails were carried up to the stars and spread all over the whole land and sea, while Octavius dreamed that the sun rose from Attia's womb" (*Divus Augustus* xciv.4, in Ihm, *Suetonii*, 108).

88. The term *hagion* could be taken as an adjective turned into a noun by the article, which would allow it to be modified by the participle: *to gennōmenon hagion* = "the holy [child] to be born" (cf. NIV "the holy one"). If the adjective is acting as a noun, we can disregard the objections raised by Moule, *Idiom-Book*, 107 (cf. Casanova, *Introducción al griego*, §177.1). Another option would be to take *hagion* as predicative: "the one to be born [will be] holy; will be called son of god" (cf. NRSV, NJB, NLT Fitzmyer,

The passage is quite sober. It does not claim that a preexistent god (or *logos*) will descend from Heaven to take human form through Mary (John 1:14), nor does it claim that the Jewish god will have direct intercourse with Mary. The text rather says that an intermediary power will implant divine life (semen?) in Mary. And this is what allows Luke to conclude: "therefore" (*dio*), that is, because the boy will be begotten by a god, "he will be called son of god" (Luke 1:35). It seems that David's dynasty alone wasn't enough for Jesus to be a divine king.

In Matthew, Mary is also depicted as "pregnant by holy spirit . . ."[89] the begotten (child) in her is by holy spirit" (1:18, 20). And this is the reason why Jesus may be called Emmanuel, that is, god with us (1:23). At this point, we should recall the words of Plutarch:

> A spirit of god (*pneuma theou*) can approach a woman and get her pregnant.[90]

The church lived in an ecosystem where kings were thought to be gods or sons of the gods. Today all these legends are disconnected from our daily experience, and modern people have little patience when preachers expect them to take these stories *literally*.[91]

4.3.4 Political Function of the Gods: To Legitimize and Advance the Monarchy

Earthly monarchies made possible the creation of gods in the image of kings (anthropomorphism). At the same time, the gods returned the favor by legitimizing human monarchies. A vital function of religion was to serve the interests of the state. The doctrine of the *divine will* remained the foundation

---

Gospel according to Luke I–IX, 334; Casanova, *Introducción al Griego*, §180.1–2). This will require the tacit presence of the copulative verb (*estai* = "will be"), as is often the case. Finally, another predicative reading would be: "the one to be born will be called holy, son of god" (ESV, Bovon, *Gospel of Luke*, 52; Creed, *Gospel according to St. Luke*, 20; Plummer, *Gospel according to St. Luke*, 25).

89. The expression *en gastri* + *echō* was the standard form to say "to be pregnant," and *ek* adds the idea of agency ("by holy spirit"). Cf. Davies and Allison, *Gospel according to Saint Matthew*, 1:200.

90. Plutarch, *Numa* 4.4 (cf. Perrin, *Plutarch's Lives*, 319). In fact, Plutarch mentions a good list of mortals having intercourse and companionship with the gods to gain wisdom and blessedness. And he finds that it is fitting and proper "that a god should have affection for a man, and a so-called love which is based upon affection, and takes the form of solicitude for his character and his virtue, is fit and proper" (Perrin, *Plutarch's Lives*, 317–21).

91. See at the end of §5.

of governments until the so-called British Glorious Revolution (1688–1689 CE), as well as the American (1775–1783 CE) and French (1789 CE) Revolutions. One of the legends about Sargon the Great (2334–2284 BCE) clearly states that "As long as Ištar will gain vic[tories for him], [Sargon will let his voice re]sound in the land. As long as Irnina[92] will attain victories for him . . . [. . . Sa]rgon will let his voice resound in the land."[93] The gods were not just the gods of nature (§1.2.3), they were the forces behind kings and empires.

One of the wall panel-reliefs of the palace of the Assyrian king Aššhur-nasir-pal II (883–859 BCE) portrays a clear image of how the gods were imagined joining their kings in the battlefield. Albrektson's comments on the sculpture are quite to the point:

> One of the most striking expressions of this idea of divine historical deeds executed through a king is found in Assyrian art. In the famous reliefs of Ashurnasirpal there is a complete conformity between the god's movements and activities and those of the king. When Ashurnasirpal draws his bow in combat, the god Ashur too, suspended in the air above the king in a winged solar disc.[94]

a. Mesopotamia

Sumer (*ca.* 1600 BCE) ascribed divine origin to its monarchy in order to legitimize the institution:

> [When the . . .] kingship had come down from heaven,
> after the lofty crown and the throne of kingship had come down from heaven . . .[95]

King Ur-Nammu (*ca.* 2112–2095 BCE) said about himself:

> For me, kingship came down from heaven!
> Sweet is the praise of me, the shepherd Ur-Nammu![96]

---

92. *Irnina* means "victory," and it is another name for goddess Ištar as the personification of war. See Westenholz, *Legends of the Kings of Akkade*, 78.

93. *Sargon in Foreign Lands* i.7–9, in Westenholz, *Legends of the Kings of Akkade*, 83.

94. Albrektson, *History of the Gods*, 49.

95. *Sumerian Flood Story* i.88–89, in Civil, "Sumerian Flood Story," 141. The *Sumerian King List* starts saying: "After the kingship descended from heaven, the kingship was in Eridug" (i.1–2, in ETCSL 2.1.1; Jacobsen, *Sumerian King List*, 71).

96. *Praise Poem of Ur-Namma* (Ur-Namma C) i.114–15, in ETCSL 2.4.1.3.

The city of Uruk and its temple claimed divine origin: "Uruk, handiwork of the gods; Eanna, the temple descended from heaven."[97] The Amorite king Šamšu-iluna (ca.1750–1712 BCE) won his victories assisted by the gods. An inscription portrays Enlil commanding Zababa and Ištar, "the doughtiest warriors among the gods," to slay the enemies of Šamšu-iluna, so that the king could bring the city of Kish (Tell al-Uhaymir) into great prominence for the glory of Enlil. So Zababa and Ištar addressed the king to inform him:

> He [Enlil] has commanded us to act as your allies to keep you safe.
> We will march at your right hand,[98]
>   we will slay your foes,[99]
>   we will deliver your enemies into your power.[100]

These warrior-gods made Šamšu-iluna victories possible: "He [= the king] slew the rebel kings, his foes, he destroyed them all ... He made all of Sumer and Akkad obedient, he made the four world regions to dwell under his command."[101]

The gods are portrayed as actively participating in the battles of their kings. They are not simple "nature gods" with no bearing on the political and military affairs of humanity. A psalm in praise of the great Tiglath-Pileser I (1114–1076 BCE) describes the gods aggressively fighting in battle at the command of Enlil:

> (So) the god [Enlil] made pride of the slaughter of the foe,
>   All the gods heard his utterance.
> Assur said: "Slaughter the enemy!"
>   "Destroy the foe!" came forth from [his] lips.
> His heart resolved on slaughter,
>   his mouth com[manded] the scattering of the wicked.
> In order to diminish their troops, he made war,
>   He drew up battle, caused mutiny (among them).
> He girded himself with awe-inspiring weapons,

---

97. *Gilgames and Agga* i.30–31, in Cooper, "Gilgamesh and Akka," 235–38. Cf. Jacobsen, *Harps that Once*, 345–55; Katz, *Gilgamesh and Akka*, 40–45.

98. Cf. "Adonay is at your right hand, and crushes the kings on the day of his wrath" (Ps 110:5; cf. Ps 60:12[14]; 81:14).

99. Yahve promises the king: "I will crush his foes before him and strike down those who hate him" (Ps 89:23).

100. *Samsuilina, King of Babylon* i.5, in Foster, *Before the Muses*, 141. Cf. Num 21:34; Deut 7:24; 20:13, etc.

101. *Samsuilina, King of Babylon* i.5, in Foster, *Before the Muses*, 141.

> He commanded his favorite to the battlefields' task,
> He made proud the weaponry of Tukulti-apil-Eshara!
> Before him (= king), Enlil leads him into battle,
> Ishtar, mistress of turmoil, aroused him to strife,
> Ninurta, foremost of the gods, positioned himself at this front,
> Nusku was slaughtering all enemies at his right,
> Adad overwhelmed the foes at his left.[102]

In a work about violence (*ca.* 765 BCE), the god Erra promises to advance the empire of the king who becomes his devotee: "Let the King who extols my name rule the world, Let the prince who discourses the praise of my valor have no rival."[103] Ashurbanipal's expansionist ideology (669–627 BCE) was founded on the doctrine of the divine will:

> ... the great gods in their council ... the lands of my enemies
> they counted into my hands. They brought all my heart's desires
> to perfect fulfilment.[104]

A hymn that talks about Ashurbanipal's coronation focuses again on divine legitimation:

> May they [= the gods] give him a just scepter
> to enlarge [his] land and people.
> May his reign be ever renewed,
> may they establish his royal throne forever.
> May they bless him day, month and year,
> may they [make] his reign [out]standing.
> [During] his years, may the rain from heaven
> and the flood from the underground depths be unfail[ling].[105]

Another story presents a violent scene in which Aššur himself saves Esarhaddon (681–669 BCE) from his enemies:

> I heard your cry and appeared as a fiery glow
> from the gate of heaven, to throw down fire and have it devour them.
> As you were standing in their midst,
> I removed them from your presence,

---

102. *Hymn to Tiglath-Pileser I* i.24–40, in Foster, *Before the Muses*, 325.

103. *Erra and Ishum* v.51, 52, in Foster, *Before the Muses*, 910–11.

104. *Historical Prism Inscriptions of Ashurbanipal*, edition B, column i, in Piepkorn, *Historical Prism Inscriptions*, 29.

105. *Ashurbanipal Coronation Prayer* i.16–22, in Foster, *Before the Muses*, 816.

drove them up the mountain
and rained fire and brimstone upon them.
I slaughtered your enemies
and filled the River with their blood.[106]

As lords of the universe, the gods claimed to have the power to protect the kings they have established. An affectionate prophecy, dedicated to Esarhaddon, mentions the assiduous care the gods had for their king:

Fear not, Esarhaddon!
I am Bel (= Marduk), I speak to you!
I watch over the supporting beams of your heart.
When your mother gave birth to you,
sixty Great Gods stood there with me, protecting you.
Sîn (= Moon) stood at your right side, Šamaš (= Sun) at your left.
Sixty Great Gods are still standing around you;
they have girded your loins.

Do not trust in humans!
Lift up your eyes and focus on me!
I am Ištar (= Venus) of Arbela.
I have reconciled Aššur to you.
I protected you when you were a baby.
Fear not; praise me!

Is there an enemy that has attacked you,
while I have kept silent?
The future shall be like the past!
I am Nabû (= god of writing), the Lord of the Stylus. Praise me![107]

---

106. *La-dagil-ili to Esarhaddon* ii.18–23, in Nissinen, *Prophets and Prophecy*, 120. Cf. Isa 34:1–3; Zeph 1:17.

107. *Bayâ to Esarhaddon* ii.16–39, in Nissinen, *Prophets and Prophecy*, 105. In a prophecy, Ištar promises Esarhaddon: "I will protect you in your palace, I will make you overcome fear and trembling. Your son and your grandson shall exercise kingship before Ninurta. I will do away with the boundaries of the countries and give them to you" (*La-dagil-ili to Esarhaddon* ii.11–6, in Nissinen, *Prophets and Prophecy*, 113).

b. Egypt

The *Stela of Thutmose III* (*ca.* 1490–1436 BCE) narrates how Amen-Re gave Pharaoh the power to conquer all the lands, including the Syro-Palestine region (Djahi). The stela says:

> The princes of all lands are gathered in your grasp,
> I stretched my own hands out and bound them for you.
> I fettered Nubia's Bowmen by ten thousand thousands,
> The northerners hundred thousand captives.
> I made your enemies succumb beneath your soles,
> so that you crushed the rebels and the traitors.
> For I bestowed on you the earth, its length and breadth,
> Westerners and easterners are under your command.[108]

c. Israel

As a weather-god, Yahve was able to unleash meteorological disasters against the enemies of his people. Nahum 1:2–6 presents Yahve as a force that will destroy Nineveh (1:1, 14) and protect Judah (1:10–13). To this end, Yahve's vindictive rage (1:2) is called upon, which can impose a destructive drought unleashing the return to Chaos (v. 4)[109] or strike with terrifying storms and lightning (vv. 3, 5–6):

> [3b]His path is in the whirlwind and the storm,
>   the clouds are the dust of his feet.
> [4]He rebukes the sea and dries it up,
>   he dries up all the rivers. [110]
> Bashan and Carmel languish,
>   and the bloom of Lebanon wither.
> [5]The mountains quake before him,
>   and the hills melt.
> The earth heaves before him,
>   the world and all who inhabit it.
> [6]Who can stand before his indignation?

---

108. *Steal of Thutmose III*, prologue 5–11, in Lichtheim, *Ancient Egyptian Literature*, 2:36.

109. For the subject of Chaos, see §1.1.4; §1.3.5–7.

110. We can clearly hear an echo coming from Ugaritic theology: the fight against Yamm (= Sea) who is also governor Nahar (= River). See §1.3.3.

> Who can endure the heat of his anger?
> His wrath is poured out like fire,
> > and the rocks are shattered by him (Nah 1:3–6).[111]

The people of Israel inherited the myth of the earthly king who demands the submission of the nations on the basis of an almighty god. Every time a king was enthroned, Yahve promised him:

> [8]Ask me, and I will give you the nations as your property,
> > and the ends of the earth as your territory.
> [9]You shall break them with an iron rod,
> > you shall smash them into pieces like a potter's vessel.
> [10]Now O kings, be prudent,
> > learn, rulers of the earth.
> [11]Serve Yahve with fear
> > and rejoice with trembling.
> [12]Kiss the son[112] lest he be angry
> > and you will perish in the way,
> for his wrath flares up quickly.
> > Happy are all those who take refuge in him (Ps 2:8–12).

Psalm 2 does not describe a friendly ruler, but instead portrays the typical violent king whose dream is to conquer the world with the help of an equally vicious god. The psalm highlights the universality of his power and the violence of his enterprise. Psalm 144 argues that Yahve is "the one who gives victory to kings."[113] And like any other god, Yahve is shown actively involved in the wars of his people (Ps 144:1–2, 5–8).

Psalm 110 contains a particularly violent scene of a god who fights for his king:

> [1]Oracle of Yahve to my adonay:
> > Sit at my right hand,
> > until I make your enemies
> > > your footstool.
> [2]Your mighty scepter

---

111. For Yahve as a weather-god, see §1.3.5–6.

112. The MT reads naššəqû-ḇar = "kiss the son" of Yahve, that is, the king (cf. v. 7). It is objected, however, the use of an Aramean word (ḇar), when the Hebrew word ben was available. A good option would be to amend the text to naššəqû-ḇəraḡlāyw. = "kiss his feet" (NRSV, NJB).

113. Ps 144:10.

> Yahve shall extend from Zion,
>> so you may rule[114] in the midst of your enemies...
> ⁵Adonay is at your right hand
>> and crushes the kings on the day of his wrath.
> ⁶He punishes the nations,
>> piling corpses,
> and shattering skulls
>> over the wide earth.

In the name of Yahve, the prophet asks the king to sit at the most prestigious place in Yahve's court. The king only needs to sit and wait for his god to fight on his behalf. Yahve himself will put his enemies as footstools, that is, he will kill or bring them down to submission (v. 1). It is Yahve who will extend his kingship for him to rule over his foes (v. 2). Like other gods, Adonay engages in warfare at the right hand of his king and shatters his enemies (v. 5). Imperial violence shows its ugly face when we are told that Yahve will fill up the world with corpses and broken skulls (v. 6). This has been a favorite psalm for violent Christianity (§5.1.1–2).

Other examples of mythic victories: Classic is the case of Exodus 14:15–25, where Yahve sows confusion among the Egyptians and personally removes (*wayyāsar*) the wheels of their chariots.[115] In a battle against a Canaanite coalition, Yahve himself caused panic among the Amorites (Josh 10:10). As a storm-god, Yahve "threw down huge stones" from Heaven. More people died by the "hailstones" than by the sword of Israel (Josh 10:11). Then Yahve told Joshua "do not be afraid of them for tomorrow at this time I will hand all of them over dead before Israel" (Josh 11:6). First Samuel 7:10 presents Yahve as a storm-warrior-god who crushes the aggressor: ... "on that day Yahve thundered with great violence against the Philistines and confounded them and were defeated before Israel."[116] Another case comes when, during the night, the Messenger of Yahve kills a hundred eighty

---

114. The impv. *rəḏēʰ* has consecutive force. Cf. Davidson, *Hebrew Syntax*, 87; Ges. § 110.c–i.

115. We find something similar in Psalm 76, where Yahve himself destroys armament, bows, shields and swords (v. 3[4]); he brings confusion among the troops (v. 5[6]) and the cavalry (v. 6[7]).

116. The verbs "thundered" (*wayyarʿēm*) and "confounded" (*wayəhummēm*) have Yahve as subject, and the agent of the passive "were defeated" (*wayyinnāḡp̄û*) is also Yahve: "they were defeated" by Yahve. A new subject only shows up in the next verse: "The men of Israel came out" (v. 11). Human action is here the response to Yahve's previous victory: "And significantly it is not an army of Israel or even Samuel himself who stampedes the invading Philistines; instead it is Yahweh ... who routs the enemy" (McCarter, *1 Samuel*, 149). Cf. Smith, *Commentary on the Books of Samuel*, 51.

thousand men in the Assyrian camp (2 Kings 19:35). Nothing new or surprising is reflected in any of these mythic stories. They just follow the well-known script of warrior-gods imitating earthly kings.

d. Mediterranean

In preparing for battle, goddess Athene covers Achilles' shoulders with her aegis and covers his head with a golden cloud which causes him to emit a gleaming flame that went up into the sky. Then Achilles shouted mightily producing great panic among the Trojans. Achilles voice was:

> strong as the sound of the trumpet when murderous foes besiege a city, such was the clearness of the brazen voice of the Aeacid. And when they heard the brazen voice of the Aeacid, the hearts of all were dismayed; and the fair-maned horses turned back their chariots for their animus foreshadowed destruction. And the charioteers were stricken with terror when they saw the inexhaustible terrifying fire that burned on the head of the magnanimous son of Peleus, for flashing-eyed Athene caused the fire to burn ... At that moment, twelve of their most courageous warriors died runned over by their own chariots and wounded by their own spears.[117]

Homer also relates the moment when Apollo himself attacked the army of King Agamemnon for having humiliated Chryse his priest:

> Angry in his heart, Apollo strode down from the peaks of the Olympus with his bow and covered quiver on his shoulders. As he moved the arrows rattled on the shoulders of the angry god, advancing like the night. He sat down apart from the ships and threw an arrow. The twang of the silver bow was frightening. He first attacked the mules and swift dogs, but then he shot his stinging arrows against the men themselves, and like never before the pyres of corpses piled up. For nine days the missiles of the god ranged through the army.[118]

Conclusion

It is clear that monarchy became the storehouse from which the ancients took a host of images and linguistic expressions to construct the conceptual

---

117. Homer, *Iliad* xviii.220–31.
118. Homer, *Iliad* i.43–49.

metaphor GOD IS KING. The abstract divine world (*target domain*) was understood in terms of the concrete earthly monarchies of the time (*source domain*). The gods became kings, and the earthly kings became gods. Most importantly, the function of the gods was to legitimize monarchy and its thirst for power. In the next chapter, we will assess the metaphors which have turned Jesus into an imperialistic warrior.

We'll never pay rent for our mansion,
The taxes will never come due,
Our garments will never grow threadbare,
But always be fadeless and new,
We'll never be hungry or thirsty,
Nor languish in poverty there,
For all the rich bounties of Heaven
His sanctified children will share.

—FREDERICK M. LEHMAN[1]

Chapter 5

CRITICAL ASSESSMENT OF THE KING METAPHOR

5.1 The Christian Warrior-God: The Foundation of Christian Tyranny

ONE OF THE MOST cherished legends of Christianity portrays Christ as the warrior-god who established Rome as a Christian Empire. It is vital at this point to remember what we have learned about the gray areas between myth and legend, history and fiction (§1.2.4), because the way Eusebius narrates the following story makes it clear that his report is both part myth and part history. It is also clear that the function of the myth was to legitimize the political power of the king: the myth of the divine will. The historical facts go like this: In July of the year 306 CE, Constantine (272–337 CE) was elected Tetrarch. In October of the same year, Maxentius (278–312 CE) encroached into power and declared war against Constantine. Taking the lead, Constantine crossed the Alps and marched up to Rome. Finally, both emperors were face to face ready to battle against each other (312 CE).

---

1. "No Disappointment in Heaven," written in 1914 by Frederick M. Lehman.

At this juncture, Eusebius inserts into his narrative the Christianized version of the warrior-god myth.[2] According to Eusebius, god himself "incited" (*anegēgermenou*) Constantine against Maxentius. During the battle god himself fought "as his ally" (*summachountos autō*). And "God himself" (*theos autos*) dragged Maxentius out into battle in order to kill him. Then Eusebius compares Constantine to Moses saying that in the same way the Egyptians sank in the Red Sea (Exod 15:4–5), Maxentius' army was defeated while fleeing from "the power of God that was with Constantine" (*ek theou meta Kōnstantinou dunamei*). Eusebius claims that Constantine's deeds were praises sung to "the Supreme God, who was the cause of his victory" (*tō panēgemoni kai tēs nikēs aitiō theō*).[3] In this narrative there is no difference between the Christian god and the warrior-gods discussed in §4.3.2 and §4.3.4.

In another place, Eusebius repeats the same story:

> While he [Constantine] was praying, God gave him a vision: a cross of light in the sky (*stauron ek phōtos en ouranō*) and an inscription exhorting him to conquer by it. So with fervent prayer and supplications, he asked him to reveal who he was and to extend his right hand to help him in the present troubles. And while he was praying with devout supplication, an extraordinary divine sign (*theosēmia*) appeared from heaven. This account would have been difficult to believe if told by any common person, but since it was the victorious emperor himself who reported it, much later, to the author of this history... Who would doubt giving credit to the report? ... He told me that about noon, when the day started to decline, he saw with his own eyes the trophy of a cross of light in the sky, above the sun, and the inscription: victory through this (*toutō nika*). When he saw it, he was amazed along with his army that followed him in this expedition and saw the miracle.[4]

---

2. See the descriptions of Enlil, Ninurta, Baal and Yahve as warrior gods in §1.1.4; §1.2.3; §1.3.3; §4.2.1.

3. Eusebio, *Historia eclesiastica* ix.9.1–9, in Migne, *Patrologiae Graecae*, 20:820–24.

4. *De Vita Constantini* i.28, in Migne, *Patrologiae Graecae*, 20:944. Lactantius (250–325 CE) narrates the story this way: "In a dream, Constantine was instructed to place the heavenly sign of God on the shields (of his soldiers) and thus go to battle. He did as he had been commanded, and marked Christ on the shields with the letter X with a vertical line rounded on top. With this sign XP, his troops stood to arms ... the hand of the Lord prevailed, and the forces of Maxentius were routed ... With great rejoicing, the senate and the people of Rome acknowledged Constantine as emperor" (Lactantius, *De Mortibus Persecutorum* 44.4–6, in Migne, *Patrologiae Latina*, 7:261). Cf. Fletcher, *Lactantius* 44.4–6, in Roberts and Donaldson, *Ante-Nicene Fathers*, 7:318.

Although Eusebius maintains that Constantine saw the miracle "with his own eyes" as well as his army, it would be foolish to believe that he's reporting historical facts, because *we know* that his narrative recycles the well-known myth of warrior-gods fighting the battles of their kings. Constantine is just another ruler in need of divine legitimation for his despotic government. And yet many Christians believe the myth to be a historical fact, as if the Christian god was *literally* fighting Constantine's battles. This is how metaphor takes control of the brain and cements the so-called foundational myth of an empire. Once a fictional narrative declares Constantine a king chosen by a god, people will "see" him this way. In order to produce such an effect, Eusebius declares that Constantine was declared supreme emperor "by God himself" (*pros autou theou*).[5] The function of the metaphor is not merely rhetorical. It is an ideological tool employed to make us think and act in a certain way. It gives us a "vision," a way of experiencing life.

In §1.2.3, we saw a similar story mixing together history and myth. We were told that Enlil gazed towards the mountains to look for the Gutians, and that he persuaded them to descend from the mountains to attack the Agade Empire. The narrative credits Enlil for the *historical* collapse of an important empire, for it was "because of Enlil" that the Gutians were able destroy their enemy. In similar fashion, Isaiah 45:1–7 blends the well-known *historical* fact of Cyrus' unstoppable conquests with the fictional perspective of a warrior-god who fights with and for his king:

> [1]Thus says Yahve to his anointed,
> > to Cyrus, the one I took by the right hand,
> to defeat nations before him,
> > and disarm kings,[6]
> to open doors before him,
> > so that gates may not close.
> [2]I myself go before you
> > and I level mountains,[7]
> I smash bronze doors
> > and I cut off iron bars,
> [3]and I give you the treasures hidden in darkness
> > and the hoards of secret places,
> so that you acknowledge that I am Yahve,

---

5. *Historia ecclesiastica* viii.13.14, in Migne, *Patrologiae Graecae*, 20:780.

6. Lit. "to strip the loins of kings."

7. "I level mountains" follows the LXX (*orē omaliō*), the Hebrew word *wahădûrîm* is not clear. 1QIsa^a also confirms it is "mountains."

the one who calls you by your name is the God of Israel.

Of course, in Babylon the warrior-god was not Yahve but Marduk who:

> searched everywhere and then he took a righteous king, his favorite, by the hand, he called out his name: Cyrus, king of Ansan; he pronounced his name to be king all over the world.[8]

It was because of Marduk that Cyrus could declare:

> I am Cyrus, king of the world, great king, mighty king, king of Babylon, king of Sumer and Akkad, king of the four quarters.[9]

According to Herodotus, Cyrus instigated the rebellion of his people against the Medes using the legend about his own supernatural birth to convince them that the gods were behind him: "Now, do as I tell you and win your freedom. For I believe that I myself was born by divine providence (*theiē tuchē*)[10] to undertake this enterprise. I hold you as people who are as good as the Medes in war and in everything else. Therefore, revolt against Astyages right now!"[11] In fact, Herodotus claimed that Cyrus himself thought he was "more than a man" (*pleon . . . anthrōpou*).[12]

A recent use of this myth comes from a retired fireman named Mark Taylor who claimed that before the U.S. presidential election of 2016 he received a message from god. His visionary experience was recounted as a true story in the movie *The Trump Prophecy*.[13] During one of his many nightmares, Taylor sees a radiant ball beaming light upon him while hearing Donald Trump talk on TV. Taylor opens his Bible to find Isaiah 45:1–7. He was convinced that the passage was a prophecy about Trump.[14] The purpose of the movie is to narrate how god revealed to Mr. Taylor that Trump is the new Cyrus, chosen to restore America to the Promised Land. Christian nationalists and fundamentalists loved the Cyrus prophecy because they yearn for a religious dictator.[15] This also shows the tremendous power of metaphor as a mind-controlling tool (§1.1.5).

---

8. *Cyrus Cylinder* i.12, in Oppenheim, "Cyrus," 315.

9. *Cyrus Cylinder* i.20, in Oppenheim, "Cyrus," 315. Cf. Kuhrt, *Ancient Near East*, 601.

10. Or: "divine necessity."

11. Herodotus, *Histories* i.126.6 (cf. Godley, *Herodotus*, 1:167).

12. Herodotus, *Histories* i.204.2.

13. The film was produced by ReelWorksStudios with the help of Liberty University, whose president, Jerry Falwell Jr., is a big supporter of Trump.

14. See the review by Rabey, "New Film."

15. See Gushee, "Trump Prophecy"; Markoe, "Did Trump Fulfill a Divine

There are many *historical* events that were wrapped in myth (§1.1.4; §1.2.3). We've seen how Enlil brought the Gutians down from the mountains to crush the Agade Empire (*ca.* 2340-2159 BCE). Yahve used Nebuchadnezzar II to punish Jerusalem for her apostasy (587 BCE). Marduk and Yahve made Cyrus the king of the world for he was "born by divine providence." And the gods also helped Cyrus conquer Croesus' kingdom (547 BCE). The gods brought about the fall of Sparta (371 BCE). The Christian god was "the cause" of Constantine's victory at the gates of Rome (312 CE), and "God himself" declared him supreme emperor. Today we find Christians declaring Trump the new Cyrus. Myth is fictional and, nonetheless, it is a fantasy that completely changes the *meaning* of any event. Once a historical event is infected by myth, it becomes the outcome of divine intervention. The event is "seen" as the work of a god and, therefore, sacred and good. Our warnings against the power of metaphor were not exaggerated (§1.1.5). Just remember that it was a metaphor that allowed criminal states to "see" Jewish and Tutsi peoples as pests who needed to be exterminated. It was metaphor that sanctioned White people to dehumanize, exploit and kill Native Americans and Africans.

5.1.1 Primitive Christianity

The Christian Bible applied to Christ two of the royal psalms discussed in chapter 4:

> Psalm 2:1-2, 7, 9 (§4.3.3.c; §4.3.4.c), quoted in Acts 4:25-26; 13:33; Hebrews 1:5; 5:5; Revelation 2:26-27; 12:5; 19:15

> Psalm 110:1 (§4.3.4.c), quoted in Acts 2:34-35; 1 Corinthians 15:25; Hebrews 1:13; 10:12-13 (cf. Ephesians 1:20-22; Colossians 3:1)

Some people believe that the Hebrew Bible depicts a warlike and irascible god, while the Christian Bible presents a loving Jesus. Although it is true that the idea of the kingdom may adopt an ethical vision (Mark 10:23-25; 12:34; Matt 5:3, 19-20; Rom 14:17, etc.) or that it could be identified with the church (Eph 1:20-23), the eschatological formulation of the kingdom describes Jesus as a totalitarian and violent king. In apocalyptic style, 1 Corinthians 15:24-25 portrays Jesus as a bellicose king who comes to exterminate his enemies. Verse 24 maintains that when "the end" comes, Christ will hand the kingdom to the Father, but only:

Prophecy?"

after having destroyed[16] all government,[17] and all authority and power.[18]

Thiselton correctly explains that these terms mean "*any* kind of structural opposition to God, whether social, political, economic, ethical, spiritual, or even (to use a problematic term) 'supernatural,' i.e., possible agencies beyond this world, although unspecified as such."[19] Then Paul uses Psalm 110 to justify (*gar*) the aforementioned destruction by declaring it mandatory: "for he [= Christ] must reign until he has put all his enemies under his feet" (1 Cor 15:25).[20] In other words, the violent concepts of the psalm are used to legitimize the universal destruction of all political structures and organizations by the "Prince of Peace."

In the book of Revelation, Christ emerges as the god of warfare, just like Ištar was "the goddess of warfare, the lady of battle." The sanguinary Jesus rides on a white horse in the company of four destructive horsemen: War, Famine, Inflation and Death (Rev 6:1-8).[21] Mounting again on his white horse, Christ appears clothed in a robe "soaked in blood" (19:13), and:

> [15]From his mouth comes a sharp sword with which to strike down the nations, and he will rule them with a rod iron; and he himself will tread the wine press of the fury of the wrath of God Almighty.[16] On his robe and on his thigh he carries inscribed the title: "King of kings and Lord of lords." (Rev 19:15-16)

This bloody king then sends an angel to invite the birds to come and eat the flesh of the rebels who opposed his totalitarian eschatological kingdom:

---

16. As in 1 Cor 6:13; 13:11; 15:26; and 2 Thess 2:8, here the verb *katargeō* means "to destroy" (NRSV, NIV, NLT) and not just "to abolish" (NJB, NASB). See Delling, "katargeō," 454; Ciampa and Rosner, *First Corinthians*, 765; Conzelmann, *1 Corinthians*, 263; Fee, *First Corinthians*, 826; Fitzmyer, *First Corinthians*, 567; Thiselton, *First Corinthians*, 1231.

17. Here the word *archē* means government (Dan 7:27; *Aristeas* i.221) or the power of government (Dan 7:14, 26).

18. These three terms refer both to secular as well as supernatural powers mentioned in apocalyptic literature, all seen as enemies of this god.

19. Thiselton, *First Epistle to the Corinthians*, 1232.

20. Paul uses here the rabbinic method in order to adapt Psalm 110 to what he wants to convey. While the psalm presents Yahve addressing the king in 1st pers. sing. (". . . until I make your enemies your footstool"), 1 Cor 15:25 makes Christ the subject of verbs now in 3rd pers. sing. (". . . he [Christ] must reign until he has put all his enemies under his feet").

21. This reminds us of Marduk's four horses: Assassin, Ruthless, Overpowering and Fast. See *En. el.* iv.52.

... eat the flesh of kings, the flesh of captains, the flesh of the mighty, the flesh of horses and their riders, the flesh of all, whether free or slave, small or great. (19:18)

In the same apocalyptic style, the Gospels talk about the "day of judgment."[22] This expression cannot be found neither in the Hebrew Bible nor in the LXX, but it began to appear during the Persian period. This new theology locates a judgment day at the end of the world, when the absolute Tyrant will throw all his adversaries in the "furnace of fire."[23] The autocrat Jesus will punish people with "eternal fire"[24] and "eternal punishment."[25] He comes to burn the chaff in "unquenchable fire" (Matt 3:12). And if someone takes refuge in the words "for God so loved the world" (John 3:16), we should remind them that in the next few verses god's love turns pretty ugly:

... but those who do not believe are condemned already, because they have not believed in the name of the only Son of God. (John 3:18, NRSV)

5.1.2 Later Christianity

If Christ is the Coming Tyrant, then he is also the king who demands obedience in the here and now. The church eagerly embraced the myth of an emperor chosen by their god to enforce religion. Constantine banned heresy and harshly repressed other religions in order to force conversions.[26] For example, the violent fight between Christians and pagans in the city of Gaza (Palestine) came to an end when Constantine issued a decree ordering the eradication of all paganism from the city, as Bishop Porphyry (347–420 CE) had requested. Pagan temples were destroyed and houses were searched in

---

22. Matt 10:15; 11:22, 24; 12:36, etc. (*1 En.* 10:6, 12; 22:4, 11, 13; *Gk. Apoc. Ezra* 2:29; 7:11; *T. Levi* 1:1; 3:3. Cf. *Sib. Or.* 3:53–54.). Cf. "the great day of judgment" (*1 En.* 97:1; 98:10; 99:15; cf. 25:4; 103:8), "the days of the true judgment" (*1 En.* 27:3), "the eternal judgment" (*1 En.* 104:5; cf. *Gk. Apoc. Ezra* 5:23), "great judgment and empire" (*Sib. Or.* 3:743). On Judgment Day, humanity will be divided in two (Matt 13:24–30, 49–50; 25:31–46), and the rebels will be thrown into the *geenna* (Matt 10:28), a place of complete darkness (Matt 22:13; *2 Ezra* 4:37; *T. Jac.* 5:9, *Sib. Or.* 4:186, etc.), where they will find weeping and gnashing of teeth (Matt 24:51; *Sib. Or.* 2:305; 8:104, 231, etc.). Cf. "the valley of burning fire" (*1 En.* 54:1).

23. Matt 13:42, 50; cf. *1 En.* 98:3.

24. Matt 25:41; cf. *4 Macc* 12:12; *3 Bar.* 4:16; *T. Zeb.* 10:13; *Sib. Or.* 8:401.

25. Matt 25:46; cf. *T. Reu.* 5:5; *T. Gad* 7:5; *T. Ab.* 11:11.

26. See MacMullen, *Christianizing the Roman Empire*; Fox, *Pagans and Christians*; Schott, *Christianity, Empire, and the Making of Religion*; Gigeser, *Making of a Christian Empire*.

order to confiscate idols and books (402 CE).[27] Ramsay MacMullen points out that the central factor that caused the eradication of paganism was imperial violence, without which pagan intransigence simply could not have been overcome. The violence against Gaza became "a sort of model for the empire as a whole." Stubborn pagans were tied up and severely tortured and taken to the provincial capital where they were killed.[28] *Vita Porphyrii* warrants the use of deadly force with the following arguments:

> But the Holy Bishop [Porphyry] said to them . . . : For even as a man who has gotten a willfully disobedient servant first admonishes him by all means to behave himself wisely and to serve him with a simple heart, but when the man finds the servant in no way obedient unto his admonition, then thereafter of necessity he lays upon him fear and blows and bonds and other such things, desiring not to destroy him but that he should be saved and acknowledge that which behooved him. Even such may you suppose God to be, enduring our disobedience with long suffering, and oftentimes persuading us for our profit both through the Scriptures and through other holy men; but when we are not persuaded, desiring in all things like a good and merciful master to keep us and not to thrust us away, he lays upon us his fear and his teaching, calling us of necessity to acknowledge that which behooves us. Therefore, the divine Scripture says: "When he slew them, then they sought him, and they returned and inquired early after God" [Ps 77:34, LXX; MT Ps 78:34]. And again it says concerning them who behave themselves unruly and stiffen their necks against God: "With muzzle and bridle you must hold their jaws, lest they come nigh thee" [Ps 31:9, LXX; MT 32:9]. It is needful, therefore, my children, that mankind be admonished by fear and threats and discipline.[29]

Following the old tradition (§4.3.3), Christianity supported the empire and the empire enforced religion via imperial decrees like a law issued by Emperor Justinian the Great (483–565 CE):

> All those who have not yet been baptized must come forward, whether they reside in the capital or in the provinces, and go to the very holy churches with their wives, their children, and their households, to be instructed in the true faith of Christians. And once thus instructed and sincerely renounced their former

---

27. For the destruction of classical culture and books, see Gaddis, *There Is No Crime*; Nixen, *Darkening Age*; O'Donnel, *Pagans*.

28. MacMullen, *Christianizing the Roman Empire*, 89.

29. Hill, *Life of Prophyry*, 83.

error, let them be judged worthy of redemptive baptism. Should they disobey, let them know that they will be excluded from the State and will no longer have any rights of possession, neither goods nor property; stripped of everything, they will be reduced to penury, without prejudice to the appropriate punishments that will be imposed on them.[30]

Perez Zagorin laments St. Augustine's (354–430 CE) endorsement of coercion as a means to conversion. "It is regrettable," he says, "that one of his major legacies to the Catholic Church was the formulation of a theory of persecution founded entirely on Christian grounds and supported with numerous examples from the Old and New Testaments."[31] Zagorin explains that Augustine finally endorsed coercion when he discovered that it works. Persecution and fear were actually bringing people to the faith! Therefore, he thought that intimidation and terror were beneficial for the soul. In support of this evangelistic strategy, Augustine quoted the Parable of the Great Dinner, in which the master orders his servants: "compel people to come in" (Luke 14:23). According to Augustine:

> ... persecution is just which the churches of Christ inflict on the wicked ... The Church persecutes by loving ... The Church persecutes in order to correct; ... The Church persecutes in order to call back from error; ... The Church, finally, persecutes and lays hold of enemies until they collapse in their vanity so that they may grow in the truth."[32]

John Calvin expressed the same sentiment in an extremely repulsive way, for it is difficult to imagine how we could happily and voluntarily serve King Jesus when the alternative is torture and death:

---

30. Decree of Emperor Justinian the Great (483–565 CE), quoted in Freeman, *Closing of the Western Mind*, 268. Cf. the *Waldense Confession* (1655), which gives expression to the popular Christian belief that the Heavenly King supports the earthly king: "God hath established kings and magistrates to govern the people, and that the people ought to be subject and obedient unto them, by virtue of that ordination, *not only for fear, but also for consciens' sake* [Rom 13:5], in all things that are conformable to the Word of God, who is the King of kings and the Lord of lords" (Schaff, *Creeds*, 3:767).

31. Zagorin, *Religious Toleration*, 32. Zagorin quotes many passages from Augustine in which he uses biblical texts to promote his idea of conversion by coercion and persecution.

32. Augustine, *Letter 185*, in Rotelle, *Saint Augustine Letters*, 185–86. Zagorin quotes Augustine saying that in the story of Acts 9:3–18 Paul "was forced by the great violence of Christ's compulsion to acknowledge and hold the truth," and "It is a wonderful thing how he who came to the gospel under the compulsion of bodily suffering labored more in the gospel than all the others who were called by words alone" (Zagorin, *Religious Toleration*, 30–31).

> Wherefore there is the greater reason that we all should with one consent prepare to obey [Christ], and with the greatest alacrity yield implicit obedience to his will. For as he unites the offices of King and Pastor towards believers, who voluntarily submit to him, so, on the other hand, we are told that he wields an iron scepter to break and bruise all the rebellious like a potter's vessel (Ps 2:9). We are also told that he will be the Judge of the Gentiles, that he will cover the earth with dead bodies, and level down every opposing height (Ps 110:6). Of this examples are seen at present, but full proof will be given at the final judgment, which may be properly regarded as the last act of his reign.[33]

Reformed theology embraced the imperial viewpoint. Question 45 of the *Westminster Larger Catechism* asks "How doth Christ execute the office of a King?" Part of the answer says:

> ... in calling out of the world a people to himself ... restraining and overcoming all their enemies ... and also in taking vengeance on the rest who know not God and obey not the gospel."[34]

Der Heidelberger Katechismus (1563 CE) promises that Christ, the second-coming judge:

> will cast all his enemies and mine into eternal damnation, but with all the elect he will take me into the heavenly joy and glory.[35]

Henry Meeter has no doubt about the truth of the mythical totalitarian king:

> If the world had remained sinless, there could be no uncertainty as to the character of the ideal state. It would be one world-state, a world empire, the kingdom of God. The type of Government would be monarchical with Adam at the head of this empire, with several lesser authorities under him. And in the new earth there will once more be a world empire under the last Adam,

---

33. Calvin, *Institutes* ii.xv.5, in Calvin, *Institutes*, 222.

34. The proof-texts are 2 Thess 1:7–8 and Ps 2:8–9. When the end of the world comes, the righteous and elect "shall see the terrible vengeance which God shall execute on the wicked, who most cruelly persecuted, oppressed, and tormented them in this world; and who shall be ... tormented in that everlasting fire which is prepared for the devil and his angels" (*Belgic Confession*, article 37, in Schaff, *Creeds*, 3:435). The "wicked" in this confession surely refers to the Catholic government that was persecuting Protestant believers; but this type of statement has been later used to fuel hatred against all non-Christians.

35. *Frage und Antwort* 52. Cf. Schaff, *Creeds*, 3:324.

Christ, as King, in which there will be the proper subordinate officers also.[36]

Diana Bass recalls a sermon that she heard about King Jesus during the commencement ceremony of a Christian university. The reading for the sermon came from Philippians 2:9–11, which portrays Jesus as the exalted King before whom all the people of the universe will be forced to bend their knee (v. 10). The preacher correctly mentioned that the word "Lord" (*kurios*) was the same word used to designate the Roman emperor, adding that when we say that Christ is Lord we are saying that Christ is Caesar. Then the preacher proclaimed that:

> ... one day Jesus—like Caesar of old—would exert his imperial will across the world and "force every living thing to its knees" to confess his name. At the end of time, God would make everyone worship him, just as everyone subject to Caesar had to pay homage to the Roman emperor—crawling backward to the imperial throne. He [= the preacher] continued likening Jesus to an imperialist warlord whose triumph over recalcitrant sinners, doubters, discontents, and rebels was assured. Emphasizing Jesus's regal glorification, he turned God into a vengeful king out to get those who had killed his son. Oddly enough, his tone was not that of a hellfire-and-brimstone evangelist. Instead, the entire lecture was delivered with stern intellectual certainty and detached professorial authority.[37]

The preacher was correct! In Philippians 2:9–11, Paul is actually using imperial images to promote a despotic king:

> ⁹Therefore, God also exceedingly exalted[38] him and granted him the name which is above all other name, ¹⁰in order that every knee should bend at the name of Jesus, in heaven and on earth and in the underworld, ¹¹and every human being[39] should confess[40] that Jesus Christ is Lord, to the glory of God the Father.

The words "above all other name" underline the complete supremacy of the Christ-Emperor. The purpose of this absolute power (v. 9) is total

---

36. Meeter, *Basic Ideas of Calvinism*, 83.
37. Bass, *Christianity after Religion*, 103–5.
38. The verb *huperpsoō* communicates the idea of god placing Jesus in the most exalted position or status in the universe.
39. Lit. "tongue" in the sense of people, regardless of their language.
40. Or: "acknowledge."

domination: "in order that" (*hina*) all people in the universe should kneel down and confess Christ as the Universal Tyrant (vv. 10–11).[41] This Jesus is like the Assyrian king Tukulti-Ninurta I (*ca.* 1244–1208 BCE):

> Your exalted power has been set over the whole world,
>   the seas and the mountains.
> With the wrath of your scepter
>   you have made to submit all regions, in all quarters.

While theocratic theologians praise the tyranny of Philippians 2:9–11, a progressive theologian may try to twist the meaning of the passage into something good. Brian McLaren overturns its meaning by saying:

> Of course, for many, those words [of Phil 2:9–11] evoke the image of a conquering king forcing the vanquished to kneel at sword point and saying, "Grovel before me and acknowledge my supremacy!" But that understanding completely undermines the thrust of all that has gone before [i.e., the humiliation of Christ in Phil 2:5–8]. It is far better, I am convinced, to understand the image like this: One day, all of humanity will become convinced that the ways of violence and domination, enslavement and exploitation, supremacy and privilege are ugly, wrong, suicidal, and ungodly.[42]

The same old autocracy also stands out in the so-called Offices of Christ by which traditional theology refers to Christ as Prophet, Priest and King.[43] These titles, says Jürgen Moltmann, "create a distance between him and the people who are his. We may note critically that these titles of sovereignty derived from an authoritarian society, and that the supremacy of the prophets, priests, and kings is accentuated when their titles are transferred to Christ." Therefore, Moltmann attempts to liberate those titles from their original culture of violence by focusing on the Jesus of history. So he asks:

> Who did the Christians listen to as their prophet? The derided Son of man from Nazareth, "a carpenter's son." Who was called God's priest? The crucified victim of the powerful on Golgotha. If, finally, all the radiance of God is conferred on the powerless man on the cross, then the crowns of the rulers on earth lose their halos. So, if society's highest titles are transferred to the

---

41. The conjunction *hina* indicates purpose followed by two subjunctives: *kampsē* and *exomologēsētai*.
42. McLaren, *Spiritual Migration*, 91.
43. For the traditional offices of Christ, see Berkhof, *Systematic Theology*, 356–59.

crucified Son of Man from Nazareth, then that is an unheard-of potential for a critical attitude toward sovereignty.[44]

5.2 Obsolete Metaphors

Before we continue, we should clarify that we are not objecting to the use of metaphor, for it happens that a great part of our worldview, morality, politics, ideals, etc., are all based on metaphors. We cannot think or talk without using metaphors. But we do reject the claim that the metaphors of Christianity are the only valid ones, and we refuse to take Christian dogma *literally*. It is like demanding us to believe that the mythological aspects of the *Odyssey* or the *Epic of Gilgameš* point to *historical events*. Modern society cannot believe anymore that Jesus was *literally* resurrected, and that he *literally* "went into heaven" (Heb 4:14) and *literally* "sat at the right hand of the throne of the Majesty in heaven" (Heb 8:1). The fastest growing demographic today are the "nones," which by the thousands are leaving the church. It is not only the greed, autocracy, corruption and hypocrisy of the church which drive the "nones" away, but it is also the insistence of taking myth *literally*, instead of recognizing that metaphor is a tool used to communicate values. Myth always points to something else, and it is not a reality in itself.

It is not only that metaphors should not be taken *literally*, but that we are dealing with *archaic* metaphors. The idea of a king-god has fallen victim to centuries of cultural change in the Western world. Wherever democracy is alive, it has created antibodies that reject statements like "your kingdom come" (Matt 6:10) which in eschatological terms means: "your violent, totalitarian kingdom come." Therefore, it is time for us to pronounce an unfavorable dictum against monarchy as a viable theological concept.

First, the conceptual metaphor GOD IS KING emerged out of specific times and places that acted as source domains (§1.1.2–3; §2.1.3; §4.1–2). However, the institutions and values that were the foundation of the king-god-metaphor are gone and, therefore, the metaphor of a king-god is an empty one.

Second, cultural conditioning made it impossible for people to imagine a king-god who was better than the earthly kings he was made to emulate. Time has exposed monarchy as an oppressive system without relevance for today. Brian McLaren correctly calls us to change our metaphorical concepts. He claims that imperial metaphors define god "by analogy to the

---

44. Moltmann, *Living God*, 120.

kings of this world who dominate, oppress, subordinate, exploit, scapegoat and marginalize." To oppose those oppressive metaphors, we should insert "into human imagination a radical new vision of God—nondominating, nonviolent, supreme in service, and self-giving."[45]

Third, the king-god metaphor is intertwined with the figure of the authoritarian male. The metaphor that represents god as a "Father" may communicate the beautiful concept of a man who provides for our needs, who protects and cares for us (Matt 6:8, 26, 32; 7:11). This metaphor instills a sense of peace and security (Rom 8:14–17). However, since the metaphor emerged within a patriarchal culture, the image also acquired undeniable destructive features. Bishop John S. Spong underlines these horrendous traits:

> The word *Father* is such a human word—so male, so dated. It elicits the traditional God images of the old man who lives just beyond the sky. It shouts of the masculinity of the deity, a concept that has been used for thousands of years to justify the oppression of women by religious institutions. That history and that practice repel me today. The Christian Church at times has gone so far as to debate whether women actually had souls and whether girl babies ought to be baptized. That Church universally relegated women to clearly defined secondary roles until the latter years of the twentieth century, when that sexist prejudice began to dissipate . . . The Church dedicated to the worship of a God who was called "Father" has consistently justified its rampant discrimination against women as the will of this patriarchal deity or, at the very least, as something idolatrously called the "unchanging sacred tradition of the Church."[46]

Today many people react negatively to expressions like "our Father" (Matt 6:9) or "I believe in God the Father," because the beneficial effects of the metaphor have been undermined by destructive cultural prejudices against women and children. Time has exposed the highly toxic elements infused into Father theology, and modern times demand that we balance the "Father" metaphor with female images of the divine. We should also use the metaphor of the "Mother" to refer to the deity. But as soon as someone suggests something like this, a cloud of male ministers locked in a rancid patriarchal world cry out "Heresy!" In vain they try to take refuge in the "normative" character of the Scriptures which makes the male image the overwhelming standard. Today this antiquarian argument falls short for we

---

45. McLaren, *Spiritual Migration*, 93.
46. Spong, *Why Christianity Must Change or Die*, 5.

recognize the Bible to be an old book that abounds in obsolete and culturally conditioned opinions.

Jürgen Moltmann has exposed the nefarious effects of this patriarchal-monarchical theology by denouncing it as the creation of a society based on an exclusively male metaphor. Moltmann reminds us that, in old times, the father was lord and owner of his wife, children and estate (*paterfamilias*). In politics, the king was the *pater patriae*, having absolute power over his subjects. In the church, there was the priest, the spiritual "father." These three fathers imposed doctrines and laws that everyone else had to obey:

> Ultimately these pyramids of family, politics and church point to the supreme authority in heaven from which they receive their legitimation, the Lord God, the Father of all. As lord and proprietor of the world God possesses fullness of power, and gives legitimation to all authority in heaven and on earth . . . This father religion produces in the individual that super-ego against which atheistic rebellion rises up, has risen up and must rise up, calling for freedom and its own responsibility, since "where the great world-ruler is, freedom has no space, not even the freedom of the children of God."[47]

The monarch-metaphor has run out of any useful application. Its toxicity is seen in the fact that Christians in the United States have the luxury of living in a somewhat democratic country and, nonetheless, Christian theology continues to induce many of its citizens to yearn for the Second Coming of an eschatological dictator. Many people do not understand how unacceptable is the image of a Jesus who comes to kill his enemies in order to impose a "peaceful" world empire.

For many Christians this expectation is not only something pertaining to the future. They feel that they have the duty to foment a theocratic government for the here and now in order to impose their religion on all citizens. The colony of Massachusetts once tried to do it:

> That if any person shall presume willfully to blaspheme the holy name of God, Father, Son, or Holy Ghost, either by denying, cursing or reproaching the true God, his creation, or government of the world; or by denying, cursing or reproaching the Holy Word of God . . . every one so offending shall be punished by imprisonment not exceeding six months and until they find sureties for the good behavior, be setting in the pillory, by

---

47. Moltmann, *History and the Triune God*, 20.

whipping, boring through the tongue with a red hot iron, or setting upon the gallows with a rope about their neck...[48]

5.3 Democratic-Secular Government versus Archaic Authoritarian Theocracy

For centuries, kings, dictators and psychopaths have found inspiration in the theology of power. Just recall the Roman senator who prophesized that divine Augustus would have "absolute power,"[49] the dream of all tyrants. So let's pause to reflect on the history of our nation. John Adams (1735–1826 CE), second President of the United States, wrote a *Defense of the Constitution of Government of the United States of America*, in which he starts his argument by mentioning the old ways in which people constructed governments:

> It was the general opinion of ancient nations, that the Divinity alone was adequate to the important office of giving laws to men. The Greeks entertained this prejudice throughout all their dispersions; the Romans cultivated the same popular delusion; and modern nations, in the consecration of kings, and in several superstitious chimeras of divine right in princes and nobles, are nearly unanimous in preserving remnants of it. Even the venerable magistrates of Amersfort devoutly believe themselves to be God's viceregents. Is it that obedience to the laws can be obtained from mankind in no other manner? Are the jealousy of power, and the envy of superiority, so strong in all men, that no considerations of public or private utility are sufficient to engage their submission to rules for their own happiness?[50]

Adams then reminds us that in ancient times people believed that the laws imposed by Minos (king of Crete) came from Jupiter; the laws of Lacedaemon (king of Sparta) were given by Apollo; the laws of Numa Pompilius (Roman king) came from Egeria, etc. All these ideas were founded on the belief that their emperors and nobles "descended from their gods." Countering the myth of divine monarchies, Adams rejects the old metaphor and establishes a new metaphor which now conceives government as the product of human reason:

---

48. This law was enacted in 1692 CE. See *Acts and Resolves of the Province of the Massachusetts Bay*, 1:297.

49. Dio Casio, *Historiae Romanae* xlv.1.4.

50. Adams, *Works of John Adams*, 4:291.

> The United States of America have exhibited, perhaps, the first example of governments erected on the simple principles of nature; and if men are now sufficiently enlightened to disabuse themselves of artifice, imposture, hypocrisy, and superstition, they will consider this event as an era in their history ... It will never be pretended that any persons employed in that service [of founding the U.S. government] had interviews with the gods, or were in any degree under the inspiration of Heaven, more than those at work upon ships or houses, or laboring in merchandise or agriculture; it will forever be acknowledged that these governments were contrived merely by the use of reason and the senses ... unembarrassed by attachments to noble families, hereditary lines and successions, or nay considerations of royal blood ... Thirteen governments thus founded on the natural authority of the people alone, without a pretense of miracle or mystery ...[51]

Since the Enlightenment and the American Revolution, our rulers ceased to be divine kings (§4.3.3). The gods—Yahve and Jesus included—stopped being the source of their authority (§4.3.4), because the U.S. government was established on a new metaphor. Our government is now "founded on the natural authority of the people alone, without a pretense of miracle or mystery." The concept of a divine monarchy is not part of the mainline culture, and does not represent our political system. The current crisis of Christian theology is its insistence on metaphors that do not arise from our culture and daily experience as *source domains*. We have evolved into a type of government opposed to absolute power. Nonetheless, the old theology continues to fight for a supremacy that is nowhere to be seen. We live in a country that walks towards democracy, diversity, civil rights, and secularism. Totalitarian Christianity awaits a despotic Jesus who will come back to kill the rebels who do not want to submit to his religion. It also works to establish a present-day authoritarian government to impose the "true" religion. But today people don't want the government to issue decrees demanding all of us "to be instructed in the true faith." Nor we need a warrior-Jesus who will come back to take "vengeance" on those who do not "obey the gospel." This archaic religion is the antithesis of a democratic society.

We need to recognize that the myth of democracy has never worked flawlessly. It is a core value that keeps growing and changing. From the very beginning, the Enlightenment ideal—"all men are created equal, that they are endowed by their Creator with certain unalienable Rights," etc.—was utterly contradicted by the atrocities of Native American genocide and the

---

51. Adams, *Works of John Adams*, 4:292–93.

slaving of Africans. Our democracy was a democracy for the Anglican-White-British male who owned land. It was not a democracy for Native Americans, enslaved Africans and women. It was not a democracy for Baptists, Presbyterians and Catholics. It was not a democracy for Germans, Irish, Italians, Mexicans, Japanese, etc. Nonetheless, the democratic ideal has been painfully and slowly moving towards a bigger umbrella of liberty and equality. Today we see tiny symbols of hope in the Western world. In England, a White prince married Meghan Markle, a biracial American actress-divorcee. The election of President Barack Hussein Obama was another modest symbol of hope. In 2015, Sherin Khankan became Denmark's first *female* imam leading a mosque. In that same year, the social justice activist Rabbi Denise Eger became the first *lesbian* president of the Central Conference of American Rabbis of the Reform movement. The Church of England appointed their first *Black female* bishop, Rose Hudson-Wilkin, in 2019.

In the overwhelmingly White-male-Christian U.S. Congress, we find small signs of a brewing democracy. In 2018 for the first time our country elected more than a hundred women to Congress. The first two Native American women were elected to the House of Representatives: Sharice Davids (D-KS, who is lesbian) and Deb Haaland (D-NM). Minnesota elected Peggy Flanagan (D-MN) as their first ever Native American woman Lt. Governor. The atheist Senator Kyrsten Sinema (D-AZ) was sworn into office by placing her hand on a law book. The Muslim Palestinian-American Rashida Tlaib (D-MI) was sworn into office placing her hand on Thomas Jefferson's copy of the Koran. Ilhan Omar (D-MN) is a Somali Muslim woman who emigrated from a refugee camp in Kenya and was voted in as Representative. However, at every turn other forces rise to oppose democracy. Racism, misogyny, homophobia, plutocracy and theocracy are all enemies of democracy for they are determined to deny those "others" full participation in society. These attacks are coupled with the constant fight against science and freedom of the press. Every month we find lawmakers proposing bills that would inject Christian proselytizing in our public schools.[52]

---

[52]. See Sokol, "Uncovering Project Blitz"; Richards, "Bible Classes in Public Schools?" The Rev. Franklin Graham has said: "I want the school boards of America in the hands of evangelical Christians within the next four to six years. And it can happen and that will have a huge impact because so many school districts now are controlled by wicked, evil people, and the gays and lesbians, and I keep bringing their name up, but they are at the forefront of this attack against Christianity in America" (quoted in Trashman, "Franklin Graham").

5.4 What Kind of God and Theology?

At the core of any theistic belief is a god constructed by anthropomorphic images. We do not necessarily object to a god created to the likeness of humankind (§2). But we need to ask ourselves: If theism does not allow us to talk about god in any other way than in human terms, what type of god do we want to create? Do we want a god created in the likeness of a totalitarian king with dreams of absolute power? Are the kings of Mesopotamia, Persia and Rome the best *source domains* for the way we envision god?[53] If we acknowledge that our concept of god is nothing more than a mirror in which we see ourselves, are we going to *imagine god* by projecting the worst of our humanity? Is god the projection of our insecurity, racism, greed, hatred and thirst for power? And why should we even bother contriving a god fashioned in terms of archaic cultures that do not fit into our modern world? We should remember Plato's warning not to portray the gods doing evil because those images "foster in our youth a strong inclination towards vileness" (§2.3.2.a).

We live in a time when global warming, nationalism, imperialism, inequality, pollution, misogyny, racism, greed, etc. threaten to destroy the world—and in some cases the world is already being destroyed. The present danger should lead us to recognize our *common humanity*. Above all religious beliefs, what unites us is the fact that we are all human beings worthy of respect and love. The White male is not the normative metaphor for what is human, and people of color are not subhuman. We need a strong universal family metaphor as a source of an egalitarian awareness that will defend the rights and welfare of all. Humanity should also feel as one with the animal and physical world. We cannot live our lives undermining nature without hurting ourselves at the same time. And it is vital for our myths to focus on the unity we have with our planet in order to protect it as it were our own child, and our myths need to be in tune with modern cosmology and science. We don't need a racist, oppressive and theocratic Jesus. We need a Christ, a Muhammad and a Yahve who receive all people without being offended by their religion, gender, race or sexual orientation. It cannot be a god who uses coercion and violence to impose his religion. Our theology needs to be interdisciplinary, for we live in a world where knowledge flourishes by observation, experimentation and rational analysis (science). Our theology needs to equip itself with the best holistic science.

---

53. For example, King Sargon the Great (2340–2284 BCE) declared himself "king of the universe," and models like these are reflected in how people conceived the gods.

5.5 Cherry-Picking on the Basis of Values

It is time for all Christians—both fundamentalists and progressives—to acknowledge that when we go to the Scriptures we are all forced to cherry-pick. We have no other option than to choose between the good and the bad that we find in the Bible. Progressive Christians should acknowledge that the criterion for this identification does not come from the Bible itself, but it comes from our current evolving democratic values. Progressive Christians cherry-pick by *looking for* inspiration in biblical passages that promote what they think is right, and ignore or twist passages that are problematic (cf. Phil 2:9, 10 above). They feel inspired by listening to texts like: "let justice flow like water and righteousness like a perpetual stream" (Amos 5:24). Progressive Christians may argue that their values come from Jesus, but I ask "Which Jesus?" Are you talking about the apocalyptic Jesus who will throw you into a "furnace of fire" (Matt 13:42, 50), the one who condemns you because you "have not believed" (John 3:18)? Or do you refer to the Jesus who says, "Come to me, all you that are weary and are carrying heavy burdens, and I will give you rest" (Matt 11:28)? On what basis do you choose between them?

Our values of democracy and human rights should help us shape our myths and our exegetical cherry-picking. We need myths that champion transparent, free and direct elections. We need a theology that supports diversity and opposes racism; metaphors that promote secular government, not theocracy; ideals that protect the rights of all Americans, minorities, women, LGBT, etc. We do not need an eschatology that talks about the "new creation" as something beyond history. Hope opens the future now in order to produce a new creation in this world.[54] Moltmann has given us some leads on how to produce a political theology oriented to social change.[55] It is within this framework that topics like democracy, health, education, human rights and the protection of the environment[56] become the explicit concretization of our mythology and eschatological hope. Therefore, the so-called kingdom is not a royal tyranny but "the realization of the eschatological *hope of justice*, the *humanizing* of man, the *socializing* of humanity, *peace* for all creation." Only in this way will Christianity be able to "gain new impulses for the shaping of man's public, social and political life."[57]

---

54. See Moltmann, *Theology of Hope*; *Crucified God*; and *Coming of God*.

55. See Moltmann, *God for a Secular Society*, and *Science and Wisdom*. Moltmann's theology helped shape the liberation theology of Leonardo Boff (see *La Trinidad* and *La dignidad de la tierra*).

56. See Moltmann, *God in Creation*.

57. Moltmann, *Theology of Hope*, 329.

However, this does not mean that we ought to bring religion *proper* into Congress. A genuine concern is how Christians debate and propose government policies *in Congress*. We should avoid daydreaming that the Bible is our only authority and source of wisdom for passing laws. For example, in the middle of a national debate, Rev. Robert Jeffress—from the First Baptist Dallas Church (Texas)—publicly defended President's Trump plan to build a wall at the southern border, by saying: "The Bible says even Heaven itself is gonna have a wall around it. Not everybody is going to be allowed in. So if walls are immoral, then God is immoral."[58] Reverend Jeffress takes refuge in an obsolete description of Heaven conditioned by the way ancient people lived: walled cities (§3.5.1-2). Do we still have walled cities in the U.S. today? Are walled cities still relevant as a metaphor for Heaven? In addition, Rev. Jeffress has decided to believe in Heaven as a place of exclusion, a place reserved only for those who follow his "true" religion. Values of exclusion also impel him to support the building of a literal wall at the southern border. Predetermined values guide him to cherry-pick and forge a doctrine of Heaven and a wall of exclusion.

Progressive Christians should not fall into the same trap, and propose legislation in Congress on the basis of religion. For example, a higher minimum wage should not be promoted arguing "Thus says the Lord." Progressives could use a moral argument based on human rights: "a person working full time should not be poor." But in promoting higher wages, they surely need to show that it is a great way of boosting the economy. They can argue that concentration of wealth in the hands of a few kills the economy, while more cash in the pockets of workers injects money into the market generating economic growth.[59] When Christians promote better education and health care, they should advance social and economic arguments. For a society to grow, it needs the largest number of happy, educated and healthy people creating and competing in the market. "Wealth creation is maximized *only* by maximizing the number of robust diverse competitors in the market ... Equality of opportunity then, isn't just a moral imperative. It's an economic imperative. Making sure everyone gets a fair shot isn't about being nice, it's bowing to necessity."[60] Besides, today the fear of climate change, school debt, part-time jobs and low paid jobs are keeping younger generations from marrying and having children. Low marriages and birthrate as well as the stagnation of salary-raises threaten our society. Stopping climate

---

58. Quoted in Martin, "Moral Question of Trump's Border Wall." Jeffress's remarks were in response to Nancy Pelosi (Speaker of the House, D-CA) who called the proposed wall "immoral."

59. Liu and Hanauer, *Gardens of Democracy*, 102-4.

60. Liu and Hanauer, *Gardens of Democracy*, 96.

change and enacting well paid jobs will boost the economy. These are not arguments made on the basis of religion *proper*.

5.6 The Quest for a Christian Worldview[61]

During the fifteenth and sixteenth centuries, the Renaissance widened the influence of humanistic-secular thought, and this marked the beginning of the never-ending conflict between church and science. Copernicus (1473–1543 CE) proposed a heliocentric cosmology (*Commentariolus*, 1530), which gained him the resolute antipathy of Martin Luther:

> People give ear to an upstart astrologer who strove to show that the earth revolves, not the heavens or the firmament, the sun and the moon. Whosoever wishes to appear clever must devise some new system which of all systems, of course, is the very best. This fool wishes to reverse the entire science of astronomy; but Sacred Scripture tell us that Josue commanded the sun to stand still, and not the earth [Josh 10:13].[62]

Faithful to the Scriptures, Calvin also defended a geocentric cosmology, saying:

> We indeed are not ignorant, that the circuit of the heavens is finite, and that the earth, like a little globe, is place in the center.[63]

William Bouwsma quotes Calvin's warnings "against those who asserted 'that the sun does not move and that it is the earth that moves and turns.' Such persons were motivated by 'a spirit of bitterness, contradiction, and faultfinding;' possessed by the devil, they aimed 'to pervert the order of nature.'"[64] However, time proved that Luther, Calvin and the Scriptures were all mistaken.

In reaction to the Enlightenment and the scientific revolution (1685–1850), James Orr (1844–1913 CE) delivered a series of conferences (the

---

61. See the valuable work by DeWitt, *Worldviews*, where he examines important issues like what is truth, empirical facts, evidence, scientific method, falsifiability, etc., and reviews how worldviews evolved from Aristotle to Newton and the twenty-first century.

62. Quoted in Langford, *Galileo, Science and the Church*, 35. Apart from his antisemitism and misogyny, Luther also hated reason: "Reason, the devil's bride, that beautiful whore, marches in and wants to be wise, and what she says she imagines to be the Holy Ghost . . . you mangy, leprous whore, you holy reason . . ." (Pelikan, *Luther's Works*, 51:373).

63. Calvin, *Genesis*, 61.

64. Bouwsma, *John Calvin*, 72.

Kerr Lectures, 1891) that were later published as *The Christian View of God and the World as Centring in the Incarnation* (1893). The book established him as the great defender of the Calvinist conservative tradition. Orr was promoting a *Christian worldview*, a system that would unify all human existence under traditional Christian dogma. He argued that it was not enough to defend Christian doctrines individually. The situation required a Christian system capable of encompassing all of reality:

> The opposition which Christianity has to encounter is no longer confined to special doctrines or to points of supposed conflict with the natural sciences,—for example, the relations of Genesis and geology—but extends to the whole manner of conceiving of the world, and of man's place in it, the manner of conceiving of the entire system of things, natural and moral, of which we form part. It is no longer an opposition of detail, but of principle.[65]

Orr claimed that all aspects of life should be understood from the point of view of the Christian god who reveals himself in the Scriptures and who has a cosmic plan of redemption with Jesus as its center. This belief system was proposed as the gravitational center unifying all truth and knowledge. Other scholars who followed his lead were Herman Dooyeweerd (1894–1977), Gordon H. Clark (1902–1985) and Francis A. Schaeffer (1912–1984), all Calvinist theologians.[66]

Abraham Kuyper (1837–1920) described how this worldview should be applied to society as a whole. First, he denounced the deadly threat that "modernism" posed to Christianity:

> There is no doubt tan Christianity is imperiled by great and serious dangers. Two *life systems* are wrestling one with another, in mortal combat. Modernism is bound to build a world of its own from the data of the natural man, and to construct man himself from the data of nature; while, on the other hand, all those who reverently bend the knee to Christ and worship Him as the Son of the Living God, and God himself, are bent upon saving the "Christian Heritage."[67]

Second, since modernism was attacking Christianity with the "vast energy of an all-embracing *life-system*," Kuyper called all Christians "to take our

---

65. Orr, *Christian View of God*, 4.

66. See Moreland and Craig. *Philosophical Foundations for a Christian Worldview*; Noebel and Edwards, *Thinking Like a Christian*.

67. Kuyper, *Lectures on Calvinism*, 11.

stand in a life-system of equally comprehensive and far-reaching power."[68] In practice, he proposed a cultural war. The following words reveal *in nuce* the core of his project:

> That in spite of all worldly opposition, God's holy ordinances shall be established again in the home, in the school, and in the State for the good of the people; to carve as it were into the conscience of the nation the ordinances of the Lord, to which Bible and Creation bear witness, until the nation pays homage again to God.[69]

5.6.1 The Obstacle of Democracy

China is officially an atheist country which is increasing its persecution of Christians, Muslims and Buddhists. This is a place where the government controls all religious personnel, publications and finances.[70] But in a democracy, Christians are free to worship and manage their own affairs. However, Kuyper's proposal seems to go far beyond the idea of private citizens coming together to worship and disseminate their faith in the context of voluntary acquiescence. The project seems to be conceived as a way of giving back to the church the huge political and cultural control that it lost. This direct attack on modern democracy is advanced by arguing that you only find "freedom" under the yoke of Christ. The key question here is how the ideal of having "god's holy ordinances" controlling home, school and state should be implemented? How do you carve god's ordinances "into the conscience" of the people until the nation pays homage to the god of this brand of Christianity? This project is not proposing a worldview at the service of the Christian community, but it has become a cultural war seeking political control in order to impose its religion on others. Kuyper's proposal makes it impossible to determine how such a worldview can be established "at home, in the school and in the state" without obliterating the *civil rights* of all the citizens who do not believe in Christianity or in Kuyper's version of it. Preaching and evangelism have never been able to convert an entire country into professed and practicing Christians. This project would need the help of a Christian political regime enforcing compulsory professions and suppressing civil liberties for the sake of religion. This worldview leads to legislating religion. The Christian worldview project has a theocratic flavor.

68. Kuyper, *Lectures on Calvinism*, 11–12.
69. Quoted in Bratt, *Abraham Kuyper*, 488.
70. See Ma, "Jailing Muslims, Burning Bibles."

During the Enlightenment, the American Revolution concluded that allowing religion to dominate society was detrimental to any real democracy. Therefore, the Framers took the executive, legislative and judiciary branches of government away from religion by introducing into the Constitution what we call today the "separation of church and state."[71] This move aimed at creating a pluralistic and democratic society that welcomes all religions—or no religion—within a secular political framework which is the foundation of democracy because it bars the government from sponsoring, imposing or promoting any religion.

The Islamic theocratic-monarchy of Saudi Arabia represents the most horrifying example of what happens when a religious worldview dominates "home, school and state." Under this theocracy, blasphemy and apostasy are penalized by capital punishment. In April 2019, Saudi Arabia beheaded thirty-seven Saudi citizens for political and religious reasons. The beheaded were mostly Shiite Muslims who were held as terrorists by the Sunni state. By contrast, in the United States, politicians and government employees are not allowed to use their office to promote religion. Our Constitution declares that "no religious test shall ever be required as a qualification to any office or public trust under the United States,"[72] referring to all U.S. senators, representatives and federal employees. Contrary to this spirit, many American Christians show an obsession with political power. In the words of Mark Labberton: "The apparent evangelical alignment with the use of power that seeks dominance, control, supremacy, and victory over compassion and justice associates Jesus with the strategies of Caesar, not

---

71. This expression sums up what Thomas Jefferson (1743–1843 CE) wrote to the Connecticut Baptist Association (January 1802) to assure them that the federal government will never persecute them or interfere with the practice of their faith, nor treat them as second-class citizens by giving preferential treatment to Anglicans. Jefferson's letter was meant to give assurance to a Baptist Church which lived in what at the time was a hostile Episcopal-Anglican country. The association wrote to President Jefferson "that no man ought to suffer in name, person, or effects on account of his religious opinions" (October 1801), and they expressed their fear that the privileges they enjoyed as a minority could be seen "as favors granted, and not as inalienable rights." To quench their fears, Jefferson wrote back: "Believing with you that religion is a matter which lies solely between Man and his God, that he owes account to none other for his faith or his worship, that the legitimate powers of government reach actions only, and not opinions, I contemplate with sovereign reverence that act of the whole American people which declared that their legislature should 'make no law respecting an establishment of religion, or prohibiting the free exercise thereof' thus building a wall of separation between Church and State." Alexander and Alexander, *American Public School Law*, 149.

72. U.S. Constitution 6.3.

with the good news of the gospel."[73] In fact, *Der Heidelberger Katechismus* answers the question "Why are you called a Christian?" by expressing the anticipation of achieving absolute power. At the end of the world, Christians will "thereafter rule eternally with him over all creatures."[74] To summarize, the practical problem of how to implement a Christian worldview without destroying the freedom of citizens remains an insolvable problem.

5.6.2 The Problem with Ancient Mythical Worldviews

The Enlightenment put an end to the clutching power that the church had over society, and this was done by merely studying the world (observation of phenomena, hypothesis predicting results, testing of the hypothesis, etc.). The ever growing amount of knowledge produced by such investigations—including Bible research—engulfed Christian beliefs into a shadow of doubt, to say the least.

The second drawback regarding the aforementioned Christian worldview seems to be that it remains oblivious to the fact that ideas like divine revelation, providence, incarnation, resurrection, etc., are mythical concepts with no basis on empirical reality. It is impossible to get access to these "realities" by means of this world. This fact should force people to recognize that Christian pretensions have no advantage over the demands of Judaism, Islam and other faiths. Behind the doctrines of Christianity there is no factual evidence which alone may reasonably exact the acquiescence of all. It is impossible to prove that Jesus was *really* born of a virgin, or that he was *actually* god incarnate, or that he walked on water, or that he was raised from the dead, and went up to Heaven, etc. On the contrary, there is ample *evidence* indicating that Christianity shared with its surrounding cultures the three well known mythical mechanisms of divinization. First, Jesus became a divine king when his mother got pregnant by a god (§3.4.1; 4.3.3e). Second, Jesus is presented as a secondary god who became a man (§2.3.3). And third, Jesus was made into a god after his death (§3.4.2). These were well-known mythological concepts applied to heroes and kings. So if we take into account that Christian dogma is metaphorical language, and that it is not construed on verifiable historical facts, and that other religions also seek cultural space for their own faiths, it is reasonably to conclude that our citizens cannot possibly be forced to accept a Christian worldview. It is not immoral to be an unbeliever, agnostic or atheist, and those who are not Christians should not be treated as outcasts. No one should be forced to act

---

73. Labberton, "Political Dealing."
74. *Frage und Antwort* 32. Cf. Schaff, *Creeds*, 3:318.

according to someone else's faith. It is impossible to build a viable worldview by appealing to the Bible or the authority of the church.

5.7 Worldviews in Collision: The Exorcism of a Possessed/Lunatic boy: Mark 9:14-29; Matthew 17:14-21; and Luke 9:37-43

To illustrate the staggering difference in outlook between the biblical worldview and our modern world, we now need to examine a story found in the Gospels. The legend talks about the healing of a person with epilepsy. Our analysis will show that our present reality defies any attempt to use the Christian belief system as a *literal* description of reality.

5.7.1 Cultural Background

a. Ancient Near East

Before examining the story about the healing of the epileptic boy, we need to use the grammatical-historical method to search for the cultural background of the story. In its excellent study, Marten Stol reports that in Mesopotamia epilepsy was known as a disease given by the god Sîn (= Moon).[75] The condition was described as an illness "fallen from heaven."[76] People also believed that the spirits of the dead (*eṭemmu*) or evil spirits (*eṭemu lemmu*) were able to come up from the Underworld to attack the living with epilepsy.[77] The disease could be given by a deputy demon of the Moon,[78] but the illness was still attributed to the hand of Sîn, as it is described in this ancient text:

---

75. Stol, *Epilepsy in Babylonia*, 5-8. See also Finkel and Geller, *Disease in Babylonia*; Geller, *Melothesia in Babylonia*; Scurlock and Andersen, *Diagnoses in Assyrian and Babylonian Medicine*.

76. In Sumerian, the expression used was an.ta.sub.ba; and in Akkadian *miqit šamê*; in both cases the meaning is "fallen from heaven." Cf. "Something fallen from heaven has 'touch' him, 'hand of his god,' he will die" ("Miqtu," 104). Another frequent term used for the illness was *bennu* (= convulsion). A text quotes a prayer asking Sîn to heal a sick person: "O Sin, let the *be-en-nu* (convulsion) which has seized him not affect him, drive it from his body" ("Bennu," 205).

77. Cf. "An evil [ghost] has seized that man, it convulses[?] him like *miqtu* disease" ("Miqtu," 104).

78. Cf. "If the hand of a ghost has seized him or if *be-en* [= convulsion] has seized him" ("Bennu," 205).

> If a patient continually turns his head to the right, his hands and his feet are stretched out, his eyes are opened wide toward the sky, spittle flows from his mouth, he makes rumbling noises, he does not know who he is at the beginning when his [confusional state] comes over him, AN.TA.ŠUB.BA (convulsion), "hand" of ^{d}Sîn.[79]

It's not surprising that Psalm 121:6 claims that Yahve is able to protect us from the Moon:

> During the day, the sun will not strike you,[80]
>   nor the moon by night.

It is easy to imagine how the heat of the sun could hurt a person during the day, but we may wonder how the moon would hurt us at night. Mitchel Dahood reminds us that "the notion that the moon beamed harmful influences was widespread in the Ancient Near East."[81]

b. Greco-Roman culture

These ideas passed into the Greco-Roman culture.[82] In his work *De Medicina*, Aulus Cornelius Celsus (*ca.* 25–50 CE) talks about a person who suffers with headaches, and recommends:

> It is well to avoid the moonlight, and especially before the actual conjunction of the moon and the sun, and to walk nowhere after dinner.[83]

Plutarch (45–120 CE) also talks about the influence that the moon has over the world:

> Thus nurses are exceedingly careful to avoid exposing babies to moonlight for, since it is full of moisture like green plants,

---

79. Labat, *Traité akkadien de Diagnostics*, 80:4–6, quoted in Scurlock and Andersen, *Diagnoses in Assyrian and Babylonian Medicine*, 493. Cf. "Miqtu," 104.

80. The hifil *hikkā^h* (from *nākā^h*) means "to smite, strike" (Exod 2:11, 13; 21:19), which many times denotes injuring blows (Deut 25:2–3; 1 Kgs 20:37; Jer 37:15; Song 5:7; Hos 6:1).

81. Dahood, *Psalms 101–150*, 202. Kraus also reminds us that "in the Babylonian world disastrous effects are ascribed to the moon god. Fever and leprosy are caused by him. But the thought can also be about the affliction of being moonstruck, which was understood to be possession by demons" (*Psalms 60–150*, 430).

82. See Preuss, *Biblical and Talmudic Medicine*; Prioreschi, *History of Medicine*; Temkin, *Falling Sickness*, and Temkin, *Hippocrates*.

83. Celso, *De Medicina* i.4.

it causes the babies to have spasms and convulsions (*spatai kai diastrephetai*). And everyone knows that it is difficult to wake up those who have gone to sleep in the light of the moon since they get stunned and doped, for the moisture poured by the moon oppress their bodies.[84]

Vettius Valens (*ca.* 120–175 CE) was an authority in Hellenistic astrology. He talks about the diseases caused by the movements of the stars. For example, he says that when the sun, the moon and mercury are situated against each other, people get their eyes injured or are affected with madness and attacks. He also mentions a man who "had injuries in irremissible places, tender feet and, most significantly, the moon made him sick" (*eselēniaszē*).[85]

In antiquity, people thought of epilepsy as "the sacred disease" (*hiera nosos*), since it was sent by gods, demons and spirits. Hippocrates championed a different view. He argued that epilepsy was produced by the flow of phlegm coming from the brain through the veins.[86] Today his diagnosis doesn't make any sense, but he was trying to find a more realistic explanation. In his treatise *De morbo sacro* (400 BCE), he says:

> I want to discuss the disease called "sacred." It appears to me that it is not more divine or sacred than other diseases. It has a natural cause and originates like any other affection. Its supposedly divine origin is due to the inexperience of people who are amazed by its peculiar character. While people still believe in its divine origin for they cannot understand it, they refute its divinity through the easy healing methods they use . . . I think the first who ascribed a sacred character to this malady were those who today are magicians, purificators, charlatans and healers who pretend being very religious and having superior knowledge. But because they roam lost and have really no cure, they take refuge and hide behind superstition, and say the disease is sacred, so their perfect ignorance is not made manifest.[87]

---

84. Plutarch, *Quaestionum Convivalium*, as found in Bernardakis, *Plutarchi Chaeronensis Moralia* iii.10.3 (658E-F, p. 135). Cf. Clement and Hoffleit, *Plutarch's Moralia*, 275–76.

85. Valens, *Vettii Valentis* 113.10 (liber ii, cap. xxxvi), in Kroll, *Vetti Valentis*, 113.

86. Hippocrates, *De morbo sacro* v.7-8; viii.1-28 (cf. Jones, *Hippocrates*, 2:151, 155–57).

87. *De morbo sacro* i.1-10; ii.1-9 (cf. Jones, *Hippocrates*, 2:138–41).

5.7.2 The Healing of a Possessed/Lunatic Boy

With this background we can now examine the story of the healing of the boy with epilepsy. Please, note that Matthew 17:15 uses the verb *selēniadsomai* = "to have the disease given by the moon, to have been stricken by the moon, to be lunatic" (the verb comes from *selēnē* = moon).

The healing of a possessed/lunatic boy

The father describes the malady and reports the incapacity of the disciples to heal the boy

Mark 9:17b–18a	Matthew 17:15–16	Luke 9:38b–40
[17b] Teacher, I brought you my son who has a dumb spirit, [18] and wherever it seizes him, it throws him to the ground; and the boy foams (at his mouth) and grinds his teeth, and becomes rigid.	[15] Lord, have mercy on my son, for he has the disease given by the moon, and he suffers terribly; for he often falls into the fire and often into the water.	[38b] Teacher, I beg you to look at my son, for he is my only child. [39] And abruptly a spirit seizes him, and at once it screams and convulses him with foam (at the mouth), and he hardly leaves him when he mauls him.
I have asked your disciples to cast it out, but they were not able to do it.	[16] And I brought him to your disciples, but they could not cure him.	[40] I begged your disciples to cast it out, but they could not.

Jesus reproaches the incredulity of the people

Mark 9:19	Matthew 17:17	Luke 9:41
19 (Jesus) answered them: You faithless generation! How much longer must I be among you? How much longer must I put up with you? Bring him to me!	[17] Jesus answered: You faithless generation! How much longer must I be among you? How much longer must I put up with you? Bring him to me!	[41] Jesus answered, saying: You faithless and perverse generation! How much longer must I be among you? How much longer must I put up with you? Bring him here!

Jesus heals the boy

Mark 9:20		Luke 9:42a

Mark	Matthew	Luke
²⁰ And they brought the boy to him. When the spirit saw Jesus, it immediately threw the boy into convulsions, and the boy fell on the ground and rolled about, foaming (at the mouth).		⁴² As (the boy) came forward, the demon threw him to the ground and convulsed him.

Mark interrupts the healing miracle to add a conversation about faith

Mark 9:21–24

²¹ Jesus asked the father: How long has this been happening? And he said: Since he was a little boy.

²² And (the spirit) often throws him into the fire or water, to kill him. But if you are able to do anything, help us out of pity for us.

²³ Jesus retorted: [what is this] "if you are able"? All things [are possible] for the one who believes.

²⁴ Immediately the father of the boy cried out: I believe, help my unbelief.

The healing is resumed

Mark 9:25–27	Matthew 17:18	Luke 9:42b
²⁵ … Jesus … rebuked the unclean spirit, saying to it: Dumb and deaf spirit, I command you: come out of him and never enter in him again.	¹⁸ And Jesus rebukes it,	⁴² But Jesus rebuked the unclean spirit and healed the boy and gave him back to his father.
²⁶ Then screaming and convulsing the boy violently, (the spirit) came out; and the boy was like dead. So that many were saying: He is dead. ²⁷ But Jesus took him by the hand and lifted him; and he stood up.	and the demon came out of him, and the boy was cure that moment.	

A quick review of the above passages shows that the evangelists differed in their descriptions of the disease:

Descriptions of the disease

Mark — The sickness was produced by "a dumb spirit" (Mark 9:17, 25), but later we are told that the spirit was also "deaf" (Mark 9:25).

Matthew — In this narrative, it is the Moon who produces the illness: the boy "has the disease given by the moon" (Matt 17:15). This important detail is washed away by translations like "he is an epileptic" (NRSV), "he is demented" (NJB), "he has seizures" (NIV, NLT). Matthew also mentions a demon (Matt 17:18).

Luke — Here we find a spirit and a demon (Luke 9:39, 42). Luke describes the symptoms of epilepsy but never mentions a dumb or deaf spirit. On the contrary, the spirit actually screams through the boy (Luke 9:39).

Origen (*ca.* 182–254 CE) is an example of how theologians purge the biblical text from what does not rhyme with their doctrinal standards. He discards Hippocrates' view that epilepsy is a brain problem. He also denies the Moon's involvement as the cause of the disease. And whether we interpret *selēnē* to be an actual goddess[88] or only a planet that communicates epilepsy, Origen rejects Matthew's view that the disease was caused by the Moon (Matt 17:15). This is his interpretation:

> Let's pay attention to what is been said [in Matthew] and let's inquire first about how we are told that the one who was a lunatic (*selēniadseszai*) had been cast into darkness and knocked down by an unclean, dumb and deaf spirit, and for what reason the expression "to be a lunatic" (*selēniadseszai*) derives its name from the great light in heaven which is next to the sun, which God appointed "to rule over the night" [Gen 1:16]. Let physicians discuss the physiology of the matter, since they think that this case is not about an unclean spirit but a bodily disorder. And investigating the nature of things, let them say that moist humours in the head are moved by a certain sympathy which they have with the light of the moon (*to selēniakon phōs*), which has a moist nature. But for us, who also believe in the gospel, this disease is caused by an unclean, dumb and deaf spirit in those who suffer it. Besides, to those accustomed—like the magicians from Egypt—to promise a cure for this illness and who, sometimes, seem to be successful, we say that perhaps, in order to slander God's creation . . . this unclean spirit watches some

---

88. Hesiod claimed that Theia and Hyperton procreated three gods: *ēelios* (Sun), *selēnē* (Moon) and *ēōs* (Dawn). See Hesiod, *Theogony* 371.

configurations of the moon and makes it appear . . . like the cause of such great evil is really not the dumb and deaf demon but the great light in heaven which was appointed to "rule by night" and which has no power to originate such a disorder among people. But all of them speak malice loftily saying that the cause of all the disorders that exist on the earth, whether in general or particular, come from the position of the stars (*tēn tōn astrōn schesin*).[89]

In antiquity, diseases were explained in terms of maladies sent by the stars (§1.1.4). The gods were a way of humanizing the *impersonal* forces of nature (§3.1). Our anthropocentric tendencies may compel us to talk about the wind in terms of a fickle friend, or to turn the season of spring into a woman, and Death into a hooded man (see §2.1.1). But to interpret this kind of language *literally* would immediately produce an irreconcilable incompatibility between our explanation and some obvious facts: the wind is not really a friend; spring is not a woman, etc.

In the Gospels, the etiology of epilepsy is understood in terms of a *literal personal agent*. It was a demon (Matthew and Luke), a spirit (Mark, Luke) or the Moon goddess (Matthew). The diagnosis demands a cure that should come from a *personal* agent in the form of a magician or exorcist who holds sufficient supernatural power to counteract the power of gods and demons. During the conflict, the spirit exhibits his power by throwing the boy into convulsions (Mark 9:20), and then the cure is achieved by way of personal confrontation: "I command you: come out of him and never enter in him again" (Mark 9:25). Metaphors enabled the ancient world to provisionally explain its environment in terms of a personal "you" who confronted people all the time.[90] It was a way of interpreting reality (§1.1.4), and we shouldn't blame the evangelists for not knowing what we know today about epilepsy.

However, we have come to a point in which it is impossible to avoid the collision between such different ways of looking at reality. Today *we know* that epilepsy is a brain disorder.[91] We know that the cause of epilepsy is not a divine *personal* agent, but a physical malady. By using anticonvulsive

---

89. *Commentaria in Evangelium secundum Mattaeum* 577–78, in Migne, *Patrologiae Graecae*, 13:1105, 1108. Cf. Patrick, *Origen's Commentary on the Gospel of Matthew*, 478.

90. See Frankfort, *Intellectual Adventure*, 4–6.

91. Epileptic seizures are produced when neurotransmitters in the brain deliver electrical signals at a speed five times the normal occurrence. These signals raid the body with incontrollable reactions. Cf. Appleton and Marson, *Epilepsy*; Kraemer, *Epilepsy from A–Z*; Bjorklung, *Epilepsy*.

drugs, the treatment is 70 percent successful. Other cases are treated with surgery.[92] Doctors today do not use exorcism to cast away the demon of epilepsy in the name of Jesus. Today we are aware that the world around us is impersonal. It is referred to as an "it," not as a "you," even when our conversation overflows in anthropomorphisms that *figuratively* humanize everything all the time.

In addition, the demon theory of epilepsy is cruel, for it blames the victim. Mark accuses the multitude and the father of unbelief (9:19–24).[93] Matthew blames the disciples (Matt 17:19–21). These days it would be callous to accuse people of unbelief, adding guilt to their suffering. If someone prays for a person with epilepsy nothing will happen, but it is not for lack of faith. Curing epilepsy is not about asking a divine person to fight against supernatural agents. What the patient needs is medical treatment.

5.8 The Current Crisis

We use historical-critical disciplines to partially bridge the cultural gulf between us and the Scriptures. These disciplines have made us aware of the jarring incompatibility between the biblical worldview and the modern world. It is not that the modern perspective has a particular antipathy just against the Bible. What happens is that it is impossible to reconcile the way in which the *entire ancient world* looked at the cosmos with the way we conceive the universe today. It is not possible anymore to accept a cosmology that *literally* believes in the *personal* gods and demons of theism who are in Heaven above and Hell below. The biblical message has come to us dressed in a mythological garb that does not make sense anymore. Paul Ricoeur calls it the "cultural vehicle" of the kerygma; and adds that we need to understand that the biblical text both reveals and occults the message of the gospel. The mythical language of the Gospels is nothing more than "the false scandal of a cultural vehicle that does not belong to us anymore."[94]

---

92. When pharmacology and surgery are not able to correct epilepsy, today's science draws upon a cerebral neurostimulator which is implanted in the skull. This dispositive watches cerebral activity, and when it detects an anomalous electric impulse, responds immediately to normalize its performance.

93. Mark does not criticize the disciples. The pl. pronoun "you" found in "you faithless generation . . . among you . . . put up with you" (v. 19) seems to refer only to the crowd and the father of the boy. The same can be said of the plural: "they brought" (v. 20). The father also demonstrates weak faith when he says "if you are able" (v. 22) and "help my unbelief" (v. 24).

94. Ricoeur, *Rule of Metaphor*, 26.

In absolute contrast to our present situation, Justin Martyr lived within a culture that made it easy for him to defend Christianity by simply arguing that the new religion was not proposing anything new. His culture allowed him to say that Jesus was conceived by a god or that Jesus was a hero who went up to Heaven:

> When we claim that the logos, the first son[95] of God, was born without [sexual] union—Jesus our teacher—and that he was crucified and died, and rose again, and ascended into heaven, we are not proposing anything new from what you call sons of Zeus: Hermes . . . Asclepius . . . who ascended to heaven, as well as Dionysius . . . Hercules[96] . . . and the Dioscuri . . . and Perseus . . . and Bellerophon who . . . rose to heaven on Pegasus' horse. What shall I say of Ariadne and those who, like her, have been declared to have been made gods?[97] And what about the emperors who die among you, whom you deem worthy of immortality,[98] and in whose behalf you produced someone who swore having seen the cremated Caesar rising to heaven from the funeral pyre?[99]

It was vital for Justin's argument to point out that the surrounding cultures of his time also believed in divine men and had "eyewitnesses" who saw them going up to Heaven. In that context, the myths and legends of the Bible were completely credible. The message of the gospel was effective because it reflected the worldview of its milieu. There was congruence between cosmology and message. The problem today is that ancient cosmologies have become obsolete and to insist on believing them *literally* creates an

---

95. Or: "offspring" (*gennēma*).

96. In §3.4.2, we quoted the myth regarding Hercules ascending to the gods in Heaven.

97. Lit. "declared to be set among the stars." For the stars as gods, see §3.1; §3.3.4a.

98. Or: "being deified" (*apazanatidseszai*).

99. Cf. Justinus, *Apologia pro Christianis*, xxi.1-3, in Migne, *Patrologiae Graecae* 6:360 (cf. Roberts and Donaldson, *Ante-Nicene Fathers*, 1:170). When Justin talks about Caesar, he refers to Caesar Augustus in the legend quoted in §3.4.2. Tertullian (160-220 CE) also argued that the Christ-fable was similar to the legends and myths of the Greco-Roman world: "Therefore, this ray of God, as it was prophesized, descending into certain virgin and made flesh in her womb, was born man and God united. This flesh formed by the Spirit is nourished, grows, talks, teaches, works, and it is the Christ. Receive meanwhile this fable, similar to some of your own, while we go on to show how Christ's claims are true, and that those [= demons] who established such [pagan] fables similar to the truth, to destroy it, knew the coming events" (*Apologeticus pro Christianis*, xxi, in Migne, *Patrologiae Latina*, 1:399; cf. Woodham, *Tertulliani*, 75; Roberts and Donaldson, *Ante-Nicene Fathers*, 3:34-5).

unbearable tension between the gospel and the world we live in. In antiquity, claims of divinity were the necessary credentials needed to become a hero or a king (§3.4; §4.3.3). But today we do not see presidents or heroes claiming to have been begotten by a god or claiming to be god. When one of our presidents dies, we do not watch the news to see how the president went up to Heaven to be deified (we could all be eyewitnesses!). Each time the church demands that we interpret the Scriptures *literally*, she loses all relevance to modern society, for the church disconnects herself from our current reality. The world she talks about doesn't exist anymore.

It should not come as a surprise that the conflict between church and science ended creating a crisis of faith. In America, Christianity, Islam and Judaism are losing their youth (Generation Z, born in 1999–2015). Young adults (Millennials, born in 1984–1998) are also leaving by the thousands every year. In March 2018, *The Economist* published an article noting the large number of people leaving Islam. The majority is second generation immigrants but adults are also experiencing a faith-crisis in growing numbers.[100] In September 2019, the organization Ex-Muslims of North America placed their first billboard in Atlanta, Chicago and Houston, saying "Nearly one in four Muslims raised in the U.S. have left Islam. Godless. Fearless. Ex-Muslim."

In January 2018, *Barna Research* reported that in America the number of atheists has doubled within the Generation Z which is now mostly a post-religious population. The *Pew Research Center* issued several studies revealing that 16 percent of young people (18–29 years old) do not believe in any god or higher power. This is the demographic with the largest number of atheists. Then 39 percent of the youth (18–29 years old), 37 percent of young adults (30–40) and 28 percent of adults (50–64) do not believe in the god of the Bible but instead only in a generic god, a higher power or spiritual force. We should also mention that 38 percent of college graduates believe only in a higher power, and 16 percent do not believe in any god at all.[101] The *Religious News Service* published an article informing us that "in a shift that stands to impact both religion and politics, survey data suggests that the percentage of Americans who don't affiliate with any specific religious tradition is now roughly the same as those who identify as evangelical

---

100. See "Number of Ex-Muslims in America Is Rising." See Zuckerman, "Secularism Hits the Arab World." In India, atheism is instilling a scientific approach that cuts across religious, class and caste lines. See Sen, "Atheist Ashram."

101. See the following studies published by *Pew Research Center*: "U.S. Public Becoming Less Religious"; "When Americans Say They Believe in God"; "Key Findings about Americans' Belief in God." This trend is also a worldwide phenomenon, according this other study: "Age Gap in Religion around the World."

or Catholic."[102] The "Nones"—people claiming no religion—are now 23.1 percent while evangelicals are below with 22.5 percent and Catholics 23 percent![103] Are we listening?

Some of the complaints raised by the younger population are: science has refuted many Christian beliefs; Christians are hypocritical; it is not possible to believe in a god who allows so much evil in the world; the church is not relevant anymore; and that they had bad experiences in the church.[104] Of all these grievances the one that stands out is the church's lack of relevance for today's world. Even among the youth who regularly attend church, we hear the protest that the church rejects science (49 percent) and that its teachings are shallow (24 percent).[105] White Evangelicals are losing thousands of people on issues like racism vs diversity; women's equality vs male dominance-privilege; LGBTQ vs heterosexual normativity; democracy vs authoritarian theocracy; oligarchy vs egalitarianism. The criticism coming from people who were insiders is quite demolishing, for they know very well the White Fundamentalist culture. They grew up in it. It was their identity. The Christian worldview started a cultural war and the movement is now in retreat.

5.8.1 Grieving Loss and Rebuilding Faith

Many fundamentalist believers try to protect their children from "the world" by resorting to home schooling. Others send their kids to Christian schools and colleges. Another tactic has been to lobby the government into supporting charter schools that would allow religion to be taught in their classrooms, diverting tax dollars from the "evil" secular public schools. But the ever increasing exodus of youth leaving the church makes it clear that it is becoming impossible to keep them in the bubble. The omnipresence of the modern world produces a crisis that eventually leads to a complete rejection of Christianity but it could also lead to a *new way of looking at religion*. Today people are thinking about religion in terms of a way of life and not as a belief system. We have argued that mythical-stories are best when

---

102. Jenkins, "'Nones' Now as Big as Evangelicals, Catholics."

103. See also, Dionne, "Survey Finds."

104. See *Pew Research Center*, "Why America's 'Nones' Don't Identify"; "Factors Driving the Growth of Religious 'Nones.'"

105. Social media is flooded with the stories of thousands upon thousands of ex-evangelicals telling their horror stories. Among many, see: http://www.fundamentallyfreeblog.com; https://exvangelicalpodcast.com; https://www.patheos.com/blogs/rolltodisbelieve; https://www.recoveringfromreligion.org.

they are used as parables in support of evolving values and ideals, instead of taking them as *literal* historical events or factual descriptions of the world.

The following story shared by Nelle Smith illustrates how unsettling and heartbreaking it is for our youth to experience the disintegration of their fundamentalist Christian worldview. Smith grew up in a fundamentalist home, and lived all her life fully immersed in the White Evangelical bubble. But then she went to college and took Geology 101. Suddenly her eyes were open. She found out that the earth had existed for billions of years. She learned that the world was not six thousand years old, nor was it created in six days. She recalls feeling this way: "there was nothing solid under me, only a great vacuum in which to flail." Every time she went to church and heard about Adam and Eve or the creation of the earth, she thought of the billions of years of evolution. Her world collapsed:

> It was the dissolution of a world. People who didn't grow up in the American evangelical bubble often don't realize what they're demanding when they ask an evangelical to accept a fact that is contradicted by their church's interpretation of the Bible. To those bought in . . . evangelicalism is not a collection of facts. It is an entire reality, based not on logic but on a web of ideas, all of which must be wholeheartedly accepted for any of it to work. It is complete unto itself, self-contained, self-justifying, self-sustaining. It's your community, your life, your entire way of thinking, and your gauge for what is true in the world. Evangelicalism feels so right from the inside.
>
> And, for an evangelical, there are no small doubts: growing up in many evangelical churches means to be told, repeatedly, that the devil will always seek a foothold and once you give him one, you're well on the road to hell, to losing your faith, to destroying your witness. That's scary stuff. To begin to doubt evangelicalism is not simply a mental exercise. For many like me, it's to feel a void opening, the earth dropping out from beneath you. It's to face the prospect of invalidating your entire existence.
>
> So know this when you talk to an evangelical: in attempting to persuade them to your point of view—even on a topic that seems minor to you—you're not asking for them to change their mind, you're asking them to punch a hole in the fabric of their reality, to begin the process of destroying their world. And, as anyone who has had the experience knows, world-destroying is not fun. It is, frankly, terrifying.[106]

---

106. See her article: Smith, "When You Argue with a Fundamentalist."

Smith's story is a clear example of the tremendous influence of metaphor. Metaphor has the power to shape the way we see and experience reality (§1.1.2; §1.1.5). However, centuries of investigation have produced such a huge amount of knowledge of the world that today we know that the old metaphors of religion cannot be taken as a *literal description* of reality. The old worldview has fallen apart (§5.2). When a worldview collapses, people feel what myth itself describes as chaos destroying a cosmos (§1.3.6–7). Smith makes this very clear when she explains that she felt like "nothing solid" was under her feet, and that she was left in "a great vacuum," or that she felt like "the earth dropping out from beneath." There are thousands upon thousands of people like Nelle Smith going through a crisis of faith, but instead of helping the youth to reshape their faith, the church has barricaded herself in the trenches, oblivious to the fact that the "party is over."

5.8.2 A Theology for the Present Age

There is no doubt that the church urgently needs an interdisciplinary theology in dialogue with the sciences. Theologians cannot anymore pronounce dictums about *reality* without consulting with those who study it. An interdisciplinary approach to theology will force the church to completely rethink its religion and even abandon many of its dogmas. But the question remains: Is it possible to articulate a Christian theology congruent with our present world? That's the challenge.

This dilemma finds a perfect example in the doctrine regarding the origin of humankind and the Fall. Let's briefly deal with this concept. We start by quoting the traditional view of the fall as it is presented in a Reformed confession:

> Man was originally created in the image of God and his understanding was adorned with true and saving knowledge of his Creator as well as of spiritual things. His heart and will were upright, all his affections pure, and the whole man was holy.[107] However, rebelling against God by the instigation of the devil, and abusing the freedom of his own will, man deprived himself from these excellent gifts. He brought upon himself blindness

---

107. We should underline here that the Catholic Church also promulgates "the original happiness of our first parents in a state of justice, integrity and immortality" (Denzinger, *Magisterio*, 512). Lutherans have also confessed that "man was created of God in the beginning pure and holy and free from sin" (*Formula of Concord*, article I,); and Calvinists have declared that "God created man, male and female, with reasonable and immortal souls, endued with knowledge, righteousness, and true holiness" (*Westminster Confession*, ch. iv.ii).

of mind, horrible darkness, futility and distortion of judgment, becoming wicked, rebellious, and stubborn in heart and will, and impure in his affections.

After the fall, man begat children in his own likeness. A corrupt stock produced a corrupt offspring. Hence all the posterity of Adam—with the exception of Christ—have derived corruption from their original parents; not by imitation—as the Pelagians of old asserted—but by the propagation of a vicious nature.

Therefore, all men are conceived in sin, and are born by nature children of wrath, incapable for any saving good, prone to evil, dead in sin, and slaves to sin. So without the regenerating grace of the Holy Spirit, they are neither able nor willing to return to God, to reform the depravity of their nature, or to dispose themselves to reformation.[108]

Apart from the fact that this doctrinal construction completely disfigures the narrative of Genesis 1–3,[109] scientific evidence has shown this doctrine to be a fantasy. Arthur Peacocke, the late scientist and Anglican priest, utterly demolished the Christian doctrine of the Fall by merely mentioning what we now know regarding evolution:

Evolution can operate only through the death of individuals. New forms of matter arise only through the dissolution of the old; new life only through death of the old. We as individuals would not be here at all, as members of the species *homo sapiens* if our forerunners in the evolutionary process had not died. Biological death was present on the Earth long before human beings arrived on the scene and is the pre-requisite of our coming into existence . . . So when St. Paul says that "sin pays a wage, and the wage is death," [Rom 6:23] that cannot possibly mean for us now *biological* death and can only mean "death" in some other sense. Biological death can no longer be regarded as in any way the *consequence* of anything human beings might have been supposed to have done in the past, for evolutionary history shows it to be the very *means* whereby they appear and so, for the theist, are created by God. The traditional interpretation of the third chapter of *Genesis* that there was a historical "Fall," an action by our human progenitors that is the explanation of biological death, has to be rejected. This means that those classical formulations of the theology of the "redemptive" work of Christ that

---

108. *Canones Synodi Dordrechtanae* iii.1–3. Cf. Schaff, *Creeds*, 3:550–97.
109. See Enns, *Evolution of Adam*.

assume a causal connection between biological death and sin must also be recast.

Those traditional interpretations concerning a historical "Fall" of humanity from a paradisiacal state have been undermined in another respect, quite apart from the general realization that the stories are mythological. For the biological-historical evidence is that human nature has emerged only gradually by a continuous process from earlier "hominids" . . . there is *no* past period for which there is reason to affirm that human beings possessed moral perfection existing in a paradisiacal situation from which there has been only a subsequent decline. All the evidence points to a creature slowly emerging into awareness, with an increasing capacity for consciousness and sensitivity and the possibility of moral responsibility . . . So there is no sense in which we can talk of a "Fall" from a past perfection. There was no golden age, no perfect past, no individuals "Adam and Eve" from whom all human beings have now descended and declined . . .[110]

In an attempt to save the doctrine of humanity's origin and fall, James Smith has tried to reformulate it in the light of what evolution teaches about the origins of the world. In dialogue with science, Smith creatively modified the doctrinal narrative in this way:

In the beginning, God created the heavens and earth. From what he seems to tell us via the book of nature, the mechanics of creational unfolding was an evolutionary process: the emergence of new life was governed by the survival of the fittest, such that biological death and animal predation are part of this process, even part of what can be acclaimed as a "good" creation. So some of the phenomena we might have traditionally described as "outcomes" of the Fall seem to be part of the fabric of a good, emerging creation.

From out this process there emerges a population of hominids who have evolved as cultural animals with emerging social systems, and it is this early population (of, say, 10,000) that constitutes our early ancestors. When such a population has evolved to the point of exhibiting features of emergent consciousness, relational aptitudes, and mechanisms of will—in short, when these hominids have evolved to the point of exhibiting moral capabilities—our creating God "elects" this population as his covenant people. The "creation" of humanity, on this picture, is the first election—the first of many (Noah, Abraham,

---

110. Peacocke, *Theology for a Scientific Age*, 221-22.

Jacob et al.). And in that covenantal election of a population, Yahweh established a relationship with humanity that involved his self-revelation to them and established moral parameters for them and for their flourishing. In being so elected, these pinnacle creatures are also deputized and commissioned as God's "image bearers"—the creator's representatives to and for creation's care and flourishing. They are charged with unfurling the latent potential enfolded into creation. And to some extent, creation now depends on their care and cultivation such that, should this emergent humanity fail to carry out its mission and obligations as articulated by God's "law," there will be "cosmic" consequences.

This original humanity is *not* perfect (the catholic theological tradition has never claimed that). They are able to carry out this mission—God's law would not be established where obedience is not possible—but they are also characterized by moral immaturity, since moral virtue requires habituation and formation, requires time. So while they are able to carry out this mission, there are no guarantees, and also nor surprises when they fail. Since we're dealing with a larger population in this "garden," so to speak, there is not one discrete event at time T_1 where "the transgression" occurs. However, there is still a temporal, episodic nature of the Fall. We might imagine a Fall-in-process, a sort of probationary period in which God is watching (not unlike the dynamics of the flood narrative in Genesis 6, a kind of second Fall narrative in the Torah). So the Fall might take place over time T_1–T_3. But there is some significant sense of before and after in this scenario.

And things change in the "after": there are cosmic effects of some discernable nature (Cp. Colossians 1–2); there is also the cosmic fallout of humanity's failure to cultivate and care for creation; and there is also some kind of (almost?) ontological shift in human nature, or at least a certain solidification of human character in a certain direction and tendency that will require the regenerating initiative of God to make rightly ordered virtue a possibility. But his regeneration and sanctification will not constitute an undoing of their created tendencies and capacities, but rather a restoration of creational possibilities and empowerment/formation to be able to realize that calling. Redemption will also require a grace that is cosmic in scope, a grace that is the outcome of the cross (Col 1:20).[111]

---

111. Smith, "What Stands on the Fall?," 61–62.

We applaud Smith's courage for trying to complement Christian doctrine with insights coming from the science of evolution. But his proposal shows how difficult it is to modify this Christian dogma without completely destroying the beauty and meaning of Genesis 1–3, to the point that his modifications ends creating an entirely different narrative. The problem that lies beneath this obsession with making Genesis compatible with evolution is the unrelenting insistence that somehow Genesis 1–3 is a *historical account* of something that really happened; the belief that these chapters contain a *literal description* of what happened in space and time at the beginning of the world. For example, under the authority of Pope Saint Pius X (1835–1914 CE), The Pontifical Commission on Biblical Matters argued, in May of 1910, that the first three chapters of Genesis were historical, for they "contain narratives of things that truly occurred; that is, narratives that correspond to objective realities and historical truths"; and that those chapters are not "fables drawn from the mythologies and cosmogonies of primitive peoples," nor are they "allegories and symbols, lacking a foundation in objective reality, given under the appearance of history."[112] The insistence on the "historicity" of the narrative is due to the fact that without a fall, the whole Christian doctrinal system seems to crumble, for "the grammar of Christian theology encapsulates the biblical narrative in a *plot* that begins with the goodness of creation, a fall into sin, redemption of all things in Christ, and the eschatological consummation of all things."[113] However, theologians seem oblivious to the fact that not only the fall but the whole doctrinal plot is mythological. Goodness of creation, redemption in Christ and the eschatological hope are all mythical concepts.

The problem with insisting in the historicity of the fall is that the effort is completely blind to *the nature of the narrative*. Genesis 1–3 is a mythological tale, just like the creation story of *Atra-ḫasīs*. The best way to interpret Genesis 1–3 is to read it against its own cultural background in the Ancient Near East, relinquishing any interference from Christian doctrine or the findings of evolution. Only then we will be able to enjoy this magnificent

---

112. Denzinger, *Magisterio*, 512. In July 2019, the Lutheran Church—Missouri Synod declared that the Bible is the Word of God and, therefore, infallible and without error. The Synod resolved to "confess and reaffirm that God created the world in six days, with a seventh day for rest, each day consisting of 24 hours." The Synod rejected the evolutionary *fact* that "death is a natural occurrence, present before the fall, not the result of Adam's sin" and, therefore, it resolved to "reaffirm that Holy Scripture teaches the historical event of the creation of the first man, Adam, who was made in the image of God, and that death came in the world as the consequence of his sin." See Lutheran Church—Missouri Synod, *Convention Workbook*, 434.

113. Smith, "What Stands on the Fall?," 51. Or: "This plot of creation, fall, redemption, and consummation constitutes the 'core' plot of biblical faith" (54).

literary work in all its beauty and significance, protected from anachronistic distortions. And then we may judge what values may be supported by this parable.

People may raise the issue that we are creating a new Jesus and a new religion. But we need to remind them that the Bible itself shows cultural shifts producing new metaphors. In the Christian Bible, we find Hellenistic views that sided with the new platonic ideas in vogue. Were the apostles and the creeds wrong in using this new source domain to form metaphors that contradicted the old ones? Hellenism was responsible for encouraging the ideas found in the creeds—god as unchangeable, impassible, incomprehensible, etc. These new ideas also distorted the interpretation of some parts of the Hebrew Bible (§2.3.3–4). We have insisted that cultural changes do not warrant distorting the meaning of Bible narratives. Just let the Bible say what it says, that's the core of the grammatical-historical method.[114] But we must insist that democracy and modern culture have made the king metaphor obsolete, and today we need to find new *source domains* to talk about god. Ancient people constructed their views of god borrowing from their own culture. We should be allowed to do the same. And this is not just an academic affair; it is a profoundly pastoral problem. We encourage ministers to confront the current crisis, and we specially urge them to listen to the youth's agony and our dying world.

---

114. Earlier, in chapters 1 and 2, we rejected the imposition of platonic interpretations to some sections of Bible, because these interpretations distort their original meaning. There are parts in the Bible which actually imagine a god who has a human body and who behaves like a human being (§2.2). We used two excursus to prove that platonic reinterpretations are wrong (§2.4 and 3.7).

GLOSSARY

Adad—See Iškur.

An—(= "heaven, sky," Sum.; **Anu**, Akk.) Supreme god of the Sumerian pantheon, king of the gods.

Anat—Goddess of war in Ugarit, and sister of Baal. She was the patroness of the warriors (Judg 3:31; 5:6). Cf. §1.3.4.

Anunnaki—(Akk.; ᵈa-nun-na, Sum.) Collective name for the gods of Mesopotamia, sometimes considered as the "great gods" who determined the fates of the universe. See Igigu, and §1.1.4; §4.2.1.

Apotheosis—Deification of a human being as part of the cult of the hero or holy person. See §3.4.2.

Apsû—(Akk.; Abzu, Sum.) "Subterranean waters" or "cosmic waters," which is the place where Enki resides. In *Enūma Eliš,* Apsu is first the husband of Tiamat. See §1.3.2; §3.1.

Ašerah—(ʾAtirat, Ugar.) Babylonian and West Semitic goddess, wife of An and mother of the gods. In the Syro-Palestine region was known as Athirat, wife of El.

Athene (Parthenos)—Greek goddess associated with wisdom, war, civilization, art, etc. She was the patroness of Athens, where she had her temple, the Parthenon.

Athirat—See Ašerah.

Atraḫasīs—(= "very wise") Babylonian myth (*ca.* 1700–1600 BCE) dealing with the creation of humankind and a hero by the same name who escapes the flood with the help of Enki. See §1.2.4.

GLOSSARY

Baal—(Ugar. *bēl, baʿlu* or *baʿal*—"Lord") Important god of Canaan and Ugarit. He was a warrior god and the god of the storm, lightning, rain, and fertility. He's also referred to as *haddu* (Hadad, Hadd or Adad), that is, "the one who thunders." See §1.3.3.

Ea—(Akk.) See Enki.

El—The word ʾēl (= "god") shares the same basic root with all other Semitic languages to refer to a god (cf. ʾilu, ilum, ʾilāh). In Ugarit, El was the head of the Pantheon, in the same way the biblical El was the head of his own council: "El is feared in the council of the holy ones" (Ps 89:7)

Enki—(= "lord of the earth," Sum.; Ea, Akk.) The most interesting Sumerian god; the one "who has no equal among the gods." He is the god of wisdom, art, creation and the waters (Abzu); the creator and defender of humankind. He is also referred to as Nudimmud ("the one who creates," the god of craftsmanship). He resides in Engur (e_2-engur—"the house of the subterranean waters") or *apsû* ("cosmic waters"). His temple was in the city of Eridu. See §2.1.3; §3.1.

Enlil—(Sum.) Chief Sumerian god, son of An (Anu). He had the executive control of the universe. His temple Ekur (= "house of the mountain") was in the city of Nippur. His name was composed of ^{d}En (= "Lord") and lil_2 (= "wind, air, atmosphere"). See §1.2.3.

Enūma Eliš—(= "when on high", Akk.) Babylonian myth. See §1.3.2.

Erra—God of war, fire, fever and plagues. See also Nergal.

Ešarra—(= "house of the universe," Akk.). Temple of the gods in Heaven.

Eṭemmu—Spirit of a dead person; a ghost.

Gilgameš—Both a legendary Sumerian king (*ca.* 2700 BCE) from Uruk and a literary work by the same name. His father was the demigod Lugalbanda and his mother the goddess Ninsum. Tradition made him into an epic divine hero known thorough several literary works: *Gilgameš Epic* (*ca.* 2100 BCE); *Enkidu and the Underworld* (*ca.* 2000 BCE) and *Gilgameš and Aga* (*ca.* 1800 BCE).

Henotheism—(*heis* = "one" + *theos* = "god") The worship of a single god but recognizing the existence of other gods.

Hero—(*hērōs*, Gk.) Human being whose deification occurs at birth or death. Cf. §3.4; 4.3.3.

Igigu—(Akk.) Collective name for the gods of Mesopotamia. Sometimes it points to proletarian gods, like in *Atraḫasīs*.

Ilu—(Akk.) God. See El.

Inana—(Sum.; Ištar, Akk.) Patroness of the city of Uruk. She was the goddess of love and war, and she's described as the evening star, the lady of all the lands.

Iškur—Sumerian storm god responsible for the fertilizing rains. In Akkadian his name was Adad; and Hadad in Ugaritic.

Ištar—See Inana.

Kothar—(= "skillful", Ugar.) God from Ugarit who plays an important role in the myth *The Baal Cycle*. Cf. §1.3.3; §2.2.4.4); §3.2.

Kulab—Twin city of Uruk that ended being annexed as a district. See Uruk.

Marduk—Supreme god of Babylon, son of Ea (Enki) and Damkina, and creator of the world. He was the god of thunder, rain and storm. His temple was known as Esagila ($e_2.saĝ.il_2$ = "sublime house" or "highest pinnacle"). Marduk was later identified with Zeus (Jupiter). See §1.3.2.

Mot—(= "death." Ugar.; *māwet* or *šəʾôl*, Heb.) God of "Death." See §1.3.4; §3.6, and Sheol.

Nergal—God of the Underworld, also identified with Erra. Husband of Ereškigal. In the Greek tradition he was known as Heracles.

Ninĝirsu—(= "Lord of Girsu") or Ninurta was known as the god of the storm, agriculture and war. Son of Enlil and patron of the cities of Lagaš and Girsu.

Ninlil—goddess wife of Enlil. In Assyria she was the wife of Ašur.

Ninsun—(nin-sun_2 = "Lady Wild Cow") Goddess who with king Lugalbanda procreated two important kings: Gilgameš and Šulgi.

Nintu(r)—($^d Nin$-tur_5 = "Lady of Maternity") Mother of the gods and creator of humankind and the fates.

Ninurta—See ᵈNin-ĝirsu.

Nudimmud—See Enki.

Nusku—God of fire and vizier of Enlil.

Šamaš—See Utu.

Sheol—(*šəʾôl*, Heb.) The Underworld, death, or the god of Death. See Mot and §3.6.

Sumer—(*šumerum*, Akk.; or kalam = "the land," Sum.) A region located in the southern part of Mesopotamia (Irak) known as the "cradle of civilization." Important cities in Sumer were Eridu, Uruk, Kiš, Nippur, Lagaš and Agade.

Tâmtu—(Akk.) "Sea, ocean, lake" or any large mass of water. See Tiamat.

Teomachia—(*theos* = "god" + *machē* = "battle, combat") Tradition about the battles among the gods.

Tiamat—One of the forms adopted by the word *tâmtu* ("sea, ocean"). It is the name of the primeval goddess who was the mother of all gods. At the beginning of the universe only Apsu and Tiamat existed. See §1.3.2

Ugarit—City of about 8,000 people known today as Ras Shamra. It was located only a mile away from the Mediterranean coast facing Cyprus, and north of Latakia, which is today the main port of Syria. To the north of the city we find Mount Saphon (5,840 feet), residence of Baal.

Uruk—(Unug or Unug-Kulab, in Sum.) City considered as the "masterpiece of the gods." The city reached a population of 60,000 people and produced famous kings, like Meš-ki-aĝ-gašer, Enmerkar, Lugalbanda, Dumuzid, Gilgameš and Ur-Nungal.

Utu—(Sum. or *Šamaš*, Akk.) Sun god, god of truth and justice. See §1.2.3; §3.1.

Yamm—(Ugar.; *yām*, Heb.) "Sea" as the god of chaos; a powerful figure who appears in several myths of Mesopotamia. See §1.3.3; §1.3.5–6.

BIBLIOGRAPHY

Aalders, G. Charles. *Genesis*. Translated by W. Heynen. Grand Rapids: Zondervan, 1981.
Abegg, Martin, P. Flint, and E. Ulrich. *The Dead Sea Scrolls Bible*. New York: Harper One, 1999.
"Abullu." In *The Assyrian Dictionary of the Oriental Institute of the University of Chicago*, edited by Ignace J. Gelb et al., 1:82–88. Chicago: Oriental Institute, 1964–2010.
Abusch, I. Tzvi. "Ghost and God: Some Observations on a Babylonian Understanding of Human Nature." In *Self, Soul & Body in Religious Experience*, edited by Albert I. Baumgarten et al., 363–83. Leiden: Brill, 1998.
Ackerman, James S. "The Rabbinic Interpretation of Psalm 82 and the Gospel of John: John 10:34." *HTR* 59.2 (1966) 186–91.
Acts and Laws Passed by the General Court of Assembly of His Majesties Province of New-Hampshire in New-England. Boston: Green, 1726.
Acts and Resolves of the Province of the Massachusetts Bay. Vol. 1. Boston: Wright & Potter, 1869.
Adams, John. *The Works of John Adams, Second President of the United States*. Vol. 4. Boston: Little & Brown, 1851.
Ahlström, Gösta W. *The History of Ancient Palestine*. Minneapolis: Fortress, 1993.
———. *Who Were the Israelites?* Winona Lake, IN: Eisenbrauns, 1986.
Akin, Daniel L. *A Theology for the Church*. Nashville: B&H Academic, 2007.
Albrektson, Bertil. *History and the Gods: An Essay on the Idea of Historical Events as Divine Manifestations in the Ancient Near East and Israel*. Originally published 1967. Winona Lake, IN: Eisenbrauns, 2011.
Albright, William F. "Archaeology and the Date of the Hebrew Conquest of Palestine." *BASOR* 58 (1935) 10–18.
———. *Archaeology and the Religion of Israel*. Baltimore: John Hopkins, 1968.
———. *The Archaeology of Palestine and the Bible*. Cambridge: American Schools of Oriental Research, 1954.
———. *The Biblical Period from Abraham to Ezra*. New York: Harper & Row, 1963.
———. *From the Stone Age to Christianity*. New York: Doubleday, 1957.
———. "The Israelite Conquest of Canaan in the Light of Archaeology." *BASOR* 74 (1939) 11–23.
Alexander, Kern, and M. David Alexander. *American Public School Law*. 6th ed. Belmont, CA: Thomson West, 2005.
Allison, Dale C. *Constructing Jesus*. Grand Rapids: Baker, 2010.

Allison, Dale C. *Night Comes: Death, Imagination, and the Last Things*. Grand Rapids: Eerdmans, 2016.

Alster, Bendt. "*Ilū awīlum: we-e i-la*, 'Gods: Men' versus 'Man: God.' Punning and the Reversal of Patterns in the Atrahasis Epic." In *Riches Hidden in Secret Places: Ancient Near Eastern Studies in Memory of Thorkild Jacobsen*, edited by Tzvi Abusch, 35–40. Winona Lake, IN: Eisenbrauns, 2002.

———. "Sumerian Literary Dialogues and Debates and Their Place in Ancient Near East Literature." In *Living Waters: Scandinavian Orientalistic Studies Presented to Professor Dr. Frede Løkkegaard*, edited by Egon Keck et al., 1–16. Copenhagen: Museum Tusculanum, 1990.

Alter, Robert. *The Books of Psalms*. New York: Norton, 2009.

———. *Genesis: Translation and Commentary*. New York: Norton, 1996.

Andersen, Francis I. "2 (Slavonic Apocalypse of) Enoch." In *The Old Testament Pseudepigrapha* edited by James H. Charlesworth, 1:91–222. New York: Doubleday, 1983.

———. *Job*. Tyndale Old Testament Commentaries. Downers Grove, IL: InterVarsity, 1976.

———. *The Sentence in Biblical Hebrew*. The Hague: Mouton, 1974.

Anderson, A. A. *The Book of Psalms*. New Century Bible. Grand Rapids: Eerdmans, 1972.

Annus, Amar, and Alan Lenzi. *Ludlul bēl nēmeqi*. State Archives of Assyria Cuneiform Texts 7. Winona Lake, IN: Eisenbrauns, 2010.

Appleton, Richard, and A. G. Marson. *Epilepsy*. Oxford: Oxford University Press, 2009.

Aquinas, Thomas. *Summa Theologica*. 5 vols. Notre Dame: Christian Classics, 1981.

Armstrong, A. H. *The Cambridge History of Later Greek and Early Medieval Philosophy*. Cambridge: Cambridge University Press, 1967.

Arnold, Bill T. *Genesis*. New Cambridge Bible Commentary. Cambridge: Cambridge University Press, 2009.

Ascalone, Enrico. *Mesopotamia: Assyrians, Sumerians, Babylonians*. Translated by R. M. G. Frongia. Dictionaries of Civilizations 1. Berkeley: University of California Press, 2007.

Attridge, Harold W. *Hebrews*. Hermeneia. Philadelphia: Fortress, 1989.

"Balaṭu." In *The Assyrian Dictionary of the Oriental Institute of the University of Chicago*, edited by Ignace J. Gelb et al., 2:46–52. Chicago: Oriental Institute, 1964–2010.

Baldwin, Joyce G. *The Message of Genesis: 12–50*. Bible Speaks Today. Downers Grove, IL: Inter-Varsity, 1986.

Baragwanath, Emily, and M. de Bakke, eds. *Myth, Truth and Narrative in Herodotus*. Oxford: Oxford University Press, 2012.

Barber, William J. *The Third Reconstruction: How a Moral Movement Is Overcoming the Politics of Division and Fear*. Boston: Beacon, 2016.

Bartlett, John R., ed. *Jews in the Hellenistic and Roman Cities*. London: Routledge, 2002.

Barr, James. "The Meaning of 'Mythology' in Relation to the Old Testament." VT 9.1 (1959) 1–10.

Barrett, C. K. *The Gospel according to St. John*. Philadelphia: Westminster, 1978.

Barton, George A. *Archaeology and the Bible*. Philadelphia: American Sunday-School Union, 1937.

Bass, Diana B. *Christianity after Religion: The End of the Church and the Birth of a New Spiritual Awakening*. New York: HarperOne, 2012.

Bauer, Walter, W. F. Arndt and F. W. Gingrich, eds. *A Greek-English Lexicon of the New Testament and Other Early Christian Literature*. Chicago: University of Chicago, 1979.
Bavinck, Herman. *Reformed Dogmatics*. Vol. 2. Grand Rapids: Baker, 2004.
Beasley-Murray, George R. *John*. 2nd ed. Nashville: Thomas Nelson, 2000.
Bekker, Immanuel. *Aristotelis Opera*. Berlin: Berolini, 1831-70.
Bekker, Immanuel, et al. *Diodori Bibliotheca Historica*. Vol. 1. Leipzig: Teubner, 1888.
Benito, Carlos A. "Enki and Ninmah and Enki and the World Order." PhD diss., University of Pennsylvania, 1969.
Bennett, William H. *Genesis*. Century Bible. Edinburgh: T. & T. Clark, 1904.
"Bennu." In *The Assyrian Dictionary of the Oriental Institute of the University of Chicago*, edited by Ignace J. Gelb et al., 2:205-6. Chicago: Oriental Institute, 1964-2010.
Berchman, R. M. *From Philo to Origen: Middle Platonism in Transition*. Brown Judaic Studies. Chico, CA: Scholars, 1984.
Berkhof, L. *Systematic Theology*. Grand Rapids: Eerdmans, 1938.
Bernardakis, Gregorius N. *Plutarchi Chaeronensis Moralia*. Vol. 4. Leipzig: Teubner, 1892.
Bertocci, Peter A. "Theism." In *Encyclopedia of Religion*, edited by Lindsay Jones, 9102-8. New York: Macmillan Reference, 2005.
Betz, Hans D., et al. *Religion Past and Present: Encyclopedia of Theology and Religion*. 4th ed. Leiden: Brill, 2007-13.
Bickerman, Elias J. *The Jews in the Greek Age*. Cambridge, MA: Harvard University Press, 1988.
Biggs, R. D. "I Will Praise the Lord of Wisdom." In *Ancient Near Eastern Texts Relating to the Old Testament*, edited by James B. Pritchard, 596-600. Princeton, NJ: Princeton University Press, 1969.
Bilby, Mark G. "The Hospitality of Dymas." In *New Testament Apocrypha*, edited by Tony Burke and B. Landau, 1:39-51. Grand Rapids: Eerdmans, 2016.
Bjorklund, Ruth. *Epilepsy*. New York: Marshall Cavendish, 2007.
Black, Jeremy A., et al. *The Literature of Ancient Sumer*. Oxford: Oxford University Press, 2004.
Black, Matthew. *Apocalypsis Henochi Graece*. Pseudepigrapha Veteris Testamenti Graece. Leiden: Brill, 1970.
Black, Max. *Models and Metaphors: Studies in Language and Philosophy*. Ithaca, NY: Cornell University Press, 1962.
Blass, F., A. Debrunner, and R. W. Funk. *A Greek Grammar of the New Testament and Other Early Christian Literature*. Chicago: University of Chicago, 1961.
Blenkinsopp, Joseph. *Abraham: The Story of a Life*. Grand Rapids: Eerdmans, 2015.
———. *Treasures Old & New*. Grand Rapids: Eerdmans, 2004.
Boff, Leonardo. *La dignidad de la tierra: Ecología, mundialización, espiritualidad*. Madrid: Trotta, 2000.
Boff, Leonardo. *La Trinidad, la Sociedad y la Liberación*. Madrid: Ediciones Paulinas, 1987.
Bottéro, Jean. *La Epopeya de Gilgamesh: El Gran Hombre que no Quería Morir*. Translated by Pedro López. Akal Oriente. Madrid: Akal, 2007.
———. *Mesopotamia: Writing, Reasoning and the Gods*. Translated by Zainab Bahrani and M. van de Mieroop. Akal Oriente. Chicago: University of Chicago Press, 1992.

———. *Religion in Ancient Mesopotamia*. Translated by Teresa L. Fagan. Chicago: University of Chicago Press, 2001.
Bottéro, Jean, and S. N. Kramer. *Cuando los Dioses Hacían de Hombres*. Translated by Francisco J. González. Madrid: Ediciones Akal, 2004.
Botterweck, G. J., et al. *Theological Dictionary of the Old Testament*. Grand Rapids: Eerdmans, 1977–2006.
Bouwsma, William J. *John Calvin: A Sixteenth-Century Portrait*. Oxford: Oxford University Press, 1988.
Bovon, François. *A Commentary on the Gospel of Luke: 1:1—9:50*. Translated by Christine M. Thomas. Hermeneia. Minneapolis: Fortress, 2002.
———. *A Commentary on the Gospel of Luke: 9:51—19:27*. Translated by Donald D. Deer. Minneapolis: Fortress, 2013.
———. *A Commentary on the Gospel of Luke: 19:28—24:53*. Translated by James Crouch. Hermeneia. Minneapolis: Fortress, 2012.
Boyd, Greg A. *God of the Possible: A Biblical Introduction to the Open View of God*. Grand Rapids: Baker, 2000.
Boyd, Greg A. *The Crucifixion of the Warrior God*. Minneapolis: Fortress, 2017.
Braithwaite, Ann, and C. M. Orr. *Everyday Women's and Gender Studies*. New York: Routledge, 2017.
Bratt, James D. *Abraham Kuyper: A Centennial Reader*. Grand Rapids: Eerdmans, 1998.
Brennan, John O. "The Ethics and Efficacy of the President's Counterterrorism Strategy." Speech at the Woodrow Wilson International Center for Scholars, April 30, 2012. https://www.wilsoncenter.org/event/the-efficacy-and-ethics-us-counterterrorism-strategy.
Brett, Mark G. *Genesis: Procreation and the Politics of Identity*. New York: Routledge, 2000.
Bright, John. *A History of Israel*. Philadelphia: Westminster, 1981.
Brooks, James A., and C. L. Winbery. *Syntax of the New Testament Greek*. Lanham, MD: University Press of America, 1979.
Brown, Raymond E. *The Gospel According to John: I–XII*. Garden City, NY: Doubleday, 1966.
———. *New Testament Essays*. New York: Image, 1965.
Brown, Francis, S. R. Driver, and C. A. Briggs. *A Hebrew and English Lexicon of the Old Testament*. Oxford: Clarendon, 1951.
Brownson, Carleton L. *Xenophon: Hellenica*. Vol. 1. Loeb Classical Library. Cambridge, MA: Harvard University Press, 1918.
Broyles, Craig C. *Psalms*. Grand Rapids: Baker, 1999.
Brueggemann, Walter. *Genesis*. Philadelphia: Westminster John Knox, 2010.
———. *Theology of the Old Testament*. Minneapolis: Fortress, 1997.
Buccellati, Giorgio. "On Poetry—Theirs and Ours." In *Lingering over Words. Studies in Ancient Near Eastern Literature in Honor of William L. Moran*, edited by T. Abusch et al., 105–34. Atlanta: Scholars, 1990.
Budge, E. A. Wallis. *Amulets and Superstitions*. New York: Dover, 1930.
Bultmann, R. *The Gospel of John: A Commentary*. Translated by G. R. Beasley-Murray. Philadelphia: Westminster, 1971.
———. *Historia de la Tradición Sinóptica*. Translated by Constantino Ruiz-Garrido. Salamanca: Sígueme, 2000.

———. *Jesus and the Word*. Translated by Louise Pettibone Smith Erminie Huntress. New York: Scribners, 1934.

Burke, Tony, and B. Landau, eds. *New Testament Apocripha*. Vol. 1. Grand Rapids: Eerdmans, 2016.

Burkert, Walter. *Structure and History in Greek Mythology and Ritual*. Berkeley: University of California Press, 1979.

Burnet, John, ed. *Platonis Opera*. Oxford: Oxford University Press, 1903.

Bury, Robert G. *Fourth Gospel and the Logos-Doctrine*. Cambridge: Heffer, 1940.

———. *Plato: Timaeus, Critias, Cleitophon, Menexenus Epistles*. Loeb Classical Library. Cambridge, MA: Harvard University Press, 1929.

———. *Plato Laws: Books 7-12*. Loeb Classical Library. Cambridge, MA: Harvard University Press, 1926.

Butler, Trent C. *Judges*. Nashville: Thomas Nelson, 2009.

Buttrick, George A., et al. *Interpreter's Dictionary of the Bible*. Nashville: Abingdon, 1962-76.

Büttner-Wobst, Theodorus. *Polybius Historiae*. 4 vols. Leipzig: Teubner, 1882-1904.

Buxton, Richard. *Imaginary Greece: The Contexts of Mythology*. Cambridge: Cambridge University Press, 1994.

Calame, Claude. *The Craft of Poetic Speech in Ancient Greece*. Translated by Janice Orion. Originally published 1986. Ithaca, NY: Cornell University Press, 1995.

Caldwell, Amy R. *Sources of Western Society: From Antiquity to the Enlightenment*. Boston: Bedford/St. Martin's, 2011.

Calvin, John. *Genesis*. Translated by John King. Geneva Series of Commentaries. Edinburgh: Banner of Truth, 1984.

———. *The Institutes of the Christian Religion*. Translated by H. Beveridge. Edinburgh: Calvin Translation Society, 1845.

Carabine, Deirdre. *The Unknown God: Negative Theology in the Platonic Tradition: Plato to Eriugena*. Eugene, OR: Wipf and Stock, 1995.

Carson, D. A. *The Gospel according to John*. Pillar New Testament Commentary. Grand Rapids: Eerdmans, 1991.

Cary, Earnest, et al. *Dio Cassius' Roman History*. Vol. 4. Loeb Classical Library. New York: Harvard University Press, 1916.

———. *Dio Cassius' Roman History*. Vol. 7. Loeb Classical Library. New York: Harvard University Press, 1924.

Cary, Henry. *Herodotus: A New Literal Translation*. New York: Harper, 1855.

Casanova, Humberto. *Introducción al griego del Nuevo Testamento*. Vol. 1. Grand Rapids: Desafío, 2001.

Cassirer, Ernst. *The Philosophy of Symbolic Forms II: Mythical Thought*. Translated by Charles W. Hendel. New Haven, CT: Yale University Press, 1955.

Cassuto, Umberto. *A Commentary on the Book of Genesis*. Skokie: Varda, 1961.

Castro, Adolfo de. *Biblioteca de Autores Españoles*. Vol. 1. Madrid: M. Rivadeneyra, 1854.

Catechism of the Catholic Church: With modifications from the Editio Typica. 2nd ed. New York: Doubleday, 1995.

Chadwick, Henry. "Philo and the Beginnings of Christian Thought." In *The Cambridge History of Later Greek and Early Medieval Philosophy*, edited by A. H. Armstrong, 137-92. Cambridge: Cambridge University Press, 1967.

Chadwick, Henry. "St. Paul and Philo of Alexandria." *BJRL* 48.2 (1966) 286-307.

Charles, R. H. *The Apocrypha and Pseudepigrapha of the Old Testament in English*. Oxford: Clarendon, 1913.
Charlesworth, James H. *Earliest Christian Hymnbook: The Odes of Solomon*. Cambridge: Charles Clarke, 2009.
Charlesworth, James H, ed. *The Old Testament Pseudepigrapha*. 2 vols. New York: Doubleday, 1983.
Chavalas, Mark W. *The Ancient Near East*. Malden, MA: Blackwell, 2006.
———, ed. *Emar: The History, Religion, and Culture of a Syrian Town in the Late Bronze Age*. Bethesda: CDL, 1996.
Chiera, Edward. *Sumerian Epics and Myths*. Vol. 3. Cuneiform Studies. Chicago: University of Chicago, 1934.
Childs, Brevard S. *Biblical Theology of the Old and New Testament*. Minneapolis: Fortress, 2011.
———. *Myth and Reality in the Old Testament*. Eugene, OR: Wipf and Stock, 1962.
Christensen, Duane. *Deuteronomy 21:10—34:12*. Word Biblical Commentary. Nashville: Thomas Nelson, 2002.
Ciampa, Roy E., and Brian S. Rosner. *The First Epistle to the Corinthians*. Pillar New Testament Commentary. Grand Rapids: Eerdmans, 2010.
Civil, Miguel. "The Sumerian Flood Story." In *Atra-ḫasīs: The Babylonian Story of the Flood*, translated by W. G. Lambert and A. R. Millard. 138–45, 167–72. Winona Lake, IN: Eisenbrauns, 1999.
Clayton, Philip. "Theism." In *Encyclopedia of Science and Religion*, edited by Wentzel Van Huyssteen et al., 880. New York: Macmillan, 2003.
Clement, Paul A., and H. B. Hoffleit. *Plutarch's Moralia*. Vol. 8. Loeb Classical Library. Cambridge, MA: Harvard University Press, 1969.
Clifford, Richard J. *The Cosmic Mountain in Canaan and the Old Testament*. Cambridge, MA: Harvard University Press, 1972.
———. *Creation Accounts in the Ancient East and in the Bible*. Washington, DC: CBQ, 1994.
———. *Psalms 73–150*. Abingdon Old Testament Commentaries. Nashville: Abingdon, 2003.
Clines, David J. A. *Job 1–20*. Word Biblical Commentary. Nashville: Thomas Nelson, 1989.
———. *Job 21–37*. Word Biblical Commentary. Nashville: Thomas Nelson, 2006.
———. *Job 38–42*. Word Biblical Commentary. Nashville: Thomas Nelson, 2011.
Cobb, John B., and David R. Griffin. *Process Theology: An Introductory Exposition*. Louisville: Westminster, 1976.
Coenen, Lothar, et al., eds. *Diccionario Teológico del Nuevo Testamento*. Salamanca: Sígueme, 1983–85.
Cohen, A., ed. *The Babylonian Talmūd: Tractate Bᵉrākōt*. Cambridge: Cambridge University Press, 1921.
Cohen, Leonard. "Anthem." *The Future*. Columbia, 1992.
Cohn, Leopold, and P. Wendland, eds. *Philonis Alexandrini Opera Quae Supersunt*. Vols. 1–6. Berlin: Reimer, 1896–1915.
Colli, Giorgio, and M. Montinari. *Nietzsche Briefwechsel*. Berlin: de Gruyter, 1975.
Collins, Adela Y. *Mark*. Hermeneia. Minneapolis: Fortress, 2007.
Collins, John J. *The Apocalyptic Imagination*. Grand Rapids: Eerdmans, 2016.

Collins, John J., and D. C. Harlow, eds. *The Eerdmans Dictionary of Early Judaism*. Grand Rapids: Eerdmans, 2010.
Collins, Johh J., and G. E. Sterling. *Hellenism in the Land of Israel. Christianity and Judaism in Antiquity*. Notre Dame, IN: University of Notre Dame Press, 2001.
Colson, F. H., and G. H. Whitaker. *Philo*. Loeb Classical Library. Cambridge, MA: Harvard University Press, 1929.
Conzelmann, Hans. *1 Corinthians*. Hermeneia. Philadelphia: Fortress, 1975.
Cook, Edward M., ed. *Targum Psalms: An English Translation*. Laramie: University of Wyoming Press, 2001.
Cook, John G. *The Interpretation of the Old Testament in Greco-Roman Paganism*. Tübingen: Mohr Siebeck, 2004.
Cooke, George A. *A Text-book of North-Semitic Inscriptions: Moabite, Hebrew, Phoenician, Aramaic, Nabatean, Palmyrene, Jewish*. Oxford: Clarendon, 1903.
Cooper, Burton Z. *The Idea of God: A Whiteheadian Critique of St. Thomas Aquinas' Concept of God*. The Hague: Nijhoff, 1974.
Cooper, Jerrold S. "Gilgamesh and Akka: A Review Article." *JCS* 33.3/4 (1981) 224–41.
———. *The Return of Ninurta to Nippur: an-gim dím-ma*. Rome: Pontifical Biblical Institute, 1978.
———. *Sumerian and Akkadian Royal Inscriptions I: Presargonic Inscriptions*. New Haven, CT: American Oriental Society, 1986.
Cooper, A., and M. H. Pope. "Divine Names and Epithets in the Ugaritic Texts." In *Ras Shamra Parallels: The Texts from Ugarit and the Hebrew Bible*, edited by S. Rummel, 3:333–469. Rome: Pontifical Biblical Institute, 1981.
Copleston, Frederick. *A History of Philosophy: Greece and Rome*. London: Continuum, 1946.
Cornelius, Izak. *The Iconography of the Canaanite Gods Reshef and Baʿal: Late Bronze and Iron Age I Periods*. Göttingen: Vandenhoeck & Ruprecht, 1994.
Corney, R. W. "Abiathar." In *IDB* 1:6–7.
Coulmas, Florian. *Writing Systems: An Introduction to Their Linguistic Analysis*. Cambridge: Cambridge University Press, 2003.
Cox, Daniel, R. Lienesch and R. P. Jones, "Beyond Economics: Fears of Cultural Displacement Pushed the White Working Class to Trump." Public Religion Research Institute, May 9, 2017. https://www.prri.org/research/white-working-class-attitudes-economy-trade-immigration-election-donald-trump/.
Craig, William L. *Reasonable Faith: Christian Truth and Apologetics*. Wheaton, IL: Crossway, 2008.
Craigie, Peter C., *Psalms 1–50*. Word Biblical Commentary. Waco, TX: Word, 1983.
Cranfield, C. E. B. *The Gospel according to St. Mark*. Cambridge Greek Testament Commentary. Cambridge: Cambridge University Press, 1977.
Crawford, Sidnie W. "Textual Criticism of the Book of Deuteronomy and the *Oxford Hebrew Bible Project*." In *Seeking Out the Wisdom of the Ancients: Essays Offered to Honor Michael V. Fox on the Occasion of His Sixty-Fifth Birthday*, edited by Ronald L. Troxel et al., 315–26. Winona Lake, IN: Eisenbrauns, 2005.
Creed, John M. *The Gospel according to St. Luke*. London: Macmillan, 1969.
Crombie, Frederick. *Origen contra Celsum*. In *The Ante-Nicene Christian Library*, vol. 22, edited by Alexander Roberts and J. Donaldson. Edinburgh: T. & T. Clark, 1879.
Cross, Frank M. *The Ancient Library of Qumran*. 3rd ed. Sheffield: Sheffield, 1995.

———. *Canaanite Myth and Hebrew Epic: Essays in the History of the Religion of Israel.* Cambridge, MA: Harvard University Press, 1973.

Dahood, Mitchell. *Psalms 1–50.* Anchor Bible. Garden City, NY: Doubleday, 1965.

———. *Psalms 51–100.* Anchor Bible. Garden City, NY: Doubleday, 1968.

———. *Psalms 101–150.* Anchor Bible. Garden City, NY: Doubleday, 1970.

Dalley, Stephanie. *Myths from Mesopotamia: Creation, the Flood, Gilgamesh, and Others.* Oxford: Oxford University Press, 2000.

Danby, Herbert. *Tractate Sanhedrin.* New York: MacMillan, 1919.

Daniels, Peter T. "The First Civilizations." In *The World's Writing Systems*, edited by Peter T. Daniels and W. Bright, 19–32. New York: Oxford University Press, 1996.

Davidson, Andrew B. *Hebrew Syntax.* Edinburgh: T. & T. Clark, 1902.

Davidson, Donald. "What Metaphors Mean." In *The Essential Davidson*, edited by Donald Davidson, 209–24. Oxford: Oxford University Press, 2006.

Davies, G. H. "An Approach to the Problem of Old Testament Mythology." *PEQ* 88 (1956) 83–91.

Davies, W. D., and D. C. Allison. *The Gospel according to Saint Matthew 1–7.* International Critical Commentary. Edinburgh: T. & T. Clark, 1988.

———. *The Gospel according to Saint Matthew 8–18.* International Critical Commentary. Edinburgh: T. & T. Clark, 1991.

———. *The Gospel according to Saint Matthew 19–28.* International Critical Commentary. Edinburgh: T. & T. Clark, 1997.

Day, John. *God's Conflict with the Dragon and the Sea: Echoes of a Canaanite Myth in the Old Testament.* Cambridge: Cambridge University Press, 1985.

———. *Yahweh and the Gods and Goddesses of Canaan.* Sheffield: Sheffield Academic, 2002.

De Claissé-Walford, Nancy, R. A. Jacobson, and Beth L. Tanner. *The Book of Psalms.* Grand Rapids: Eerdmans, 2014.

De Jonge, M., ed. *Testamenta XII Patriarcharum.* Leiden: Brill, 1970.

De Moor, Johannes C. *The Rise of Yahwism: The Roots of Israelite Monotheism.* 2nd ed. Bibliotheca Ephemeridum Theologicarum Lovaniensium. Leuven: Leuven University Press, 1997.

De Moor, Johannes C., and Klass Spronk, eds. *An Anthology of Religious Texts from Ugarit.* Leiden: Brill, 1987.

Dearman, J. Andrew. *The Book of Hosea.* New International Commentary on the Old Testament. Grand Rapids: Eerdmans, 2010.

Deissmann, A. *New Light on the New Testament: From Records of the Graeco-Roman Period.* Edinburgh: T. & T. Clark, 1908.

Delitzsch, Franz. *Biblical Commentary on Psalms.* Grand Rapids: Eerdmans, 1955.

———. *A New Commentary on Genesis.* Edinburgh: T. & T. Clark, 1888.

DeMello, Margo. *Animals and Society: An Introduction to Human-Animal Studies.* New York: Columbia University Press, 2012.

Denzinger, Enrique. *El Magisterio de la Iglesia.* Barcelona: Herder, 1955.

Dever, William. "How to Tell a Canaanite from an Israelite." In *The Rise of Ancient Israel*, edited by Hershel Shanks, 27–56. Washington, DC: Biblical Archaeology Society, 1992.

———. *Who Were the Early Israelites and Where Did They Come From?* Grand Rapids: Eerdmans, 2003.

DeWitt, Richard. *Worldviews: An Introduction to the History and Philosophy of Science.* Oxford: Wiley-Blackwell, 2010.
Dibelius, Martin. *Die Formgeschichte des Evangeliums.* Tübingen: Mohr, 1933.
Dibelius, Martin and H. Conzelmann. *The Pastoral Epistles.* Hermeneia. Minneapolis: Fortress, 1972.
Dietrich, M., O. Loretz, and J. Sanmartín, eds. *The Cuneiform Alphabetic Texts from Ugarit, Ras Ibn Hani and Other Places.* Münster: Ugarit, 1995.
———, eds. *Die Keilalphabetischen Texte aus Ugarit. Teil 1 Transkription.* Alter Orient und Altes Testament 24/1. Kevelaer: Butzon und Bercker; Neukirchener, 1976.
Dillon, John M. *The Middle Platonists, 80 B.C. to A.D. 220.* Ithaca: Cornell University, 1996.
Dionne, Brittany. "Survey Finds More and More Americans Do Not Believe in God." WBRC, April 11, 2019. http://www.wbrc.com/2019/04/11/survey-finds-more-more-americans-do-not-believe-god/.
Dodd, C. H. *The Interpretation of the Fourth Gospel.* Cambridge: Cambridge University Press, 1953.
Dods, Marcus. *The City of God.* Works of Aurelius Augustine 2. Edinburgh: T. & T. Clark, 1871.
Dombart, B. *De Civitate Dei.* Vol. 2. Sancti Aurelii Augustini. Leipzig: Teubner, 1892.
Dombart, B., and A. Kalb. *De Civitate Dei.* Vol. 1. Sancti Aurelii Augustini. Leipzig: Teubner, 1863.
Dozeman, Thomas B. *Exodus.* Eerdmans Critical Commentary. Grand Rapids: Eerdmans, 2009.
Driver, Godfrey R. *Semitic Writing from Pictograph to Alphabet.* London: Oxford University Press, 1976.
Driver, Godfrey R., and John C.L. Gibson, *Canaanite Myths and Legends.* Edimburgo: T. & T. Clark, 1977.
Driver, Samuel R. *The Book of Genesis.* Westminster Commentaries. London: Methuen, 1909.
———. *A Treatise on the Use of the Tenses and Some Other Syntactical Questions.* London: Oxford University Press, 1892.
Driver, S. R., and George B. Gray. *The Book of Job.* International Critical Commentary. Edinburgh: T. & T. Clark, 1921.
Duff, J. D. *Silius Italicus Punica.* Loeb Classical Library. Cambridge, MA: Harvard University Press, 1927.
Dundes, Aland. *The Flood Myth.* Berkeley: University of California Press, 1988.
Dunn, James D. G. *The Epistles to the Colossians and to Philemon.* New International Greek Testament Commentary. Grand Rapids: Eerdmans, 1996.
Dupont-Sommer, André. *The Essene Writings from Qumran.* Gloucester: Peter Smith, 1973.
Ebeling, E., et al. *Reallexikon der Assyriologie und Vorderasiatischen Archäologie.* 16 vols. Berlin: de Gruyter, 1932.
Ebeling, Erich. *Keilschrifttexte aus Assur religiösen Inhalts.* Vol. 1. Deutsche Orient-Gesellschaft: Ausgrabungen der Deutschen Orient-Gesellschaft in Assur. Leipzig: J. C. Hinrichs, 1919.
Edmonds, John M. *Elegy and Iambus 1.* Loeb Classical Library. Cambridge, MA: Harvard University Press, 1931.

Edwards, Lorwerth E. S., et al. *The Cambridge Ancient History: Prolegomena and prehistory.* Vol. 1. Cambridge: Cambridge University Press, 1970.

Edzard, Dietz-Otto. "Mesopotamien. Die Mythologie der Sumerer und Akkader." In *Götter und Mythen im Vorderen Orient*, edited by H. W. Haussig, 17–140. Wörterbuch der Mythologie 1. Stuttgart: Ernst Klett, 1965.

———. "Sumerische Komposita mit dem Nominalpräfix nu-." *ZA* 55 (1962) 102–3.

Eichrodt, Walter. *Teología del Antiguo Testamento.* 2 vols. Madrid: Cristiandad, 1975.

Eissfeldt, Otto. "El and Yahweh." *JSS* 1 (1956) 25–37.

———. *The Old Testament: An Introduction.* New York: Harper & Row, 1965.

Eliade, Mircea. *Myth and Reality.* New York: Harper & Row, 1963.

———. *The Sacred and the Profane: The Nature of Religion.* New York: Harcourt, 1959.

Eliot, Thomas S. *Four Quartets.* Orlando: Harcourt, 1943.

Emlyn-Jones, Chris, and W. Preddy. *Plato's Republic.* Loeb Classical Library. Cambridge, MA: Harvard University Press, 2013.

Engberg-Pedersen, Troels. *Paul and the Stoics.* Louisville: Westminster John Knox, 2000.

Enns, Peter. *The Evolution of Adam: What the Bible Does and Doesn't Say about Human Origins.* Grand Rapids: Brazos, 2012.

Epstein, Ezekiel I., ed. *The Babylonian Talmud.* London: Soncino, 1935–52.

Erickson, Millard J. *Christian Theology.* Grand Rapids: Baker, 2013.

Etheridge, John W. *The Targums of Onkelos and Jonathan ben Uzziel on the Pentateuch: Genesis and Exodus.* London: Longman, 1862.

Evans, Craig, A., and H. D. Zacharias. *Old Testament Pseudepigrapha: Greek and English.* Grand Rapids: Eerdmans, 2015.

Evans-Pritchard, Edward E. *Nuer Religion.* London: Oxford University Press, 1970.

Evelyn-White, Hugh G. *Hesiod: Homeric Hymns and Homerica.* Loeb Classical Library. Cambridge, MA: Harvard University Press, 1914.

Farber, Gertrud. "'Inanna and Enki' in Geneva: A Sumerian Myth Revisited." *JNES* 54.4 (1995) 287–92.

Fee, Gordon D. *The First Epistle to the Corinthians.* New International Commentary on the New Testament. Grand Rapids: Eerdmans, 2014.

Feldman, Louis. *Jews and Gentile in the Ancient World: Attitudes and Interactions from Alexander to Justinian.* Princeton, NJ: Princeton University Press, 1983.

Festinger, L. *A Theory of Cognitive Dissonance.* Stanford, CA: Stanford University Press, 1957.

Feuerbach, Ludwig. *Essence of Christianity.* London: Trübner, 1881.

Finkel, Irving L., and Markham J. Geller, eds. *Disease in Babylonia.* Leiden: Brill, 2007.

Finkelstein, Israel, and N. A. Silberman. *The Bible Unearthed.* New York: Simon and Schuster, 2001.

Fishbane, Michael. *Biblical Myth and Rabbinic Mythmaking.* Oxford: Oxford University Press, 2003.

Fisher, William B. *The Middle East: A Physical, Social, and Regional Geography.* Cambridge: Cambridge University Press, 1978.

Fitzmyer, Joseph A. *First Corinthians.* Anchor Bible. New Haven, CT: Yale University Press, 2008.

———. "Further Light on Melchizedek from Qumran Cave 1." *JBL* 86.1 (1967) 25–41.

———. *The Gospel according to Luke: I–IX.* Anchor Bible. New York: Doubleday, 1981.

———. *The Gospel according to Luke: X–XXIV.* New York: Doubleday, 1985.

Fletcher, William. *Lactantius*. In *The Ante-Nicene Fathers*, vol. 7, edited by Alexander Roberts, and J. Donaldson, 301–22. Edinburgh: T. & T. Clark, 1886.
Foster, Benjamin O. *The History of Rome*. Vol. 1. Cambridge, MA: Harvard University Press, 1919.
Foster, Benjamin R. *The Age of Agade: Inventing Empire in Ancient Mesopotamia*. London: Routledge, 2016.
———. *Before the Muses: An Anthology of Akkadian Literature*. Bethesda, MD: CDL, 2005.
———. *The Epic of Gilgamesh*. New York: Norton, 2001.
———. "Self-Reference of an Akkadian Poet." *JAOS* 103.1 (1983) 123–30.
Fowler, Harold N. *Theaetetus, Sophist*. Vol. 7 of *Plato in Twelve Volumes*. Loeb Classical Library. Cambridge, MA: Harvard University Press, 1921.
Fox, Everett. *The Five Books of Moses*. New York: Schoken, 1995.
Fox, Robin L. *Pagans and Christians*. New York: Knopf, 1987.
Frankfort, Henri. *Cylinder Seals: A Documentary Essay on the Art and Religion of the Ancient Near East*. London: Macmillan, 1939.
Frankfort, Henri, et al. *The Intellectual Adventure of Ancient Man*. Chicago: University of Chicago, 1946.
Frayne, Douglas R. *Old Babylonian Period (2003–1595 BC)*. Toronto: University of Toronto Press, 1990.
———. *Pre-Sargonic Period: Early Periods (2700–2350)*. Toronto: University of Toronto Press, 2008.
Frazer, James G. *Apollodorus*. 2 vols. Loeb Classical Library. Cambridge, MA: Harvard University Press, 1921.
———. *Ovid's Fasti*. Loeb Classical Library. Cambridge, MA: Harvard University Press, 1931.
Freely, John. *Flame of Miletus: The Birth of Science in Ancient Greece*. London: Taurus, 2012.
Freeman, Charles. *The Closing of the Western Mind: The Raise of Faith and the Fall of Reason*. New York: Vintage, 2002.
Fretheim, Terence E. *The Book of Genesis*. In *New Interpreter's Bible*, vol. 1, edited by William M. McPheeters et al. Nashville: Abingdon, 1994.
———. *The Suffering of God: An Old Testament Perspective*. Overtures to Biblical Theology. Philadelphia: Fortress, 1984.
Freud, Sigmund. *The Future of an Illusion*. Translated by Gregory C. Richter. New York: Norton, 1961.
———. *Totem and Taboo*. Translated by Abraham A. Brill. New York: Moffat, Yard, 1918.
Friedman, Richard E. *Commentary on the Torah*. New York: HarperOne, 2001.
Frye, Northrop. *Myth and Metaphor*. Charlottesville: University Press of Virginia, 1990.
Gaddis, Michael. *There Is No Crime for Those Who Have Christ: Religious Violence in the Christian Roman Empire*. Berkeley: University of California Press, 2005.
Gagné, Renaud. "Literary Evidence—Poetry." In *The Oxford Handbook of Ancient Greek Religion*, edited by Esther Eidinow et al., 83–96. Oxford: Oxford University Press, 2015.
Galling, Kurt, et al. *Religion in Geschichte und Gegenwart*. 3rd ed. Tübingen: Mohr-Siebeck, 1958.
Garbini, Giovanni. *Myth and History in the Bible*. Sheffield: Sheffiled Academic, 2003.

García, Florentino. *The Dead Sea Scrolls Translated.* Grand Rapids: Eerdmans, 1996.
García, Florentino, and E. J. C. Tigchelaar. *The Dead Sea Scrolls: Study Edition.* 2 vols. Grand Rapids: Eerdmans, 1997, 1998.
Gaster, Moses. "Two Thousand Years of a Charm against the Child-Stealing Witch." *Folk-lore* 11.2 (1900) 129–62.
Gaster, Theodor H. "An Ancient Eulogy on Israel: Deuteronomy 33:3–5, 26–9." *JBL* 66 (1947) 53–62.
———. *Myth, Legend, and Custom in the Old Testament.* New York: Harper & Row, 1969.
Gaylord, H. E. "3 (Greek Apocalypse of) Baruch." In *The Old Testament Pseudepigrapha*, vol. 1, edited by James H.Charlesworth, 653–80. New York: Doubleday, 1983.
Geertz, Clifford. "Religion as a Cultural System." In *Anthropological Approaches to the Study of Religion*, edited by M. Banton, 1–44. London: Routledge, 1966.
Gelb, I. J., et al., eds. *The Assyrian Dictionary of the Oriental Institute of the University of Chicago.* Chicago: Oriental Institute, 1964–2010.
Geller, Markham J. *Melothesia in Babylonia: Medicine, Magic, and Astrology in the Ancient Near East.* Berlin: de Gruyter, 2014.
Geller, Stephen A. "Some Sound and Word Plays in the First Tablet of the Old Babylonian *Atramḫasis* Epic." In *The Frank Talmage Memorial*, vol. 1, edited by Barry Walfish, 63–70. Haifa: Haifa University Press, 1993.
Genouillac, H. de. *Textes religieux sumériens du Louvre.* 2 vols. Textes Cunéiformes. Paris: Paul Geuthner, 1930.
George, A. R., and F. N. H. Al-Rawi. "Tablets from the Sippar Library. VI. Atra-hasis." *Iraq* 58 (1996) 147–90.
———. "Tablets from the Sippar Library. VII. Three Wisdom Texts." *Iraq* 60 (1998) 187–206.
George, Andrew R. *The Babylonian Gilgamesh Epic: Introduction, Critical Edition and Cuneiform Texts.* 2 vols. Oxford: Oxford University Press, 2003.
———. *Babylonian Topographical Texts.* Leuven: Peeters, 1992.
———. *The Epic of Gilgamesh.* London: Penguin, 1999.
Gerstenberger, Erhard S. *Psalms, Part 2, and Lamentations.* Forms of the Old Testament Literature. Grand Rapids: Eerdmans, 2001.
Gibbs, Raymond, ed. *The Cambridge Handbook of Metaphor and Thought.* Cambridge: Cambridge University Press, 2008.
Gigeser, Elizabeth D. *The Making of a Christian Empire: Lactantius and Rome.* Ithaca, NY: Cornell University Press, 2000.
Gildersleeve, Basil L. *The Apologies of Justin Martyr, and the Epistle to Diognetus.* New York: Harper, 1877.
Gill, Roma. *Shakespeare: Measure for Measure.* Oxford: Oxford University Press, 2001.
Ginsberg, H. L. "Poems about Baal and Anath." In *Ancient Near Eastern Texts Relating to the Old Testament*, edited by James B. Pritchard, 129–42. Princeton, NJ: Princeton University Press, 1969.
Glassner, Jean-Jacques. *The Invention of Cuneiform: Writing in Sumer.* Baltimore: John Hopkins University Press, 2003.
Godley, A. D. *Herodotus.* Vol. 1. Loeb Classical Library. Cambridge, MA: Harvard University Press, 1926.
Goetze, A., and S. Levy. "Fragment on the Gilgamesh Epic from Megiddo" *Atiqot* 2 (1959) 121–28.

Goldingay, John. *Old Testament Theology.* Downers Grove, IL: InterVarsity, 2006.
———. *Psalms 42–89.* Baker Commentary on the Old Testament Wisdom and Psalms. Grand Rapids: Baker, 2007.
Good, Edwin M. *Genesis 1–11. Tales of the Earliest World.* Stanford, CA: Stanford University Press, 2011.
Goodenough, Erwin R. *By Light, Light: The Mystic Gospel of Hellenistic Judaism.* New Haven, CT: Yale University Press, 1935.
Gottwald, Norman K. *The Hebrew Bible in Its Social World and in Ours.* Atlanta: Scholars, 1993.
———. *The Tribes of Yahweh: A Sociology of the Religion of Liberated Israel, 1250–1050 BCE.* Maryknoll, NY: Orbis, 1979.
Grabbe, Lester. *Judaic Religion in the Second Temple Period: Belief and Practice from the Exile to Yavneh.* London: Routledge, 2000.
Graf, Fritz. "Myth." In *Ancient Religions,* edited by Sarah I. Johnston, 45–58. Cambridge, MA: Belknap Press of Harvard University Press, 2007.
Graham, Daniel W. *Explaining the Cosmos: The Ionian Tradition of Scientific Philosophy.* Princeton, NJ: Princeton University Press, 2006.
Gray, John. *The Legacy of Canaan: The Ras Shamra Texts and Their Relevance to the Old Testament.* 2nd ed. Leiden: Brill, 1965.
Green, Alberto R. W. *The Storm-God in the Ancient Near East.* Winona Lake, IN: Eisenbrauns, 2003.
Green, Douglas J. *"I Undertook Great Works": The Ideology of Domestic Achievements in West Semitic Royal Inscriptions.* Forschungen zum Alten Testament. Tübingen: Mohr Siebeck, 2010.
Green, H. Benedict. *The Gospel according to Matthew.* Oxford: Clarendon, 1975.
Green, William H. *The Unity of the Book of Genesis.* London: Scribner's, 1895.
Greenstein, Edward L. "Kirta." In *Ugaritic Narrative Poetry,* edited by Simon B. Parker, 12–48. Chico, CA: Scholars, 1997
Gregory, Richard L. *Eye and Brain.* Princeton, NJ: Princeton University Press, 1997.
Grudem, Wayne A. *Systematic Theology: An Introduction to Biblical Doctrine.* Grand Rapids: Zondervan, 2000.
Gruen, Erich S. *Heritage and Hellenism: The Reinvention of Jewish Tradition.* Berkeley: University of California, 1998.
Gundry, Robert H. *Mark: 9–16.* Grand Rapids: Eerdmans, 1993.
———. *Matthew: A Commentary on His Literary and Theological Art.* Grand Rapids: Eerdmans, 1982.
Gunkel, Hermann. *Creation and Chaos in the Primeval Era and the Eschaton.* Translated by K. William Whitney Jr. Grand Rapids: Eerdmans, 2006.
———. *Genesis.* Translated by Mark E. Biddle. Mercer Library of Biblical Studies. Macon, GA: Mercer, 1997.
———. *Introducción a los Salmos.* Originally published 1966. Translated by Juan M. Díaz. Clásicos de la Ciencia Bíblica. Valencia: Edicep, 1982.
Gushee, David P. "The Trump Prophecy." *Sojourners Magazine,* May 2019. https://sojo.net/magazine/may-2019/trump-prophecy.
Guthrie, Kenneth S. *Numenius of Apamea: The Father of Neo-Platonism.* London: George Bell, 1917.
Guthrie, William K. C. *A History of Greek Philosophy: The Earlier Presocratics and the Pythagoreans.* Cambridge: Cambridge University Press, 1962.

Haag, Herbert. "Ben in the Semitic Languages." In *Theological Dictionary of the Old Testament*, edited by G. J. Botterweck et al., 2:147–59. Grand Rapids: Eerdmans, 1975.

Habel, Norman C. *The Book of Job*. Old Testament Library. Philadelphia: Westminster, 1985.

Habicht, Christian. *The Hellenistic Monarchies*. Ann Arbor: University of Michigan Press, 2006.

Hagner, Donald A. *Matthew 1–13*. Word Biblical Commentary. Dallas: Word, 1993.

———. *Matthew 14–28*. Word Biblical Commentary. Nashville: Thomas Nelson, 1995.

Hallo, William W. *The World's Oldest Literature: Studies in Sumerian Belles-Lettres*. Leiden: Brill, 2010.

Hallo, William W., and K. L. Younger Jr. *The Context of Scripture*. Vol. 1: *Canonical Compositions from the Biblical World*. Leiden: Brill, 2003.

Hamilton, Victor P. *The Book of Genesis: 18–50*. New International Commentary on the Old Testament. Grand Rapids: Eerdmans, 1995.

Hamori, Esther J. *When Gods Were Men: The Embodied God in Biblical and Near Eastern Literature*. Berlin: de Gruyter, 2008.

Harris, Elizabeth. *Prologue and Gospel: The Theology of the Fourth Evangelist*. Edinburgh: T. & T. Clark, 2004.

Hartley, John E. *Genesis*. New International Biblical Commentary. Grand Rapids: Baker, 2000.

Hartshorne, Charles. *The Divine Relativity: A Social Conception of God*. New Haven, CT: Yale University Press, 1948.

———. *A Natural Theology for Our Time*. La Salle: Open Court, 1967.

———. *Omnipotence and other Theological Mistakes*. Albany: State University of New York Press, 1984.

Hays, John H., and Sara R. Mandell. *The Jewish People in Classical Antiquity*. Louisville: Westminster John Knox, 1998.

Heidel, Alexander. *The Babylonian Genesis*. Chicago: University of Chicago Press, 1951.

———. *The Gilgamesh Epic and Old Testament Parallels*. Chicago: University of Chicago, 1963.

Heimpel, Wolfgang, "Mythologie." *RAVA* 8.7/8 (1997) 537–64.

———. "The Sun at Night and the Doors of Heaven in Babylonian Texts." *JCS* 38.2 (1986) 127–51.

Held, Colbert C. *Middle East Patterns: Places, Peoples and Politics*. Boulder, CO: Westview, 2006.

Hendel, Ronald. "The Nephilim Were on Earth: Genesis 6:1–4 and Its Ancient Near East Context." In *The Fall of the Angels*, edited by C. Auffarth et al., 11–34. Leiden: Brill, 2004.

Hendriksen, William. *The Gospel of Mark*. Grand Rapids: Baker, 1975.

Hengel, Martin. *Judaism and Hellenism*. Philadelphia: Fortress, 1974

Heppe, Heinrich. *Reformed Dogmatics*. Eugene, OR: Wipf & Stock, 2007.

Herdner, A., ed. *Corpus des tablettes en cunéiformes alphabétiques découvertes à Ras Shamra-Ugarit de 1929 à 1939*. Paris: Imprimerie Nationale, 1963.

Hess, Richard S., et. al. *Critical Issues in Early Israelite History*. Winona Lake, IN: Eisenbrauns, 2008.

Hicks, R. D. *Diogenes Laertius: Lives of Eminent Philosophers*. 2 vols. Loeb Classical Library. Cambridge, MA: Harvard University Press, 1972.

Hilberg, Raul. *The Destruction of the European Jews*. Vol. 3. New Haven, CT: Yale University Press, 2003.
Hill, David. *The Gospel of Matthew*. New Century Bible Commentary. Grand Rapids: Eerdmans, 1972.
Hill, George F. *The Life of Porphyry, Bishop of Gaza*. Oxford: Clarendon, 1913.
Hitchens, Christopher. *Mortality*. New York: Twelve, 2012.
Hoffner, H. A. "Enki's Command to Atraḫasis." In *Kramer Anniversary Volume: Cuneiform Studies in Honor of Samuel Noah Kramer*, edited by Barry L. Eichler et al., 241–45. Kevelaer: Butzon & Bercker, 1976.
Hölbl, Günther. *A History of the Ptolemaic Empire*. New York: Routledge, 2001.
Horowitz, W., and W. G. Lambert. "A New Exemplar of Ludlul Bēl Nēmeqi Tablet I from Birmingham." *Iraq* 64 (2002) 237–45.
Horowitz, Wayne, and Takayoshi Oshima. *Cuneiform in Canaan: Cuneiform Sources from the Land of Israel in Ancient Times*. Jerusalem: Hebrew University of Jerusalem, 2006.
Horowitz, Wayne. *Mesopotamian Cosmic Geography*. Winona Lake, IN: Eisenbrauns, 2011.
———. "Stars, Cows, Semicircles and Domes: Astronomical Creation Myths and the Mathematical Universe." In *A Woman of Valor: Jerusalem Ancient Near East Studies in Honor of Joan Goodnick Westenholz*, edited by W. Horowitz et al., 73–85. Madrid: Consejo Superior de Investigaciones Científicas, 2010.
Horst, Friedrich. *Die Zwölf kleinen Propheten*. Tübingen: Mohr, 1964.
Hossfeld, Frank-Lothar, and E. Zenger. *Psalms 51–100*. Hermeneia. Minneapolis: Fortress, 2005.
Hruša, Ivan. *Ancient Mesopotamian Religion: A Descriptive Introduction*. Münster: Ugarit, 2015.
Hume, David. *Hume: Dialogues Concerning Natural Religion: And Other Writings*. Originally published 1779. Cambridge: Cambridge University Press, 2007.
———. *Natural History of Religion*. Originally published 1757. Stanford: Stanford University Press, 1956.
Hund, Wulf D., et al. *Semianization: Apes, Gender, Class, and Race*. Zürich: Lit, 2015.
Ihm, Maximilian. *C. Suetonii Tranqulli Opera*. Vol. 1: *De Vita Caesarum*. Leipzig: Teubner, 1907.
Isaac, E. "(Ethiopic Apocalyse of) Enoch." In *The Old Testament Pseudepigrapha*, edited by James H. Charlesworth, 1:5–90. New York: Doubleday, 1983a.
"Irkallu." In *The Assyrian Dictionary of the Oriental Institute of the University of Chicago*, edited by Ignace J. Gelb et al., 7:177–78. Chicago: Oriental Institute, 1964–2010.
Izre'el Shlomo. *Adapa and the South Wind: Language Has the Power of Life and Death*. Winona Lake, IN: Eisenbrauns, 2001.
———. *The Amarna Scholarly Tablets*. Groningen: Styx, 1997.
Jackson, A. V. Williams. *Zoroastrian Studies*. New York: AMS, 1965.
Jacobsen, Thorkild. "The Battle between Marduk and Tiamat." *JAOS* 88.1 (1968) 104–8.
———. "The Chief God of Eshnunna." In *Tell Asmar and Khafaje*, edited by Henri Frankfort et al., 51–59. Chicago: University of Chicago Press, 1932.
———. "The Eridu Genesis." *JBL* 100 (1981) 513–29.
———. *The Harps that Once . . . : Sumerian Poetry in Translation*. New Haven, CT: Yale University Press, 1987.
———. "Primitive Democracy in Ancient Mesopotamia." *JNES* 2.3 (1943) 159–72.

———. *The Sumerian King List*. Chicago: University of Chicago Press, 1939.

———. "Sumerian Mythology: A Review Article." *JNES* 5.2 (1946) 128–52.

———. *Toward the Image of Tammuz and Other Essays on Mesopotamian History and Culture*. Cambridge, MA: Harvard University Press, 1970.

———. *The Treasures of Darkness: A History of Mesopotamian Religion*. New Haven, CT: Yale University Press, 1976.

Jaeger, Werner. *The Theology of the Early Greek Philosophers*. Oxford: Clarendon, 1947.

Jastrow, Morris. *The Religion of Babylonia and Assyria*. Boston: Ginn, 1898.

Jenkins, Jack. "'Nones' Now as Big as Evangelicals, Catholics in the US." *Religion News Service*, March 23, 2019. https://religionnews.com/2019/03/21/nones-now-as-big-as-evangelicals-catholics-in-the-us/.

Jones, Lindsay. *Encyclopedia of Religion*. New York: Macmillan Reference, 2005.

Jones, Robert P. *The End of White Christian America*. New York: Simon & Schuster, 2016.

Jones, W. H. S. *Hippocrates*. Vols. 1–2. Loeb Classical Library. Cambridge, MA: Harvard University Press. 1923.

Jowett, Benjamin. *The Dialogues of Plato*. Vol. 1. Oxford: Oxford University Press, 1892.

Jung, Carl G. *The Archetypes and the Collective Unconscious*. 2nd. ed. New York: Bollingen/Princeton, 1980.

Jüngel, Eberhard. *God's Being Is in Becoming*. Grand Rapids: Eerdmans, 1983.

Katz, Dina, *Gilgamesh and Akka*. Groningen: Styx, 1993.

Kautzsch, E., and A. E. Cowley. *Gesenius' Hebrew Grammar*. Oxford: Clarendon, 1910.

Kayser, Carl L. *Flavii Philostrati Opera*. Vol. 1: *Philostratus the Athenian*. Leipzig: Teubner,1870.

Keil, C. F. *The Pentateuch*. Grand Rapids: Eerdmans, 1951.

Kilmer, Anne D. "Fugal Features of Atraḫasis: The Birth Theme." In *Mesopotamian Poetic Language: Sumerian and Akkadian*, edited by Marianna E. Vogelzang and H. L. J. Vanstiphout, 127–39. Groningen: Styx, 1996.

———. "The Mesopotamian Concept of Overpopulation and Its Solution as Reflected in Mythology." *Orientalia* 41.1 (1972)160–77.

———. "Notes on Akadian *Uppu*." In *Essays on the Ancient Near East in Memory of Jacob Joel Finkelstein*, edited by Maria de Jong Ellis, 129–38. Hamden: Archon, 1977.

———. "Speculations on Umul, the First Baby." In *Kramer Anniversary Volume: Cuneiform Studies in Honor of Samuel Noah Kramer*, edited by Barry L. Eichler et al., 265–70. Kevelaer: Butzon & Bercker, 1976.

King, L. W. *The Seven Tablets of Creation, or The Babylonian and Assyrian Legends concerning the Creation of the World and of Mankind*. London: Luzac, 1902.

Kingsley, Peter. *Ancient Philosophy, Mystery and Magic: Empedocles and Pythagorean Tradition*. Oxford: Oxford University Press, 1995.

———. *Reality*. Inverness: Golden Sufi Center, 2003.

Kirk, Geoffrey S. "On Defining Myth." In *Sacred Narrative: Reading in the Theory of Myth*, edited by Alan Dundes, 53–61. Berkeley: University of California Press, 1984.

Kirk, Geoffrey S., et al. *The Presocratic Philosophers: A Critical History with a Selection of Texts*. Cambridge: Cambridge University Press, 1983.

Kittay, Eva F. *Metaphor: Its Cognitive Force and Linguistic Structure*. Oxford: Oxford University Press, 1987.

Klijn, A. F. J. "2 (Syriac Apocalypse of) Baruch." In *The Old Testament Pseudepigrapha*, edited by James H. Charlesworth, 1:615–52. New York: Doubleday, 1983.
Kline, Meredith G. "Divine Kingship and Genesis 6:1–4." *WTJ* 24:2 (1962) 187–204.
Knafl, Anne K. *Forming God: Divine Anthropomorphism in the Pentateuch*. Winona Lake, IN: Eisenbrauns, 2014.
Knowles, Murray, and Rosamund Moon. *Introducing Metaphor*. New York: Routledge, 2005.
Koehler, Ludwig, et al., eds. *Hebräisches und Aramäisches Lexicon zum Alten Testament*. Leiden: Brill, 1967–1990.
Köneke, Vanessa. *Psychology of Self-Insight: Motivated Reasoning and Self-Deception*. Norderstedt: Grin, 2009.
Kornaros G., and I. Kalamaridēs, eds. *Iōannou tou Damaskēnou. Ekdosis tēs Orzodoxou pisteōs*. Atenas: Typois Ph. Karampinē kai K. Vapha, 1859.
Köstenberger, Andreas J. *John*. Baker Exegetical Commentary on the New Testament. Grand Rapids: Baker, 2004.
Kövecses, Zoltán. *Metaphor*. Oxford: Oxford University Press, 2010.
———. *Where Metaphors Come From: Reconsidering Context in Metaphor*. Oxford: Oxford University Press, 2015.
Kraemer, Guenter. *Epilepsy from A–Z: Dictionary of Medical Terms*. Stuttgart: Georg Thieme, 2004.
Kramer, Samuel N., and John Maier. *Myths of Enki, The Crafty God*. New York: Oxford University Press, 1989.
Kramer, Samuel N. "Gilgamesh and Agga." *AJA* 53.1 (1949)1–18.
———. "Gilgamesh and Agga." In *Ancient Near Eastern Texts Relating to the Old Testament*, edited by James B. Pritchard, 44–47. Princeton, NJ: Princeton University Press, 1969.
———. *Gilgamesh and the Huluppu-Tree: A Reconstructed Sumerian Text*. Chicago: University of Chicago Press, 1938.
———. "The Sumerian Deluge Myth: Reviewed and Revised." *AS* 33 (1983) 115–21.
———. *Sumerian Mythology: A Study of Spiritual and Literary Achievement in the Third Millennium B.C.* Philadelphia: University of Pennsylvania Press, 1961.
———. *The Sumerians: Their History, Culture, and Character*. Chicago: University of Chicago Press, 1963.
Kraus, Joachim-Hans. *Psalms 1–59*. Continental Commentary. Minneapolis: Fortress, 1993.
———. *Psalms 60–150*. Continental Commentary. Minneapolis: Fortress, 1993.
Krebs, Robert E., and Carolyn A. Krebs. *Groundbreaking Scientific Experiments, Inventions, and Discoveries of the Ancient World*. Westport, CT: Greewood, 2003.
Kristeller, Paul O. *Greek Philosophers of the Hellenistic Age*. New York: Columbia University Press, 1993.
Kroll, Wilhelm. *Vetti Valentis Anthologiarum*. Berlin: Weidmann, 1908.
Kruse, Colin G. *John*. Tyndale New Testament Commentary. Downers Grove, IL: InterVarsity, 2003.
Kuhrt, Amélie, *The Ancient Near East*. London: Routledge, 1995.
"Kullatu." In *The Assyrian Dictionary of the Oriental Institute of the University of Chicago*, edited by Ignace J. Gelb et al., 8:504–6. Chicago: Oriental Institute, 1964–2010.
Kunda, Ziva. "The Case for Motivated Reasoning." *Psychological Bulletin* 108.3 (1990) 480–98.

Kuyper, Abraham. *Lectures on Calvinism*. Grand Rapids: Eerdmans, 1931.
Kvanvig, Helge S. *Primeval History: Babylonian, Biblical, and Enochic. An Intertextual Reading*. Leiden: Brill, 2011.
Labat, René. *Traité akkadien de diagnostics et pronostics médicaux*. Leiden: Brill, 1951.
Labberton, Mark. "Political Dealing: The Crisis of Evangelicalism." Speech given to evangelical leaders, April 16, 2018, Wheaton College, Chicago. https://www.fuller.edu/posts/political-dealing-the-crisis-of-evangelicalism/.
Laessøe, Jørgen. "The Atraḫasīs Epic: A Babylonian History of Mankind." *BO* 13.4 (1956) 90–102.
Lake, Kirsopp. *Apostolic Fathers*, vols. 1 and 2. Loeb Classical Library. Cambridge, MA: Harvard University Press, 1912–13.
Lakoff, George. "The Contemporary Theory of Metaphor." In *Metaphor and Thought*, edited by Andrew Ortony, 202–51. Cambridge: Cambridge University Press, 1993.
———. "What Is a Conceptual System?" In *The Nature and Ontogenesis of Meaning*, edited by Willis F. Overton and David S. Palermo, 41–90. Hillsdale: Lawrence Erlbaum, 1994.
Lakoff, George, and Mark Johnson. *Metaphors We Live By*. Chicago: University of Chicago, 1980.
———. *Philosophy in the Flesh: The Embodied Mind and Its Challenge to Western Thought*. New York: Basic, 1999.
Lamb, Walter R. M. *Plato*. Vol. 12: *Charmides, Alcibiades, 1 and 2, Hipparchus, The Lovers, Theages, Minos, Epinomis*. Loeb Classical Library. Cambridge, MA: Harvard University Press, 1927.
Lambert, Wilfred G. *Babylonian Creation Myths*. Winona Lake, IN: Eisenbrauns, 2013.
———. *Babylonian Wisdom Literature*. Oxford: Oxford University Press, 1960.
———. "Interchange of Ideas between Southern Mesopotamia and Syria-Palestine as Seen in Literature." In *Mesopotamien und seine Nachbarn*, edited by Hans J. Nissen and J. Renger, 311–16. Berlin: Reimer, 1983.
———. "Mesopotamian Creation Stories." In *Imagining Creation*, edited by Markham J. Geller and M. Schipper, 15–60. Leiden: Brill, 2008.
———. "Der Mythos im Alten Mesopotamien, sein Werden und Vergehen." *ZRG* 26 (1974) 1–16.
———. "New Evidence for the First Line of Atra-ḫasīs." *Orientalia* 38 (1969) 533–38.
———. "The Reign of Nebuchadnezzar I: A Turning Point in the History of Ancient Mesopotamian Religion." In *The Seed of Wisdom: Essays in Honour of T. J. Meek*, edited by W. S. McCullough, 3–13. Toronto: University of Toronto Press, 1964.
———. "The Relationship of Sumerian and Babylonian Myth as Seen in Accounts of Creation." In *La circulation des biens, des personnes et des idées dans le Proche-Orient ancien: Actes de la XXXVIIIe Rencontre assyriologique internationale, Paris, 8-10 juillet 1991*, edited by D. Charpin and F. Joannès, 129–35. Paris: Editions Recherche sur les civilisations, 1992.
———. "Studies in Marduk." *BSOAS* 47.1 (1984) 1–9.
———. "The Theology of Death." In *Death in Mesopotamia*, edited by Bendt Alster, 53–66. Copenhagen: Akademisk Forlag, 1980.
Lambert, Wilfred G., and A. R. Millard. *Atra-ḫasīs: The Babylonian Story of the Flood*. Originally published 1969. Winona Lake, IN: Eisenbrauns, 1999.
———. *Cuneiform Texts from Babylonian Tablets in the British Museum*. Babylonian Literary Texts 46. London: Trustees of the British Museum, 1965.

Lamberton, Robert. *Homer the Theologian: Neoplatonist Allegorical Reading and the Growth of the Epic Tradition.* Berkeley: University of California Press, 1986.

Landsberger, Benno, and J. V. K. Wilson. "The Fifth Tablet of Enuma Eliš." *JNES* 20.3 (1961) 154-79.

Langdon, Stephen. *Sumerian Liturgies and Psalms.* University Museum Publications of the Babylonian Section 10.4. Philadelphia: University Museum, 1919.

Lange, Armin, and E. M. Meyers, eds. *Light Against Darkness: Dualism in Ancient Mediterranean Religion and the Contemporary World.* Göttingen: Vandenhoeck & Ruprecht, 2011.

Langford, Jerome J. *Galileo, Science and the Church.* Ann Arbor: University of Michigan Press, 1992.

Lapinkivi, Pirjo. *Ištar's Descent and Resurrection.* Neo-Assyrian Text Corpus Project. Winona Lake, IN: Eisenbrauns, 2010.

Lawson, E. Thomas, and R. N. McCauley. *Rethinking Religion: Connecting Cognition and Culture.* Cambridge: Cambridge University Press, 1990.

Leick, Gwendolyn. *The Babylonians: An Introduction.* London: Routledge, 2002.

———. *Sex and Eroticism in Mesopotamian Literature.* London: Routledge, 1994.

Lemche, Niels P. *Ancient Israel: A New History of Israelite Society.* Sheffield: JSOT, 1988.

———. *Early Israel: Anthropological and Historical Studies on the Israelite Society before the Monarchy.* Leiden: Brill, 1985.

———. *The Old Testament between Theology and History: A Critical Survey.* Louisville: Westminster John Knox, 2008.

Lenz, John R. "Deification of the Philosopher in Classical Greece." In *Partakers of the Divine Nature*, edited by Michael J. Christensen and J. A. Wittung, 47-62. Madison, WI: Fairleigh Dickinson University Press, 2007.

Lesher, J. H. *Xenophanes of Colophon: Fragments.* Toronto: University of Toronto Press, 1992.

Levine, Lee. *Judaism and Hellenism in Antiquity.* Seattle: University of Washington Press, 1998.

Levi-Strauss, Claude. *The Savage Mind.* Translated from the French. Chicago: University of Chicago Press, 1966.

Lewis, C. S. *Mere Christianity.* New York: Harper Collins, 2001.

Lewis, Theodore J. "The Birth of the Gracious Gods." In *Ugaritic Narrative Poetry*, edited by Simon B. Parker, 205-14. Chico: Scholars, 1997.

———. "CT 13 33-34 and Ezequiel 32: Lion-Dragon Myths." *JAOS* 116.1 (1996) 28-47.

Lichtheim, Miriam. *Ancient Egyptian Literature.* Vol. 1: *The Old and Middle Kingdoms.* Berkeley: University of California Press, 1973.

———. *Ancient Egyptian Literature.* Vol. 2: *The New Kingdom.* Berkeley: University of California Press, 1976.

———. *Ancient Egyptian Literature.* Vol. 3: *The Late Period.* Berkeley: University of California Press, 1980.

Lichty, Erle. "Demons and Population Control." *Expedition* 13 (1971) 22-26.

Litke, Richard L. *A Reconstruction of the Assyro-Babylonian God-Lists, An: dA-nu-um and An: Anuša amēli.* New Haven, CT: Yale Babylonian Collection, 1998.

Liu, Eric, and Nick Hanauer. *The Gardens of Democracy.* Seattle: Sasquatch, 2011.

Liverani, Mario. *Israel's History and the History of Israel.* London: Equinox, 2005.

Locke, John. *An Essay Concerning Human Understanding.* London: Tegg, 1836.

Lohse, Eduard. *Die Texte aus Qumran: Hebräisch und Deutsch.* München: Kösel, 1971.

Long, A. A., and D. N. Sedley. *Hellenistic Philosophy: Stoics, Epicureans, Sceptics.* Berkeley: University of California Press, 1986.
———. *The Hellenistic Philosophers.* 2 vols. New York: Cambridge University Press, 1987.
Longman, Tremper, III. *Genesis.* The Story of God Bible Commentary. Grand Rapids: Zondervan, 2016.
———. *How to Read Genesis.* Downers Grove, IL: InterVarsity, 2014.
———. *Psalms.* Tyndale Old Testament Commentaries. Downers Grove, IL: InterVarsity, 2014.
Luschnig, C. A. E., and H. M. Roisman. *Euripides' Alcestis.* Norman: University of Oklahoma Press, 2003.
Lundbom, Jack R. *Deuteronomy.* Grand Rapids: Eerdmans, 2013.
Luz, Ulrich, *Matthew 1–7.* Continental Commentary. Minneapolis: Fortress, 2007.
———. *Matthew 8–20.* Continental Commentary. Minneapolis: Fortress, 2001.
———. *Matthew 21–28.* Continental Commentary. Minneapolis: Fortress, 2005.
Lutheran Church—Missouri Synod. *Convention Workbook: Reports and Overtures 2019.* July 20–25, 2019, Tampa, FL. https://files.lcms.org/wl/?id=q3sr9s4o5Ou9WSVibBi0Hwv27NV8xv25.
Ma, Alexandra. "Jailing Muslims, Burning Bibles, and Forcing Monks to Wave the National Flag: How Xi Jinping Is Attacking Religion in China." *Business Insider*, December 2018. https://www.businessinsider.my/how-xi-jinping-is-attacking-religion-in-china-2018-11/.
MacKenzie, Roderick A. F. "Before Abraham Was . . ." *CBQ* 15.1 (1953) 131–40.
Mack-Fisher, Loren R. "A Survey and Reading Guide to the Didactic Literature of Ugarit: Prolegomenon to a Study on the Sage." In *The Sage on Israel and the Ancient Near East*, edited by John G. Gammie and Leo G. Perdue, 67–80. Winona Lake, IN: Eisenbrauns, 1990.
MacMullen, Ramsay. *Christianizing the Roman Empire.* New Haven, CT: Yale University Press, 1984.
Maisels, Charles K. *The Emergence of Civilization: from Hunting and Gathering to Agriculture, Cities and the State in the Near East.* New York: Routledge, 1990.
Malina, Bruce J., and R. L. Rohrbaugh. *Social-Science Commentary on the Gospel of John.* Minneapolis: Fortress, 1998.
Malinowski, Bronislaw. *Magic, Science and Religion.* Garden City, NY: Doubleday, 1948.
March, F. A. *Athenagoras.* New York: Harper, 1876.
Marchant, Edgar C. *Xenophontis opera omnia.* Vol. 2. 2nd ed. Oxford: Clarendon, 1901.
Marcus, Joel. *Mark 1–8.* Anchor Bible. New Haven, CT: Yale University Press, 2000.
Marshall, I. Howard. *Commentary on Luke.* New International Greek Testament Commentary. Grand Rapids: Eerdmans, 1978.
Marsman, Hennie J. *Women in Ugarit & Israel: Their Social & Religious Position in the Context of the Ancient Near East.* Leiden: Brill, 2003.
Martin, Dale B. *New Testament History and Literature.* New Haven, CT: Yale University Press, 2012.
Martin, Michel. "The Moral Question of Trump's Border Wall." *All Things Considered*, NPR, January 27, 2019. https://www.npr.org/2019/01/27/689191255/the-morality-question-of-trump-s-border-wall.
Mathews, Kenneth A. *Genesis 1—11:26.* New American Commentary. Nashville: B&H, 1996.

Matouš, L. "Review of Lambert-Millard Atrahasis." *Archiv Orientální* 38 (1970) 74–6.
Mayes, A. D. H. *Deuteronomy*. New Century Bible Commentary. Grand Rapids: Eerdmans, 1979.
Mays, James L. *Psalms*. Old Testament Library. Louisville: John Knox, 2011.
McCann, J. Clinton. *Psalms*. Nashville: Abingdon, 1996.
McCarter, P. Kyle, Jr. *1 Samuel*. Anchor Bible. New Haven, CT: Doubleday, 1980.
McLaren, Brian D. *The Great Spiritual Migration*. New York: Convergent, 2016.
McConville, J. G. *Deuteronomy*. Apollos Old Testament Commentary. Downers Grove, IL: InterVarsity, 2002.
McKenzie, John L. "Myth and the Old Testament." *CBQ* 21.3 (1959) 265–82.
Meeter, H. Henry. *The Basic Ideals of Calvinism*. Grand Rapids: Baker, 1990.
Mellaart, James. *The Neolithic of the Near East*. New York: Scribner, 1975.
Mendenhall, George E. "'Change and Decay in All Around I See': Conquest, Covenant, and 'The Tenth Generation.'" *BA* 39.4 (1976) 152–57.
———. "The Hebrew Conquest of Palestine." *BA* 25.3 (1962) 65–87.
———. *The Tenth Generation: The Origins of the Biblical Tradition*. Baltimore: Johns Hopkins University Press, 1973.
Meyer, August W. *Critical and Exegetical Hand-Book to the Gospel of John*. Edinburgh: T. & T. Clark, 1883.
Meyer, Rudolf. *Gramática del hebreo bíblico*. Barcelona: CLIE, 1989.
Michalowski, Piotr. *The Lamentation over the Destruction of Sumer and Ur*. Winona Lake, IN: Eisenbrauns, 1989.
———. "Tokenism. Review of Before Writing by Schmandt-Besserat." *AA* 95.4 (1993) 996–99.
Migne, Jacques P. *Patrologiae Graecae*. Vol. 6: *S. Justinus philosophus et martyr, Tatianus S. Justini Discipulus, Athenagoras Atheniensis, philosophus christianus, S. Theophilus Antiochenus Episcopus, Hermias*. Paris: Imprimerie Catholique, 1857.
———. *Patrologiae Graecae*. Vol. 8: *Clementis Alexandrini*. Paris: Imprimerie Catholique, 1857.
———. *Patrologiae Graecae*. Vol. 11: *Origenes*. Paris: Imprimerie Catholique, 1857.
———. *Patrologiae Graecae*. Vol. 13: *Origenes*. Paris: Imprimerie Catholique, 1857.
———. *Patrologiae Graecae*. Vol. 20: *Eusebii Pamphili*. Paris: Imprimerie Catholique, 1857.
———. *Patrologiae Graecae*. Vol. 21: *Eusebius Pamphili: Praeparatio Evangelica*. Paris: Imprimerie Catholique, 1857.
———. *Patrologiae Graecae*. Vol. 25: *S. Athanasius Alexandrinus*. Paris: Imprimerie Catholique, 1857.
———. *Patrologiae Latina*. Vol. 1: *Quinti Septimii Florentis Tertulliani Presbytery Carthaginiensis opera omnia*. Paris: Imprimerie Catholique, 1844.
———. *Patrologiae Latina*. Vol. 7: *Lucii Caecilii Firmiani Lactantii Opera Omnia*, vol. 2. Paris: Imprimerie Catholique, 1844.
———. *Patrologiae Latina*. Vol. 22: *Sancti Aurelii Augustini*. Paris: Imprimerie Catholique, 1845.
———. *Patrologiae Latina*. Vol. 24: *Sancti Aurelii Augustini*. Paris: Imprimerie Catholique, 1865.
———. *Patrologiae Latina*. Vol. 38: *Sancti Aurelii Augustini*. Paris: Imprimerie Catholique, 1863.

Miller, Patrick D. *The Divine Warrior in Israel*. Atlanta: Society of Biblical Literature, 2006.

———. *The Religion of Ancient Israel*. Louisville: Westminster John Knox, 2000.

"Miqtu." In *The Assyrian Dictionary of the Oriental Institute of the University of Chicago*, edited by Ignace J. Gelb et al., 10:103–5. Chicago: Oriental Institute, 1964–2010.

Moltmann, Jürgen. *The Church in the Power of the Spirit: A Contribution to Messianic Ecclesiology*. Minneapolis: Fortress, 1993.

———. *The Coming of God: Christian Eschatology*. Minneapolis: Fortress, 1996.

———. *The Crucified God: The Cross as the Foundation and Criticism of Christian Theology*. London: SCM, 1974.

———. *God for a Secular Society: The Public Relevance of Theology*. London: SCM, 1999.

———. *God in Creation: An Ecological Doctrine of Creation*. London: SCM, 1985.

———. *History and the Triune God*. London: SCM, 1991.

———. *The Living God and the Fulness of Life*. Louisville: Westminster John Knox, 2015.

———. *Science and Wisdom*. London: SCM, 2003.

———. *Theology of Hope: On the Ground and the Implications of a Christian Eschatology*. London: SCM, 1967.

———. *The Trinity and the Kingdom: The Doctrine of God*. London: SCM, 1981.

———. *The Way of Jesus Christ: Christology in Messianic Dimensions*. Minneapolis: Fortress, 1993

Moran, William L., ed. and trans. *The Amarna Letters*. Baltimore: John Hopkins University Press, 1992.

———. "Atrahasis: The Babylonian Story of the Flood." *Biblica* 52.1 (1971) 51–61.

———. "The Creation of Man in Atrahasis 1.192–248." *BASOR* 200 (1970) 48–56.

———. "Notes on the Hymn to Marduk in Ludlul Bel Nemeqi." In *Studies in Literature from the Ancient Near East: Dedicated to Samuel Noah Kramer*, edited by Jack M. Sasson, 255–60. AOS 65. New Haven, CT: American Oriental Society, 1983.

———. "Some Considerations of Form and Interpretation in Atra-ḫasis." In *Language, Literature, and History: Philological and Historical Studies Presented to Erica Reiner*, edited by Francesca Rochberg-Halton, 245–56. AOS 67. New Haven, CT: American Oriental Society, 1987.

More, Brookes. *Ovid. Metamorphoses*. Boston: Cornhill, 1922.

Moreland, James P., and William L. Craig. *Philosophical Foundations for a Christian Worldview*. Downers Grove, IL: InterVarsity, 2003.

Morris, Brian. *Anthropological Studies of Religion*. Cambridge: Cambridge University Press, 1987.

Morris, Thomas V. *Our Idea of God*. Downers Grove, IL: InterVarsity, 1991.

Morton, Samuel G., et al. *Types of Mankind: Ethnological Researches*. Philadelphia: Lippincott, Grambo, 1854.

Most, G. W. *Hesiod: The Shield, Catalogue of Women, other fragments*. Cambridge, MA: Harvard University Press, 2007.

———. *Hesiod: Theogony, Works and Days, Testimonia*. Cambridge, MA: Harvard University Press, 2006.

Moule, C. F. D. *An Idiom-Book of New Testament Greek*. Cambridge: Cambridge University Press, 1959.

Moulton, James H., and G. Milligan. *The Vocabulary of the Greek Testament Illustrated from the Papyri and Other Non-Literary Sources.* London: Hodder and Stoughton, 1919.

Moulton, James H., and Nigel Turner. *A Grammar of New Testament Greek.* Vol. 3: *Syntax.* Edinburgh: T. & T. Clark, 1963.

Mowinckel, Sigmund. *The Psalms in Israel's Worship.* Grand Rapids: Eerdmans, 1962.

Mullen, E. Theodore. *The Divine Council in Canaanite and Early Hebrew Literature.* Chico, CA: Scholars, 1980.

Murphy, Frederick J. *Apocalypticism in the Bible and Its World.* Grand Rapids: Baker, 2012.

Murray, A. T. *Homer: Odyssey, Books i–xii.* Loeb Classical Library. Cambridge, MA: Harvard University Press, 1998.

———. *Homer: Odyssey, Books xiii–xxiv.* Loeb Classical Library. Cambridge, MA: Harvard University Press, 1999.

———. *The Iliad: i–xii.* Loeb Classical Library. Cambridge, MA: Harvard University Press, 2003.

———. *The Iliad: xiii–xxiv.* Loeb Classical Library. Cambridge, MA: Harvard University Press, 1999.

Murray, Gilbert. *Euripidis Fabulae.* Vol. 2. Oxford: Clarendon, 1913.

Mutz, Diana C. "Status Threat, Not Economic Hardship, Explains the 2016 Presidential Vote." Proceeding of the National Academy of Sciences of the Unites States of America. https://www.pnas.org/content/115/19/E4330.

"Mūtu." In *The Assyrian Dictionary of the Oriental Institute of the University of Chicago*, edited by Ignace J. Gelb et al., 10.2:316–9. Chicago: Oriental Institute, 1964–2010.

"Našû." In *The Assyrian Dictionary of the Oriental Institute of the University of Chicago*, edited by Ignace J. Gelb et al., 11.2:80–112. Chicago: Oriental Institute, 1964–2010.

Nelson, Richard D. *Deuteronomy.* Old Testament Library. Louisville: Westminster John Knox, 2002.

Nelson-Pallmeyer, Jack. *Jesus against Christianity.* Harrisburg, PA: Trinity, 2001.

Neusner, Jacob. *The Incarnation of God: The Character of Divinity in Formative Judaism.* Philadelphia: Fortress, 1988.

Newsome, James D. *Greeks, Romans, Jews: Currents of Culture and Belief in the New Testament World.* Philadelphia: Trinity, 1992.

Nickelsburg, George W. E. *Ancient Judaism and Christian Origins.* Minneapolis: Fortress, 2003.

———. *Jewish Literature between the Bible and the Mishnah: A Historical and Literary Introduction.* Minneapolis: Fortress, 2011.

———. *Resurrection, Immortality, and Eternal Life in Intertestamental Judaism and Early Christianity.* Grand Haven, MI: Harvard Divinity School, 2006.

Nickelsburg, George W. E., and J. C. VanderKam. *1 Enoch.* Minneapolis: Fortress, 2012.

Niditch, Susan. *Folklore and the Hebrew Bible.* Minneapolis: Fortress, 1993.

———. *Judges.* Old Testament Library. Louisville: Westminster John Knox, 2008.

Niese, Benedikt. *Flavii Iosephi Opera.* Berlin: Weidmann, 1885–94.

Nissen, Hans J. *The Early History of the Ancient Near East, 9000–2000.* Chicago: University of Chicago Press, 1988.

Nissinen, Martti. *Prophets and Prophecy in the Ancient East.* Atlanta: Society of Biblical Literature, 2003.

Nixen, Catherine. *The Darkening Age: The Christian Destruction of the Classical World*. Boston: Houghton Mifflin Harcourt, 2018.

Noebel, David, and C. Edwards. *Thinking Like a Christian: Understanding and Living a Biblical Worldview*. Nashville: B&H, 2002.

Noth, Martin. *Estudios sobre el Antiguo Testamento*. Originally published 1966. Translated from German. Salamanca: Sígueme, 1985.

"The Number of Ex-Muslims in America Is Rising." *The Economist*, March 15, 2018. https://www.economist.com/united-states/2018/03/15/the-number-of-ex-muslims-in-america-is-rising.

O'Day, Gail R., and S. E. Hylen. *The Gospel of John*. Westminster Bible Companion. Nashville: Abingdon, 1995.

O'Donnel, James J. *Pagans: The End of Traditional Religion and the Rise of Christianity*. New York: Ecco, 2015.

O'Donnell, Svenja. "May Says She'll Seek 'Red, White and Blue' Brexit as Talks Near." *Bloomberg*, December 6, 2016. https://www.bloomberg.com/news/articles/2016-12-06/may-says-she-ll-seek-red-white-and-blue-brexit-as-talks-near.

O'Grady, Patricia F. *Thales of Miletus: The Beginning of Western Science and Philosophy*. London: Routledge, 2002.

O'Meara, Dominic. *Platonopolis: Platonic Political Philosophy in Late Antiquity*. Oxford: Clarendon, 2003.

Oates, David, and Joan Oates. *The Rise of Civilization*. Oxford: Elsevier Phaidon, 1976.

Oden, Robert A. *The Bible Without Theology*. San Francisco: Harper & Row, 1987.

———. "Divine Aspirations in Atrahasis and in Genesis 1–11." *ZAW* 93 (1981) 197–216.

Oesterley, William O. E. *The Psalms: Translated with Text-Critical and Exegetical Notes*. London: SPCK, 1959.

Oldfather, C. H. *Diodorus of Sicily*. Vol. 2. Loeb Classical Library. Cambridge: Cambridge University Press, 1925.

Oppenheim, "Cyrus." In *Ancient Near Eastern Texts Relating to the Old Testament*, edited by James B. Pritchard, 315–16. Princeton, NJ: Princeton University Press, 1969.

Orr, James. *The Christian View of God and the World as Centring in the Incarnation*. Edinburgh: Andrew Eliot, 1893.

Ortony, Andrew, ed. *Metaphor and Thought*. Cambridge: Cambridge University Press, 1993.

Oshima, Takayoshi. *Babylonian Prayers to Marduk*. Tübingen: Mohr Siebeck, 2011.

Otto, Rudolf. *Das Heilige: Über das Irrationale in der Idee des Göttlichen und sein Verältnis zum Rationalen*. Munich: Verlag Beck, 1963.

———. *The Idea of the Holy*. Translated by John W. Harvey. 2nd. ed. New York: Oxford University Press, 1950.

Paine, Thomas. *The Age of Reason: Being an Investigation of True and Fabulous Theology*. Boston: Josiah P. Mendum, 1852.

Pakkala, Juha. *God's Word Omitted: Omissions in the Transmission of the Hebrew Bible*. Göttingen: Vandenhoeck & Ruprecht, 2013.

Pàmias, Jordi. "The Reception of Greek Myth." In *Approaches to Greek Myth*, edited by Lowell Edmunds, 42–83. Baltimore: Johns Hopkins University Press, 2014.

Pannenberg, Wolfhart. *Basic Questions in Theology*. Minneapolis: Fortress, 1970.

———. *Systematic Theology* 1. Grand Rapids: Eerdmans, 1991.
———. *Systematic Theology* 2. Grand Rapids: Eerdmans, 1994.
———. *Systematic Theology* 3. Grand Rapids: Eerdmans, 1997.
Pardee, Dennis. "The 'Aqhatu Legend." In *The Context of Scripture*, vol. 1: *Canonical Compositions from the Biblical World*, edited by Hallo, William W. and K. L. Younger, 343–52. Leiden: Brill, 2003.
———. "The Ba'lu Myth." In *The Context of Scripture*, vol. 1: *Canonical Compositions from the Biblical World*, edited by Hallo, William W. and K. L. Younger, 241–74. Leiden: Brill, 2003.
———. "The Kirta Epic." In *The Context of Scripture*, vol. 1: *Canonical Compositions from the Biblical World*, edited by Hallo, William W. and K. L. Younger, 333–43. Leiden: Brill, 2003.
Parker, Simon B. "Aqhat." In *Ugaritic Narrative Poetry*, edited by Simon B. Parker, 49–80. Chico, CA: Scholars, 1997.
———. "Baal Fathers a Bull." In *Ugaritic Narrative Poetry*, edited by Simon B. Parker, 181–86. Chico, CA: Scholars, 1997.
Parpola, Simo. *The Standard Babylonian Epic of Gilgamesh*. Helsinki: Neo-Assyrian Text Corpus Project; Winona Lake, IN: Eisenbrauns, 1997.
Patrick, John. *Origen's Commentary on the Gospel of Matthew*. In *The Ante-Nicene Fathers*, vol. 9, edited by Alan Menzies, 297–410. New York: Scribner's, 1896.
Paul, Shalom M. "Gates of the Netherworld." In *A Woman of Valor: Jerusalem Ancient Near Studies in Honor of Joan Goodnick Westenholz*, edited by W. Horowitz, 163–70. Madrid: Consejo Superior de Investigaciones Científicas, 2010.
Peacocke, Arthur. *Theology for a Scientific Age*. Minneapolis: Fortress, 1993.
Pelikan, Jaroslav J., et al, eds. *Luther's Works*. Vol. 2: *Lectures on Genesis 6–14*. Saint Louis: Concordia, 1960.
———, et al., eds. *Luther's Works*. Vol. 51: *Sermons*. Saint Louis: Concordia, 1986.
———. *Whose Bible Is It? A Short History of the Scriptures*. London: Penguin, 2005.
Perdue, Leo G. *Scribes, Sages, and Seers: The Sage in the Eastern Mediterranean World*. Göttingen: Vandenhoeck & Ruprecht, 2008.
Perowne, J. J. Stewart. *The Book of Psalms*. London: George Bell, 1878.
Perrin, Bernadotte. *Plutarch's Lives*. 11 vols. Cambridge, MA: Harvard University Press, 1914–26.
Perry, Mervin et. al. *Western Civilization: Ideas, Politics, and Society*. Boston: Wadsworth, 2013.
Pettinato, Giovanni. *Das altorientalische Menschenbild und die sumerischen und akkadischen Schöpfungsmythen*. Heidelberg: Universitätsverlag, 1971.
———. "Die Bestrafung des Menschengeschlechts durch die Sintflut." *Orientalia* 37 (1968) 165–200.
Pew Research Center. "The Age Gap in Religion around the World." June 13, 2018. https://www.pewforum.org/2018/06/13/the-age-gap-in-religion-around-the-world/.
———. "The Factors Driving the Growth of Religious 'Nones' in the U.S." September 14, 2016. https://www.pewresearch.org/fact-tank/2016/09/14/the-factors-driving-the-growth-of-religious-nones-in-the-u-s/.
———. "Key Findings about Americans' Belief in God." April 25, 2018. https://www.pewresearch.org/fact-tank/2018/04/25/key-findings-about-americans-belief-in-god/.

———. "U.S. Public Becoming Less Religious." March 15, 2018. https://www.pewforum.org/2015/11/03/u-s-public-becoming-less-religious/.

———. "When Americans Say They Believe in God, What Do They Mean?" April 25, 2018. https://www.pewforum.org/2018/04/25/when-americans-say-they-believe-in-god-what-do-they-mean/.

———. "Why America's 'nones' don't identify with a religion." August 8, 2018. https://www.pewresearch.org/fact-tank/2018/08/08/why-americas-nones-dont-identify-with-a-religion/.

Pfeiffer, Robert H. "I Will Praise the Lord of Wisdom." In *Ancient Near Eastern Texts Relating to the Old Testament*, edited by James B. Pritchard, 434–37. Princeton, NJ: Princeton University Press, 1969.

———. "An Oracular Dream concerning Ashurbanipal." In *Ancient Near Eastern Texts Relating to the Old Testament*, edited by James B. Pritchard, 451. Princeton, NJ: Princeton University Press, 1969.

Piaget, Jean. *The Child's Conception of the World*. New York: Harcourt Brace, 1929.

Piepkorn, Arthur C. *Historical Prism Inscriptions of Ashurbanipal*. Chicago: University of Chicago Press, 1933.

Pitard, Wayne T. "Canaanite Literature." In *From an Antique Land: An Introduction to Ancient Near Eastern Literature*, edited by Carl S. Ehrlich, 255–311. Lanham, MD: Rowman & Littlefield, 2009.

Plantinga, Richard, et. al. *An Introduction to Christian Theology*. Cambridge: Cambridge University Press, 2010.

Plummer, Alfred. *A Critical and Exegetical Commentary on the Gospel according to St. Luke*. Edinburgh: T. & T. Clark, 1922.

Poebel, Arno. *Historical Texts*. Vol. 4. Publications of the Babylonian Section. Philadelphia: University Museum of Pennsylvania, 1914.

Pope, Marvin H. *Job*. Anchor Bible. Garden City, NY: Doubleday, 1965.

Postgate, J. N. *Early Mesopotamia: Society and Economy at the Dawn of History*. London: Routledge, 1992.

Potts, Timothy. *Civilization: Ancient Treasures from the British Museum*. Canberra: Australian National Gallery, 1990.

Preuss, Julius. *Biblical and Talmudic Medicine*. Northvale: Jason Aronson, 1993.

Prioreschi, Plinio. *A History of Medicine: Roman Medicine*. Omaha: Horatious, 1998.

Pritchard, James B. *Ancient Near Eastern Texts Relating to the Old Testament*. Princeton, NJ: Princeton University Press, 1969.

Propp, William H. C. *Exodus 19–40*. Anchor Bible. New York: Doubleday, 2006.

Provan, Iain. *Discovering Genesis: Content, Interpretation, Reception*. Grand Rapids: Eerdmans, 2015.

"Puḫru." In *The Assyrian Dictionary of the Oriental Institute of the University of Chicago*, edited by Ignace J. Gelb et al., 12:485–93. Chicago: Oriental Institute, 1964–2010.

Punter, David. *Metaphor: The New Critical Idiom*. London: Routledge, 2007.

Rabey, Steve. "New Film Highlights Belief that Trump's election Was God's Plan." *Religion News Service*, September 26, 2018. https://religionnews.com/2018/09/26/film-trump-prophecy-mark-taylor-gods-plan-liberty-university/.

Rackham, Horace. *Aristotle Politics*. Loeb Classical Library. Cambridge, MA: Harvard University Press, 1932.

———. *Aristotle's The Nicomachean Ethics*. Loeb Classical Library. Cambridge, MA: Harvard University Press, 1934.

Radau, Hugo. *Early Babylonian History Down to the End of the Fourth Dynasty of Ur.* Oxford: Oxford University Press, 1900.
Rampell, Catherine. "The Demographic Time Bomb that Could Hit America." *Washington Post*, December 31, 2018. https://www.washingtonpost.com/opinions/can-the-us-avoid-japans-demographic-disaster/2018/12/31/1f29ba66-0d3f-11e9-8938-5898adc28fa2_story.html?utm_term=.f5c48d4eb9de.
Rasimus, Tuomas, et al. *Stoicism in Early Christianity*. Grand Rapids: Baker, 2010.
Renger, J. "Review of W. G. Lambert and A. R. Millard, Atra-ḫasīs: The Babylonian Story of the Flood." *JNES* 32.3 (1973) 342–44.
Reno, R. R. *Genesis*. Grand Rapids: Baker, 2010.
Richards, Erin. "Bible Classes in Public Schools? Why Christian Lawmakers Are Pushing a Wave of New Bills." *USA Today*, January 23, 2019. https://www.usatoday.com/story/news/education/2019/01/23/in-god-we-trust-bible-public-school-christian-lawmakers/2614567002/.
Richards, Ivor A. *The Philosophy of Rhetoric*. Oxford: Oxford University Press, 1936.
Ricoeur, Paul. "Evil." In *Encyclopedia of Religion*, edited by Lindsay Jones, 5:2897–904. New York: Macmillan, 2005.
———. *El Lenguaje de la Fe*. Buenos Aires: Editorial La Aurora, 1978.
———. *The Rule of Metaphor: Multi-disciplinary Studies of the Creation of Meaning in Language*. Toronto: University of Toronto Press, 1977.
———. *The Symbolism of Evil*. Translated by Emerson Buchanan. Boston: Beacon, 1967.
Riley, Gregory J. *One Jesus, Many Christs: How Jesus Inspired Not One True Christianity but Many*. New York: HarperSanFrancisco, 1997.
Riley, Henry T. *The Comedies of Plautus*. Vol. 2. London: George Bell, 1881.
Roberts, Alexander, and J. Donaldson, eds. *The Ante-Nicene Fathers*. Vol. 3: *Latin Christianity: Its founder, Tertullian*. New York: Charles Scribner's Son, 1903.
———.*The Ante-Nicene Fathers*. Vol. 7. Edinburgh: T. & T. Clark, 1886.
Roberts, Alexander, and J. Donaldson.*The Ante-Nicene Fathers*. Vol. 1. Edinburgh: T. & T. Clark, 1885.
Roberts, Jimmy J. M. "The Davidic Origin of the Zion Tradition." *JBL* 92.3 (1973) 329–44.
———. *First Isaiah*. Hermeneia. Minneapolis: Fortress, 2015.
———. *Nahum, Habakkuk, and Zephaniah*. Old Testament Library. Louisville: Westminster John Knox, 1991.
Robertson, A. T. *A Grammar of the Greek New Testament in the Light of Historical Research*. Nashville: Broadman, 1934.
Robertson, Robin. *Jungian Archetypes: Jung, Gödel, and the History of Archetypes*. York Beach, ME: Nicolas-Hays, 1995.
Rodkinson, Michael L. *Babylonian Talmud*. 2nd. ed. New York: Boston New Talmud, 1903.
———. *New Edition of the Babylonian Talmud: Tract Sanhedrin*. New York: New Talmud, 1902.
Römer, Willem H. Ph. "Mythen und Epen in sumerische Sprache." *TUAT* 3.3 (1993) 351–559.
Roos, A. G. *Flavii Arriani Anabasis Alexandri*. Leipzig: Teubner, 1907.

Rosenthal. "Eshmunʿazar of sidon." In *Ancient Near Eastern Texts Relating to the Old Testament*, edited by James B. Pritchard, 662. Princeton, NJ: Princeton University Press, 1969.
Ross, Allen. *Genesis*. Carol Stream, IL: Tyndale, 2008.
Ross, W. D. *Aristotle's Metaphysics*. Oxford: Clarendon, 1924.
Rotelle, John E. *Saint Augustine, Letters 156–210*. New York: Augustinian Heritage Institute, 2004.
Roth, Martha T. *Law Collections from Mesopotamia and Asia Minor*. Atlanta: Scholars, 1995.
Routledge, Robin. *Old Testament Theology*. Downers Grove, IL: InterVarsity, 2008.
Roux, Georges. *Ancient Iraq*. London: Penguin, 1992.
Rowe, Ignacio M. "Scribes, Sages and Seers in Ugarit." In *Scribes, Sages, and Seers: The Sage in the Eastern Mediterranean World*, edited by Leo G. Perdue, 95–108. Göttingen: Vandenhoeck & Ruprecht, 2008.
Rowley, H. H. *The Book of Job*. New Century Bible Commentary. Grand Rapids: Eerdmans, 1976.
Rowton, M. B. "The Sumerian King-List." In *The Cambridge Ancient History*, vol. 1: *Prolegomena and Prehistory*, edited by Lorwerth E. S. Edwards et al., 200–201. Cambridge: Cambridge University Press, 1970.
"Rubbû." In *The Assyrian Dictionary of the Oriental Institute of the University of Chicago*, edited by Ignace J. Gelb et al., 14:393–94. Chicago: Oriental Institute, 1964–2010.
Rubinstein, Mark. "C. S. Lewis and Proof by Metaphor." *FI* 35.4 (2015) 14–15.
Runia, David T. *Philo in Early Christian Literature*. Minneapolis: Fortress, 1993.
———. *Philo of Alexandria and the Timaeus of Plato*. Leiden: Brill, 1986.
Ryan, John K. *The Confessions of Saint Augustine*. New York: Doubleday, 1960.
Sailhamer, John H. *Genesis*. Expositor's Bible Commentary. Grand Rapids: Zondervan, 2008.
"Šalāhu." In *The Assyrian Dictionary of the Oriental Institute of the University of Chicago*, edited by Ignace J. Gelb et al., 17.1:196–202. Chicago: Oriental Institute, 1964–2010.
Salmond, S. D. F., ed. *John of Damascus. Exposition of the Orthodox Faith*. Grand Rapids: Eerdmans, 1993.
Sandys, John, *Pindar. The Odes of Pindar Including the Principal Fragments*. Loeb Classical Library. Cambridge, MA: Harvard University Press, 1937.
Sarna, Nahum M. *Genesis*. Philadelphia: Jewish Publication Society, 1989.
Sauren, H. "Nammu and Enki." In *The Tablet and the Scroll: Near Eastern Studies in Honor of William W. Hallo*, edited by Mark E. Cohen et al., 198–208. Bethesda: CDL, 1993.
Sayce, Archibal H. *An Elementary Grammar with Full Syllabary and Progressive Reading Book of the Assyrian Language in the Cuneiform Type*. London: Samuel Bagster, 1875.
Schaeffer, Claude F-A. "Les fouilles de Minet el Beida-et de Ras Shamra, Grand stele (haut.: 1m 42) de BAAL, au foudre." *Syria* 14.2 (1933) 93–127.
Schaff, Philip, ed. *The Creeds of Christendom with a History and Critical Notes*. 3 vols. New York: Harper & Row, 1931.
———, ed. *Nicene and Post-Nicene Fathers*. Vol. 6: *St. Augustine, Harmony of the Gospels*. New York: Christian Literature, 1888.

Schleiermacher, Friedrich. *On Religion*. Translated by Richard Crouter. Cambridge: Cambridge University Press, 1988.

———. *Über die Religion: Reden an die Gebildeten unter ihren Verächtern*. Berlin: Johann Friedrich Unger, 1799.

Schmandt-Besserat, Denise. *Before Writing*. Vol. 1: *From Counting to Cuneiform*. Austin: University of Texas Press, 1992.

Schmidt, Brian B. *Israel's Beneficent Dead: Ancestor Cult and Necromancy in Ancient Israelite Religion and Tradition*. Winona Lake, IN: Eisenbrauns, 1994.

Schnackenburg, Rudolf. *El Evangelio según San Juan*. Barcelona: Herder, 1980.

———. *The Gospel of Matthew*. Grand Rapids: Eerdmans, 2002.

Schökel, Luis A., and Cecilia Carniti. *Salmos II*. Madrid: Cristiandad, 1996.

Schökel, Luis A., and J. L. Sicre. *Job*. Madrid: Cristiandad, 1983.

———. *Profetas*. 2 vols. Madrid: Cristiandad, 1980.

Schott, Jeremy M. *Christianity, Empire, and the Making of Religion in Late Antiquity*. Philadelphia: University of Pennsylvania Press, 2008.

Schubart, J. H. C. *Pausaniae Decriptio Graeciae*. Vol. 1. Leipzig: Teubner, 1881

Schürer, Emil. *Historia del pueblo judío in el tiempo de Jesús*. Madrid: Cristiandad, 1985.

Schwarz, Hans. *Eschatology*. Grand Rapids: Eerdmans, 2000.

Schwemer, D. "The Storm-Gods of the Ancient Near East: Summary, Synthesis, Recent Studies,Part I." *JANER* 7 (2007) 121–68.

———. "The Storm-Gods of the Ancient Near East: Summary, Synthesis, Recent Studies, Part II." *JANER* 8 (2007) 1–44.

Scott, Ernest F. *The Fourth Gospel: Its Purpose and Theology*. Edinburgh: T. & T. Clark, 1908.

Scurlock, Joann, and B. R. Andersen. *Diagnoses in Assyrian and Babylonian Medicine: Ancient Sources, Translations, and Modern Medical Analyses*. Chicago: University of Illinois Press, 2005.

Sedley, D. N. "The Ideal of Godlikeness." In *Plato: Ethics, Politics, Religion, and the Soul*, edited by Gail Fine, 309–28. Oxford: Oxford University Press, 1999.

Seland, Torrey. *Strangers in the Light: Philonic Perspectives on Christian Identity in 1 Peter*. Leiden: Brill, 2005.

Sen, Priyadarshini. "Atheist Ashram on Lord Krishna's Home Turf Roils Indian's Hindu Nationalists." *Religion News Service*, June 19, 2019. https://religionnews.com/2019/06/19/atheist-ashram-on-lord-krishnas-home-turf-roils-indias-hindu-nationalists/.

Sennett, James F., ed. *The Analytic Theist: An Alvin Plantinga Reader*. Grand Rapids: Eerdmans, 1998.

Seybold, K. *Introducing the Psalms*. London: T. & T. Clark, 1990.

Shaked, Shaul. "Iranian Influence on Judaism: First Century B.C.E. to Second Century C.E." In *The Cambridge History of Judaism*, vol. 1: *Introduction and Persian Period*, edited by W. D. Davies and L. Finkelstein, 308–25. Cambridge: Cambridge University Press, 1984).

Siegert, Folker. "Early Jewish Interpretation in a Hellenistic Style." In *Hebrew Bible: The History of Its Interpretation*, edited by M. Sæbø, 130–98. Göttingen: Vandenhoeck & Ruprecht, 1996.

"Šimtu." In *The Assyrian Dictionary of the Oriental Institute of the University of Chicago*, edited by Ignace J. Gelb et al., 17.3:11–19. Chicago: Oriental Institute, 1964–2010.

Sinclair, Peter. "It's the Data (Not Just Models), Scientists Emphasize." *Yale Climate Connections*, May 23, 2017. https://www.yaleclimateconnections.org/2017/05/its-the-data-not-just-the-models-scientists-emphasize/.

Sjöber, Ake W. "In the Beginning." In *Riches Hidden in Secret Places: Ancient Near East Studies in Memory of Thorkild Jacobsen*, edited by T Abusch, 229–47. Winona Lake, IN: Eisenbrauns, 2002.

Skinner, John, *A Critical and Exegetical Commentary on Genesis*. International Critical Commentary. Edinburgh: T. & T. Clark, 1930.

Smith, Barry D. *The Oneness and Simplicity of God*. Eugene, OR: Pickwick, 2014.

Smith, David L. *Less Than Human: Why We Demean, Enslave, and Exterminate Others*. New York: St. Martin's, 2011.

Smith, Henry P. *A Critical and Exegetical Commentary on the Books of Samuel*. Edinburgh: T. & T. Clark, 1899.

Smith, James K. A. "What Stands on the Fall?" In *Evolution and the Fall*, edited by William T. Cavanaugh and James K. A. Smith, 48–64. Grand Rapids: Eerdmans, 2017.

Smith, Mark S., and W. T. Pitard. *The Ugaritic Baal Cycle*. vol. 2. Leiden: Brill, 2009.

Smith, Mark S. "The Baal Cycle." In *Ugaritic Narrative Poetry*, edited by Simon B. Parker, 81–180. Chico, CA: Scholars, 1997.

———. *The Early History of God: Yahweh and the Other Deities in Ancient Israel*. Grand Rapids: Eerdmans, 2002.

———. *How Human Is God?* Collegeville, MN: Liturgical, 2014.

———. "Mythology and Myth-Making in Ugaritic and Israelite Literatures." In *Ugarit and the Bible*, edited by George J. Brooke et al., 293–341. Münster: Ugarit, 1994.

———. *The Origins of Biblical Monotheism: Israel's Polytheistic Background and the Ugaritic Texts*. Oxford: Oxford University Press, 2001.

Smith, Nelle. "When You Argue with a Fundamentalist, You Don't Know What You're Asking For." *Religion Dispatches*, March 27, 2018. http://religiondispatches.org/when-you-argue-with-a-fundamentalist-you-dont-know-what-youre-asking-for/.

Snell, Daniel C., ed. *A Companion to the Ancient Near East*. Oxford: Blackwell, 2005.

———. *Life in the Ancient Near East, 3100–332 B.C.E.* New Haven, CT: Yale University Press, 1998.

Soggin, J. Alberto. *A History of Ancient Israel*. Philadelphia: Westminster, 1985.

Sokol, Samantha. "Uncovering Project Blitz: Fighting a Secret, Coordinated Legislative Strategy to Undermine Religious Freedom In the States." *Americans United*, June 5, 2018. https://www.au.org/blogs/wall-of-separation/uncovering-project-blitz-fighting-a-secret-coordinated-legislative.

Sommer, Benjamin D. *The Bodies of God and the World of Ancient Israel*. Cambridge: Cambridge University Press, 2009.

Sommerfeld, Walter. *Der Aufstieg Marduks: Die Stellung Marduks in der babylonischen Religion des zweiten Jahrtausends v. Chr*. Alter Orient und Altes Testament 213. Kevelaer: Burzon & Becker, 1982.

Speiser, Ephraim A. "The Creation Epic." In *Ancient Near Eastern Texts Relating to the Old Testament*, edited by James B. Pritchard, 60–72. Princeton, NJ: Princeton University Press, 1969.

———. *Genesis*. Anchor Bible. Garden City, NY: Doubleday, 1981.

Spencer, Herbert. *Illustrations of Universal Progress: A Series of Discussions.* New York: Appleton, 1865.
Spencer, W. G. *De Medicina. Celsus.* Loeb Classical Library. Cambridge, MA: Harvard University Press. 1971.
Spiro, Melford E. "Religion: Problems of Definition and Explanation." In *Anthropological Approaches to the Study of Religion*, edited by Michael Banton, 85–126. London: Tavistock, 1966.
Spong, John S. *Why Christianity Must Change or Die.* San Francisco: HarperSanFrancisco, 1998.
Starr, Ivan. *Queries to the Sungod: Divination and Politics in Sargonid Assyria.* London: University of Helsinki Press, 1990.
Stec, David M. *The Aramaic Bible: The Targum of Psalms.* London: T. & T. Clark, 2004.
Stein, Robert H. *Studying the Synoptic Gospels: Origin and Interpretation.* Grand Rapids: Baker, 2001.
Steinkeller, Piotr. "An Ur III Manuscript of the Sumerian King List." In *Literatur, Politik und Recht in Mesopotamien: Festschrift für Claus Wilcke*, edited by W. Sallaberger et al., 267–86. Wiesenbaden: Harrassowitz, 2003.
Stol, Marten. *Birth in Babylonia and the Bible: Its Mediterranean Setting.* Groningen: Styx, 2000.
———. *Epilepsy in Babylonia.* Groningen: Styx, 1993.
Talon, Philippe. *The Standard Babylonian Creation Myth: Enūma Eliš.* Winona Lake, IN: Eisenbrauns, 2005.
"Tâmtu." In *The Assyrian Dictionary of the Oriental Institute of the University of Chicago*, edited by Ignace J. Gelb et al., 18:150–58. Chicago: Oriental Institute, 1964–2010.
Tanner, Beth L., Nancy De Claissé-Walford, and R. A. Jacobson. *The Book of Psalms.* Grand Rapids: Eerdmans, 2014.
Tate, Marvin E. *Psalms 51–100.* Word Bible Commentary. Waco, TX: Word, 1990.
Taylor, J. Glen. *Yahweh and the Sun: Biblical and Archaeological Evidence for Sun Worship in Ancient Israel.* Sheffield: JSOT, 1993.
Tcherikover, Victor. *Hellenistic Civilization and the Jews.* Grand Rapids: Baker, 2011.
Temkin, Owsei. *The Falling Sickness: A History of Epilepsy from the Greeks to the Beginnings of Modern Neurology.* Baltimore: Johns Hopkins University Press, 1971.
———. *Hippocrates in a World of Pagans and Christians.* Baltimore: Johns Hopkins University Press, 1991.
Terrien, Samuel. *The Psalms: Strophic Structure and Theological Commentary.* Grand Rapids: Eerdmans, 2003.
Tetlow, Elisabeth M. *Women, Crime, and Punishment in Ancient Law and Society.* Ancient Near East 1. New York: Continuum, 2004.
Thackeray, Henry St. J. *Josephus.* Vol. 1: *The Life, Against Apion.* Loeb Classical Library. New York: Putnam, 1926.
Thayer, Joseph H. *A Greek-English Lexicon of the New Testament.* New York: Harper, 1889.
Theissen, G. *The Miracle Stories of the Early Christian Tradition.* Minneapolis: Fortress, 1983.
Thiessen, Henry C. *Lectures in Systematic Theology.* Grand Rapids: Eerdmans, 1979.
Thiselton, Anthony C. *Companion to Christian Theology.* Grand Rapids: Eerdmans, 2015.
———. *The First Epistle to the Corinthians.* Grand Rapids: Eerdmans, 2000.

Thompson, Stith. "Myths and Folktales." In *Myth: A Symposium*, edited by T. A. Sebeok, 104–10. Philadelphia: American Folklore Society, 1955.

Thompson, Thomas L. *The Mythic Past*. New York: MJF, 1999.

Thomsen, Marie-Louise. *The Sumerian Language: An Introduction to Its History and Grammatical Structure*. Copenhagen: Akademisk, 1984.

Tigchelaar, Eibert. "'Lights Serving as Sings for Festivals' (Genesis 1:14b) in Enuma Eliš and Early Judaism." In *Creation of Heaven and Earth: Re-Interpretation of Genesis 1 in the Context of Judaism, Ancient Philosophy, Christianity, and Modern Physics*, edited by Geurt H. van Kooten, 31–48. Leiden: Brill, 2005.

Tillich, Paul. *Systematic Theology*. Chicago: University of Chicago Press, 1951.

Tomasino, Anthony J. *Judaism Before Jesus: The Events & Ideas that Shaped the New Testament World*. Downers Grove, IL: InterVarsity, 2003.

Towner, Philip H. *The Letters to Timothy and Titus*. Grand Rapids: Eerdmans, 2006.

Towner, W. S. *Genesis*. Westminster Bible Companion. Louisville: Westminster John Knox, 2001.

Tredennick, Hugh. *Aristotle Metaphysics*. Loeb Classical Library. Cambridge, MA: Harvard University Press, 1935.

Trump, Donald. "Remarks by President Trump at a California Sanctuary State Rountable." May 16, 2018. https://www.whitehouse.gov/briefings-statements/remarks-president-trump-california-sanctuary-state-roundtable/.

Tsedaka, Benyamim. *The Israelite Samaritan Version of the Torah*. Grand Rapids: Eerdmans, 2013.

Turretin, Francis. *Institutes of Electic Theology*. Phillipsburg, NJ: P&R, 1992.

"Ultimate Mars Challenge." *NOVA*, November 14, 2012. WGBH Media Library and Archives. https://www.pbs.org/wgbh/nova/video/ultimate-mars-challenge/.

Unamuno, Miguel de. *The Tragic Sense of Life in Men and Nations*. Princeton, NJ: Princeton University Press, 1972.

Van de Mieroop, Marc. *The Ancient Mesopotamian City*. Oxford: Oxford University Press, 1999.

———. *A History of the Ancient Near East, ca. 3000–323 BC*. Blackwell History of the Ancient World. Malden, MA: Wiley-Blackwell, 2007.

Van der Toorn, Karel. "Cuneiform Document from Syria-Palestine. Texts, Scribes and Schools." *ZDPV* 116 (2000) 97–103.

Van Koppen, Frans. "The Scribe of the Flood Story and His Circle." In *The Oxford Handbook of Cuneiform Culture*, edited by Karen Rabner and Eleanor Robson, 140–66. Oxford: Oxford University Press, 2011.

Van Seters, John. *The Biblical Saga of King David*. Winona Lake, IN: Eisenbrauns, 2009.

———. *Prologue to History*. Louisville: Westminster/John Knox, 1992.

VanderKam, James C., and W. Adler. *The Jewish Apocalyptic Heritage in Early Christianity*. Minneapolis: Fortress, 1996.

Vangemeren, Willem A. *Psalms*. Grand Rapids: Zondervan, 2008.

Vanstiphout, Herman L. J. "Debate between Summer and Winter." In *The Context of Scripture*, vol. 1: *Canonical Compositions from the Biblical World*, edited by William W. Hallo and K. L. Younger, 584–88. Leiden: Brill, 2003.

———. "Enūma eliš 1:3." *NABU* 4 (1987) 52–53.

———. "Enūma eliš V Lines 15–22." *JCS* 33.3 (1981) 196–98.

———. "Lore, Learning and Levity in the Sumerian Disputations: A Matter of Form, or Substance?" In *Dispute Poems and Dialogues in the Ancient and Medieval Near East*, edited by Gerrit Reinink et al., 23–46. Leuven: Peeters, 1991.

———. "Mesopotamian Debate Poems: A General Presentation (Part I)." *Acta Sumerologica* 12 (1990) 271–318.

———. "Mesopotamian Debate Poems: A General Presentation (Part II)." *Acta Sumerologica* 14 (1992) 339–67.

Vermes, Geza. *The Complete Dead Sea Scrolls in English*. London: Penguin Classic, 2004.

Von Rad, Gerhard. *Deuteronomy*. Old Testament Library. Philadelphia: Westminster, 1966.

———. *Genesis*. Old Testament Library. Philadelphia: Westminister, 1972

———. *Teología del Antiguo Testamento*. Vol. 1. Salamanca: Sígueme, 1982.

Von Soden, W. "Der Mensch bescheidet sich nicht: Überlegungen zu Schöpfungserzählungen in Babylonien und Isreal." In *Symbolae biblicae et Mesopotamicae Francisco Mario Theodoro de Liagre Böhl dedicatae*, edited by M. A. Beek et al., 349–58. Leiden:Brill, 1973.

Von Wahlde, Urban C. *The Gospel and the Letters of John*. Vol. 2. Grand Rapids: Eerdmans, 2010.

Wallis, Faith, ed. *Medieval Medicine*. Toronto: University of Toronto Press, 2010.

Waltke, Bruce K. *Genesis: A Commentary*. Grand Rapids: Zondervan, 2001.

———. *An Old Testament Theology: An Exegetical, Canonical, and Thematic Approach*. Grand Rapids: Zondervan: 2007.

Waltke, Bruce K., and M. O'Connor. *An Introduction to Biblical Hebrew Syntax*. Winona Lake, IN: Eisenbrauns, 1990.

Walton, John H. *Genesis*. NIV Application Commentary. Grand Rapids: Zondervan, 2001.

Ward, W Hayes. *Cylinders and Other Ancient Oriental Seals in the Library of J. Pierpont Morgan*. New Haven, CT: Yale University Press, 1920.

Wasserman, Nathan. *Style and Form in Old-Babylonian Literary Texts*. Leiden: Brill, 2003.

Watson, Wilfred G. E. and N. Wyatt. *Handbook of Ugaritic Studies*. Leiden: Brill, 1999.

Watts, Fraser. *Psychology, Religion, and Spirituality*. Cambridge: Cambridge University Press, 2017.

Watts, John D. W. *Isaiah 1–33*. Word Biblical Commentary. Waco, TX: Word, 1985.

Weber, Otto. *Altorientalisch Siegelbilder*. Vol. 1: *Text*. Leipzig: J. C. Hinrich, 1920.

———. *Altorientalisch Siegelbilder*. Vol. 2: *Abbildungen*. Leipzig: J. C. Hinrich, 1920.

Weinstein, Adam. "Gays 'Make God Want to Vomit': Meet Santorum's Honorary Florida Chairman." *Mother Jones*, January 22, 2012. Reclaiming America for Christ 2003, organized by Dr. James Kennedy and the Presbyterian Church of Coral Ridge, Ft. Lauderdale, Florida. https://www.motherjones.com/politics/2012/01/rick-santorum-oneal-dozier-florida-gay/.

Weiser, Arthur. *The Old Testament: Its Formation and Development*. Translated by Dorothea M. Barton. New York: Association, 1961.

———. *The Psalms*. Old Testament Library. Philadelphia: Westminster, 1962.

Wenham, Gordon J. *Genesis 1–15*. Word Biblical Commentary. Nashville: Thomas Nelson, 1987.

Werblowsky, R. J. Zwi. "Anthropomorphism." In *The Encyclopedia of Religion*, edited by Lindsey Jones, 1:388–92. 2nd ed. New York: Macmillan, 1987.

Westen, D., et al. "Neural Bases of Motivated Reasoning: An fMRI Study of Emotional Constraints on Partisan Political Judgment in the 2004 U.S. Presidential Election." *Journal of Cognitive Neuroscience* 18 (2006) 1947–58.

Westenholz, Aage. "The Sumerian City-State." In *A Comparative Study of Six City-State Cultures*, edited by M. H. A. Hansen, 23–42. Copenhagen: Kongelige Danske Videnskabernes Selskab, 2002.

Westenholz, Joan G. *Capital Cities: Urban Planning and Spiritual Dimension*. Jerusalem: Bible Land Museum Jerusalem, 1998.

———. *Legends of the Kings of Akkade*. Winona Lake, IN: Eisenbrauns, 1997.

Westermann, Claus. *Genesis 1–11*. Continental Commentary. Minneapolis: Augsburg, 1984.

———. *Genesis 12–36*. Continental Commentary. Minneapolis: Augsburg, 1985.

Whitacre, Rodney A. *John*. IVP New Testament Commentary. Downers Grove, IL: InterVarsity, 1999.

White, Andrew D. *A History of the Warfare of Science with Theology in Christendom*. New York: Appleton, 1896.

Whitehead, Alfred N. *Process and Reality: An Essay in Cosmology*. New York: Free Press, 1978.

Wicksteed, Philip H., and Francis M. Cornford. *Aristotle: The Physics*. Vol. 2. Loeb Classical Library. Cambridge, MA: Harvard University Press, 1934.

Wierenga, Edward R. *The Nature of God: An Inquiry into Divine Attributes*. Ithaca, NY: Cornell University Press, 1989.

Wiesel, E. *Night*. Originally published 1958. Translated by Marion Wiesel. New York: Hill and Wang, 2008.

Wiggermann, F. A. M. "Tišpak, His Seal, and the Dragon mušḫuššu." In *To the Euphrates and Beyond: Archaeological Studies in Honour of Maurits N. van Loon*, edited by O. Haex et al., 117–33. Rotterdam: Balkema, 1989.

Wilcke, Claus. "Weltuntergang als Anfang: Theologische, anthropologische, politisch–historische und ästhetische Ebenen der Interpretation der Sintflutgeschichte im babylonischen Atram-hasīs-Epos." In *Weltende: Beiträge zu Kultur und Religionswissenschaft*, edited by A. Jones, 63–112. Wiesbaden: Harrassowitz, 1999.

Wills, Garry. *Saint Augustine Confessions*. New York: Penguin, 2006.

Winer, Georg B. *A Treatise on the Grammar of the New Testament*. Edinburgh: T. & T. Clark, 1882.

Winter, Steve L. *A Clearing in the Forest: Law, Life, and Mind*. Chicago: University of Chicago Press, 2001.

Wintermute, O. S. "Jubilees." In *The Old Testament Pseudepigrapha*, edited by James H. Charlesworth, 2:35–142. New York: Doubleday, 1983.

Wise, Michael, et al. *A New Translation of the Dead Sea Scrolls*. New York: HarperOne, 2005.

Wiseman, D. J. "A New Text of the Babylonian Poem of the Righteous Sufferer." *AS* 30 (1980) 101–7.

Wöhrle, Georg. *The Milesians:Thales*. Berlin: de Gruyter, 2014.

Wolf, Hans W. *Hosea*. Hermeneia. Philadelphia: Fortress, 1974.

Wolkstein, D., and S. N. Kramer. *Inanna: Queen of Heaven and Earth her Stories and Hymns from Sumer*. New York: Harper & Row, 1983.

Wolohojian, Albert M. *The Romance of Alexander the Great by Pseudo-Callisthenes*. New York: Columbia University Press, 1969.

Wolpert, Lewis. *The Unnatural Nature of Science: Why Science Does Not Make Sense.* Cambridge, MA: Harvard University Press, 1992.
Wolterstorff, Nicholas. *Inquiring about God.* Cambridge: Cambridge University Press, 2009.
Wood, Simon P. *Clement of Alexandria: Christ the Educator.* Washington, DC: Catholic University of America Press, 1954.
Woodham, H. A. *Tertulliani Liber Apologeticus.* Cambridge: J. Deighton, 1850.
Work, Telford. *Deuteronomy.* Brazos Theological Commentary on the Bible. Grand Rapids: Brazos, 2009.
Wright, George E. *Arqueología Bíblica.* Madrid: Cristiandad, 1975.
———. "The Literary and Historical Problem of Joshua 10 and Judges 1." *JNES* 5.2 (1946) 105–14.
Wyatt, Nicholas. *The Mythic Mind: Essays on Cosmology and Religion in Ugaritic and Old Testament Literature.* London-Oakville: Equinox, 2005.
———. *Religious Texts from Ugarit.* 2nd ed. London: Sheffield Academy, 2002.
———. "The Titles of the Ugaritic Storm-God" *UF* 24 (1992) 403–24.
Xeravits, Géza G. "Son of God." In *The Eerdmans Dictionary of Early Judaism*, edited by John J. Collins and D. C. Harlow, 1248–49. Grand Rapids: Eerdmans, 2010.
Zagorin, Perez. *How the Idea of Religious Toleration Came to the West.* Princeton, NJ: Princeton University Press, 2003.
Zerwick, Maximilian. *Biblical Greek.* Rome: Scripta Pontificii Instituti Biblici, 1963.
Zimmermann, Bernhard, and A. Markantonatos, eds. *Crisis on Stage: Tragedy and Comedy in Late Fifth-Century Athens.* Berlin: de Gruyter, 2012.
Zuckerman, Phil. "Secularism Hits the Arab World," *Psychology Today*, July 3, 2019. https://www.psychologytoday.com/us/blog/the-secular-life/201907/secularism-hits-the-arab-world.

INDEX OF ANCIENT SOURCES

I. Ancient Near East

Adab to Enlil for Šulgi
i.19   178

Adapa and the South Wind
167f.

Admonitions of Šūpē-awīlin to his son
168

Against a Curse
i.3   23

Against an Impending Evil
i.1-2   23

Against a Known Sorcerer
i.1-2   23

Against a Snake
i.2   23

Against Ghosts
i.10   23

Anzu
167

Ashurbanipal coronation prayer
i.16-22   186

Assurbanipal's War against Teumman
i.37-38   174

Atraḫasīs
24, 27, 61, 132, 168, 237, 239
i.101   169
i.122   132
i.219   24
i.364-367   106
III.iii.36   132
III.vii.1-8   9

Babylonian Prayer
HSM 7494   150

Barton cylinder
16

Bayâ to Esarhaddon
ii. 16-39   187

Before Creation
16

Index of Ancient Sources

Bilgames and the Netherworld
I.1–10   49f.

Bilingual Story of Creation
I.7–20   16, 132

Bridal Sheets
16

Cursing of Agade
21
i.100–48   22
i.149–75   22

Cyrus Cylinder
i.12   196
i.20   196

Debate between Summer and Winter
i.9   150

Descent of Ištar
i.1–15   155
i.15   156

Dream concerning Ashurbanipal
v.54–59   61

Enki and the World Order
70

Enki, Namma and Ninmaḫ
16
I.52   60

Enlil and Ninlil
i.134   174
i.142–53   20
i.143–54   170

Enūma Eliš
16, 32f., 87, 149, 167, 169, 237f.

i.1–6   33
i.21–25   33
i.23, 109   33
i. 55–78   33
i.85–104   33
i. 105–110   33
i.120–122   33
i.125–146   33
ii. 160–2   169
iii.133–136   60
iv.13–14   33
iv.28   169
iv.35–64   33
iv.39, 42–7   32
iv.50   33f., 44
iv.52   198
iv.101–104   34
iv.101–4, 135–38   37
iv.123–v.76   34
iv.139–44   46
iv.145–6   149
v.9, 10   150
v.47–66   33
v.50–1   33
v.77–116   32
v.113   169
v.117–156   32
v.127–129   150
vi.39–81   32
vi.92–120   32
vi.121–vii.144   32

Epic of Gilgameš
8, 16, 23, 67, 91, 110, 132, 153, 167f., 172, 205, 238
i.50   178
ii.171–300   132
v.135–79   23
vi.1–9   68
ix.48   179
ix.38–41   153
x.7   179
x.77–81   24
x.305   8
x.319–322   9
x.321, 323   155
xi.221   150
xii.83f.   153

Erra and Ishum

iv.13	150
iv.123	154
v.51, 52	186

Fourth prayer of the household

150

Gilgameš and Agga

	132
i.30-31	185

Gudea Cylinder A

241-253	169f.

Hammurabi Code

	23, 167, 173
i.1-5	169

Hymn to Enlil

i. 92-4	19
i.100-3	20
i.110-3	21
i.114-21	21

Hymn to Inana

I.18	177

Hymn to Marduk

K. 3,352	46

Hymn to Tiglath-Pileser I

i.24-40	186

Inana, Gilgameš and the Ḫuluppu tree

16

Inscription of Ashurbanipal

edition B column i	24

Inscription of Damiq-ilīšu

E4.1.15	165

Inscription of Djedkhonsefankh

1-5	170

Inscription of Eshmunazar

CIS i.3, line 9	135

Inscription of Lipit-Eštar E4.1.5.3

i.28	178

Inscription of Narām Sîn

i.1-8	178

Inscription of Nebneteru

right side: 5-7	170
left side: 5-8	150

Inscription of Yeḥimilk

KAI 4	135

La-dagil-ili a Esarhaddon

ii.11-16	187
ii.18-23	187

Lament over the Destruction of Sumer and Ur

I.364-5	132

Laws of Lipit-Ishtar

xxi.5-17	23

Laws of Ur-Nammu

A.i.32	178

Lion-Serpent

i.8-9	31

Ludlul bēl nēmeqi

	24, 85, 167f.
i.23	25
i.29-33	25
i.55	178

Index of Ancient Sources

Ludlul bēl nēmeqi (continued)
ii.36-37 — 154
ii.40-43, 48 — 25
ii.46-47
iii.51-4 — 25

Lugalbanda in the Mountain Cave
— 23
i.433 — 132

Marduk: The creator of the world
— 16

Myth of King Etana
— 167

Nergal and Ereškigal
— 168

Poem of the Early Rulers
— 168

Poetical Steal of Thutmose III
Epilogue 3-5 — 179

Praise Poem of Šulgi
A i.6 — 178

Praise Poem of Ur-Nammu
I.114-115 — 184

Samsuilina, King of Babylon
i.5 — 185

Sargon, King of Battle
i.18 — 172

Sargon, Lord of the Lies
i.1-4 — 175

Šamaš Hymn
i.2, 9, 17, 27, 58, 101 — 126

Slaying of Labbu, see Lion-Serpent

Song of the Hoe
i.94-106 — 19

Steal of Thutmose III
Prologue 5-11 — 188

Stela of Taimhotep
1-3 — 170

Stela of Treasurer Tjetji
17-20 — 133

Sumerian King List
i.1-2 — 176, 184

Transference of the arts to Unug
B.6-15 — 58

Tukulti-Ninurta Epic
i. (= A obv.) 18-20 — 179
v. (= A rev.) 16-8 — 175

Victory Stele of Narām-Sîn
— 177

Vulture Stele of Eannatum
iv.9-12 — 177

Ziudsura: The Sumerian version of creation and the flood
— 16
i.88-89 — 184

II. Ugarit
Aqhat

	75
CAT 1.17.i.6-8	135
1.17.i.39-40	73
1.17.v.2-33	74
1.17.v.4-5	144
1.17.vi.29	34
1.19.iv.22-25	127, 152

Atonement Ritual

KTU 1.40	136

Baal Cycle

	16, 36, 239
CAT, 1.2.i.13-14	136
1.2.i.18, 34	35
1.2.i.14, 20, 31	134
1.2.iii.19—20	135
1.2.iv. 7-10	36
1.2.iv.11-14	129
1.2.iv.25-27	37
1.3.i.2-4	37
1.3.i.15-17	60
1.3.i.22	134
1.3.ii.40	35
1.3.iii.26-28	35
1.3.iii.32	129
1.3.iii.37-40	37
1.3.iv.32	129
1.3.v.8	60
1.3.v.32-5	171
1.4.i.23-6	129
1.4.iii.12-14	136
1.4.iii.14	133
1.4.iv.43-4	35
1.4.v.3-5	60
1.4.v.6-9	36
1.4.v.46-7	129
1.4.v-vi	129
1.4.vi.53-54	60
1.4.vii.35-39	34
1.4.viii.7	153
1.4.viii.15	129
1.5.ii.21-3	34
KTU 1.5.i.1-8	39
1.5.i.9	129
1.5.i.14-19	38
1.5.v.6-8, 14-17	39
1.5.v.8	129
1.6.i.6-8	35, 40
1.6.i.36	60
1.6.ii.15-23	38
1.6.iii.10-13, 20-21	40
1.6.iii.12-13, 20-21	36, 40

Baal fathers a bull

CAT 1.10.i.3, 4	126f., 133f., 152

Epic of Kirta (Keret)

CAT 1.14.ii.22-4	151
1.15.ii.7, 11	139
1.15.iii.2-4, 13-15	136
1.16.i.6-8	134
1.16.i.6-9	35
1.16.i.22-23	180
1.16.iii.7-8	35, 142

III. Apocrypha and Pseudepigrapha
Aristeas

i.221	198

Baruch

4:8, 10	99

2 Baruch

51:5, 10	115

3 Baruch

4:16	199
11:1-2	152

4 Baruch

9:6	99

Book of Giants

	168

Sirach

8:16	102
24:1-9	94
45:2	146

1 Enoch

	111
6:1-2	113
6:1-7	127
6-11	112, 115
7:1	113
7:1-2	113
9:8-9	113
10:6,12	199
12-16	112, 115
12:2-3	112
20:1-8	112
22:4, 11, 13	199
25:4	199
37-71, 92-105	115
54:1	199
86:1-6	127
91:1	199
98:3	199
98:10	199
99:15	199
103:8	199
104:5	199

2 Enoch

20:1	152

1 Esdras

4:20	

2 Ezra (Gk. Apocalypse of Ezra)

2:29	199
4:37	199
5:23	199
7:11	199
7:97-98	125

Jubilees

4:15, 22	112
5:1	115
7:21	112
10:5	112
11:18-22	

2 Maccabees

1:25	99
5:21	180
9:8	180

3 Maccabees

5:51	156
6:12	99
7:16	99

4 Maccabees

12:12	199

Psalms of Solomon

16:2	156

Sibylline Oracles

2:305-6	199
3:53-4	199
3:743	199
4:186	199
8:104, 231	199
8:401	199

IV. Hellenistic Jewish Literature

Josephus

Antiquitates Judaicae

i.73	114
xii.125	180
xviii.14	153, 156

Contra Apionem

ii.167	99

De Bello Judaico

iii.374-75	156

Philo of Alexandria

De Abrahamo

i.113	79
i.118	79

De agricultura
i.51   95

De confusione linguarum
i.146   95

De Fuga et Inventione
i.112   95
i.137   96

De gigantibus
i.6   114

De migratione Abrahami
i.102-3   96

De mutatuione nominum
i.54   99

De opificio mundi
i.31, 35   96
i.100   100

De posteritate Caini
i.15   100
i.28   100

De sacrificiis Abelis et Caini
i.8   146
i.9-10   146, 147

De specialibus legibus
i.81   95

De Vita Mosis
i.158   146
ii.288-292   147

Legatio ad Gaium
i.6   99

Legum Allegoriarum
i.51   100
ii.2   95, 100
ii.33   100
iii.96   95

Quis rerum divinarum heres sit
i.79   96
i.206   95
i.188   95
i.205   96

Quod deus sit immutabilis
i.52   109
i.54   109
i.55   109
i.57   95, 109

Targum of Psalms
Psalm 82:1, 6   158f.

Targum Onkelos
Genesis 6:1, 2   117f

Targum Pseudo Jonathan
Genesis 32:24, 30   84

Testament Reuben
5:5   199
5:6-7   112

Testament Levi
1:1   199
3:3   199

Testament Zebulun
10:13   199

Testament Naphtali
3:5   112

Testament Gad
7:5   199

Testament of Abraham
A iii.6   99

Testament of Abraham (continued)

11:11	199

Testament of Jacob

5:9	199

The Book of Wisdom (of Solomon)

2:12-20	148
4:7-18	148
5:1-5	148
5:5	66, 142, 148
7:21-28	96
7:22-27	94
7:30-8:1	94
16:13	156

V. Qumran

1QIsa^{a}col. xlii	44
1QapGen 2.1, 16	112
1QIsa^a 45.7	195
1QH 3.16-18	156
1QM 1.10	134
1QM 10.11	136
1QM 12.7	136
1QM 14.16	137
1QM 15.14	136
1QM 18.2	136
4Q37	140, 141
4Q181	134
4Q201 frag. 1, col. 3	113
4Q201 frag. 1, col. 4	113
4Q511	134
4Q511, frag. 35	115
4Q534.1ii+2, 15	112
4QDeut^j	66, 140-2
11Q13	137, 157
11Q13.9	136
11Q13.11	158
CD 2.18	112

VI. Rabbinic Literature

Babylonian Talmud

Avodah Zarah 5a	160
b. Berakoth 11a	90
Sabbath 127.a	69
Sanhedrin i.9	159

Midrash Rabbah

Ex. 32:7	160

VII. Greco-Roman Literature

Apollodorus

Epitome

E1.23	154

Library

ii.4.2-3	39

Aristotle

Ars Poetica

1457b	

Metaphysics

xii.1073a	100
1091b.5	171

Physics

viii.6	100

Politics

i.1252b27	61, 164

Cornelio Celso

De Medicina

i.4	220

Diodorus Siculus

Bibliotheca Historica

iv.9.1	144
iv.10.7	145
iv.38.1-5	146

Index of Ancient Sources

Diogenes Laertius
Lives

viii.21	92

Dio Cassius
Historiae Romanae

xlv.1.2-5	182
xlv.1.4	208
xlv.6.7	147
lvi.41.9	148
lvi.46.2	148

Euripides
Alcesti

4	48
25	154
743	154

Flavius Arrianus
Anabasis Alexandri

vii.30.2-3	144

Herodotus
Historiae

i.32.9	26
i.34.1	26
ii.122.1	154

Hesiod
Catalogue of Women

xxii.25-7	146

Theogony

71	152, 172
180-1	67
240-5	144
371	224
461, 919	150
687	151
820-68	39
881-6	172

Works and Days

122-4	141
249-54	141

Hippocrates
De morbo sacro

i.1-10	221
ii.1-9	221
v.7-8	221
viii.1-28	221

Homer
Hymn 5 to Aphrodite

55	143
165	143
195-8	144

Iliad

i.43-9	191
i.131	143
i.176	181
i.418	144
i.489	143
i.493-5	151
i.528-30	60
i.570	150
ii.98, 445	181
ii.116, 350, 403	64
ii.196	181
ii.410	151
ii.669	172
ii.821	144
iii.16, 27, 30	143
v.373	150
v.646	156
v.663	143
v.375-7	151
vii.23	172
viii.18-22	92
viii.438	133
xvii.672	91
xviii.220-31	191

Iliad (continued)

xix.155	143
xx.68	172
xx.127	143
xxiv.217	143

Odyssey

i.16-7, 88-9	26
i.17-8	25
i.105	72
i.118-143	73
ii.100	91
ii.352	143
iii.208-10	25
iii.416	143
iv.834	156
v.3	133, 174
vii.197	143
ix.269-70	69
xiv.173	143
xiv.55-6	69
xvii.483-487	70

Numenius

Peri tagathou

i.xiii	93

Numenii Fragmenta

2.xix	101

Ovidus Nason

Fasti

vi.505	72
vi.505-35	72

Metamorphoses

xi.221-4	144

Pausanias

Descriptio Graeciae

2.24.4	172

Pindar

Pythian

i.53	143
iv.58	143

Plato

Cratylus

398d	143

Epinomis

985a	99

Laws

xii.941b	88

Phaedo

79a	154

Republic

ii.377e	88
ii.378b	88
ii.379a	89
ii.379b	89
ii.379e	89
ii.380c	90
ii.381c	100
ii.381d	90
ii.382e	91
iii.388a	89
iii.388b-c	89
iii.390c	89
iii.391d-392a	89

Sophist

216a-b	70

Theaetetus

153c-d	92
176a-b	92

Timaeus

39-40	126

Plautus
Amphitryon or Jupiter in Disguise

i.3   84

Plutarch
Numa

4.4   183

Plutarchi Chaeronensis Moralia

iii.10.3 (658E-F)   221

Polybius
Historiae

xii.23.4-5   145
xxxvii.17.4   87

Pseudo Callisthenes
Romance

281   145

Silius Italicus
Punica

vii.170-4   71

Suetonius
Divus Julius

lxxxviii.1-4   147

Divus Augustus

c.4   148

Titus Maccius Plautus
Amphitryon or Jupiter in Disguise i.3   84

Titus Livius
History of Rome

i.16.1-3   148

Vettius Valens
Vettii Valentis 113.10   221

Xenophanes
Curfrag.tlg-0267.11   88

Xenophon
Oeconomicus

x.1   88

Hellenica

v.4.1   27

VIII. Early Christian Literature

Apostle's Creed
206

Athanasian Creed
97

Athenagoras
Legatio pro Christianis xxiv.40   114

Clement of Alexandria
Christ the educator

3.2.14   114

Eusebius
Historia Ecclesiastica

ix.9.1-9   194

De Vita Constantini

i.28   194

INDEX OF ANCIENT SOURCES

Praeparatio Evangelica viii.10
    94

Hospitality of Dymas
3940   71

John of Damascus
Ekdosis tēs Orthodoxou pisteōs

2   98

Justin Martyr
Apologia I

v.48   114
xxi.1–3   227

Apologia II

v.88   114

Lactantius
De Mortibus Persecutorum 44.4–6
    194

Origen of Alexandria
Commentaria in Evangelium secundum Mattaeum

577–578   225

Saint Augustine
Confessionum

iv.16.31   97

De civitate dei

viii.6   101
xv.23   116

Letters

185   201

De Trinitate

v–vii   101
vi.v.7   101
xv.7–8   101

Sermo 52

vi.16   105

Saint Thomas Aquinas
Summa Theologica

I. Q.3   101, 105
I. Q.51.1–3   119
I. Q.51.3, ad.1   119
I. Q.51.3, ad.6   119

Shepherd of Hermas
Similitude

ix.27.2–3   148
ix.27.3   115

Tertullian
Apologeticus pro Christianis

xxi   227

Apologeticus adversus gentis

xxii.2   114

INDEX OF BIBLE CITATIONS

Hebrew Bible

Genesis

1	45, 50	6:1ff.	112, 127
1–3	16, 232, 235	6:1-2	66, 110f., 112, 119f., 142
1:1-3	45	6:1, 4	66, 111
1:1, 3	45	6:1-4	66, 67, 110f., 116, 118, 157
1:2	43, 44, 45, 50	6:2	64, 111, 117
1:3	45	6:2, 4	66, 142
1:3-31	45	6:3, 4	111
1:9	45	6:4	66, 117, 144
1:16	224	6:5-7	68
2	45	6:6	109
2-3	62	6:6-7	109
2:1	45	11:5	152
2:18, 20	11	11:5, 7	81
3	53	11:29	66
3:3	53	11:30	75
3:4	53	12:1-3, 7	79
3:6	111	12:18	64
3:7-13	65	12:19	66
3:8	64, 65	14:17-20	140
3:8-13	63, 65	15:1	161
3:9	63, 65	15:2, 8	76
3:10	65	16:2	66, 75
3:11	65	17:1	64
3:13	53, 65	17:1, 9, 15	79
3:14	53	18	65, 69, 75
3:16	11	18-19	62, 69, 115
4:1, 17, 24	82	18:1	78, 79
4:17, 25, 26	116	18:1-8	78, 83
4:19	66	18:1-16	76, 80
5:3, 28	116	18:2	78
6	114, 121, 234	18:2, 4, 5, 8, 9	77
6:1	117	18:3	76, 77, 79
		18:4-5	78
		18:5-8	119
		18:6, 7	78

Genesis (continued)

18:8	126
18:9	80
18:9-16	80
18:10	78, 80
18:10b-11	77
18:10-15	80
18:12-13	80
18:12-15	77
18:13	80
18:13-14	80
18:16	78, 80
18:17-20	81
18:17-21	80
18:17-19:25	81
18:17-33	81
18:20-21	65
18:21-22	81
18:22	126
18:23-32	81
18:23-33	80
18:27, 31	76
18:33	81
19:1-25	81
19:1	81
19:1-3	83, 119
19:2	77
19:5	83
19:6-8	83
19:8	82
19:10	83
19:12	83
19:12-14	83
19:15-17	83
19:18	77
19:24	152
19:24, 25	83
21:33	98
24:3	170
28:13	76
30:3	66
32:22-31	83
32:22-23, 31	84
32:24	84
32:24-29	62
32:25	84
32:25, 26	83
32:26	84
32:27-28	85
32:28	85
32:31	85
38:8	66

Exodus

2:11, 13	220
3:2	59, 78
3:4-9	59
3:5	61
3:7	59
3:8	59, 81
4:22	116
4:23	116
4:24-26	85
7:1	146
9:23, 28, 29, 44, 34	48
12:12	141f., 35
14:2, 9	
14:4, 5	
14:15-25	122, 190
15:3	174
15:4-5	194
15:4-10, 15, 16	174
15:6-7	174
15:8	174
15:10	174
15:11	137, 142, 174
15:12	153, 174
16:10	59
18:11	142
19:11	94
19:22	101
19:24	101
20:3	142
20:22	152
21:19	220
24:9-11	60
24:11	60
24:16	117
24:33-34	62
31:18	103
32	102
32:1-8	103
32:7-14	102f.
32:7	160
32:8	103
32:9	103

INDEX OF BIBLE CITATIONS 291

32:10	104	33:2-3	29
32:11	104	33:26	36, 41
32:11-12		33:26-28	42
32:12	104	33:28	41
32:13	104	34:5	146
32:20	160	34:6	146
32:25-29	104		
32:30-35	104	*Joshua*	
33:2	160		
33:7-11	78	5:13	61
33:11	106	5:13-15	61, 122
34:14	142	5:14	61
		5:15	61
Leviticus		6:2	61
		6:2-5	61
9:23	59	10:10	190
25:8-55	157	10:11	152, 190
		10:12	127
Numbers		10:13	214
		11:6	190
12:8	106	14:6	75
14:10	78		
16:42	59	*Judges*	
21:34	185		
22:22-24	53	5:4-5	29
23:19	66, 68	5:8	127
24:24	48	9:8-15	8
33:7	35	9:13	60
		13:1-25	75
Deuteronomy		13:2	75
		13:3	29, 75
4:19	126, 140	13:3-5	75
5:31	146	13:3, 9, 13, 15-18, 20	75
7:24	185	13:3-21	29
14:1	116	13:3-5	75
20:13	185	13:6	62
25:2-3	220	13:6-7	75
26:15	152	13:6,10	75
29:29	140	13:8	75
31:15	59	13:8, 11	75
32:5, 20	116	13:10	76
32:7	140	13:11	76
32:7-9	140	13:12-14	76
32:7-14	140	13:14-14	
32:8	66, 141f.	13:15	76
32:8-9	140f., 160	13:16	76
32:9	141	13:19-20	29
32:10-12	140	13:20	76
32:13-14	140	16:1	66
33:1	75		

1 Samuel

2:27	75
3:10	76
7:10	190
7:11	190
9:6, 10	75
12:17	48
15:10	161
21:1-8	123
26:19	66

2 Samuel

5:2	165
5:24	63
7:4	161
7:14	66, 180
11:2	111
22:12	151
22:13	42
24:11	161

1 Kings

8:27	62
12	102
12:22	75, 161
12:28	103
13:1, 4-8, 11, 12, 14	75
13:20	161
14:6	63
16:1	161
17:2, 8	161
18:1	161
19:9	161
20:35	66
20:37	220
21:18-24	6
22	6
22:5-6	6
22:6, 10-12	
22:19	7, 126, 130
22:19-22	6, 18, 126
22:20	126
22:38	6

2 Kings

2:3, 5, 15	66
4:1, 38	66
4:8-17	78
6:32	63
14:9	8
15:5	39
19:35	191
20:4	161

1 Chronicles

9:30	66
22:11	180
26:32	161
28:6	180

2 Chronicles

26:21	39
30:27	152
32:15	142

Ezra

1:2	170
4:1	67

Nehemiah

3:8	66
9:6	126
9:17	68
9:17-18	103
12:23	67

Job

1:1-2:10	16
1:6	66, 133, 136, 142
1:6-12	7, 18
2:1	66, 133, 136, 142
2:1-6	7
3:8	43
4:18	129
5:1	137, 142
7:9-10	155
7:11-12	43
7:12	37
9:8	47
9:5-13	45
10:8-13	45
10:21	155
11:10	25
12:13-25	45

15:15	137, 142	29	40
16:22	155	29:1	66, 133, 137, 142
25:1-6	45	29:1-2	40
25:5-14	45	29:1-11	41
25:6	66	29:3-5, 7-9	40
26:1	45	29:3, 10	40
26:5-14	45	32:9[LXX]	200
26:10-13	46	33:5	23
26:12	44	33:7	45
30:26	90	44:20	142
33:12	99	45:2-6	165
34:17	99	45:3	165
36:15	11	45:3-4	165
37:3	36	45:6	181
38	46	46:7	36
38:6-7	127	47:3, 8	171
38:7	66, 127, 133, 142	47:8	6
38:8	46	48:3	171
38:8-11	46	49:15	38
38:11	46, 48	55:15	154
38:17	156	58:5	43
40:23	46	58:11	23
		60:12	185
Psalms		63:9	153
		65:7	47
2	189	68:34	36
2:1-2, 7, 9	197	72	175
2:7	179f.	72:8-11	175
2:8-9	202	74	10, 46
2:8-12	189	74:4-8	47
2:9	202	74:9	47
5:3	171	74:12	36, 47
7:7	158	74:12-14	47
7:7-9	158	74:13-14	36, 47
9:8	23	74:14	37, 48
9:13	156	74:15-17	47
10:16	6, 171	76:3	190
11:4	66, 152, 171	76:5	190
14:2	66	76:6	190
18	36	76:8	25
18:2	7	77:16	48
18:10	81	77:16-18	48
18:10-14	42	77:18	48
18:11	36	77:34[LXX]	200
18:13	41	78:23, 24	152
18:14	36, 48	78:25	142
21:1	142	78:34	200
23:4	5	78:70-72	165
24:8	174		

Psalms (continued)

80:17	66
81:14	185
82	11, 18, 30, 110, 138f., 141f., 157f.
82:1	18, 139, 142, 158f.
82:1-2	158
82:1, 6	131, 142, 158
82:2	158
82:2-7	140
82:5, 8	159
82:6	142, 159, 160, 181
82:6-7	159
82:8	159
83:15	33
86:8	142
86:13	154
88:6	155
88:12	155
89	137
89:5	142
89: 5, 7	135, 138
89:5-8	18, 137
89:6	66, 138, 142
89:6, 7	171
89:7	133, 142, 238
89:8	131
89:8-9	47
89:23	175, 185
89:26, 27	180
90:2	99
91:13	31
93	47
95:3	129, 131, 171
93:4	47
96:5	142
97:7	171
103:6	23
103:8-9	68
103:19	171
103:19-22	163
103:20	130, 142
103:21	7, 126
104:3	44
104:7	48
104:26	47
104:33	34
106:8-9	47
107:5, 9	38
110	189, 198
110:1	190, 197
110:1-6	189f.
110:2	190
110:5	185, 190
110:6	190, 202
110:7	189
118:15	3
119:67, 71	11
121:6	220
135:5	171
135:6	43
138:1	142
139:7-12	62
141:7	38
144	189
144:1, 2, 5-8	189
144:5	81
144:6	48
144:10	189
145:9	163
146:7	23
148:1-3	127
148:7	43

Proverbs

1:12	38
8:1-36	96
8:22-31	94
8:27	43
9:18	154
22:24-25	102
27:20	38
29:22	102

Ecclesiastes

7:14	25

Song of Solomon

5:7	220
16:2	156

Isaiah

1:2, 4	116
1:10	161
1:14	101

5:14	38
5:20	90
6:1	6, 60, 152, 171
6:1-4	78, 130
6:1-5	62
8:9	42
13:21	48
14:9	38, 154
14:13	134
14:13, 14	134
14:14	134
19:1	36, 44
23:10	42
23:13	48
24:19	47
24:21	126, 142
26:4	99
27:1	43
28:15, 18	38
29:6	33
29:8	38
30:1, 9	116
30:6	31
30:30	33
33:21	48
34:1-3	187
34:14	48
38:10	156
40:28	99
42:14	101
43:10-11	131
44:6	131
44:6, 8	131
44:15, 17	126
45:1-7	195f.
45:5-7, 14, 18, 21	131
45:7	25, 90
45:21	131
46:1	32
46:9	131
51:9-10	44
51:10	43
52:7	157
54:15	25
61:1	157
63:6	102
63:15	152
64:1-2	81
66:1	62
66:15	34

Jeremiah

1:2	161
2:29	102
8:4-5	102
9:20	38
10:13	36
18:8-10	68
20:7	7
23:18, 22	6
23:19	34
23:23-24	62
26:3	68
37:15	220
50:2	32
51:44	32

Lamentations

3:37-39	25

Ezekiel

1:26	171
1:26-28	62
14:9	7
30:9	48
31:14	153
32:2	31
32:2-8	31
32:4-6	31
32:6	31

Daniel

2:18, 19	170
4:8	135
4:8, 9, 18	18, 142
4:13, 23	112
4:14[11]	
4:17	112, 142
5:11	18, 135, 142
7	37
7:9	60
7:13, 22	60
7:14, 26	198
7:18	135
7:27	198

Daniel (continued)

8:11	61
8:13	137
9:14	163
10:13, 20–21	140
11:12	136
11:30	48
11:36	137
11:37	142
12:1	140

Hosea

1:1	161
6:1	220
11:1–2	107
11:1	116
11:12	136, 142
12:4	84
13:14	38

Joel

1:1	161
2:11	42

Amos

3:5–6	25
5:19	31
5:24	212
7:7	76
7:14	66
9:1	76

Jonah

1:1	161
3:9, 10	68
4:2	68

Micah

1:1	161

Nahum

1:1, 14	188
1:2	102, 188
1:2–6	188
1:3, 5, 6	188
1:3–6	189
1:4	188
1:10–13	188

Habakkuk

1:11	142
2:5	38
3:3, 7	29
3:6, 9, 12	44
3:8–9, 15	37
3:8, 11	48
3:8, 15	44
3:9, 11	44
3:10	44

Zephaniah

1:1	161
1:17	187
3:17	101

Haggai

1:1	161

Zechariah

1:1	161
1:7–17	60
1:8, 10	61
1:8–11	61
1:9	61
1:11, 12	61
3:1–5	61
3:4, 9	130
5:6	130
5:8	130
5:9	130
5:11	130
6:1–7	34
9:14	48
14:5	136, 142

Malachi

2:17	101

Christian Bible

Matthew

1:18, 20	183
1:23	183

INDEX OF BIBLE CITATIONS

2:13-15	70
3:12	199
3:17	152, 179
5:3, 19-20	197
5:16, 45	152
5:12	156
5:34	152
6:8, 26, 32	206
6:9	152, 206
6:10	205
7:11	152, 206
10:15	199
10:28	199
11:22, 24	199
11:23	156
11:28	212
12:36	199
13:24-30, 49-50	199
13:42, 50	199, 212
16:18	156
17:5	179
17:14-21	219
17:15	10, 122, 222, 224
17:15-16	222
17:17	222
17:18	223, 224
17:19-21	226
22:13	199
22:30	115, 118f.
23:22	152
24:51	199
25:31-46	199
25:41	199
25:46	199
27:24	14

Mark

2:25-26	123
2:26	123
9:1-8	145
9:14-29	219
9:17b-18a	222
9:17, 25	224
9:19	222, 226
9:19-24	226
9:20	222, 225f.
9:21-24	223
9:22	226
9:24	226
9:25	224f.
9:25-27	223
10:23-25	197
12:25	119
12:34	197
14:22	62
16:5	115

Luke

1:27, 32	182
1:31-33	182
1:33-35	
1:34	182
1:35	182f.
8:25	180
9:37-43	219
9:38b-40	222
9:39	224
9:39, 42	224
9:41	222
9:42a	222
9:42b	223
14:23	201
16:23, 26	156
23:43	156

John

1:1-10	96, 109, 149
1:14	183
1:18	60, 96
1:49	182
3:16	199
3:18	199, 212
10:33-36	161
10:33	161
10:34	161
10:34-36	161
10:35	110, 157, 161
11:27	182
20:31	182

Acts

2:24	54
2:34-35	197
4:25-26	197
9:3-18	201

Acts (continued)

13:33	197
14:11	61, 69
17:23	99
28:1	69

Romans

1:20	99
6:9	54
6:23	232
8:14–17	206
13:5	201
14:17	197
16:26	98

1 Corinthians

6:13	198
13:11	198
15:24	197
15:24–25	197
15:25	197f.
15:26	54, 198
15:55	54

2 Corinthians

5:1	156
12:2	152

Ephesians

1:20–22	197
1:20–23	197

Philippians

2:5–8	204
2:9	203
2:9–11	203f.
2:9, 10	212
2:10	149, 203
2:10–11	204

Colossians

1–2	234
1:5	156
1:15	60, 99
1:15–18	97
1:20	234

3:1	197

2 Thessalonians

1:7–8	202
2:8	198

1 Timothy

1:17	60, 99
3:2	69
6:16	105

Hebrews

1:5	197
1:13	197
4:14	152, 205
5:5	197
8:1	152, 205
8:2	152
9:1	152
9:11	152
9:23	152
9:24	153
10:12–13	197
11:27	99
13:2	69, 76

1 Peter

1:4	156
4:9	69

1 John

4:20	60

Jude

14	14

Revelation

1:18	156
1:20	126
2:26–27	197
6:1–8	198
11:13	152, 170
11:19	152
12:5	197
13:1–10	37
16:11	152

19:13	198	19:18	199
19:15	197	22:16	145
19:15-16	198		

INDEX OF AUTHORS

Aalders, G. C.,, 116
Abegg, M., 44, 90, 140
Ackerman, J.S., 160
Adams, J., 208
Ahlström, G.,, 29
Akin, D.L.,, 120
Albrektson, B.,, 19, 184
Albright, W.F., 29, 112
Allison, D., 184,
Alster, B.,, 8
Alter, R.,, 30, 84, 112
Andersen, B. R., 219f.
Andersen, F.I., 43, 103, 152
Anderson, A.A., 159
Annus-Lenzi, 24, 154, 178
Appleton-Marson, 225
Aquinas, T.,, 97, 101, 105, 119
Arnold, B.T.,, 112
Ascalone, E.,, 177f.
Attridge, H.W.,, 69

Baldwin, J.G. 76
Barlett, J.R., 93
Barr, J., 19
Barrett, C.K., 161
Bass, D.B., 203
Bavinck, H., 59, 106f,
Bekker, I., 144-6,
Bennett, W.H., 112
Berchman, R.M., 97
Berkhof, L., 120, 204
Bernardakis, G.N., 221
Bertocci, P.A., 57
Bickerman, E.J., 93
Biggs, R.D., 24

Bilby, M.G., 71
Bjorklung, R., 225
Black, J.A., 19, 22, 24, 49, 70, 132, 155, 170
Black, Max, 2
Blenkinsopp, J,., 76, 79, 140
Boff, L., 212
Bottéro, J., 68, 87, 129, 163, 166
Bottéro-Kramer, 9, 32, 150,
Bouwsma, W.J., 214
Bovon. F., 183
Bratt, J. D., 216
Brennan, John, 13
Brett, M.G., 112
Brown, R.E., 157
Brownson, C.L., 27
Broyles, C.C., 159
Brueggemann, W., 79, 84, 111f.,
Bultmann, R., 96, 149, 161
Burkert, W., 28
Burnet, J., 143
Bury, R.G., 88, 96, 126
Butler, T.C., 60
Büttner-Wobst, 87, 145
Buxton, R., 2, 28

Calame, C., 86
Caldwell, A.R., 122
Calvin, J., 105, 109f., 116, 201f., 214
Carson, D.A., 161
Cary, E., 147f., 182
Cary, H.,, 26
Casanova, H., 182f.
Cassuto, U., 63, 65, 112
Castro, A., 53

INDEX OF AUTHORS

Chadwick, H., 95, 97,
Charlesworth, J.H., 94,
Chavalas, M.W., 164, 168
Chiera, E., 131
Childs, B.S., 16, 67
Christensen, D., 141
Ciampa-Rosner, 198,
Civil, M., 174, 184
Clayton, P., 56f.
Clifford, R.J., 138, 159
Clines, D. J. A., 43, 45, 47
Cobb, J.B., 108
Cohen, A., 90
Cohen, L., 1
Cohn-Wendland, 95
Colli-Montinari, 162
Collins, J.J., 157
Collins-Sterling, 93
Colson-Whitaker, 79, 95f., 99f., 114, 146,
Conzelmann, H., 198
Cook, J.G., 93
Cooke, G.A., 135
Cooper, B.Z., 108
Cooper, J.S., 47, 70, 132, 177, 185
Cooper-Pope, 35,
Copleston, F., 86
Corney, R.W., 123
Coulmas, F., 166
Craig, W.L., 123
Craigie, P.C., 36
Crawford, S.W., 141
Creed, J.M., 183
Cross, F.M., 60, 140

Dahood, M., 137f., 159, 166, 220
Dalley, S., 32, 150, 154f., 168
Danby, H., 159
Davidson, A.B., 103, 106, 190
Davidson, D., 3
Davies, G.H., 19
Davies-Allison, 193
De Claissé-Walford, 138
Delitzsch, F., 63, 83, 159
Delling, G., 198
Denzinger, E., 62, 231, 235
Dever, W., 29
Dibelius-Conzelmann, 105

Dillon, J.M., 91, 93
Dodd, C.H., 96
Dods, M., 116
Dombart, B., 101, 116
Donaldson, J., 114, 194, 227, 247
Dozeman, T.B., 102
Dozier, O'Neal, 15
Driver, G.R., 166
Driver, S. R., 44, 63, 106, 112
Driver-Gibson, 35f., 39f., 127, 135f., 151-3
Duff, J.D., 71
Dundes, A., 16
Dunn, J.D.G., 96
Dupont-Sommer, A., 134

Edmonds, J.M., 88
Eichrodt, W., 93, 159
Eissfeldt, O., 17, 19, 140
Eliade, M., 1, 16, 49f.
Emlyn-Jones-Preddy, 88
Engberg-Pedersen, T., 97
Enns, P., 232
Erickson, M.J., 120
Etheridge, J.W., 84, 118
Evelyn-White, 143

Fee, G. D., 198
Feldman, L., 93
Festinger, L.,, 124
Finkel-Geller, 219
Finkelstein-Silberman, 29
Fitzmyer, J.A., 157, 182, 198
Foster, B.O., 148
Foster, B.R., 8f., 23f., 28, 31f., 132, 149f., 155, 167, 168, 172, 175f., 178f., 185f.
Fowler, H.N., 70, 92
Fox, E.,, 141
Fox, R., 199
Frankfort, H., 23, 57, 225
Frayne, D.R., 165, 178
Frazer, J.G., 39, 72, 154
Freely, J.,, 86
Freeman, C., 201
Fretheim, T.,, 59, 63, 79, 102, 112
Freud, S.,, 55, 128
Frye, N., 2

INDEX OF AUTHORS

Gagné, R.,, 92
García, F.,, 113
García-Tigchelaar, 136, 158
Gaster, M.,, 10
Gaster, Th.H., 41f., 140
Gaylord, H.E., 152
Geertz, C., 51
Geller, M.J., 219
George, A.R., 9, 23, 49, 67, 132, 153, 168, 179
George-Al-Rawi, 24
Gerstenberger, E.S., 140
Gibbs, R.,, 2
Gildersleeve, B.L., 114,
Glassner, J-J., 166
Godley, A.D., 154, 196
Goetze-Levy, 168
Goldingay, J, 112, 140, 159
Goodenough, E.R., 93
Grabbe, L., 93
Graf, F., 28
Graham, F., 210
Graham, D.W., 86
Green, A.R.W., 34, 36, 44
Green, D.J., 135
Green, W.H., 116
Greenstein, E.L., 35, 134, 136, 142, 151
Gregory, R.L., 55
Grudem, W.A., 120, 123
Gruen, E.S., 93
Gunkel, H., 43, 63-5, 76, 80, 84, 112, 140
Guthrie, K.S., 93, 101
Guthrie, W.K.C., 86

Haag, H.,, 111
Habel, N.C., 43, 45f.
Hallo, W.W., 8, 32
Hamilton, V.P., 76, 79
Hamori, E., 79
Harris, E.,, 96
Hartley, J.E., 76
Hartshorne, C., 108
Hays-Mandell, 93
Heidel, A., 31f.
Heimpel, W., 16, 150
Hendriksen, W.,, 123

Hengel, M.,, 93
Heppe, H., 59
Hess, R.S.,, 29
Hicks, R.D., 92
Hilberg, R., 14
Hitchens, C.,, 54
Horowitz, W.,, 32
Horowitz-Lambert, 24
Horowitz-Oshima, 168
Horst, F., 135f.
Hossfeld-Zenger, 48, 159
Hruša, I., 87
Hume, D., 50-3, 105

Ihm, M.,, 147f., 182

Jackson, A.V., 157
Jacobsen, Th., 16, 19-21, 31-3, 126, 131f., 155, 165, 170, 174, 176f., 184f.
Jaeger, W.,, 91
Jones, W.H.S., 221
Jung, C.G., 2
Jüngel, E., 108

Katz, D., 132, 185
Keil, C.F., 116
Kilmer, A.D., 168
Kingsley, P., 91
Kirk, G.S., 1, 27, 86
Kittay, E.F., 2
Klijn, A.F.J., 115
Kline, M. G., 118
Knafl, A.K., 59, 63
Köneke, V., 124
Kornaros-Lakamaridēs, 98
Köstenberger, A.J.,
Kövecses, Z., 2-5
Kraemer, G., 225
Kramer, S.N., 19, 21f., 70, 132, 167
Kramer-Maier, 58
Kraus, J-H., 47f., 159, 163, 166, 220
Kristeller, P.O., 92
Kroll, W., 221
Kruse, C.G., 161
Kuhrt, A., 21, 164, 177f., 196
Kunda, Z., 124
Kuyper, A.,, 215f.

Lake, K., 70
Lakoff, G.,, 4f., 12
Lakoff-Johnson, 2-4, 12
Lamb, W.R.M., 99
Lambert, W. G., 1, 8, 24, 31-4, 77, 87, 126, 132, 150, 154f., 168, 178
Lambert-Millard, 9, 27
Lamberton, R., 93
Lange-Meyers, 157
Langford, J.J., 214
Lapinkivi, P., 155
Lawson-McCauley, 55, 58
Leick, G., 164
Lemche, N.P., 29
Lenz, J.R., 91
Levine, L., 93
Levi-Strauss, C., 128
Lewis, C.S., 14
Lewis, Th., 31, 127
Lichtheim, M., 133, 150, 170, 179, 188
Lipiński, E., 43
Liverani, M., 29
Lohse, E., 134, 156
Long, A.A., 92f.
Longman, T., 112, 115, 159
Long-Sedley, 93
Lundbom, J.R., 140f.
Luther, M., 116, 214

Mack-Fisher, L.R., 168
Maisels, C.K., 164
Malina-Rohgbaugh, 161
Malinowski, B., 51, 55
March, F.A., 114
Marchant, E.C., 88
Martin, D.B., 157
Martin, M., 213
Mathews, K., 116
Mayes, A.D.H., 141
Mays, J. L., 141, 159
McCann, J.C., 159
McCarter Jr., P. K., 190
McConville, J.G., 141
McKenzie, J., 19
Meeter, H. H., 202
Mellaart, J., 164
Meyer, A.W., 161
Michalowski, P., 132, 166

Migne, J.P., 94, 97, 105, 114, 194f., 225, 227
Miller, P.D., 129, 130, 131
Moltmann, J.,, 108, 204f., 207, 212
Moran, W.L., 24, 167
Moreland-Craig, 215
Morris, B.,, 55
Morris, T.V., 108
Most, G.W., 39, 67, 141, 144, 146, 172
Moule, C.F.D., 160, 182
Mowinckel, S., 159
Murphy, F.J., 157
Murray, A.T., 25, 60, 70, 72, 91, 133, 156, 172, 174,

Nelson, R.D., 141
Nelson-Pallmeyer, 104
Neusner, J., 63
Newsome, J.D., 93
Nickelsburg, G.W.E., 148, 157
Nickelsburg-VanderKam, 127
Niditch, S., 64, 75
Niese, B., 114
Nissen, H.J., 164
Nissinen, M.,, 174, 187
Noebel-Edwards, 215
Noth, M.,, 180

O'Day, G.R., 161
O'Donnel, J.J., 200
O'Donnell, S.,, 14
O'Grady, P.,, 86
O'Meara, D., 91
Oates-Oates, 164
Oden, R.A., 19
Oesterley, W.O.E., 137, 139
Orr, J., 214f.
Ortony, A., 2
Oshima, T.,, 46
Otto, R., 105

Pakkala, J., 141
Pàmias, J., 86
Pannenberg, W., 108
Parker, S.B., 34, 73f., 126f., 133, 135, 144, 152
Parpola, S., 67
Patrick, J., 225

INDEX OF AUTHORS

Peacocke, A., 232
Pelikan, J., 117, 214
Perrin, B., 183
Perry, M., 86
Pettinato, G., 27, 133,
Pfeiffer, R.H., 24, 61
Piaget, J., 55
Piepkorn, A.C., 24, 186
Pitard, W.T., 135, 166
Plantinga, R., 108,
Plummer, A., 161
Pope, M.H., 43, 45
Postgate, J.N., 131, 176
Preuss, J., 220
Priorechi, P., 220
Provan, I., 112

Rackham, H., 61, 164
Radau, H., 177
Rasimus, T., 97
Renger, J., 27
Reno, R.R., 116
Richards, E., 210
Richards, I.A., 2
Ricoeur, P., 2, 10, 226
Riley, G.J., 157
Riley, H.T., 84
Roberts, J.J.M., 44, 102, 134
Roberts-Donaldson, 194, 227
Robertson, P., 11
Robertson, R., 2
Rodkinson, M.L., 69, 159
Roos, A.G., 144
Ross, A., 118f.
Roth, M.T., 23, 169, 178
Routledge, R.,, 112
Roux, G., 164
Rowley, H.H., 43, 45
Rubinstein, M., 14
Ruiz, D., 114
Runia, D.T., 95, 97
Ryan, J.K., 97

Sailhamer, J.H., 76, 116
Sandys, J., 143
Sarna, N., 82, 112
Sayce, A.H.,, 166

Schaff, P., 59, 97, 98, 108, 201, 202, 218, 232
Schleiermacher, F., 105
Schmandt-Besserat, D., 166
Schmidt, B.B., 180
Schmidt, P.O., 14
Schnackenburg, R., 161
Schökel-Carniti, 137, 140, 159
Schökel-Sicre, 43, 45f., 136
Schubart, J.H.C., 172
Schürer, E., 93
Scott, E.F., 199
Scurlock-Andersen, 219f.
Sedley, D.N., 91
Seland, T., 97
Sennet, J.F., 59
Seybold, K., 47
Shaked, S., 87
Siegert, F., 92
Skinner, J., 63, 65, 77, 112
Smith, B.D.,, 108
Smith, D.L., 15
Smith, H.P., 190
Smith, J.K.H.,, 233-5
Smith, M.S., 16, 19, 30, 35-7, 39f., 44, 59f., 62, 129, 133-6, 140, 171,
Smith, N., 230f.
Smith-Pitard, 135
Snell, D.C., 164
Soggin, A., 29
Sommer, B.D., 59, 62
Sommerfeld, W., 32
Speiser, E.A., 32, 64f., 82, 112
Spencer, H., 58
Spiro, M.E., 58
Spong, J.S., 206
Stec, D.M., 158
Stein, R.H., 121
Steinkeller, P., 176
Stol, M., 177, 219

Talon, P., 32
Tanner, B.L., 47, 138, 159
Tate, M.E., 47f., 140, 159
Taylor, J.G., 127
Taylor, M., 196
Tcherikover, V., 93
Temkin, O., 220

Terrien, M.E., 138
Thiessen, G., 123
Thiselton, A.C., 198
Thompson, S., 28
Thompson, T.L., 19
Tigchelaar, E., 136
Tillich, P., 105
Tomasino, A.J., 97
Towner, P.H., 105
Towner, W.S., 79, 112
Tredennick, H., 100, 171
Tsedaka, B., 77
Turretin, F., 120

Unamuno, M., 50

Van de Mieroop, M.,, 164
Van der Toorn, K., 168
Van Seters, J., 27-30
VanderKam-Adler, 97
Vangemeren, W.A.,
Vanstiphout, H.L.J., 8, 150
Vermes, G., 113, 115, 158
von Rad, G., 19, 76, 112, 141, 180
Von Wahlde, U.C., 161

Waltke, B.K., 76, 119f.,
Walton, J.H., 79, 117
Wasserman, N., 467
Watts, F., 55
Watts, J.D.W., 134

Weiser, A.., 17, 19, 159
Wenham, G.J., 65, 112, 121
Werblowsky, R.J., 57f.
Westen, D., 124
Westenholz, A., 164
Westenholz, J.G., 172, 184
Westermann, C., 64, 77f., 84, 112
Whitacre, R.A., 161
Whitehead, A.N., 108
Wierenga, E.R., 108
Wills, G., 97
Winter, S. L., 3-5
Wintermute, O.S., 114
Wise, M., 113, 115, 134, 156, 168
Wiseman, D.J., 24
Wöhrle, G., 86
Wolohojian, A.M., 145
Wolpert, L., 54
Wolterstoff, N., 59
Wood, S.P., 114
Woodham, H.A., 227
Work, T., 141
Wright, G., 18
Wyatt, N., 19, 30, 35f., 38, 136, 142, 153, 180

Xeravits, G. G

Zimmermann-Markantonatos, 91
Zobel, H-J., 141

INDEX OF SUBJECTS

Abraham, 72, 75-81, 83, 85, 103, 122, 126, 233
Abullu, 150
Adad
   Arrow/lightning, 57
   Fighting for his king, 186
   Humanized, 57
   Storm-god, 34
Akkadian
   Assyrian writing, 167
   Akkadûm, 167
   Babylonian writing, 167
   Classical period, 167
   Debates and fables, 8
   Empire, 173
   International influence, 167
   Literature, 167f.
Amen-Re
   Begets Thutmose III, 179
   Confers the king universal power, 188
   King of the gods, 170
   Lord of thrones, 170
Anat
   Defeats and kills Mot, 37, 40
   Saves Baal, 40
Ancient Near East
   Agriculture, 164
   Definition, 6
   Empires, 173
   Epilepsy, 219f.
   Important gods, 8, 34, 129, 174
   Humanized gods, 59f., 63, 66f., 79
   International language, 167

   Region sharing the same mythical world, 121
   Sacred myths, 92
   Theology, 19, 87, 140, 153, 163, 167f.
Angel(s)
   angelos, 129
   Assign to the nations, 93, 141
   Attacks Moses, 85
   Bodies, 119
   Death, 160
   Drink and eat, 79, 119
   Fallen, 114, 116, 118f.,
   Feminine, 130
   Fights with Jacob, 84
   Foreign visitors, 69, 78
   Get marry, 67, 113-5, 119
   Gods, 18, 129, 134, 142
   Hierarchies, 128ff.
   Human becoming, 92
   Host of heaven, 127
   Logos, 95
   Lust, 113f.
   malʾak, 129
   Mediators, 93
   People becoming, 70, 92
   Possessing kings, 118f., 120
   Procreating, 114-6, 120, 128
   Psalm 82, 157f.
   Seven stars, 127
   Sexual relations, 112-9
   Sin, 113ff., 131
   Sons of god, 112
   Spiritual, 79, 115, 118-20
   Tormented, 202

Angel(s) *(continued)*
  Watchmen, 112
  Visits Mary, 182
  Yahve's council, 18, 134
Anthropomorphism (theistic)
  As problem, 85ff., 92
  Based on our bodily experience, 55f.
  Beard, 60
  Cognitive medium/model, 55
  Conceptual metaphor, 58
  Etymology, 52
  Eyebrows, 60
  Fundamental metaphor of Theism, 17f., 56, 122, 162
  Garments, 23, 57, 60,
  General definition, 52
  Glyptic art, 23, 57, 84
  Gods drink and eat, 60, 72, 75, 79, 119, 122, 135
  Gods have human emotions, 68f., 106
  Gods idealized human beings, 58, 87, 90, 101, 106
  Gods procreate, 66f.
  Gods with human bodies, 59ff., 92, 122
  Hair, 60
  Humanity of god, 58
  Humanizing of nature, 128
  Incarnation, 63, 108
  King metaphor, 162
  Materialization of, 15, 62f., 79
  Monarchy, 163, 169, 183
  More than a figure of speech, 63
  Not equal to monotheism, 57
  Not infantile, 55
  Only way to talk about god, 107
  Procreation, 67
  Source domain, 58
  Target domain, 58
  Theistic definition, 56f.
  Unavoidable for theism, 106f., 125
  Universal experience, 52ff.
Anthropopathism, 52
Anu/An
  Head of the pantheon, 169
  King of heaven, 169

Apollo
  Arrows, 122, 191
  Attacks an army, 191
  Engendered Augustus, 181f.
  Giver of laws, 208
  Lord, 172
  Sends Hercules to heaven, 145f.
arṣ, see Earth
  Baal Lord of 35
  Underworld, 39, 153
Assembly/council
  Divine, 35, 130-3, 139, 168
  El, 18, 139, 142, 158
  God, 159
  Gods, 8, 18, 132f., 138
  Holy ones, 18, 135, 158
  Human, , 31f.
  Judgment, 132
  Meeting, 6, 133, 150
  Most high, 94
  Puḫru, 131f.
  Sons of El, 133, 136
  Stars, 126f., 133f., 139
Aššur
  Directs the universe, 174
  Fights for the king, 185f.
  Rains fire, 187
  Warrior-god, 186f.
Athena
  Chariot, 151
  Fire, 191
  Horses, 151
  Humanized, 26
  Spear, 151
  Visit, 26, 72
  Warrior-goddess, 151, 191
Baal
  Assistants, 129
  Clouds of, 36
  Death, 39f.
  Descends to the underworld, 35
  Fertility god, 35f., 40, 57, 142
  Humanized, 57
  Important god, 34
  King, 35, 170f.
  Lightning, 35f.
  Lord, 34, 36, 40
  Master, 34

INDEX OF SUBJECTS 309

Mighty, 35
Mountain, 134
Most high, 35
Offspring of El, 34
Rain, 35-6, 39f., 142
Resurrection, 40
Rider/charioteer of the clouds, 35-7
Saphon, 35
Storm-god, 34f.
Thunder, 35-6, 39
Titles, 34f.
Voice, 36
Vs Mot, 8, 37ff.
Vs Yamm, 8, 16, 31, 33, 34ff.
Warrior-god, 35, 57
Weather-god, 8, 35
Chaos, *see* cosmos
Transformed, 49
Christian/Platonic god
  Almighty, 59, 98, 101
  Creator, 98, 109, 231
  Does not repent, 109f.
  Eternal, 59, 98-101, 108,
  Formless, 100
  Idealized human being, 101, 106
  Immutable, xix, 59, 66, 90, 98f., 101, 106
  Impassible, 98f., 108, 236
  Incomprehensible, xix, 59, 98f., 105f., 236
  Indivisible, 98, 100
  Infinite, 59, 98, 106f.
  Love, 199
  No emotions, 109
  No magnitude, 100
  No passions whatsoever, 109
  No rage, 109
  Not controlled by wrath, 109
  Not humanized, xix, 87, 90
  No physical body, 16, 60, 78f., 84, 97-9, 100f., 106f., 109, 119
  Omnipotent, 97, 109
  Omniscient, 108, 109
  One, 17, 19, 30, 51
  Perfect, 90, 98, 106, 108
  Problems with, 105, 108
  Simple, 59, 90f., 98-101, 105f., 108,
  Spiritual, 59, 78, 98, 106

Transcendent, 90, 92f., 95-7, 104, 106, 108-10
Unchangeable, 98-101, 236,
Uncreated, 95, 98-100
Unmoved mover, 59, 100
Cosmos
  logos as creator, 95-7, 109
  Structure, 49
  Threated, 47, 50, 231
  Vs chaos, 10, 49, 51
  Views, 226
Creation
  Babylon, 32, 150
  By acts of separation, 49f.
  By Enlil, 19
  By the gods, 24
  By Yahve, 44-7, 50
  Failed, 68, 85
  God, 126
  Good, 233, 235
  Humankind, 231
  Marduk, 34
  Myths, 16
  Opposed to chaos, 47, 49
  Theomachia, 47
  World, 16, 34, 49, 95, 141, 233
Cuneiform
  Akkadian, 167
  Development, 166
  First writing system, 166
  Theological influence, 167
Death
  Angel of, 160
  Anthropomorphism, 8, 53-5, 225
  Baal, 39f.
  Divinization, 145, 149, 218
  Established by the gods, 8, 24, 26
  Evolution, 232
  Explained by myth, 9, 16, 37ff.
  Fate of humankind, 153
  Fear of, 50
  Gates, 156
  Gods, 138
  Humanized, 38
  Hungry, 37f.
  Impersonal, 11, 54f.
  Māwet, 38
  Metaphor, 10

Death *(continued)*
  Moira, 91
  Mot, 37ff., 129, 153
  Overpowering, 8
  Personification, 38
  Punishment, 153, 232f.
  Righteous, 148
  Ruler of men, 8
  Sheol/ *šəʾôl*, 38
  Šīmtu, 91
  Vs life, 47-9, 51
Dogma/doctrine
  Anticipates conclusions, 64, 120
  Basis for worldview, 215
  Fall of humankind, 231-6
  Imaginary time, 120
  Imposed on the population, 207
  Metaphoric nature, 218
  Mythical causality, 10
  No factual evidence, 218
  Progressive revelation, 104
  Transcendence, 108
  Vitiates Bible interpretation, 59, 64, 120, 124, 235
  Vs anthropomorphism, 101, 104
  Vs evidence, 108, 120, 123
  Vs reality, 231
Earth
  Actions of the gods happen on, 28, 80
  Amen-Re is Lord, 170
  Augustus is king, 181
  Baal is Lord, 35f., 37, 40
  Christ creator, 96, 233
  Christian-god creator, 98
  Christian god kills people, 202
  Christian-god's empire, 202f.
  Death, 232
  Earth-Of-No-Return, 155
  Elyon is King, 181
  Enki is Lord, 126
  Enlil is Lord, 20, 170, 174
  Escaping, 91
  Evil, 91
  Fertilized by Baal, 35f.
  Geocentric system, 214
  Gods come down to, 127
  King of Israel, 189
  Life on, 40
  Marduk is King, 169
  Male dominion, 207
  Naram-Sin king, 177
  Not six thousand years old, 230
  Šamaš King of the, 23, 174
  Separated from heaven, 49f.
  Sophia rules, 94
  Thutmose III is king, 188
  Under the supervision of gods, 141
  Underworld is under the, 153, 156
  Yahve is Lord, 170
  Yam born of the, 46
El (Ugaritic)
  Father, 40, 151
  Gracious, 40
  Head of the pantheon, 34, 129
  Humanized, 60, 122
  Issues a decree, 73
  Sides with Yamm, 36
  Sons of, 111, 133, 136, 179f.
  Wise, 60
Enki/Ea
  Drunk, 60
  Father of Marduk, 33
  God of culture, etc., 126, 174
  God of the city of Eridu(g), 58, 176, 178, 184
  Humanized, 57, 106, 126
  Nudimmud, 126
  Omniscient, 58
  Visits the cities, 70
Enlil
  Controls human life, 21
  Controls historical events, 21f.
  Fertility-god, 20f.
  King of the gods, 20, 170
  Rain, 20f.
  Storm-god, 22, 34, 175
  Warrior-god, 20, 22, 34
  Weather-god, 19
Epilepsy
  Cure, 225f.
  Given by the Moon, 10, 122, 219ff.
  Given by a demon or spirit, 219f., 225
  Healing of an epileptic boy, 222ff.
  Hippocrates, 221f.

Impersonal/physical disorder, 225f.
Personal agent, 225
Sacred disease, 221
Selēniadsomai/Selēnē, 221f., 224,
'Ereṣ, see Earth Underworld, 38, 153, 174
Erṣetu, see Earth, 153
Evangelicals/Fundamentalists
  Bubble, 229
  Percentage in US population, 228f.
  Search for power, 217
  Vision of the world, 230
  Want a religious dictator, 196
  Want to control Public Education, 210
  White, 229f.
  Youth leaving, 229f.,
Faith
  Acceptance by, 86, 149, 226
  Act of, 14, 107, 223
  As doctrine, 110, 123, 200f., 209, 216, 218, 235
  Biblical, 235
  Christ of, 149
  Crisis, xvii, 228, 231
  Evolving, 104
  Language, xvii
  Losing, 230
  Scripture, 214
  Rebuilding, 229, 231
  Trust, 128
Gods' attributes in the ANE
  Almighty, 25, 64, 189, 198,
  Anger, 25, 44, 103, 189
  Body, 33, 52, 58-63, 85, 128, 149, 179, 236
  Creator, 16, 40, 56, 64, 94f., Emotions, xix, 63, 68f., 104
  Eternal, 24, 36, 41, 59, 98-101, 108
  Fury, 104, 198
  Humanized, xix, 9, 23, 38, 51, 59f., 68, 78, 83-5, 101f., 125, 128, 163f., 225
  Love, 16, 33, 58, 67, 75, 101, 107, 130, 144, 169, 177, 181, 183
  Make love with humans, 67, 114, 143, 176
  Marduk's body, 33
  Moaning, 101
  Not immutable, 59, 66
  Not infinite, 59
  Not omnipotent, 68f., 85
  Not omniscient, 65-9, 108f.
  Omniscient, 22
  Personal/impersonal, xix, 9-11, 25, 47f., 56-58, 125-8, 225f.
  Rage, 44, 101f., 104, 188
  Rejoice, 101
  Repentance, 68, 103f., 109f.
  Wrath, 34, 46, 103f., 185, 189f.
  Yahve's body, 59, 62, 65, 75, 85
God(s)
  Conceptual metaphor, xx, 2, 6, 6, 58, 125, 129, 162f., 168, 191f., 205
  Control life and death, 8
  Control the life of individuals, 24-6
  Control history/universe, xviii, 19, 24, 26f., 36, 85, 114, 238
  Control nature, xviii, 22, 27, 32, 46, 85,
  Cosmic rulers, 24, 35, 95, 100, 137, 156, 170f., 174
  Established death, 8
  Fight for their kings, 185, 189f., 195
  Fire, 199
  Function, 129, 183-92, 193
  Glyptic art, 23, 57, 85
  Holy ones, 134-8, 142, 146, 148, 158, 171, 174
  Idealized human beings, 58, 65, 87f., 90, 101,106
  Kings, xx, 6, 129, 163, 168, 169f., 192, 205
  Nomen naturae and *officii*, 128f.
  Personal relationship, 107
  Procreate, 67, 85, 114-21, 127f., 176, 178, 224
  Proletarian, 61, 239
  Sign, 91, 194
  Sons of El, 111, 133f., 136f., 139, 158
  Sons of Elohim, 18, 127
  Sons of Elyon, 139, 142, 158
  Sons of god, 66, 116-8, 141, 148

God(s) *(continued)*
  Sons of the elohim, 66, 110-2, 116-9
  Sons of the gods, 40, 66, 110f., 117f., 136-8, 140-2, 171, 183
  Sons of Zeus, 111
  Sophia, 93, 96
  Stars, 6, 10, 57, 115, 126f., 133f., 139, 147, 152, 182, 225, 227
  Storm, 22, 32-7, 40-2, 44, 47f., 57, 142, 174f., 188, 190, 238
  Warriors, xx
  Watchmen, 112
  Wrath, 109, 198
Heaven
  Abode of the gods, xviii, 115, 126f., 133, 145, 150-2, 163, 171, 207, 226
  Angels fell/came down, 114f., 127
  Bolts, 150
  City, 149
  Created, 44f., 98, 233
  Drips dew, 42
  Enlightenment, 209
  Epilepsy, 219
  Ešarra, 149
  Gate(s), 150, 152, 186
  Geocentric, 214
  Gods, 113
  Gods act in/from, 7, 18, 28, 121f., 138, 152, 190, 194
  Gods come down from, 59, 70, 81, 127, 150f., 183
  Heroes go to, 145-8, 227
  Host, 6, 18, 127, 142
  Humanized, 135, 137
  Kingship descends from, 176, 184f.
  Levels, 152
  Logos, 96
  Mountain, 149, 151
  Opposed to hell, 157
  Opposed to the underworld, 153
  Overheats, 39
  Palace/temple, 149, 152
  Pantheon, 111
  Pillars, 45
  Rains oil, 36, 40
  Righteous go to, 93, 115, 156
  Separated from earth, 49f.
  Sons of, 127
  Sophia, 94
  Staircase, 150
  Stars, 126f.
  Upwards or up there, 134, 149, 151, 153, 181
  Uranus, 88
  Walled city, 150f., 213
Hero(s)
  Achilles, 143f.
  Aeneas, 144
  Alexander, 144f.
  Atrahasis, 27
  Caesar Augustus, 145, 147f.
  Daniel, 73f.
  Definition, 143
  Demigod by birth, 143
  Distortion, 88f.
  Divine credentials, 228
  Divinization at death, 145f.
  Elijah, 145
  Gods, 142, 163
  Hercules, 144-6
  Jesus, 145, 148f., 218, 227
  Julius Caesar, 145, 147
  King, 67, 136, 143
  Kirta, 136
  Marduk, 32
  Moses 145-7
  Myth, 28
  Narrative about, 2
  Procreated by a god, 112, 117, 143ff., 176
  Samson, 75
  Šulgi, 178
  Teaching about 87
  Telemachus, 143
  Washington, George, 177
Human(s)
  Anthropomorphism, 52, 57-63, 85f., 169, 211, 225f.
  Appearance, 115
  Assemblies, 131
  Began to multiply, 66, 110, 116f.
  Bodily experience, 3, 55f.
  Controlled by the gods, xviii, 7, 10, 19, 25f., 30, 185

INDEX OF SUBJECTS 313

Controlled by Enlil, 21, 185
Controlled by Ištar, 187
Controlled by Marduk, 25, 187
Controlled by Utu, 23
Create civilization, 164
Create agriculture, 164
Create first writing system, 166, 183
Create monarchy, 164
Create religion, 51
Create the gods, 176
Creation of, 49f.
Daughters of, 66, 110-14, 117
Dehumanized, 15, 197, 211
Divinization, 91
Experience of evil, 10
Exterminated, 68
Fall, 231-5
Father, 206
Go to the underworld, 153
Gods, 111, 117ff.
Gods as idealized, xix, 87-90, 101, 106
Gods supervise, 70, 140f.
Heroes, 117, 144f.
King, 176
Main cognitive model, 55
Metaphor for the divine, xviii, 3, 5, 20, 26, 48, 56-64, 90, 107, 109, 125-8, 163-5, 168f., 211, 225f.
Nature, 128
Origin, 231-5
Reason, 208
Rights, 212f.
Soul, 43, 92f., 96, 100, 109, 122, 146-8, 156, 201, 206, 231
Source domain for the divine, 58
Spirit, 43, 181, 219
Threaten and assaulted, 8, 11, 24, 46
Visited by gods, 69ff., 121f.
Women, 111, 116
World, 111
Worthy of respect, 211
Yahve as, 76ff.
Interpretation
Babylonian and Assyrian context, 167f.
Cognitive dissonance, 124

Cultural background/context, xx, 69, 121, 131, 168, 205, 219, 235
Cultural change, 205, 236
Cultural gulf, 226
Cultural prejudice, 206
Distorted, 59, 61, 112, 119-21, 236
Dogma 101, 104
Exorcism of a boy as case study, 219ff.
Evidence, 18f., 79, 86, 122-5, 214, 218, 232f.
Genesis 6:1-4 as case study, 110ff., 120
Grammatical-historical, 101, 104, 108, 110, 236
Hellenistic context, 92f., 96, 99, 100, 105, 149, 221, 236
Infallibility of the Bible, 121-3, 235
Infallibility of the church, 122
Integrity of, 104, 110
Platonic, xix, 59, 104, 116ff.
Prejudices/presuppositions, 17, 65, 110, 119f., 121-3, 157, 206, 208
Psalm 82 as case study, 138ff., 157ff.
Rabbinic, 160f., 198
Sumerian context, 16, 32, 121, 125, 129, 150, 155, 166-9, 173, 176, 184, 219
Systematic theologians, 120
The fall, 231ff.
Ugaritic context, 36, 42, 44, 48, 111f., 127, 137f., 153, 159, 188
Ištar/Inana
Cares for the king, 187
Descends to the underworld, 154
Gate of the underworld, 155
Helps Gilgameš, 132
Humanized, 68
Seduces Gilgameš, 67
Visits Enki, 58
Warrior-goddess, 122, 174, 184f., 198
Wedding, 16
Jesus Christ
Ascended to heaven, 152f., 203, 205, 218, 227
Begotten by a god, 183
Blood, 62

Jesus Christ *(continued)*
   Creator, 96
   Destroys his enemies, 198, 202
   Emperor, 203
   Faith, 149
   His church persecutes, 201
   Image of god, 96
   In the Eucarist, 62
   King, 202, 204
   Logos, 96f.
   Priest, 204
   Proclaimed, 149
   Prophet, 204
   Second coming, 30
   Secondary god, 96
   Son of god, 161, 182f., 199
   Tyrant, 193, 199, 204, 212
   Warrior-god, 193-5, 198, 209
   World Empire, 202f.
King
   Almighty, 181
   Anger, 181
   Baal
   Begotten by a god, 145, 177f., 180, 182
   Demigod, 143, 147
   Demon possessed, 118f., 120
   Divinized, 145f., 177, 227
   Dominion, 172, 174f.
   Empire, 11, 21f., 26, 92 167, 172ff., 184, 186, 193, 195, 197, 200, 207
   Eternal, 179
   Firstborn of god, 181
   Flesh of the gods, 178
   Function of, 165, 172
   Image of god, 179
   Judge, 165
   Legislator, 165
   Powerful, 26, 165, 167
   Priest, 165
   Provider, 165
   Son of god, 148, 176, 180,
   Tyrant, 134, 208
   Warrior, 165
   Wrath, 175
Life, *see* death
   Established by the gods, 8
   Eternal, 24
   Provided by Baal, 35
   Vs death, 8
Literal approach
   Disfiguration of reality, 55, 128, 183, 219, 225, 228
   God as Father, 7
   Literal expressions, 66
   Not accepted, 86, 94, 149, 205, 219, 226f., 231
   Taking myth as fact, 12, 62, 195, 225, 230, 235
   Yahve as king, 7
Marduk
   Anger, 25
   Arrows, 33f.
   Built Babylon, 150
   Chariot, 32f., 44
   Clouds, 32
   Fire, 33
   Flames, 46
   Head of the pantheon, 32
   Horses, 34
   King of heaven 169
   Lightning, 32, 33
   Rain, 33
   Sovereign, 25
   Storm-god, 32-4, 44
   Thunderstorm, 33
   Warrior-god, 196
   Winds, 32f.
Mesopotamia
   Agriculture, 131, 164
   Armies, 164
   Assemblies, 131
   Cradle of civilization, 164
   Cuneiform, 166, 167
   Empire, 173
   Epilepsy, 122, 219
   Influence on Israel, 168f.
   First writing system, 166
   Health, 9
   Literature, 27, 166f.
   Source domain, 211
   Theological agenda, 166-8
   Theology of the monarchy, 184
Metaphor
   Become obsolete, 11, 205, 207, 213, 227, 236

INDEX OF SUBJECTS

Bodily foundation, 3, 55f.
Cautionary warning, 12ff., 195
Cognitive mechanism, xvii, 12, 51, 55, 108, 169
Conceptual, xx, 2-7, 58, 90, 94, 100, 107, 120, 125, 129, 152, 162-5, 168, 171, 174, 191, 205, 209, 211
Correspondence, 4
Cultural conditioning, xx, 6, 163, 183, 205, 207, 209, 213
Definition, 2f.
Extended, xvii, 1f., 7, 30, 56, 121, 125
Language of the Bible, xvii, xix, 7, 17, 30, 61f., 107, 109f., 218, 225
Mind controlling nature, xviii, 12, 15, 195-7, 226
More than rhetoric, 3f., 12, 17, 63, 195
Misunderstanding, 3, 12
Myth, xvii, 2
Power, 12, 15, 196f., 231
Shapes understanding and experience, 3f., 12, 15, 55, 231
Source domain, 4-6, 13, 56, 58, 129, 163, 192, 205, 209, 211, 236
Target domain, 4-6, 13, 58, 163, 192
Monarchy
  Anthropomorphism, 169
  Conceptual metaphor, 6, 191
  Descends from heaven, 176
  Divine, xix, 7, 129, 163, 205
  Legitimation, 183ff.
  Not our current system, 209
  Obsolete, 205
  Political government, 131, 163f., 205
  Saudi Arabia, 217
  Source domain, 6, 129, 163, 176, 192
Moon (Sîn, *Selēnē*)
  Fights for the king, 187
  Geocentric system, 214
  God or goddess, 125f., 127
  Strikes with disease, 10, 122, 219ff.
Mot
  God of the underworld, 37, 153

Hungry, 37f.
Killed by Anat, 40
Swallows Baal, 39
Vs Baal, 8, 37f.
Warrior-god, 39
Myth
  Boundaries, 27f
  Collective significance, 2
  Cultural conditioning, 121, 131, 168, 205f., 219
  Cultural norms, 11
  Cultural vehicle, 226
  Definition, xvii, 1f.
  Explanatory function, 10f.
  Extended metaphor, 1f., 7, 30, 56, 121, 125
  Faulty definitions, 16ff.
  Functions, 1, 8, 10f., 70, 88
  Guilt and evil, 10
  Imaginary, 6f., 107, 120, 176
  Imitates this world, xx, 7, 129, 191
  Legends, 27
  Life and death, 8, 51, 156
  Literary genre, 2, 162
  Monarchy xix, 6f., 129, 131, 162ff., 205, 209
  Muthos, 1, 86
  Narrative nature, 1f., 5-7
  Political function, 183, 192f., 195
  Polytheistic, 17f.
  Popular use, 2
  Stories about origins, 16
  Stories about the gods, xvii, 1, 8, 29, 85, 162
  Theism, 31, 56
  Theological narrative, 1
  Theomachia, 31ff.
  Values and virtues, 2, 11, 51, 88, 90, 205, 212f., 230, 236
Ninurta/Ningirsu
  Humanized, 57
  Fights for the king, 186
  Legitimizes the king, 187
  Son of Enlil, 19, 179
  Storm-god, 34, 47
  Warrior-god, 34, 169
Platonism
  Anthropomorphism, 90, 101, 107

Platonism (continued)
- Cultural context, 236
- Distorts interpretation, 78, 94, 101, 110, 115f.
- Divinization of humankind, 91
- Effects, 87, 89
- Function of myth, 88f.
- God idealized human being, xix, 90
- God is invisible, 60, 105
- God is not physical, 59, 67, 87, 90, 97, 100f., 109
- God is not the cause of evil, 89, 211
- God's attributes, 98f.
- God's transcendence, 90, 92, 95, 105
- Hellenism influence, 92f., 96, 100, 105, 149, 236
- Influence in Christianity, 96f.
- Influence in Judaism, 93, 98
- Intermediary god, 93
- Leaves us without god, 105, 107
- Logos, 95f., 109, 149
- Rejects immoral gods, 88f.
- Simplicity of god, 90, 95
- Standard for theology, 89f.
- Virtues, 89

Providence/Divine will, 25, 183, 186, 196f., 218

Puḫru, see assembly

Šamaš
- Humanized, 23, 126, 150
- Intervenes in history, 22f., 126
- King of heaven, 23, 126
- Meaning, 22
- Protects the king, 187
- Ruler of the universe, 174

Sumer
- Empires, 173
- First writing system, 166
- History and theology, 168
- Kingship descent, 184

Theism
- Anthropomorphic images, 59
- Atheism, 105
- Definition xviii, 56
- Language, xvii, 30
- Fundamental metaphor, 17f., 56, 122, 162
- Not equal to monotheism, 56

Theology
- Adoptionism, 180, 182
- Akkadian, 167
- Anthropomorphic, 101, 106
- Apocalyptic, 157, 199
- Begins at Sumer, 166, 168, 176
- Babylonian, 46
- Before Israel, 19
- Christian classical, 59, 87, 97f., 101, 104, 204, 207, 209, 235
- Father, 206
- For the present age, 231ff.
- Hellenistic, 96
- Imperial, 180f., 202, 207f.
- Interdisciplinary, 211, 231
- Mesopotamian, 168
- Mythical, 30
- Narrative, 1
- Negative, 92
- Persian, 131
- Platonic, 89
- Preconceptions, 119
- Science, 211
- Traditional, 16
- Ugaritic, 44, 48, 188
- What kind, 211f.

Tamtû, 33

Tiamat
- Battles with Marduk, 32ff.
- Cosmic waters, 33
- Killed by Marduk, 34
- Meaning of the word, 33
- Mother of all the gods, 33

Underworld
- All people go, 91, 145, 153
- Anat, 40
- *Arallû*, 153
- Arṣ, 39, 153
- Baal, 35, 38-40
- *Chthonios*, 154
- Description, 154
- *'Ereṣ*, 153
- *Erṣetu*, 153
- Fate, 91
- Gate, 156
- Hades, 154
- Hungry, 38

INDEX OF SUBJECTS

Kurnugê, 154
Māwet, 38
Moira, 91
Mot, 37, 153
 No escape, 154f.
 Part of the universe, 149, 203
 Personification, 38
 Place for the wicked, 156
 Seclusion, 153
 šəʾôl 38, 154
 šimtu, 91
 Spirits, 219
 Under the earth, 153f.
Utu, see Šamaš
Visits of the gods
 Anthropomorphism, 62
 Athena, 26, 72f.
 Bacchus, 71
 Hospitality 69ff.
 Jupiter, Poseidon and Mercury, 72f.
 Kothar, 73f.
 Man-god, 75f.
 Patron gods, 70
 Vs transcendence, 90
 Yahve, 75, 76ff.
Worldview/Cosmology
 Ancient, 218, 226f., 231
 Anthropomorphism
 Bible, xi, xvii, 30, 219, 226
 Christian, 215f., 218, 230
 Cultural conditioning, 227
 Cultural control, 216
 Cultural war, 216, 229
 Cultural shift, 236
 Disintegration, 230f.
 Geocentric, 127, 214
 Greek, 86
 Heliocentric, 214
 Human Rights
 In Collision, 208, 219, 226f.
 Metaphors, 205
 Modern, xx, 211, 226
 Monarchy, 163
 Mythic, 218
 Obsolete, 11, 149, 205, 207, 213, 227, 236
 Problems, 218
 Saudi Arabia, 216

Secular, 86, 208f., 212, 214, 217, 229
Theocracy, 216f.
Yahve
 Anger, 189
 Arrows, 42, 44, 48
 Body, 59
 Chariot, 34, 44
 Cherub, 42
 Clouds, 42, 44, 48, 188
 Confers political dominion, 175
 Eats and drinks, 77, 122
 El, 18, 29, 41, 47, 68, 85, 99, 102, 129, 134-7, 139, 171, 181, 142, 158, 171, 181
 Father, 107
 Feet, 63, 65, 77-9, 99, 109, 188
 Fertility god, 41f.
 Fight for the king, 33, 165f., 175, 189f.
 Fights with Jacob, 83ff.
 Fire, 34, 41f., 59, 189
 Flames, 34, 41
 Fury, 34
 Hail, 41f.
 Head of the pantheon, 18, 129f., 134, 171
 Hears, 65
 Horses, 44
 Hurricane, 34
 King of heaven, 41f., 170
 King of the gods, 129
 Legs, 65, 108
 Lightning, 36, 42, 44, 48, 188
 Rage, 44, 188
 Rain, 34, 41, 44, 48, 152
 Repents, 68f.
 Storm, 188
 Storm-god, 36, 40, 42, 48, 174, 190
 Talks, 59, 65, 79, 122
 Throne, 6, 60, 130, 152, 163, 166, 171
 Thunder, 40-2, 48, 190
 Thunderstorm, 40, 42
 Visits Abraham, 76ff.
 Voice, 36, 40-2, 48, 152
 Warrior god, 42, 44, 48, 61, 174, 190, 195

Yahve *(continued)*
    Wind, 34, 42, 44, 174
    Wrath, 34, 103f., 185, 189f.
Zeus
    Arrows/lightning, 48
    Chariot, 133
    Clouds, 151
    King of heaven, 172
    King of the gods, 172
    Lightning, 48, 151
    Master of gods and men, 172
    Thunder, 133, 172, 174
    Horses, 133

www.ingramcontent.com/pod-product-compliance
Lightning Source LLC
Chambersburg PA
CBHW050615300426
44112CB00012B/1517